CABINET
GOVERNMENT
IN AUSTRALIA, 1901–2006

Professor Patrick Weller AO is the ANZSOG Premier of Queensland Chair of Governance and Public Management and director of the Centre for Governance and Public Policy at Griffith University, where he has held a chair of politics since 1984. He is a graduate of Oxford University, and has a doctorate from the Australian National University. He is a leading authority on the way that governments and executives work, the levers that leaders use to exercise authority, and the power and influence of officials in the national and international arenas. In the past 30 years his systematic studies of ministers, prime ministers and the public service have contributed substantially to our understanding of executive government in Australia and overseas. Patrick Weller's extensive work on Australian politics includes his popular biographies *Malcolm Fraser PM* and *Dodging Raindrops – John Button: A Labor Life* and his collective study, *Australia's Mandarins: the frank and the fearless?*. His most recent popular book, *Don't Tell the Prime Minister* (Scribe, 2002), focused on the 'Children Overboard' Affair. Weller was elected a fellow of the Academy of the Social Sciences in Australia in 1996. In 2002 he was appointed an Officer of the Order of Australia for his contribution for 'service through research in political science and public administration and for extending knowledge of executive government'.

ANZSOG Program on Government, Politics and Public Management

The Australia and New Zealand School of Government (ANZSOG) is a network initiative of five jurisdictions (the Australian and New Zealand governments, New South Wales, Victoria and Queensland) and nine universities. Established in 2003, ANZSOG represents a new and exciting prospect for the development of world-class research and teaching in the public and community sectors.

ANZSOG has announced an extensive research program that promotes innovative and cutting-edge research in partnership with academia and the public sector (<http://www.anzsog.edu.au>). In association with UNSW Press, ANZSOG has undertaken to publish a series of books on contemporary issues in Australian government, politics and public management. Titles in this program will promote high-quality research on topics of interest to a broad readership (academic, professional, students and general readers) and will include teaching texts relevant to the ANZSOG consortia in the areas of government, politics and public management.

Series editors are Professor John Wanna and Professor R.A.W. Rhodes, Research School of Social Sciences, Australian National University, Canberra.

Recent titles include:

- *Terms of Trust: Arguments over Ethics in Australian Government* by John Uhr.
- *Yes, Premier: Labor Leadership in Australia's States and Territories* edited by John Wanna and Paul Williams.
- *Westminster Legacies: Democracy and Responsible Government in Asia and the Pacific* edited by Haig Patapan, John Wanna and Patrick Weller.
- *The Australian Electoral System: Origins, Variation and Consequences* by David M. Farrell and Ian McAllister.
- *Fighting Crime Together: The Challenges of Policing and Security Networks* edited by Jenny Fleming and Jennifer Wood.

CABINET GOVERNMENT
IN AUSTRALIA, 1901–2006

Practice, Principles, Performance

PATRICK WELLER

A UNSW Press book

Published by
University of New South Wales Press Ltd
University of New South Wales
Sydney NSW 2052
AUSTRALIA
www.unswpress.com.au

© Patrick Weller 2007
First published 2007

This book is copyright. Apart from any fair dealing for the purpose of private study, research, criticism or review, as permitted under the Copyright Act, no part may be reproduced by any process without written permission. Inquiries should be addressed to the publisher.

National Library of Australia
Cataloguing-in-Publication entry

> Weller, Patrick, 1944– .
> Cabinet government in Australia, 1901–2006: practice, principles, performance
>
> ISBN 0 86840 874 3.
>
> ISBN 978 0 86840 874 3.
>
> 1. Cabinet system - Australia - History. 2. Australia - Politics and government - History. I. Title.
>
> 320.494

Cover   Photograph provided courtesy of AUSPIC
Printer Griffin

CONTENTS

Acknowledgments … vi
Prologue: Cabinet in 1901 and 2006 … 1
1 Understanding cabinet government … 6

Part 1 ⌁ The Australian experience

2 Setting the arrangements: 1901–14 … 20
3 Stretching the limits: 1914–23 … 33
4 Consolidation, with hiccups: 1923–41 … 52
5 Fighting war and managing mavericks: 1941–49 … 77
6 An emperor and three pale shadows: 1949–72 … 95
7 Dashed hopes: 1972–75 … 122
8 Working all hours: 1976–83 … 135
9 Contrasting styles: 1983–96 … 159
10 Discipline and control: 1996–2006 … 177

Part 2 ⌁ The cabinet system

11 Cabinet, party and parliament: The threads of accountability … 192
12 The rules of cabinet … 214
13 Making policy in cabinet … 232
14 The power of prime ministers: Cabinet as contest … 249
15 Core executives: Is Australian cabinet different? … 268
16 Conclusion: Trends and futures for cabinet government … 281

Appendix 1 … 286
Appendix 2 … 289
References … 293
Bibliography and source notes … 309
Index … 316

ACKNOWLEDGMENTS

In 1974 the Royal Commission on Australian Administration was about to hear the evidence of Sir John Bunting, secretary of the Department of the Prime Minister and Cabinet, and his deputy, Geoff (later Sir Geoffrey) Yeend. Because the proceedings of cabinet were still covered by a veil of secrecy, the public gallery at the commission was cleared. From memory I was the only person in the gallery, so I left. That afternoon I had an appointment with Geoff Yeend. He commented that, as they had only talked about cabinet processes, the need to hold a closed session had been unnecessary. He then went through the principal issues that had been covered in the morning, all of which became public when the transcript was eventually released. That meeting really whetted my appetite; my interest in the processes of cabinet government has now lasted for over 30 years, so I owe that, and more, to the late Sir Geoffrey Yeend. Over the years too I have benefited from a number of conversations with those two great public servants and secretaries to the cabinet: Mike Codd and Michael Keating.

Many others have contributed since, far too many to list here. Over the period since 1974 I have written a number of books and articles on Australian politics, many of which have touched on the processes of cabinet government and thus provide some of the foundation for this study. In *Politics and Policy in Australia* (1979), Geoff Hawker, R.F.I. Smith and I wrote about the cabinet of the Whitlam government; my chapter here draws on that account, and I am grateful to Geoff and Bob for their agreement in allowing me to use some of the ideas expressed there. I wrote on cabinet in *Fraser PM* (1989). For that book Malcolm Fraser kindly gave me access to the cabinet documents of his government. The version here only uses the material included in that book and thereby put on the public record. I remain grateful for the privilege of that original access.

For two earlier books, *Can Ministers Cope*, written with Michelle Grattan in 1981, and *Australia's Mandarins* (2001), I extensively interviewed both ministers and departmental secretaries. The insights from those volumes provided me with many of the inside views of government that I hope are reflected in this book. For all those interviews and all those hours, for the patience and the humour, again I express my thanks.

More specifically for this volume, John Wanna, Haig Patapan and Peter Hamburger have read versions of some or all chapters and provided me with sage advice. John Nethercote, on holiday in Sicily, went through the text in great detail, and, with his eye for detail and his encyclopaedic knowledge of Australian politics and history, both saved me from many mistakes and added invaluable insights to the analysis.

I would particularly like to thank Catherine Althaus who worked through the final text and prepared it for the publishers with great patience and a mastery of detail. Paula Cowan was my research assistant the whole way, exploring the archives, sorting the cabinet microfiche, filling the gaps. The book would never have been completed without Paula's assistance.

And the rest, as they say, is down to me alone.

PROLOGUE:
CABINET IN 1901 AND 2006

There were nine in the first Australian cabinet sworn in on 1 January 1901, the dawn of a new century and a new country. All were male and experienced. Six of them had been premiers of their states. None of them had yet been elected. They were chosen by the new prime minister to begin the process of establishing a new national government while an election was held. Two of them would be gone when parliament eventually convened. One died on 10 January, setting a record for ministerial brevity that was seldom beaten; another decided he preferred to remain as premier of Tasmania and did not contest the poll. Both were replaced with members elected from their state in the first Commonwealth election of 27–28 March 1901.

For the members of this first Australian national cabinet, the business of establishing an administration may have been new, but the procedures of governing followed established practice. George Turner, the treasurer, had twice been premier of Victoria. William Lyne had led New South Wales (NSW). As the premier of the original colony and largest state, he had been the first person invited to form the ministry. John Forrest had dominated the fledgling state of Western Australia, serving as premier for the previous decade. Charles Kingston had spent six years leading South Australia. Experienced, hardened in politics, these state veterans knew precisely how governments should work and where they stood in the political world. The two leading members of the cabinet, Edmund Barton and Alfred Deakin, had less ministerial and administrative experience than their older colleagues. Not for nothing was it called a 'Cabinet of Kings'.

'Kings' is what some of these new ministers had indeed been. The principle of 'responsible cabinet government' had been accepted almost without debate in the constitutional conventions. There had been one dissident. The chair of the convention had moved a motion to test whether cabinet government should be retained. He wanted the parliament to elect the ministers and make policy, while ministers administered their departments. He thought too much power lay with the premiers. When ministers disagree, he asked:

> Who decides now? Why, that modern autocrat, the Premier. Why should the direct representatives of the people delegate to one man that power and those responsibilities with which they have been entrusted by the people?

There is nothing new about challenging the balance of power between ministers and premiers. It was inherent in the system of cabinet government. No one seconded the motion and it lapsed. Cabinet government was accepted without further debate.

The 'Kings' had hotly contested the formation of the initial cabinet. The new Governor-General initially asked the NSW premier, William Lyne, to form a cabinet. From his sick bed in Victoria Alfred Deakin sought to thwart Lyne, refusing to serve himself and encouraging Barton sometimes to refuse and sometimes to join. Eventually Lyne returned the commission, unable to gather a cabinet. With due process restored, in Deakin's eyes at least, the champion of federation, Edmund Barton, became the first prime minister and minister for external affairs, three months before he knew who would be in the first parliament.

Cabinet government had developed naturally in each of the colonial governments, derived from the British experience, even as it matured there. Cabinet meetings were to be held regularly and decisions were collective. The ministers had to maintain support in the newly elected House of Representatives. There is no sign that they asked what these processes meant or considered in any detail alternative structures of decision-making. The transition was smooth because of their experience and their expectations.

So what would cabinet government mean for those original ministers? First, they would see the cabinet as the high point of the political game, the source of power and authority. As they rose through the political ranks, from hopeful candidate to member of parliament, then from colonial minister to premier, they were conscious of where power lay.

The system created a number of power relationships. The first was between the members of cabinet. Prime ministers are almost always surrounded by their potential successors; even when they choose their ministers, they will still select the most powerful of their colleagues. The selection of ministers, even for the first Commonwealth cabinet, had been controversial. A disappointed candidate had to be compensated with the offer of the first speakership of the House of Representatives. Cabinet was both individual ambition and the party prize. Only the party that could control the House of Representatives either with a majority of its own, or, as occurred until 1909, with the support of a third force, could form a government.

Many ministers saw themselves as potential prime ministers. They often regarded themselves as partners, not subordinates; they had statutory responsibility for the implementation of the legislation under their portfolio. They were elected and had independent status. Distance from home meant that for federal ministers politics soon became a full-time occupation; there was little opportunity for many of them to retain a separate professional life, unless it was a sheep station or occasional legal practice. Managing the politics of the cabinet, the fears and ambitions, the personalities and the factions, the crises and the routine, became a primary responsibility of every prime minister.

Cabinets depend for their continued existence on the support of their party in parliament. As long as the party remains disciplined, that support will be retained. By federation the tradition had developed that the parliamentary parties should meet, elect their leaders and discuss tactics. Implicit in that contract was the assumption that the parliamentary parties could also withdraw that support and effectively sack their leaders. In May 2001 the federal Labor Party could celebrate the centenary of its first party meeting in May 1901; other parties had similar, if not so formalised, processes. Regular meetings meant that party management was a significant part of cabinet government. Whether the party meetings (for the Labor Party, the caucus) should be able to direct the cabinet was a matter of continuing dispute. The interdependence of cabinet and party was recognised from an early stage.

Parliament had to be managed too. In the first nine years cabinet had to negotiate with other parties, but not with individuals; thereafter it could usually be guaranteed a majority in the House of Representatives. It had no such assurance in the Senate. Elected by a different system that, in the first 49 years, could deliver overwhelming majorities to one side or the other, sometimes the Senate was dominated by the Opposition. Since the introduction of proportional representation in 1949, the numbers were always close; from 1980 to 2005 neither government nor the Opposition had a majority. It was still largely party politics, not state interests, that determined the outcomes.

Cabinet, party and parliament are the three arenas that prime ministers had to manage. In this trinity the cabinet is the pinnacle of the political system. Getting there and staying there are the fixations for political leaders and their supporters. That is what politics is about: the exercise of government power. It is what a study of cabinet needs to explain. The exercise of power within a political system is hard to analyse because it is often so intangible. Interactions between ministers and their leader are daily occurrences; ministers may agree today because of what they fear may otherwise happen tomorrow. Relationships are continuous; personalities dominate. The use of power may be part of the atmosphere, always implicit, seldom having to be expressed.

Barton was late for his first cabinet meeting; he was chided for his lack of punctuality by the meticulous Deakin. Yet it was to set the precedent that prime ministers would decide when cabinet meetings were held and on what conditions they would be run. Administration was informal; the NSW premier made space available for the new prime minister in the NSW parliament and Barton claimed that he carried the administration of Australia in his brief case.

With a small cabinet and limited responsibilities the running of government business could be easy. There were no extant records until early 1902, when Deakin was acting prime minister during Barton's visit to Britain for the coronation of Edward VII. Cabinet and the ministry were the same. Ministers were responsible for putting decisions into effect. Yet tensions still remained. Barton might find the company of some of his colleagues congenial; he would talk late into the night with Deakin, his close friend and ministerial colleague Richard O'Connor and Forrest. But there was constant antagonism between the strong minded Kingston and Forrest until Kingston's resignation in 1903 was greeted with a sigh of relief by his colleagues.

By 2006, after 100 years of cabinet government, the informality of proceedings has largely disappeared. The terms of government are the same: prime ministers summon ministers to cabinet meetings for collective discussions on the problems facing the government. But the structures of cabinet government are very different. There are more ministers, organised into tiers of senior and junior ranks. Managing the processes of cabinet has become more complex. Rules of procedure dictate what can be brought to cabinet and in what form. The agenda may be no longer than in the past, but it has increased in complexity and range. The difficulties of putting Australian problems in an international and regional context are growing. New technology and better communications have shrunk problems of distance, but demand quicker reaction time. Cabinet DNA may be the same, but the environment in which cabinets function has changed beyond immediate recognition.

How did the small and intimate cabinet of 1901 develop into the complicated bureaucratic machine of 2006? This is the principal question this book seeks to address. In some respects cabinet development may be easy to chart. Rules and procedures, statistics and records, can be discovered, read and analysed. In other respects, changes may be less tangible; it is harder to identify whether the dynamics of cabinet changed to the same degree, in the distribution of authority, in the opportunity for ministers to influence the general debate, in the capacity of cabinet to develop sensible and agreed policy conclusions. How effectively did cabinets work then and now? Were the relationships different, or simply more complex? Is cabinet government still viable in modern circumstances? Those questions, too, are the subject of this book.

1 UNDERSTANDING CABINET GOVERNMENT

Cabinet government is a term that is taken for granted. Australia has cabinet government, our textbooks say, as though that is the end of it. Cabinet government is usually contrasted with presidential government. The one is collective, the other individual. In the one, prime ministers are said to be *primus inter pares*, the first among equals, working with ministerial colleagues in the governing of the country. Presidents, on the other hand, have personal power; they and they alone must be persuaded to act. Those images are too simple; prime ministers may in reality be more effective than presidents, even though their authority is nominally exercised through responsible ministers and their influence may be indirect. Presidents may well be more restricted in what they can achieve, working with divided powers and independent congresses.

Even within the world of cabinet government the variations in power are vast. How and when cabinet is consulted; the degree to which decisions are made by cabinet; the authority of the prime ministers: these will all change from country to country and even, within the one country, from prime minister to prime minister. To describe a country as being governed by cabinet provides a broad description but no set of rules or map of power. It does not tell anyone how to govern, or provide a set of normative rules that determines when cabinet government is properly applied.

Cabinet government is part normative, part descriptive, part perception. It provides a general description, available for manipulation and shaping. It will mean different things to the participants in the political system, whether supporting officials, outer ministers, or backbench politicians, and to those outside, the press and academics. What they look for will determine what they see and what judgments are made; different schools of thought will direct attention to different parts of the system. Depending on what the observer expects, they may be more or less satisfied with what they find. The academic debate on the topic gives at least five different ways of interpreting cabinet government, each of which emphasises a different part of the political architecture.

But even before those interpretations are explored, there is a prior consideration. Is a study to be an analysis of cabinet *government* or of *cabinet* government? That is, should it be a broad study of the government of the country that is nominally considered as having cabinet government, in contrast to presidential government, for instance? Or should it be a more precise analysis of the way that the cabinet works within the general framework of parliamentary and political processes? The first might explore the rise and fall of governments, the exercise of the regal prerogatives, the principles of ministerial and collective responsibility, the workings of political parties and the principles of governing. Cabinet government becomes a description of government itself. In that analysis the cabinet itself plays a subordinate role, just one part of the political architecture. In the second, the meetings of cabinet, the application of collective government, the challenges that cabinet must meet, and the links between the cabinet and other parts of the political community are seen from the perspective of the cabinet members — the concern is the ability of the cabinet, however described, to operate effectively.

Encel's study, *Cabinet Government in Australia*, with the first edition in 1962 and a second in 1974, fits the first mould. It describes the circumstances and the fortunes of governments. It explores the application of constitutional principles such as ministerial and collective responsibility. It touches briefly on the supporting structures. Cabinet itself remains a black box with little consideration of the way that it operated. That was understandable for two reasons. First, there were comparatively few general accounts of the fate of governments that were concerned with the interaction of party, parliament and ministry. The book thus filled a vacuum. Second, there were few documents that provided evidence of the way that cabinet worked. There were no consolidated cabinet documents; the National Archives had not yet undertaken its Herculean task of identifying and of collecting the series of documents that now make up the twentieth-century cabinet record. Even if it had, the records were then covered by a 50-year rule that would have limited access to any documents beyond the first decades. To write a broad account was both necessary and inevitable, given the availability of sources.

Times have changed; a far wider range of sources is now available. If Encel wrote a study of cabinet *government*, this book is a study of *cabinet* itself, a consideration of the problems of cabinet decision-making and management. It is an account of the challenges at the centre of government, for prime ministers, ministers and those officials who serve there; it looks out from cabinet to the political world beyond. Party politics certainly is the foundation stone of Australian government, but here the concern is primarily the way it shapes and directs the working of cabinet itself. The driving questions for this book are concerned with the way Australia is governed and the capacity of ministers satisfactorily to undertake the multiple roles that the system of cabinet government requires of them.

The different ways in which cabinet can be conceptualised are important because each approach asks different questions and therefore will come to conclusions about the efficacy of cabinet on the basis of its prior assumptions. Even if it is imposing a slightly artificial neatness, each approach can be traced back to different disciplinary assumptions about government and the way that governments should work. The discussion here draws on evidence not only from Australia, but also from Britain and Canada. Debate on cabinet in Australia has been less vigorous than the analysis in those countries. In part that may be because in those countries the continuing viability of cabinet as an institution is under more open challenge. As a consequence the insights developed there can be used to ask questions about challenges and performance associated with Australian cabinet government.

There are then five ways at least in which cabinet government can be viewed.

1 **Cabinet government as constitutional actor, as part of the political architecture, enmeshed with party and parliament, with the analytical focus on responsibility and accountability: a constitutional theory or legal approach**

Cabinet is seen as the zenith of the party and parliamentary battle. The concern is how it relates to party and parliament, and where the lines of accountability lie. Cabinet is thus seen as the focus for the application of two basic constitutional doctrines that define the proper lines of accountability: collective and ministerial responsibility to parliament. These doctrines may be described in normative terms proposing what ministers should do or in pragmatic terms, explaining how these ideas are applied and for whose benefit.

These doctrines were conventions, an agreed code of behaviour; they were never legally binding. How the conventions associated with collective and ministerial responsibility may have been altered, what debates occurred about their applicability, and whether they had a different impact over time is a matter for debate. Cabinet emphasises the collectivity, ministers working together resolving disputes, finding common ground. In principle the conventions were accepted from the beginning. The Constitutional Convention debates talked often about the responsibility of ministers to parliament. Whether the responsibility was the *individual* responsibility of ministers for the activities in their portfolios or the *collective* responsibility of cabinet, *both* doctrines were accepted by those founding fathers as essential to the working of the Constitution. Cabinet was the link between the government and the parliament; Bagehot famously called it 'a hyphen which joins, a buckle which fastens, the legislative part of the State to the executive part of the State. In its origins it belongs to the one, in its functions it belongs to the other'. The original ministers had all been members of parliament; they knew the rules and expectations and they understood how best to maintain their standing there.

Both these conventions have a basis in practical politics. Ministers must be members of parliament. So they must explain and justify what they and their departments do. From the very beginning of the federal parliament, party discipline ensured that usually the government won any vote. Ministers would rarely be forced to resign by parliamentary action. They never resigned because of the failings of their departments; that has always been a phantom test.

Collective responsibility is as much a convenience as a constitutional principle, even if formally promoted as such. If ministers were to disagree in public, the coherence and unity of government would soon decay. So they stand together and seek to ensure that their fights, of which there are bound to be many, stay private. Expedient practice, interpreted for convenience, builds into constitutional convention.

This relationship between minister and parliament has been a focal point for debate in Britain with its unwritten constitution. Its meaning is just as uncertain in Australia where neither the prime minister nor the cabinet is mentioned in the Constitution, and ministerial power is derived from section 64, the appointment of ministers by the Governor-General to administer a department of state. In Britain, Mackintosh spends some time considering the links between the cabinet, the parliament and the crown. Encel is almost entirely concerned with party links and the meaning and practice of ministerial or collective responsibility.

Often critiques develop around the concept of how the system *ought* to work. Some critics refer to standards by which behaviour should be judged.

Talking of Canada, Richard French called these analysts 'theorists', interested in how governing ought to work (in contrast to the 'pragmatists' who are concerned to see that government works better).

The basic questions are: what is the meaning of constitutional and ministerial responsibility and how are they applied to cabinet? What impact do they have on the workings of cabinet? How is the executive held accountable to the legislature? The Opposition, knowing how vague the Westminster model is, still asks: are practices consistent with the Westminster system?

2   Cabinet as a formal administrative institution, based on rules and routines: a public administration or positional approach

How should the cabinet be run? All the original ministers had experience of cabinet and they understood the central role of premiers. Cabinets were run by the rules determined by these premiers; it was collective and intended to meet regularly. But, at the turn of the twentieth century, that was about as far as the rules went. What should go to cabinet or be decided elsewhere; who makes these decisions and how? In what form should they be presented? Often control over *how* something is done may be close to control over *what* is done. Procedures and rules shape expectations and affect outcomes.

Cabinet began as an informal meeting of ministers, but over the years the pressure of business and the demands on the time of ministers required that proceedings became more formal. The development of cabinet handbooks that include the rules and conventions of cabinet have burgeoned, particularly after the establishment of a cabinet secretariat in wartime (the 1914–18 war in Britain; the 1939–45 war for Canada and Australia). Membership of cabinet shapes the roles and choices of ministers; expectations have been created by the historical development of cabinet rules. Prime ministers initially devised those rules and they are at liberty to alter and adjust them, but they do so warily.

This approach is the traditional institutional study of the structure and organisation of an established body. It leads to some fundamental questions. To what extent has the routinisation and bureaucratisation changed the way that cabinet works? Has it changed the manner and location of decisions? What impact do rules and routines have on the policy outcomes emerging out of cabinet?

An additional component is an analysis of the supporting departments or agencies that provide advice to the cabinet as a collectivity or to the prime ministers. Does the prime minister need a department? Should the central agencies support the cabinet as a collectivity, and how can that support be organised? The institutional arrangements vary from nation to nation; it is not significant (except in terms of political presentation) whether the supporting agency is called a department (as in Australia) or an office (Canada and Britain). What matters is what services they provide and to whom: do they serve the prime minister, or the cabinet as a collective, or in some way both? There is no doubt that the support at the centre has grown, in both non-partisan officials and political appointees who have personal connections with prime ministers and ministers. It is easy to assume that institutional existence means as a matter of course that the position of prime ministers has been strengthened. That need not be so. It is also possible to conclude there is still a hole at the centre, and that prime ministers often need more advice. Solutions to the problem of helping prime ministers are invariably posed in institutional terms because they provide clear steps that can be taken. It is easier to propose a body to provide collective advice than to exhort prime ministers to limit themselves or to undertake only those particular roles that are somehow seen by the observer as proper. Institutions provide potential; that potential still needs to be exercised.

3 **Cabinet as a forum for policy decisions that require the best available information and coordination to ensure those ministers are well-informed when making the decisions: a public policy approach**

If cabinet is the centre of decision-making, how well does it do that task? That is, what are the systems through which the decisions are made and how well informed are the decisions? Cabinet government makes heroic assumptions about the capacity of ministers. Those who have risen through a political process by counting the numbers are somehow assumed to have the ability to make sensible decisions on policy matters. Many ministers know nothing of the policy areas of the departments to which they are appointed. Yet there is no apprenticeship. The day they arrive they are asked to make decisions of importance. Some ministers have the intrinsic ability to make decisions; others selected by this process find themselves incapable of rising to the occasion. All of them need help.

The challenge is how to provide sufficient support for the ministers to promote sensible decisions. For many decades this support was provided by the public service; at times bureaucratic power, exercised through pliant ministers, was seen as dominant. More recently other players have entered the game of advising: ministerial advisers and think tanks now offer answers and solutions from their own viewpoint. Ministers have more choices.

There is also a matter of coordination. Cabinet pulls together the political and the administrative. It decides – sometimes legitimises – policy. Cabinet is responsible for ensuring a degree of consistency across programs and a common political and economic strategy. It can be judged by the quality of the policies and the effectiveness of the governance of the country. How, then, are cabinet's advisory processes, its control of information, its capacity to determine good policy settled? Can these processes be improved?

Those who provide this emphasis are French's 'pragmatists'. Amid the furore of politics, cabinets are accepted as the principal decision-making body in the polity. That raises questions about their ability to collect and synthesise the necessary data, to determine priorities, allocate expenditure or work effectively in other areas. There is concern about how to prevent fragmentation or excessive segmentation. There are even challenges to the usefulness of collective decision-making. Edmund Dell, a former British minister, has questioned the notion of collective decision-making, suggesting it is largely a fraud as most ministers have neither the knowledge nor the inclination to become actively involved in subjects beyond their portfolio. In response, Sir John Hunt, Secretary to the British Cabinet from 1974–79, argued that the inefficiencies were counterbalanced by the value of discussion as a means of ensuring support, with cabinet acting as the cement that held the government together.

Cabinet procedures will always in part reflect the working style of prime ministers; but those who work for prime ministers are constantly thinking about ways cabinet might be run better. Academics, too, propose better ways. Lindquist and White suggest that in Canada too little attention has been given to the organisation and running of cabinet as a complex organisation, if it is to work more strategically. The questions arising from this body of literature are therefore: how is support for decision-making organised? What advice is provided? To whom? How have those systems for advising cabinet as a collectivity been managed and to what effect?

4 **Cabinet as a political battleground, as a contest for position, power, policy and reputation; and in which incentives and resources are the best means for explaining action: a political science approach**

Prime ministers are often referred to as 'the first among equals'. That phrase has never been true. Cabinet is a forum in which unequals compete. There are several interpretations of the distribution of power in cabinets.

One debate refers to the issue of prime ministerial government. Some argue that power has shifted to the prime minister. These commentators examine the degree to which prime ministers have increased their authority and usurped the influence of individual ministers. The most sophisticated addition to the debate has been the two books by Michael Foley on the British 'presidency'. Foley explores the 'stretching of the leadership' and the consequential relations between prime ministers and their colleagues. His is, as his subtitle notes, a study of the politics of public leadership and elections. He is less concerned with the balance of the internal decision-making or the continuing functions of the cabinet system.

Others either assert that the proper term is 'ministerial government', at least in Britain, and that cabinet government can readily be reasserted after the demise of a dominant prime minister such as Thatcher.

A third line of argument has asserted that cabinet now provides greater collective impact. In Australia, Bunting proposed that as early as the 1960s cabinet had displaced ministers as the principal locus of decision-making.

Which of these interpretations best suits the Australian cabinet and are there trends that can be identified? Are these phenomena new, or merely more readily identified?

Finally there is an analysis of the levers of power that can be used in the cabinet system, such as the organisation of cabinet, the impact of federalism, access to ministerial positions, the use of cabinet committees, the provision of advice to the leaders or to the cabinet as a collectivity. Each of these levers can be interpreted as weapons in the pursuit of influence and advantage. The crucial questions are therefore: who really decides? How has the balance of power in cabinets changed? Has the position of prime minister been strengthened? What are the resources and incentives that can be applied by the different actors?

5   Cabinet as an arbiter and patchwork of influence: a network analysis

It should not be assumed that only ministers or cabinet are powerful. The cabinet operates within a network of institutions, many of which can exercise authority. They may be better informed, have greater access to the levers of power, have statutory authority and be there for far longer. In the early days when the scope of government was limited, when a public service barely existed, ministers may have been able to make many of the key decisions. But as the range of issues became greater, programs were more extensive and technical skills became more necessary, so the capacity changed. Other players became significant. Central agencies and prime ministerial offices may now be more important than junior ministers. We need to see whether the locus of power has shifted to the extent that the cabinet becomes, in Bagehot's terms, a dignified, rather than a working, part of the political system.

Rhodes developed the concept of the core executive to explain how decisions are made in Britain, drawing into the analysis those key advisers and civil servants. He argued that:

> The label 'cabinet government' was the overarching term for (some of) these institutions and practices but it is inadequate and confusing because it does not describe accurately the effective mechanisms for achieving coordination. At best it is contentious, and at worst seriously misleading, to assert the primacy of cabinet among all organisations and mechanisms at the heart of government.

Burch and Holliday, too, regard the cabinet as part of a set of interlocking institutions that need to be understood as a whole. They discuss the broader notion of the cabinet system as a set of arenas over which ministers and others fight for authority and influence. Here the cabinet is just part of, even if sometimes the key feature of, the process that determines what happens in the system of governing. Rhodes argued that the resolution of conflict may be undertaken in any part of that system. The principal questions in this approach are: how do the influences and interactions combine? Are they assembled in cabinet or elsewhere in the system? What contribution does cabinet make to decisions; that is, who coordinates and resolves conflict?

The assumption here is that the role of cabinet is to resolve conflict at the centre of government. That assumption has been questioned. Andeweg asks why the resolution of conflict, rather than, say, representation should be regarded as the primary function given precedence in the study of cabinet. He has a point: discussing cabinet in Canada *without* analysing pressures of representation would be of limited credibility. But if the need to resolve conflict is granted, then as an analytical device for understanding the centre of government, the concept of the core executive has value. Cabinet will never be the sole source of authority; there is value in providing a corrective for the notion that cabinet alone determines what may happen. The concern is to identify who makes the crucial decisions in a range of cases. But the approach is about influence in government, where cabinet is one player, rather than about cabinet itself.

That may be a useful analytic tool, but it will not carry much weight with ministers. For participants, cabinet *is* different. Appointment to cabinet is the sign of success for ministers, particularly in Britain and Australia where there are tiers of ministers and only the senior sit in cabinet. It is the target of ambition for politicians. Cabinet decisions, however they are made and whoever is initially responsible, have weight and legitimacy within the bureaucracy, usually greater than decisions emerging from other forums; they are the currency of government. If cabinet meetings had no practical or useful function, they would be discontinued. But they are held, frequently and without question. Why? Even if cabinet may now serve different functions from those of the nineteenth and twentieth centuries – and what these functions may be is an empirical question – its existence remains important. Cabinet needs to be understood within the broader framework of the core executive and its significance assessed.

These five different criteria may lead to contrasting judgments about whether the cabinet is working well, and hence varying conclusions about what is required for cabinet to be improved. *Constitutional theorists* will explore the relations between cabinet and other parts of the political system: cabinet government in their view works to the extent the cabinet is responsible to and responsive to the needs of the broader political system. The *public administration school* will ask what procedures govern behaviour and whether the rules are being applied, whether the institutional and supporting arrangements are adequate or effective. The *public policy advocates* will explore how cabinet makes policy decisions and whether it has the capacity to fulfil a range of functions that require a broader outlook; they may argue it should have a strategic or priority-setting capacity. The power realists will look at the political outcomes and ask whether the balance of power may be, or should be, altered. *Network analysts* will ask whether cabinet is indeed a centre of real authority or whether that power has been ceded to others on strategic positions. Hence 'solutions' for a cabinet that does not live up to expectations may be better rules, more sophisticated coordination and more effective accountability.

This discussion illustrates that there are several ways that cabinet can be considered and that the different models will concentrate in turn on:

- responsibility and accountability
- procedures and rules
- approving or deciding policy outcomes
- power among the players
- networks of influence.

These are useful analytical distinctions, each based on different approaches and they will shape the second half of the book. They are all a means to an end: the interpretation of cabinet government. None of them provides a working definition of cabinet government. They mean little to practitioners who are instinctive rather than analytic in their exercise of power. Getting to power and staying there are the fixations for political leaders and their supporters.

How do practitioners react when asked about the nature of cabinet government? Officials from central agencies that support cabinets provide a different type of definition aimed at what cabinets are required to achieve. These officials offer a pragmatic emphasis:

- Cabinet government is the arrangements the prime minister makes to ensure that decisions are made in the interests of the general, rather than the individual minister, with a view to presenting a unified program for legislation and supply (Canada).
- Cabinet government is a shorthand term for the process by which government determines its policy and ensures the political will to implement it (Britain).
- Cabinet government is collective government and must establish a coherent set of policies consistent with its strategic directions; it needs policy coherence and political support (Australia).

All these definitions are process neutral. They accept the need for political support and for coherent policy, but appreciate that the mix will change from time to time. How the prime ministers use cabinets to achieve these objectives will differ from person to person. Some prime ministers take initiatives as individuals; others work through the cabinet. Some discuss policies in a meeting of ministers; others work in and around the cabinet. The definitions have a realistic ring, and an acknowledgment that there is no single way that cabinet government must be organised and run.

In French's terms, officials are pragmatists rather than theorists. They see the need for a prime ministerial overview, but do not seek to prescribe what prime ministers should do or how they do it. Whether a study has, in these terms, a theorist or pragmatic approach makes a difference to the emphasis of the analysis; it will lead to a different set of questions. The theorists might ask why cabinets have failed to live up to the proper standards and expectations of the Constitution or to the prescriptions of the Westminster system; they seek an ideal. The pragmatist will ask what the cabinets are doing, how they perceive the issues and whether or how they could do it better.

Analysing Australian cabinets

This book explores the institution of the Australian cabinet from two angles. In the first half it provides an account of the evolution of cabinet, of the way the institution developed and the pressures that drove change: from that small and often informal meeting of colleagues to the highly institutionalised structure of 2006. The chapters are chronological, organised by governments, as they document the changes that occurred. In those first decades there were no centralised cabinet records. The National Archives culled the files to collate a series of documents that cabinet would most likely have seen. They remain incomplete (there was no filing system that could be described as complete anyway), but they are the best available. In those early years, then, the picture must be little more than a series of snapshots. In the 1940s, 1950s, 1960s and early 1970s the records are much fuller. The intention nonetheless is to provide evidence of the way that cabinet worked and the pressures upon it. I have not tried to cover everything that cabinet might have determined. The emphasis remains on how cabinet procedures functioned.

After 1974 the 30-year non-disclosure rules cut in and there is no formal access to cabinet documents given they have not yet been released. However, I have been observing and writing on the ways of the Australian cabinet since 1974. In the late 1980s, when I was writing a study of Malcolm Fraser as prime minister, he kindly gave me access to the cabinet papers of his government. I have used here only those details that were put on the record in my book *Malcolm Fraser PM*. In support of that project and several other books on ministers, prime ministers and departmental secretaries, I have interviewed senior officials and ministers on a regular basis over 30 years. The later period therefore relies in part on that earlier research.

The second half of the book draws on this historical evidence to provide a series of insights into the way that cabinet works in Australia. It seeks to explore the five themes that have been developed above. I ask questions about:

- cabinet as a focus of responsibility, as part of the political system (Chapter 11)
- cabinet as a set of rules and bureaucratic practices, and their implications for its workings (Chapter 12)

- cabinet as a maker of policy, and the search for better decision-making (Chapter 13)
- cabinet as a centre for political power, particularly the weight of prime ministers and their ability to drive the cabinet agenda (Chapter 14)
- cabinet as a network of influences and relationships (Chapter 15).

This last chapter also develops the question of whether cabinet itself remains a crucial forum or whether, consistent with the implications of the core executive, it has become, in Bagehot's terms, a dignified but not effective part of the Constitution. To illustrate how cabinet government in Australia reflects some of its local traditions, this chapter is explicitly comparative. It asks whether cabinet is a more powerful institution than its equivalent bodies in similar systems of government in Canada and the United Kingdom, and what accounts for the variations.

In each government the emphasis is often on the early years because that was where the style of that government was established. Cabinets often became set in their ways, with ministers reluctant to change their *modus operandi*. New ministers, by contrast, and particularly those with no previous cabinet experience, were more prepared to experiment. I also seek to identify the style and impact of different prime ministers, as the way they presided determines the way that cabinet works. At the same time I have sought to keep the narrative simple, avoiding cluttering the text with too many of the myriad of minor players who had momentary, even if significant, roles in Australia's cabinet story.

The concern here is not to ask how Australia is governed, but to inquire how cabinet works, what its influence is, under what constraints it operates, and what impact it has.

PART 1

THE AUSTRALIAN EXPERIENCE

2 SETTING THE ARRANGEMENTS: 1901–14

Cabinet took off in full stride. The first executive council met on 1 January 1901. The new private secretary to the prime minister, Atlee Hunt, then wrote out the first government gazette in longhand, establishing the departments of state. For three months there was no parliament to which ministers had to answer and an election had to be fought. Yet the ministers had to undertake all those rare activities required to create a new level of government, almost without support. Barton's office space was temporary.

> Lyne, as minister for home affairs but still premier of New South Wales, provided for Barton by sending his secretary off on leave and commandeering his room. The prime minister's business was conducted by Atlee Hunt on a table set up in an ante-room of Parliament House which was used as a thoroughfare. Privacy was impossible, documents went astray, and in later years Barton was wont to reminisce that when he travelled from Sydney to Melbourne he could carry the whole federal archives in his Gladstone bag.

In these first months cabinet met regularly as it had to plan a whole legislative program and establish a government almost without officials.

There is no record of quite how often the cabinet met in the first year. In May 1902 Barton went to an imperial conference in Britain that was intended to coincide with the coronation. Deakin, as acting prime minister and chair of cabinet, began to keep records. They are not extensive. On the left-hand side of each page is the date and a list of items. On the top of the right-hand side is a list of those ministers who attended, usually four or five only. Opposite each item was the outcome. It was always brief: 'considered', 'deferred', or 'decided'. Where there were decisions, they were summarised in a word or two, never more than two or three lines. There were no other minutes. The decisions were recorded by the minister on the paper from which they read and then sent back to the officials.

Barton may have maintained a similar record in the first 15 months of his cabinet, but, if so, it did not survive. On his return from Britain, Barton continued Deakin's practice. There are, in the first decade, records of all the period in which Deakin was prime minister, but none for the Watson, Reid or Fisher governments. However, what does exist, with the records collected in the cabinet files, allows some appreciation of the rhythm and content of the cabinet meetings.

In 1903 cabinet did not meet until 26 February and only once after 20 October, as an election was held in December. Between those dates cabinet met 51 times; meetings were heaviest in the winter months as the principal pieces of foundation legislation were developed. In May and August there were eight meetings each month.

July was the busiest month because it was the occasion of the greatest tension. There were 12 meetings that month. Six of them had only one item on the agenda: the Conciliation and Arbitration Bill where there was a major division between Kingston and the other members of cabinet. Time after time Barton recorded merely that the bill was 'further discussed' or 'further considered'. Sometimes parts were agreed. On 23 July he noted that 'Mr Kingston resigns, accepted 24 July'. The next week he records that the bill was 'further discussed and settled'. The relief is almost palpable.

The impression is almost cosy, as, by modern standards, it was. Four or five people, far from home in distant parts of Australia, were meeting regularly to establish the skeleton of a new government. Some of the issues were trivial: who would pay the phone bill of the Governor-General: 'send it to the treasurer', determined the prime minister. Or a cryptic note about an exchange of letters between the Governor-General and the prime minister on 'the subject of raising the Marquis of Tullibardine's horse'. 'The matter was discussed in cabinet', but there is no report of what was actually arrived at. Others were to be perennial matters of controversy, even 100 years later. What travel costs should be paid for ministers? Should travel be paid for the wives of parliamentarians? There were the usual begging letters from companies asking 'what concessions your Government would be prepared to extend to an American company that is willing to invest $20,000,000 in

Australia in the iron industry'. Barton annotated such requests with the simple instruction: 'To cabinet'.

Some issues were of broader significance. The Governor-General cabled London on 12 April 1901:

> Federal cabinet first sitting Melbourne decided unable recommend [Colonial Secretary Joseph] Chamberlains suggestion send Boer prisoners Tasmania other business unimportant Turner absent slight illness.

The records suggest a continuing conversation in which ministers brought issues to the attention of their colleagues. Barton used to note who brought the items to cabinet. Most often it was the prime minister himself; Lyne, Minister for Home Affairs, was the next most frequent. The cabinet often chose to continue debate, with items deferred or delayed, even when the final outcome was an item being referred to the minister for action. Sometimes issues were not reached. Since the agenda in those first years never had more than 12 items, usually only six or seven and occasionally only one, the emphasis seems to have been on discussion rather than expedition.

Even so the cabinet suffered from leaks. In April 1901 the Colonial Secretary complained that he was reading in the London newspapers cables detailing actions by the cabinet to induce the Colonial Office to negotiate with France over the sale of Kergualen Island. In 1903, in a cable to the Colonial Secretary, Barton condemned the leaking:

> That it has been published is due, I fear, to treachery. I am now causing a full enquiry to be made into the matter and, should that enquiry, as I hope, result in the detection of the offender, he would be promptly and severely punished.

It was to be the first of many such leak inquiries.

In other policy areas, Barton established an all too common theme for cabinets: how to keep control of expenditure. In June 1903 he complained to ministers that the estimates were too high:

> It appears to me undesirable that the expenditure of the Government should be increased to anything like the extent mentioned, and I shall be pleased if you will examine the Estimates with great care, in order that reductions may be effected wherever practicable, as it is my particular wish that Parliament shall not be asked to sanction any expenditure which is not absolutely essential for the proper performance of the work of Government.

The process was *ad hoc* and almost random with a degree of disorder. On 11 December 1902 Barton wrote to his private secretary:

> Mem
>
> There is a matter I told you I would bring up at tomorrow's cabinet. Do you remember what it is? I've been cudgelling my brains over it but can't recall it. When I go to Sydney next week I will take all the papers connected with the conference & any other matters which arose during my visit to England. I may not want the discussions. By the way, is the abstract finished? I should like to have a copy in every colleague's hands before returning to Sydney ...
>
> If anything of great importance suggests itself to you as a matter on which cabinet should ruminate before we rusticate, let me know in time to put it in my little list. Another cabinet this year may be out of the question. Then there is the matter of presiding over Executives when H.E. is in Adelaide and seeing that he is well informed on Executive matters. Remind me.

Relying on his personal secretary to remember items for cabinet indicates how little support, whether secretarial or official, Barton had. On return from the London conference he provided cabinet with a 70-page report – in his own handwriting.

Cabinet was from the beginning concerned with political tactics and manoeuvres. That was a matter of necessity. In its first nine years no government had a majority in the House of Representatives. Cabinets had to rely on support from a third party, usually (except for 1904–05) the Labor party. Determining parliamentary tactics – and ensuring a common view – were thus immediate necessities for the new cabinet. Barton discussed the opening of parliament, sitting days, the Governor-General's speech and the organisation of the election campaign with his ministers. When he took over in October 1903, Deakin brought the election dates and electoral program to cabinet for discussion, in between agreeing on Melbourne Cup Day (Australia's greatest horse race) to 'let officers go when they can be spared'.

Cabinet was also intent on ensuring that it made the crucial decisions and did not want to cede authority to officials. On a number of occasions ministers consciously brought items within their competence to cabinet for a policy decision; on a payment to a senior officer of the Defence department the minister said: 'I think it would be well to submit this to cabinet so that a ruling may be obtained to guide me in future cases'.

The transition from Barton to Deakin was seamless. On 24 September Barton noted:

> I announced to the cabinet that having offered the office of chief justice of the High Court to Sir Samuel Griffith who has indicated his willingness to accept it, I have decided to resign the Office of Prime Minister and to place myself in the hands of my colleagues, indicating also that Mr O'Connor has placed in the hands of the prime minister his resignation of the office of Vice President of the Ex Council.

Barton and O'Connor were duly appointed as justices of the High Court. It was to be the first of only three orderly and uncontested hand-overs from one prime minister to another in the next century.

Deakin's legacy: Consolidating cabinet procedures

After the election of 1903 the parliamentary situation became more uncertain. Deakin continued in office until April when he was replaced by the first Labor government led by Chris Watson. After a mere three months the non-Labor parties combined to displace Watson and George Reid headed a coalition government that was an amalgam of free traders and protectionists. For most of its time in government parliament was in recess. As soon as it met the government was doomed; Labor threw its support behind Deakin who resumed office in July 1905 and stayed there until Labor decided to bring him down in November 1908. Another brief Labor cabinet, headed by Andrew Fisher, from November 1908 to June 1909, survived long enough for the non-Labor parties to combine officially, return to office and lose the April 1910 election handsomely. From June 1909 the modern party system, in which Labor and non-Labor faced one another, was essentially created.

Cabinet seemed unaffected. But the links between cabinet and caucus became an issue for the first time. Protectionist prime ministers had met their parties in regular meetings, but the Labor caucus had greater ambitions to share power with cabinet. In 1904 the Labor caucus authorised Watson to accept the commission to form a government and then agreed to give him a free hand in the selection of his ministry. He consulted with his senior colleagues, Billy Hughes and Egerton Batchelor, before he chose ministers. They had a range of experience: Dawson and Fisher had been ministers in the week-long Labor government in Queensland in 1899; Batchelor had been a minister in South Australia. Caucus immediately put on the books a demand for a discussion of the relationship between cabinet and caucus, though no conclusions were reached. It initially opposed any idea of a coalition, although it later authorised Watson to negotiate towards an alliance with Deakin. He declined the offer to talk.

Caucus met 17 times while Watson was prime minister. It never directly sought to direct cabinet, although it did appoint a delegation to the minister of external affairs to discuss the Immigration Restriction Bill. Limitations instead came from the state branches. When the caucus sought to gain some electoral quarantine for those non-Labor members who gave them support in parliament, the state branches of Victoria and Queensland refused to endorse any offer of immunity. When the government was under threat by a reunited opposition, Watson reported to caucus the thinking of the cabinet. On 6 July, he declared that if either of two amendments to the Conciliation and Arbitration Bill were carried the government would ask for a dissolution of parliament and, if that was refused, would resign. The caucus agreed. On 28 July, in discussion of the key amendment on which the government was eventually to fall, a motion to amend the cabinet's proposal was lost by ten votes to nine. Backbenchers believed they had an active role as partners to cabinet.

Ministers were scarcely regular attendees at caucus meetings. Hughes did not attend any meetings after 26 May, missing 13 in a row. Dawson came to only one of the 17, Mahon only to the first three. The prime minister spoke at eight of the 17, including the one where he thanked the supporters just prior to the government's resignation. Senator Gregor McGregor, the near-blind leader of the government in the Senate, was the link between the cabinet and the more radical members. The relationship was not close enough for the radical backbenchers. In the next years they successfully sought at national conference to institutionalise rules by which the supremacy of caucus over cabinet was clearly accepted, including the election of ministers by the caucus.

Of the proceedings of the Watson cabinet there is little record. Hughes wrote many years later:

> Just what we talked about at that first Labour Cabinet meeting has passed from my mind, which is not to be greatly wondered at; for although we contrived to maintain that outward placidity of demeanour which, tinged with the suggestion of encyclopaedic knowledge and thinly veiled authority, is the hallmark of ministers, we were, in sober fact, as worked up and nervous as young soldiers going into battle. Anyway, whatever we were talking about

> was forgotten the moment our leader, Mr Watson, the new prime minister, entered the room and seated himself at the head of the table. All eyes were riveted on him; he was worth going miles to see ... He was the perfect picture of the statesman, the leader. He inspired us all with courage; when he began to speak we hung upon his words, and agreed with all he said before he had finished saying it. Like Master, like man; we patterned ourselves upon him, sartorially and in every other way; and to such good purpose that ... even our bitterest opponents freely admitted that we looked the part and our ministerial manners left nothing to be desired.

Some issues that did come to cabinet illustrated that a new government was in power. The cabinet approved overtime payment for Sunday work. But no records have survived that document the activities of that first Labor cabinet.

There are none at all for the short-lived Reid-McLean cabinet either. But there were occasions when the rights of the executive over the other branches of government were called into account. The attorney-general used his control of the purse to try to limit to one the number of staff that the justices of the High Court took with them when they travelled to hear cases. The chief justice exploded in anger declaring that this was an attempt to interfere with the administration of justice. The affair was smoothed over when Deakin returned to power, but it indicated the need for all parts of the system to mark out their territory and determine what was suitable behaviour.

The second Deakin government, from July 1905 to November 1908, further established the norms of cabinet government. In the first month of the new government, cabinet met nine times, as it settled its priorities and prepared a statement for parliament that established its program. In one week it met four days in succession. For the rest of the year it met roughly weekly, holding three or four meetings a month with seven or so issues on each agenda. Deakin also created a cabinet sub-committee of three ministers, to gather the necessary information on rural products bounties and then report back and advise on action; it was the first committee to which I can find any reference. Over the next months a number of issues were referred to this sub-committee. In the first five months of 1906, the cabinet only met once a month, before shifting into weekly mode once parliament had met. In September and October cabinet discussed the program and policy for the elections.

In March 1907 Deakin travelled to the Imperial conference. After he returned in June, he was ill for a long period. He did not attend a cabinet meeting between his departure in March and early November. On several occasions in the 15 meetings he missed, cabinet decided to inform him what they had decided or to ask advice on what could be done. Even when the treasurer, Sir John Forrest, resigned after his return from England, protesting about the continued reliance of the government on Labor support, there seemed little pressure on Deakin to attend. Nor did he seek to run the cabinet from afar. That was not Deakin's style. In 1908 he held fewer meetings, often only one a month, sometimes with a large agenda (not all of which was covered) and then never more than three times a month. By this stage the style of government was set. In October the budget was brought to cabinet and settled with a large tick. In November cabinet decided to discuss the political situation created by the withdrawal of support by Labor. Cabinet 'decided to challenge House on Tuesday'. Deakin moved a motion, declaring that if the government lost it would resign. It did.

In June 1909 the non-Labor parties finally merged after extensive negotiations and considerable angst. The combined parties, rather contemptuously, voted the government from office amid accusations of being Judas (from its own backbench) and withering contempt from Hughes. Deakin took office for the third time, as the only person under whose leadership the different sections were prepared to unite. In the first month of office the cabinet had to determine where it stood in terms of the program already before the parliament; it seems to have been in almost permanent session, meeting 12 times in June alone, ticking through the bills ('Proceed', 'Proceed, Push on', recorded Deakin against one item after another as the cabinet pushed through its decisions). Thereafter, with the direction set, the pace of meetings could be more relaxed, once or twice a month. It considered the budget 'in detail'. In the last meetings it had to appoint the High Commissioner in London and Deakin noted 'Sir John Forrest desires not to be considered'. The old enemy, George Reid, was chosen instead. That apart, meetings in early 1910 were spent discussing election dates and the policy speech. After defeat in the elections, Deakin held two final cabinets: to announce the government's resignation and to farewell his colleagues.

Deakin may have been by this stage a senior citizen; of those whose company he enjoyed in 1901 only Forrest was left, and he had resigned in 1907 to pressure Deakin to break with Labor. His secretary commented that 'out of office he was jolly and genial, but in office he was reserved and kept all at arm's length'. That did not prevent Deakin from imposing detailed controls on ministers; for instance, he wanted all answers to parliamentary questions sent to him for approval in advance. Not all ministers appreciated such close attention.

Labor in office: Tackling the caucus–cabinet relationship

The new Labor government, elected in 1910 with majorities in both houses, created new problems for cabinet. In the Watson government caucus had been quiet, even reverential; it sent delegates to meet ministers, rather than demanding action through motions in the party room. Even though its opponents accused the cabinet of being in thrall to caucus there was little evidence of such bondage in practice. Watson claimed: 'There is no truth to the suggestion by Mr Reid that the Ministry has to submit matters to Caucus, though on several occasions, as a matter of courtesy after something has been decided upon, it has reported to caucus'.

By the end of 1910 the Labor backbenchers had much greater confidence and strength and sought to exercise the power that the party rules nominally gave them. Initially in 1910, there was a degree of cooperation between cabinet and caucus; four caucus committees were set up to consider legislation before it went to parliament. Sometimes a bill received extensive discussion and led to amendments from backbenchers.

But, as ministers found their feet and caucus its capacity, there were severe clashes. In September there was a long discussion of the relationship between caucus and cabinet after the Works Estimates had been pushed through the House in an all-night sitting. A motion 'that this party sincerely hopes that the method adopted to push the Works Estimates through in one sitting should not occur again' was discussed over four sessions before it was withdrawn. For most of the parliament, relations seem to have been quite good, perhaps because Fisher accepted the right of caucus to discuss strategy and tactics, but also because, as Childe suggests, the government's program reflected the sentiments of the Labor movement and cabinet tried, usually successfully, to implement the party platform. There were still some limits. When an MP demanded in 1912 that caucus consider all significant appointments, the debate on the motion extended over three days before Fisher ruled that, as the motion was 'not a party question no vote could be taken'. An attempt to overturn his ruling was eventually lost and some cabinet discretion was retained.

The Labor government thus brought a new dimension to cabinet government. Prime ministers have always worked closely with their supporters, particularly in those early years when parliamentary support was uncertain and all legislation had to be negotiated through the House. The tight interconnectedness of party and cabinet was emphasised. After 1904 the Labor caucus elected ministers. Watson had been allowed to select his own, but the 1905 interstate conference resolved that future Labor cabinets be elected. In 1908 Watson had tried to give Fisher the same freedom he had exercised, but his motion was defeated by 24 votes to 17. By 1910 election of ministers was accepted practice.

So, too, was the regular attendance of the prime minister and his colleagues at the weekly meetings of caucus. Fisher presided over about half the meetings in 1910 and most of the meetings in 1911 and 1912. Access for backbenchers was thus constant and the prime minister was always aware of the views, backed by the capacity to vote, of his party. But caucus only met when parliament was sitting. There were no meetings between 25 November 1910 and 30 August 1911, or between 15 December 1911 and 12 June 1912 when the new parliamentary sessions began. For much of the year cabinet was unencumbered by meetings of caucus. Even so, there was a level of integration between party and cabinet that was at that time unique and that made the process of governing more complex. If it was difficult in times of peace under a consensus leader such as Andrew Fisher, it was to prove to be more contentious under the mercurial Billy Hughes in wartime.

Up to the Fisher government, support for the prime minister and the cabinet had primarily been provided by a branch of the Department of External Affairs. In the first six months, as the federal government was being established, Atlee Hunt, the secretary of that department, sent out a number of memoranda under the title of the Prime Minister's Department, but it never had any formal status, nor was it provided for in the Estimates. Since Barton, Deakin (in his first two stints) and Reid were also external affairs ministers, and much of their activity concerned interactions with the British Colonial Secretary, this was logical. The department could readily deal with correspondence, and to a lesser extent, state premiers, as required. The prime ministers themselves were served by a single private secretary; first, Atlee Hunt (for a brief period), quickly followed by T.R. Bavin (later a Nationalist premier of New South Wales) and then Malcolm Shepherd filled that position. Shepherd recalled later that in those early days he only provided secretarial support to Deakin. He would not have presumed to offer policy advice.

Following Watson's precedent, Fisher took the treasury as well as being prime minister; he appointed a separate minister for external affairs. That decision raised the question of how he ought to be advised on matters referred to him as prime minister. In 1910 he instructed that the external affairs department be divided into two sections, one of which was to serve him as prime minister. As the head of external affairs noted, all the papers submitted to the prime minister in his role as prime minister, that is, questions for cabinet or executive council and matters concerning the Governor-General or state premiers, were to go to this section, which was effectively the prime minister's office (PMO). Fisher noted that 'I do not consider that at the present time the circumstances warrant the establishment of a separate department, though that may become necessary at some later date'. Shepherd was appointed as head of that section.

A year later the change occurred. On 11 April Fisher decided to create a separate Prime Minister's Department under Shepherd and required that provision for it be made in the 1911–12 Estimates. He argued that 'included in the department will be the Executive Council, the Auditor-General and I suggest the Public Service Commissioner'. In the face of criticism, justification was provided by the Labor leader in the Senate: 'it had been found absolutely necessary, in the interests of good government, that the prime minister should have some place entirely separated from the treasury where he could transact the business which rightly belongs to his office, without being harassed by the work of that Department'. The head of government had to sign all the inter-governmental correspondence. When another minister became minister for external affairs, 'the prime minister became divorced from the records that ought to be available to him'.

The decision identified a central element of the prime ministership. There are responsibilities that the prime minister must fulfil which are broader than the scope of any one department, even the Treasury. They are concerned with the running of the government and the overview of the government's progress; prime ministers must organise and direct cabinet and deal with the state premiers. For these activities they need advice and Fisher thought he could get it more readily from a small department headed by Shepherd. Later prime ministers agreed with this diagnosis. From the beginning the department was created to serve the prime minister, not the collective cabinet. This initial decision determined the character of future arrangements.

In 1913 Labor narrowly lost its majority in the House but still dominated the Senate. Joseph Cook formed a cabinet for which few details can be found. Much of the time was spent provoking the Labor Senate and engineering a double dissolution election. As the double dissolution election, called by Cook, was being fought, Europe went to war.

How Australia was to react to the war was to be a decision for cabinet, if cabinet could be brought together. An anonymous account in the cabinet records notes many of the difficulties caused by a crisis during an election:

> The Defence Schemes of Great Britain and the Dominions provided that, if a great war seemed imminent, the British government would cable to the Governor-General of each Dominion that there was 'danger of war'; later, if the war arrived, it would so inform him by a second telegram. On receiving the first message the Dominion would, if it so decided, order a precautionary stage of mobilisation, taking steps to protect seaports, railway bridges and other vital points.
>
> On July 30th the first of these messages arrived. The Governor-General, Sir Ronald Munro-Ferguson, was in Sydney, where his Official Secretary deciphered it. It happened that the Government was in the midst of an election campaign. The prime minister, Joseph Cook, was about to leave for an important election rally in the country; the Minister for Defence, Senator Millen, was in Sydney. [Major, later Sir Brudenall] White was at Defence headquarters in the Victoria Barracks, Melbourne. The message notifying 'danger of war' and the need to take precautionary measures did not come to him, but two hours later, shortly after 5 p.m. on the 30th, he heard of it from the Navy Office, which, in turn, had learnt of it from the British admiral commanding the China station, and also from New Zealand.

Even then there were misunderstandings as the telegram had been wrongly deciphered and the minister for defence thought no further action was required.

> The Governor-General meanwhile had telegraphed to the prime minister suggesting that the Cabinet should be summoned so that the British Government might know what support to expect from Australia. But the prime minister had not the key to the cipher and had to telegraph to Melbourne to have the message deciphered. When at last on August 1st he learnt its contents he ordered a cabinet meeting to be summoned in Melbourne for Monday August 3rd. Meanwhile another message had come from the British Government asking that precautionary steps should be taken at defended ports. The prime minister hurrying back to Melbourne at last learnt that the telegrams received were matters of intense urgency. He called the service chiefs to him on the morning of the 2nd; but the most important of them, White,

> having been called from his office to Sydney, could not be present till cabinet met after the arrival of the Sydney express on August 3rd ... At the cabinet meeting were five of the ten ministers ... The meeting was wholly concerned with the naval and military aid which could be given to Britain in the event of war.

Then the cabinet had to decide the level of commitment that could be made.

> When the prime minister turned to White and asked if he had any plan for sending a force from Australia in such an emergency, he spoke to the only man who had studied the matter and could advise him with a certainty; White's plans for cooperation with New Zealand were in his private drawer, ready for emergency. A force of 12,000 men of all arms could be raised and organised for service abroad, he said, and he could guarantee to have them ready for sailing in six weeks.

But the decision was made as much on the basis of national pride as military analysis.

> Mr Cook was determined that Australia's contingent should be bigger than this. New Zealand and Canada had already offered contingents and the Canadian offer was reported to be of 30,000 men. Mr Cook asked White if 20,000 could be sent. The reply was that they could and that was a fair prospect that they would be ready to sail in six weeks. Cabinet decided to offer them and that Australia should bear the cost of sending and maintaining them.

The decision was thus eventually made, if after a chaotic process and without too much thought. Decision-making by this partial cabinet was on the run.

Then there rose the question of paying for the commitment when parliament was not sitting and an election was being held. The treasurer, Sir John Forrest, suggested to the prime minister that, as the Governor-General had executive authority, an Order in Council authorising the treasury to pay for mobilisation might be the proper course. Cook noted back on 21 August that: 'Cabinet agrees that in all the circumstances it should assume the responsibility'. Forrest tartly noted on the file: 'Action accordingly, but ministers would not have been relieved of any responsibility by the procedure I recommended'.

Cook lost the election. Fisher came into government and war.

3 STRETCHING THE LIMITS: 1914–23

Fisher was prime minister for the first year of the war. It had started while the election was being held, after the calling of a double dissolution, created by Labor's use of its majority in the Senate. Labor had a clear majority of nine in the 75-member House of Representatives and held 31 of the 36 Senate positions. The opposition to the cabinet was to come from behind, not from the Opposition, as the exigencies of wartime clashed with some of the cherished principles and prejudices of Labor members. The question always uppermost was whether the demands of security took precedence. Hughes always thought it should; the chasm was unbridgeable.

The split between the party and some members of cabinet began early. In Labor's first majority Fisher government caucus wanted a direct influence but usually worked with the ministers. This time the backbenchers challenged cabinet more directly. In the first three months caucus voted on the issues to be included in the Governor-General's speech, on the values at which a land tax should apply, and on the eligibility for pensions. When parliament was sitting, backbencher involvement was detailed and continuous. Caucus did not meet between December 1914 and April 1915 while parliament was prorogued; governing was primarily by regulation. But thereafter the criticism of government decisions was constant. Debate of sugar tariffs lasted over five sessions through three meetings. Even Fisher's ruling that members could not be bound as it was a tariff question did not calm the intensity. Eventually no vote was taken but the battlelines were drawn. At the next meeting, 14 June, the executive had asked that 'the attitude of certain members be discussed at Caucus'. Instead of backing cabinet, caucus demanded 'That in future all Government measures be submitted for the consideration of caucus before their presentation to parliament and that the nature of these measures when so presented to parliament shall be as a duly constituted meeting by majority may decide'. Then, on the formal motion 'That the Chairman now leave the Chair', a barrage of criticism ensued in a meeting constantly reconvened during the next three days.

In part this constant battle with caucus may have been a reason behind Fisher's decision to quit as prime minister. He had chaired most of the caucus meetings in the first six months of his government, but only did so once after July 1915. On 30 October he told the caucus that 'owing to the strain on his health during the last two years he had decided to be an applicant for a position in the public service, namely the position of High Commissioner [in London]. He had been unanimously selected by his colleagues ... he would ask them to appoint a successor and hoped they would give that gentleman the same consideration they had shown him'. The last point was pure ritual. He had become tired by the pressure and, according to George Pearce, was furious that he had been forced to break an agreement with the Opposition under pressure from the Australian Workers Union (AWU). He had had enough.

Caucus alone was perhaps not the problem. Although little remains of cabinet records, it seems Fisher's time was not as easy as it had been in his previous term. In the initial months the cabinet was likely to have been hectic, if judged by the range of issues that came up for discussion. Ministers decided to allow the naturalisation of enemy aliens over the age of 60. They approved the proposition in a cable from the High Commissioner that relayed Kitchener's request that the First Australian Imperial Force (AIF) be landed and trained in Egypt, as there was no proper accommodation available in England; as a doctor reported: 'to house Australian troops in tents in mid-winter on this windswept area [Salisbury Plain] after long voyage in troopships passing through tropics and subtropics would be criminal'. They also were concerned about the details of immigration. When the pearlers in Broome wanted to keep their native divers, cabinet determined on 11 November 1914: 'pearlers who lay up boats may return their coloured crews. On conclusion of war they may each obtain the number of coloured men employed at the time the boats were laid up, but the total number of permits now operating must not be exceeded when work is resumed and the conditions under which permits are issued to be reviewed prior to 30-6-1918'. When the mayor of Broome appealed against the decision, Fisher noted: 'Cabt regrets unable take action desired'.

Often the note of the decision made by the minister included the administrative follow-up that was required. In December the minister for external affairs told his secretary that cabinet 'decided that syphilis should be a notifiable disease in all the territories of the Commonwealth including Norfolk Island and Canberra. Please notify Home Affairs Department as to Canberra'. The Secretary, Atlee Hunt, in turn noted:

> Inform Home Affairs accgly. Inform Papua and Norfolk Island. Says AGs Dept now drafting measure for N.I. When its terms are settled will send copy for their inform.t [information]. Ascertain from AGs Dept when drafting maybe expected.

There were tensions between Fisher and Hughes from the beginning. Fisher may have led, but Hughes was becoming the dominant figure. For instance, in February 1915 the prime minister was in New Zealand. He cabled Hughes as acting prime minister:

> Cabinet approved Deakin as commonwealth representative Panama Exhibition. Deakin called on me day or two prior to my leaving Melbourne. On strength above I spoke him as the Commonwealth representative. Cannot go back on that. Apart from that serious aspect think him specially suited speak for us in America present critical time. Think any other decision costly blunder. Official engagements prevent immediate return. Cable urgently. All well, Fisher.

Hughes's response was not exactly accommodating:

> Cabinet will consider whole position tomorrow. Your cable will be brought before ministers. I quite understand the position.

The next day:

> Cabinet considered matter at length this morning. Ministers feel very strongly that they were misled and they fear deliberately misled by suppression of material facts but in view of your cable desire to know whether you were aware of contents of ... the ... letter forwarded by you to Mahon [External Affairs Minister] before your final intervention with Deakin and whether you consider in all the circumstances Deakin should still act for the Commonwealth.

Fisher insisted and Deakin duly went, but Fisher's authority did not seem strong.

Ministers came to cabinet with a single copy of the proposals they wanted cabinet to consider. It could come in any form. It might be a formal memorandum from the department, a letter from a member of the public seeking action, or an oral report.

In April 1915, the Secretary of External Affairs, Atlee Hunt, wrote to his minister that 'I have three matters for cabinet ...'. Two were requests for naturalisation from German-born residents who had been in the country from the time they were one year of age. He also wanted a reply to the British Colonial Secretary on the New Hebrides. The minister noted that cabinet had agreed to grant naturalisation in these cases. Not everything came to cabinet. The British High Commissioner wanted Australia to take 100 Syrian refugees, the Minister for External Affairs asked if it could be submitted to cabinet, Fisher was 'unable to comply with request'.

Other issues routinely went to cabinet committees. Questions of compensation for accidental death, special treatment or support for British wives of Australian troops were all sent to a committee to determine what would be done. The assistant minister and the vice-president of the executive council, both effectively ministers without portfolio, decided whether special treatment was desirable and what the level of compensation should be.

Once a decision was taken, the minister made a note of what was decided, usually on the covering memorandum, although external affairs minister, Hugh Mahon, once complained that the 'Prime minister took possession of Secretary's memo on the subject' and presumably took it with him when he left. The minister had to make a separate note of the decision. On other occasions the department secretary had to ask the minister to endorse the memo with the cabinet decision as a means of gaining authority to act, or even to find out what had been decided.

Consistently, information or endorsement came from three sources: the ministers' notes, a message from the prime minister, or a memo from his department. For instance, on 17 February 1915 the secretary of the Prime Minister's Department formally recorded:

> It was decided that the Minister for Defence be authorised to take such steps as he thinks necessary to intern enemy subjects in Australia who are fit for military service.

Then he sent a copy to the Defence Department, 'by direction for favour of attention'.

When Fisher resigned, Hughes was elected party leader and prime minister without opposition. Within ten days, Hughes's style of leadership became obvious. The Labor government had proposed a referendum for the states to transfer power to the federal government for the management of the war. Although the plans were advanced and a date set, no one seemed keen to proceed, certainly not the Labor premiers of New South Wales and Queensland. Caucus met on 4 November, a meeting that lasted well into the evening. After it closed, Hughes met the premiers and they all agreed that the states would pass legislation to transfer the necessary powers to the national government (although how they were going to pass the legislation through hostile upper houses was never announced; it was an excuse to get the government off the hook). Hughes then reconvened caucus (not cabinet) at 10.35 p.m. to get its approval to postpone the referenda; caucus agreed by 51 votes to 6. A week later Hughes told the caucus that he had been invited to go to England and thought it desirable to accept. Only three members voted against the proposal.

In the next year caucus barely met. There were three meetings in May 1916 and three more in August and September. On 14 November the caucus met and split over conscription, with Hughes leading his supporters out of the party and eventually into a Nationalist coalition. For the cabinet, the lack of caucus meetings must have been a relief, for caucus was always rebellious and difficult to manage. Even at the meeting where Hughes was elected unopposed as leader, caucus rejected his proposal that only one minister be elected to replace the departing Fisher. Instead a spill of all positions was passed and two ministers were dropped. The instigators of the spill, William Webster and the egregious King O'Malley, were elected in place of two incumbents. By the next May the two had fallen out and the three caucus meetings that month were dominated by charges that Webster and one of the defeated ministers, Archibald, were levelling at O'Malley for his administration of the development of Canberra as the federal capital. There was no collective responsibility as ministers traded accusations and the acting prime minister, Senator George Pearce, sought to quell the brawls.

Hughes had left Australia in January 1916 and did not return until 31 July. By that stage the great debate on conscription had split the caucus. In May Hughes had asked that conscription not be discussed by caucus until he returned. When he did, the issue had divided not just caucus but the party as a whole. In August caucus met over four days. On the final day it met at 2.30 p.m. and ran for 12 hours, finishing at 2 a.m. the next morning, with a compromise that no one would be called up for the next month and then, if recruitment numbers were enough, not until after the referendum on conscription. The compromise only passed by 23 to 21. In September Frank Tudor, minister for trade and customs and the next Labor leader, resigned from the ministry. In late September Hughes still presided over the party meeting, even though he had been expelled from the party by the NSW executive. By the next caucus in November any semblance of unity had collapsed. Hughes accused his opponents of treachery and led the walkout.

What of cabinet in this period? It does seem that there was still an expectation that collective responsibility should be applied. In August, the treasurer, William Higgs, wrote to his former leader Fisher in London: 'I shall vote against conscription in cabinet and in caucus if allowed by Cabinet's practice or decision to do so'. But Hughes did not want to discuss conscription there. He held two cabinet meetings in Melbourne the week he got back from England in August, but did not formally discuss the topic. As he wrote to Keith Murdoch, journalist and future press baron, that week: 'A large majority of our party in the parliament are frightened out of their lives – many of course dare not call their souls their own. I'm not even sure of the cabinet!' He was right; half the cabinet left with him, the other five stayed with the Labor party. In such a momentous battle, cabinet took second place to caucus and the political leagues outside the parliament.

Yet when Hughes was away in England, Pearce, even though a senator, was acting prime minister and chaired the cabinet. The systems worked effectively and with a degree of routine. Cabinet met at least weekly, sometimes more often, on occasion convening on consecutive days. The decisions were sent to ministers either from Pearce himself or from the secretary of the Prime Minister's Department who wrote that 'he was instructed by the acting prime minister to inform you cabinet has agreed ...'. Pearce sometimes sought to follow up cabinet decisions: he wrote to the attorney-general; 'At the meeting of cabinet held 16 May 1916 it was agreed that the Commonwealth should take what action it could to prevent the word "Anzac" being used for commercial or trade purposes. Will the Acting Attorney-General advise what action can be taken?' At times Pearce annotated a letter that had been taken to cabinet for consideration with instructions to the secretary of the department for action. Thus cabinet decided not to approve the establishment of a branch of the National City Bank of New York in Australia and agreed to disenfranchise persons of enemy birth for the period of the war and 12 months thereafter. Any exceptions had to be considered by cabinet.

Hughes was kept informed of decisions by cable; in May, for instance, he was sent a cable: 'Cabinet has approved gen[eral] principle War Profits tax on lines of English bill, to be operative for financial year ending June'. Pearce also asked, somewhat hopefully in May: 'Should be glad to know whether you can fix a definite date for your return'. Given the behaviour of caucus, he was looking forward to handing back the reins of government. He brought some order to the process of government.

Hughes as Nationalist prime minister

After Hughes and his 25 supporters walked out of the Labor party, the prime minister immediately appointed a new cabinet from among their group as a National Labor government. Unwilling to face parliament as a minority government, he opened tortuous negotiations with the Liberal Opposition. He exploited divisions among their leaders, particularly between Cook and Forrest, to merge the two parties into a new Nationalist organisation. Hughes, even though leader of the smallest group, was able to hang on to the prime ministership. The former Liberals provided six of the 11 ministers. The two-party structure, with cabinet relying on a majority, was quickly reinstated.

For the first 15 months after the Labor government split, including the 1917 election, Hughes remained in Australia, with cabinet run according to his own rules. Hughes would ensure that cabinet endorsed his views. When the British demanded that Australian troops, like all others, be shot for desertion, and that their 'privileged position be ended', cabinet 'decided they would not approve at this juncture to amend the Defence Act to conform with Army Act in references to sentences of death as punishment for desertion'.

In 1918 Hughes once again chose to go to Britain. This time he was away for 15 months, from 26 April 1918 to 23 August 1919. W.A. Watt, ex-premier of Victoria and treasurer, was acting prime minister. The tension between the two crackled over the telegraph lines. Watt was organised, careful and proper; Hughes was the precise opposite. As a former premier, Watt knew how he thought a cabinet should be run. Hughes only gave lip service to the concept of collectivity.

M.L. Shepherd, secretary of the Prime Minister's Department, approved of the way Watt ran cabinet:

> He was the most methodical of all prime ministers and had fixed times for each of the Heads of Departments with whom he had to

deal. He was treasurer as well as acting prime minister. His method of dealing with cabinet was ideal. Each minister would submit matters for discussion which it was my duty to classify and list. In this classification the ministers took it in turn to have first say. Decisions were noted by Watt in the space provided on the agenda for that purpose, and at the conclusion of the meetings all would be handed to me to type on the relevant file, which Watt would sign before returning to the Department. In this way there was no chance of argument later about the decision. In some previous cabinets each minister noted his own decisions, which did not always coincide with what other ministers thought had been settled.

Indeed cabinet seems to have been well organised and smoothly run. There was a degree of collective government. Pearce once noted to his department:

Cabinet had decided not to allow race meetings on week days in metropolitan areas with certain indicated exceptions. I do not propose to receive deputations on this point. The decision is not mine but a collective decision of cabinet and objections thereto should be sent to the head of government by those interested.

Such discipline and control was bound to lead to clashes with Hughes. Watt believed that Hughes should consult cabinet before making decisions overseas. Hughes thought cabinet should consult him before finalising decisions. The first clash occurred quickly. Watt cabled Hughes on 24 May:

Re finance, hope you will not mind me suggesting you not do anything involving finance on a large scale without consulting me.

He noted cabinet considered [General Birdwood's] views on military issues and felt it should accept his advice:

Will you carefully consider how new arrangement works, get White's view and advise me from England. At present this matter secret.

Hughes responded on 21 June.

I have received no cables from you since my departure from America. Should be glad to be kept closely in touch with the Government action and policy. Most embarrassing to learn of the things done by Government through columns of English press.

I suggest, in order that we may be able to represent Australia effectively, all important decisions of Cabinet be communicated to me before action is taken unless subject matter is such as precludes delay; that copies all cables to and from Colonial Office be sent me and that no action be taken on matters that gravitate around this end until we have opportunity of advising you.

Strictly confidential. Matters relating to war unsatisfactory. I fear Australian interests have suffered ... My opinion absolutely essential change all this. Am looking into matters war and general very closely.

Watt agreed in principle, but found the demands for delays outrageous. He cabled on 24 June:

I will see that you are kept posted on essential matters that may affect your representation in England. Surely you can get copies of cablegrams to and from Colonial Office in London, thus avoiding enormous expense of repeating both. One of my messages to you in America cost over 100 pounds.

Astonished at your suggestion that important decisions of Cabinet be communicated to you before any action is taken. I think you must trust myself and other colleagues to tell you of matters if it is considered advisable.

Watt often called Cabinet to discuss items in Hughes's cables that could be vague: 'very secret. I am not yet satisfied with plan campaign for war ... We must not have any more Passchendales', he once wrote.

Watt tried to maintain a process by which cabinet discussed items. Thus on 6 and 9 August Watt cabled:

... re AIF command: have consulted Pearce Minister for Defence, he concurs with you, am submitting matter Cabinet tomorrow and will cable result.

Cabinet considered your views AIF command and adopted numbers one to five inclusive recommendations contained in your telegram August 1st.

Watt and Hughes simply had different ideas about what the prime minister's prerogatives were. Hughes could write on 4 September that 'I am now giving closest attention to all such matters and will advise from time to time the policy that appears necessary leaving Cabinet to decide'. Watt felt that cabinet was left out and, in a foreshadowing of later war coverage by Cable News Network (CNN), complained on 3 October:

> Ministers naturally very pleased with rapid changes in war situation but are obliged to take all our information from the press. Ordinary war cables are now generally four or five days old. Can you arrange to keep us posted, so that parliament, which is sitting, may at least receive official confirmation of press cables.

Often ministers had to deny rumours, doubtless created by Hughes' less than diplomatic behaviour. Watt wrote on 21 August: 'Labor journalists here are reprinting report of alleged interview with you re conscription. Do you authorise me contradict statement re conscription'.

There were many misunderstandings, to put it at the most polite. Cabinet thought that a minister could usefully be sent to Britain to deal with much of the routine required by the needs of demobilisation and repatriation. On 31 August Watt said cabinet was 'slightly in dark' regarding the necessity for sending across a minister to assist Hughes. 'Cabinet agreed before you went. Do you want minister there?' Watt asked on 3 October. Hughes saw no need and declared a minister was not required. But later he complained he was left with all the work. Watt reminded him of the original plan and 'You have evidently forgotten the substance of our cable correspondence ... you cabled you had assumed command'.

Hughes had clear views when he wanted action, even on domestic matters:

> Shipping Bill. I hope you will not proceed during my absence. I initiated this Line. I have my ideas as to how it should be run.

Watt replied:

> Shipping Bill: cabinet decided to postpone as long as possible until definitely known whether you will arrive during session. If found you cannot return within that time, Bill must be proceeded with or definite promise broken.

But cabinet still had to ask for the chance to add their view even on the most crucial of issues, such as the Peace Plan:

> Your colleagues unanimously think, in view of rapid change in situation and prospects of early important events that you should remain in Britain. There will be no trouble in Party or country.
>
> If you wish it, Ministers will be glad give you their views on some President Wilson's fourteen peace points. They feel strongly that articles 2, 3, and 5 would be distinctly unacceptable to Australian people and menacing to their future safety and prosperity.

Hughes did not necessarily wait for a reply when he asked for views. On 8 November, Watt wrote:

> Immediately on receipt your telegram 6th November Cabinet called together. While considering it we were apprised of your utterance on question, as telegraphed by Herald representative. This greatly embarrassed us, as I understood you would await colleagues' views before defining any public utterance ... Apart from this, Cabinet unanimously share your surprise and indignation that conditions of peace should be decided without consultation with Dominions.

And again in January 1919:

> On several occasions lately there have appeared in press cables reports of alleged interviews or alleged utterances by you on matters of gravest moment to Australia. Sometimes they contain declarations of Australian policy which Government as Government has never considered, including list of Aus demands at Peace conference, so I asked Cabinet to deliberate, with the result I am now authorised to advise you as follows ...
>
> When considering this report, I again felt the embarrassment of having to deal with such matters after declarations had been made upon them by yourself and not as subjects for consultation between cabinet and yourself.

The cabinet often had to take Hughes's word for what was happening; thus on 11 April:

> Unanimous view of colleagues that if facts or developments are as you describe or fear, Cabinet supports your view as expressed.

At times Watt insisted that no decision was final until cabinet agreed. On the sale of wheat:

> Your telegram November 11th: wheat: was astonished at its contents ... In the meantime I do not regard the wheat as sold and hope you will do nothing until further advised.

Cabinet had on one occasion 'been waiting patiently for some information concerning destination of German West Pacific Islands'. When cabinet did express a clear opinion in time, Hughes was often begrudging in his agreement. He wanted to take an aggressive stance on Nauru; cabinet advised him to be more delicate. Hughes finally wrote:

> In the face of your telegram I could not of course follow the only course that would have given us full control of Nauru and its phosphates. I am quite sure I should have succeeded had Cabinet supported me. As it did not, I have been perforce compelled to make best of bad job.

Watt was caught in the middle. He not only had to deal with a rampant prime minister, but with the party behind him. In October, he:

> ... discussed war situation with Party yesterday. Informed them of Cabinet telegram to you. Party unanimously approved that you should remain in Britain this war crisis.

He had to fend off rumours of challenges to the leadership:

> Secret. Pearce has just shown me Censor's copies of press cables despatched by Age and Sun correspondents to London during last three weeks of November. I consider them venomous and totally misrepresentative of the position here. Allusions to movement to effect change of leadership of Party entirely without warrant. I know nothing of it and will have nothing to do with it if it arises.

There was the occasional political crisis. When the minister for the navy Jens Jensen was criticised by a royal commission for his own behaviour in rorting tendering processes on behalf of a close colleague, Watt told Hughes:

> All members furnished with report Saturday. Cabinet met and considered matter very fully Monday; meeting lasted whole day and evening Jensen attended and stated his case fully. Cabinet decided unanimously that best course was for Jensen to resign.

Jensen refused. So Watt:

> Called Cabinet together and decided only course was to invite Governor-General cancel his commission ... Give me your views on matter.

Jensen was forced out.

Watt also had to brief the party. Sometimes their potential reaction concerned him. He wrote in May:

> Shipbuilding. Impossible summon cabinet but Poynton Minister for Home and Territories and I have discussed matter afresh and

> prepared to authorise you arrange for construction of three steamers of type mentioned on best terms possible. We are, of course, taking risks with party who are scattered over Australia in going this far and for strategic reasons at this stage we think it better to cut out passenger accommodation. When we meet party in July, may be able to convince them to give us a free hand.

But they were in 'splendid temper' in June 1919. On political tactics, Cabinet had to determine the date for re-opening parliament; when Hughes wanted it delayed, Watt took it to cabinet for decision.

At times Watt was close to breaking. In December he wrote 'I have had eight months' leadership and am very sick of it. The sooner you return the better I will be pleased'. In April he asked if Hughes had considered his retirement. Hughes turned on the charm:

> I confess at once that prospect of your retirement fills me with dismay. The problems facing Commonwealth are tremendous. There is *trouble* inside the party. I am very sick of everything and am little disposed to fight desperate battles inside as well as outside. I too want a rest ... my dear Watt, I know your health must be bad for you are not the kind of man to leave the ranks without great cause, but can you not leave things as they are until I return.

But Hughes had not changed his style. In June Watt complained about interference in the Honours list:

> You must see that it is quite impossible to run matters of this kind or any kind in this way. Knowing that I was dealing with matter surely proper thing was to consult so that views could be co-ordinated. What is the explanation?

Hughes denied the claim, and said that anyway, Watt was late with the list. Having to deny rumours that Hughes was going to rejoin the Labor party was perhaps the last straw. When Hughes returned, Watt was greatly relieved.

As Watt discovered the next year, only prime ministers could get away with such high-handed behaviour. In 1920, he was sent to Britain to fulfil a number of obligations as treasurer. He complained long and hard that he had not been kept informed of negotiations in Australia and that he was seldom given a free hand. 'Boiled down', he wrote, 'your determination appears to be that I must touch nothing except the things on my list, and even on these, decide nothing without referring to you. I cannot accept that position, which is that of an official and not a Minister'. The angry exchange of cables constantly referred back to the degree of control that had been exercised over Hughes while he had been in Britain. Hughes replied to Watt's complaints with a certain degree of satisfaction; he prepared paragraph after paragraph in which he rebutted Watt's complaints one after another. Satisfied with the demolition of Watt, each paragraph signed off with a 'So much for that'. He gave several examples of the way that he had been forced to back off by cabinet. The examples, he argued:

> Amply demonstrate that the opinion of the Government was then, and is now, that it is impossible to give an absolutely free hand to representatives overseas and that the Government is and must remain in Melbourne. You will not forget this rule applied even while I, as prime minister, along with the ministers for Navy and Defence, was in London and Cook and I were in widest sense of the term plenipotentiaries. Having said so much, let me say further to you: I am merely following the rule which you yourself insisted upon. You will admit, I think, that the rule is a sound one.

His memories were naturally selective, as he had constantly fought against any referral to cabinet and had with ill-grace accepted some of their decisions. Watt's memory without the cables gave a better account than Hughes' selective quotations from them. Hughes' general tenor was self-satisfied, and vindictive, recalling West Australian writer Tom Hungerwood's description of Hughes as 'cold as sea ice, vain as a peacock, cruel as a butcherbird, sly as a weasel and mean as catshit'. Watt, a decent if limited man, out of his depth in this type of company, would have agreed.

However, Hughes had a point when he argued:

> I put it to you, as one man to another that as prime minister I may fairly claim to be consulted before any variation is made in Peace Treaty with which I had so much to do and with the details of which you cannot be as familiar as I am myself. Reference to cables files show that in every stage of the Peace discussions I acted in fullest concert with the Cabinet and took no important step without first obtaining their views.

Amid all the complaints Watt correctly diagnosed the difference. 'You are the head of government and I a subordinate minister'. Unable to accept the restrictions on his freedom of action, unable to accept 'the rule' on which he had insisted, he cabled his resignation from London. Hughes had locked cabinet in behind him, passing round Watt's cables and gaining endorsement for his replies. Prime ministers can get away with behaviour that no minister can survive. Collective responsibility is what a prime minister declares it to be, particularly in relation to his own activities.

Watt's organisation nevertheless carried over into the next years. Cabinet continued to be held weekly, sometimes more often, particularly at the beginning of the year. An agenda was circulated each week. It included a list of items that had been sent to the PMO for consideration by cabinet. Each agenda was organised around ministers, first listing those items nominated by the prime minister, then by the treasurer, then the next minister. In practice, it was not so much an agenda for the next meeting as a compendium of those issues that ministers wanted discussed at some stage. Items could stay on the list for weeks on end before they were reached, if they ever were. The appointment of a high commissioner to London sat there for three months at the beginning of 1921.

The prime minister still wrote the decision on the submission, whether it appeared as a letter, a more formal submission, or a note from the minister. Where they could, his department officials would put together a collection of decisions, but they depended on being briefed on what had happened in the meeting, and that did not always occur. Sometimes a minister required his department to follow up the decision. So the head of home affairs wrote to the secretary of the prime minister's department asking him to write to state premiers to implement a decision cabinet had taken on rail passes. There remained a degree of randomness in application of the systems. An apparent improvement in process was not necessarily transferred into better practice.

The style of Hughes can also be identified in his interaction with Stanley Bruce. In December 1921 he wanted to recruit Bruce to cabinet. As a Gallipoli veteran and businessman Bruce would give weight and credibility to a cabinet in decline.

Here are Hughes's letters, which were written in his typical scrawl, attempting to recruit Bruce to cabinet:

> My dear Captain Bruce, Welcome home!! Things here are in a state of flux: & a censure motion, under cover of an amendment to reduce the estimates by £2800,000, has been moved by Dr Page & is to be supported by the Labor Party whose motion to reduce the Defence estimates was defeated by an overwhelming majority. The Division should take place this evening & the probabilities are that the Gov will only win by the casting vote of the

> Chairman. This as you know is the state of parties 38 to 37 the same as it has been during the greater part of this Parl.
> What I write about however is independent of the division and it is to ask if you will accept a position in the gov, which if defeated as is improbable, must go to the country & I offer you the position of Minister for Trade and Customs ... Will you accept. I am relying on your promise and I do most strongly urge you in the interests of the Commonwealth and good times to do so.

Bruce pointed out that as a large importer there might be a conflict of interest, but said it would be difficult to refuse if he were offered the role of treasurer. So Hughes switched his offer. He still had to settle the arrangements with other ministers. Twice on 15 December he wrote to Bruce:

> I thought it best not to telephone otherwise some bright spirit in my Department — and there are one or two — might have put two and two together with the result that there could have been a par in the papers in the morning and there may be one anyhow. We did nothing at the Cabinet relating to the reformation. Until Green [Walter Massy Greene] returns there is no situation to develop and no news, tomorrow one ought to hear something and so be able to shape one's course definitely and it will be the next week or I'm no prophet.

Later that day:

> Cabinet making is like some deaths — an agony long drawn out & I had hoped to have completed all arrangements by today, but this has been found impossible. Green has gone to Adelaide 'to see a man'. He won't be back until tomorrow and it certainly looks as though it will be next week before we can fix things up. I hope you won't mind; it's really not my fault.

And finally, dramatically, on 21 December 1921:

> The hour has struck: the knell has sounded to summon thee from the country house to the gilded hall of kings, or their representative. The Hour is 3 p.m. this day. All is prepared: the execution will be prompt and painless. Be thou there. By order of yours most sincerely, W.M.Hughes

Bruce was sworn in as treasurer.

Once in office Bruce was appalled by what he saw of the processes of cabinet. His memories are colourful:

When I joined the Government, I discovered that Cabinet meetings were strange and mysterious affairs, where really nothing was seriously discussed. I believed this was felt by all ministers other than the prime minister, but no one moved. I accordingly went into the ring and I obtained Cabinet's agreement to there being a formal agenda for cabinet meetings, every minister who had an item on the agenda having to circulate a paper outlining the proposals before the item was discussed by cabinet.

When these proposals were put to the prime minister, he cordially accepted them – with, I am sure, the mental reservation that he had not the slightest intention of allowing anything of the sort to happen. An attempt was made to put the new proposals into operation, but the prime minister completely defeated them. He continued his usual practice of arriving anything up to half an hour late and then producing some new, and generally wild, scheme. Cabinet would then proceed to discuss his new scheme before going anywhere near the agenda and, generally speaking, the whole of the meeting was devoted to the attempt to dissuade the prime minister from his latest brainwave.

Or he would approach the agenda like a hen picking corn. He would dart at the subjects that interested him, regardless of their position on the agenda, and the other items would be neglected or held over.

To overcome the problem of the cabinet's sitting around waiting for the prime minister to arrive, it was suggested to him that when it was impossible for him to be on time for a meeting, that cabinet should proceed with the agenda under the chairmanship of the next senior minister. This also the prime minister agreed to. On two or three occasions it worked quite well. Decisions were reached on a number of matters that were listed for consideration. The prime minister, however, managed to defeat this plan also. His method was, on his arrival at a cabinet meeting, to ask what had been decided. He would then begin to wonder whether the decision was entirely wise. Because of his extraordinary influence over cabinet members, he was invariably successful in getting decisions reversed.

After these abortive efforts, I came to the conclusion that with an eccentric genius like Billy Hughes it was impossible to have any well-regulated procedure for the cabinet. I ceased to put Treasury items on the agenda, and simply went ahead and did whatever I thought was necessary.

Indeed, Bruce did send little to cabinet while Hughes was prime minister. In 1921, he only listed half a dozen issues, and one of those, on parliamentary refreshment rooms' deficits, sat there for three months before the end of the parliament. Nor, when he did take items, were they particularly helpful. When Tasmania asked for a grant, and Tasmanian minister John Earle circulated an appeal to his fellow ministers for support, Bruce's memo to cabinet was positively laconic. He spelt out the comparative situation of all the states and noted that 'the facts set out above more or less give the necessary information to form an opinion'. He concluded: 'The question which has to be considered by Cabinet is whether any further assistance should be given to Tasmania in order to enable it to make its own financial contribution'. There was little in the way of a recommendation there.

On another occasion Hughes wanted to spend about £8 million. Bruce described the result:

> In the picture he drew, this was going to solve practically every problem that faced Australia. In the discussion that followed I strongly opposed the prime minister's plan, and I think at the beginning I had the majority of the Cabinet on my side. The discussion went on for a considerable period, and one by one those who had supported my view were weaned away. By about 4 p.m. I was left without a supporter.
>
> When we reached this point I said that apparently Cabinet was quite determined to give effect to the prime minister's proposals, and to that I could offer no objection. But, I said, as I was the Finance Minister and responsible for the policy, it would have to be carried out by a new Finance Minister. I, being opposed to the expenditure, could not possibly accept responsibility for it.
>
> The prime minister's reply was characteristic: 'You are defying the whole cabinet.' I replied that I was doing nothing of the sort. It was for cabinet to decide what it wanted to do, and having decided on this particular thing it was entitled to have its policy carried into effect. It was obvious, however, that you could not carry through a great policy of this sort with a treasurer who was totally opposed to it, so they would have to get themselves another treasurer.
>
> This statement, one would have imagined, must precipitate a complete crisis. But the prime minister's only reply was 'Oh!' and then: 'Anyhow, it's getting late, and we had better catch our trains.' [The Easter recess was about to begin, and cabinet ministers were returning to their home states.] On this, the cabinet meeting broke up.

> I went home and told my wife that, thank God, I was now rid of being a member of the Government, a prospect that pleased her greatly. I continued in that blissful state over the Easter holidays. After Easter, I expected to hear something from the prime minister. From that day to this I have never heard a word. The policy was dropped, without the prime minister's giving any indication to the members of the cabinet who had supported him of why he had dropped it, or any other form of enlightenment. And I continued as treasurer.
>
> I should imagine this must be a unique episode in Cabinet government.

Even if all his ideas were not accepted, Hughes allowed nothing to pass with which he did not agree. On 2 May 1921 cabinet agreed, in response to the British government's representations, and subject to the prime minister's approval, that the number of Maltese admitted to Australia should be raised from 260 to 500 a year. The prime minister turned down this proposal, but declared 'he had no objection to Northern Italians'; a month later the superintendent of immigration was still asking what he should do. Whimsical seems a fair description of this mode of decision-making in which many decisions were provisional until endorsed by the prime minister.

Eventually Hughes' prime ministership came to an end, because he lost his majority in the House of Representatives. To govern he needed Country Party support. The Nationalist ministers were keen to keep him as leader. The Country party leader, Dr Earle Page refused to serve under him. Eventually, and reluctantly, the Nationalists replaced Hughes with Bruce.

Hughes redefined the prime ministership and the role of cabinet. While his predecessor, Fisher, had worked largely in collaboration with colleagues, Hughes brought an imperious style and a vicious whimsy to the role that was unprecedented. In part that may have been a consequence of war, but it also reflected the style and personality of a leader who brooked no opposition and had little patience for other views. In the end that lack of consideration made him unacceptable as the leader of the coalition, but only after a seven-year roller-coaster of a ride for his cabinet and his colleagues.

4 CONSOLIDATION, WITH HICCUPS: 1923–41

In the 16 years after the fall of the mercurial Hughes, more systematic cabinet processes were gradually adopted. It was a combination of personality and precedent. Hughes's execution at the hands of the Country Party and, finally, of his own supporters was a timely warning of what could happen to a prime minister who too often and for too long rode roughshod over his ministers. It was also because it suited future prime ministers Bruce and Lyons to work in that way. Between the two, the Scullin government provided an example of how badly a cabinet could be organised.

The Bruce–Page cabinet set the precedent for most future non-Labor governments; it provided a stable coalition, seen as a partnership. The coalition agreement was short and simple: the parties would keep their own identities: the portfolios to be held by each party were identified. Page would be second in seniority and act as prime minister whenever such a position was needed and it would be known as the Bruce–Page ministry. There were six Nationalist and five Country party ministers. Due to a combination of electoral defeat and reconstruction, Bruce only selected two ministers from the last Hughes cabinet, one of whom was the ever-present Senator George Pearce, a minister for all but three of the years between 1910 and 1937.

Bruce: Businessman as leader

Bruce, 39 and with only a year of ministerial experience, wanted a smooth operation. He was a decorated soldier and regarded himself as a businessman, the only businessman thus far to become prime minister. He was an example of a person who sought to bring systematic practices to the process of governing, mainly as a contrast to Hughes, in part because he saw it as the way to make the system work better. Reminiscing on his approach, he emphasised the process and the oversight:

> When the change of Government took place in 1923, we introduced an orderly method of handling Cabinet business. We adopted the idea of a definite agenda and the circulation of papers by ministers in respect of any item they had put down. I, however, added to this procedure an arrangement that any Minister with an item down who had circulated a paper had to see the prime minister privately before the cabinet meeting. This worked admirably and is a tip that anyone running a Government might well give heed to.
>
> Notwithstanding the provision that papers had to be circulated by the Minister in respect to any of the items, it was obvious at Cabinet meetings that the majority of his colleagues had not read his paper. With our system, however, that was not frightfully material. I always allowed a discussion for half an hour or some limited period and then came into the ring myself, being fully informed in the matter by reason of my private conversation with the Minister concerned beforehand. The weight of the prime minister definitely on the side of the Minister, in the face of the rest of the Cabinet – the majority of whom had not read the paper and did not know what it was all about – proved in practice to be quite decisive and we got through a great deal of work with minimum time.

In his analysis Bruce touched on all the substantive issues that face a prime minister in ensuring good decisions: how to appreciate the problems and their likely outcome; whether to ensure that all colleagues are informed; how to tie them into the result, whether or not in an informed manner; and when the prime minister should be involved.

As prime minister he annotated the submissions with the official decision. These were then sent to the departments. Sometimes lengthy decisions were drafted by the prime minister in cabinet and then passed on to the support staff. At the same time a second minister kept a further consolidated record of decisions that was then lodged with the Prime Minister's Department. It is a comment on the process that there were often distinct differences between the decision recorded by the prime minister and those by the unofficial secretary, the Vice-President of the Executive Council,

J.A. Atkinson. In January 1925 Major Marr took over the role of cabinet notetaker and made it considerably more formal, with typed lists of decisions initialled by the prime minister.

Cabinet met regularly. At the beginning of the year, and often during July when the budget was being formulated, there would be a string of meetings, perhaps four or five on consecutive days. When parliament was sitting, cabinet would meet weekly. The agenda could be extensive because it was in effect a running list of those items which ministers wanted discussed by cabinet; listing did not ensure that the submission would be raised at the next meeting. A list of decisions shows that cabinet often only determined half a dozen issues. Occasionally there was an effort to clear the list, with a wide range of 20 or more decisions on a number of less significant topics. At the other end of the spectrum were a number of meetings dedicated to the discussion of single items. Moreover, there was sometimes discussion without decision, a process of estimating what was at issue and what the alternatives might be. This was cabinet at its most deliberative, although Bruce's comments notwithstanding, there is no estimate of the quality or impact of such lengthy debate.

In 1927 there was the first formal step to create a cabinet secretariat and a set of rules. On 28 November cabinet appointed Sir Neville Howse, then an Honorary Minister, to carry out the duties of secretary to cabinet. Ministers were circulated with a letter describing how cabinet should work and what the expectations on them were. Officials in the Prime Minister's Department had prepared a draft. The prime minister then went through the document amending it where necessary and initialling each paragraph when he was satisfied. This first set of rules, like every other one as the procedures developed, was part of the prime minister's prerogative to determine when and how the cabinet should be run.

The variations between the draft from officials and Bruce's final wording illustrate the official desire for order contrasted against the political need for cohesion and flexibility. Bruce added a clause to allow ministers to tell the secretary of cabinet if they wanted to 'absent themselves from a cabinet meeting'. Officials wanted due notice for all submissions. Bruce decided to waive these demands 'in matters of extreme urgency', but required that ministers advise the secretary they wanted to bring up an item without notice.

Treasury officials, following British practice, wanted tight treasury control, proposing that:

> The Secretary will not place questions on the list of waiting subjects until they have been discussed in their financial aspects between the Department concerned and the Treasury.

Bruce softened the stance:

> It would greatly facilitate Cabinet business if, before submitting questions for Cabinet decision, they have been discussed in their financial aspects between the Department concerned and the Treasury.

Treasury did not give up. In 1934, Lyons, both prime minister and treasurer, gave Treasury the access it wanted. He wrote to ministers:

> In view of the difficulties and delays that are liable to arise by reason of the submission to Cabinet of proposals involving expenditure before the Treasury have investigated them, I would be glad if Ministers would be good enough to submit all such proposals to the Treasury before they take the form of submissions to Cabinet. I feel that the strict adherence to this principle will enable the Treasury to express itself adequately on proposals for new expenditure – and will, in the end, save time.

The prime minister approved the agenda for each meeting. The secretary summoned ministers and kept records that 'should be as short as possible and apart from the decision itself will be limited to such explanation as is indispensable to render the decision intelligible'. The secretary would communicate the decisions to ministers. 'The duty of the Secretary will end after he has communicated the decision to the Minister'. All decisions would be circulated to ministers and should be kept secret; the secretariat had no responsibility to follow up the decisions.

The draft from officials emphasised that 'No mention will be made of the views of individual Ministers and the principle of the collective responsibility must be carefully maintained'. It also suggested that, 'In exceptional cases, by decision of Cabinet, a statement by a Minister may be reproduced and annexed to the minutes of decisions after the approval by the Prime Minister'. Bruce excised the second suggestion; there were to be no alternative or individual views after cabinet made a decision.

Bruce added a clause: 'two or more Ministers may be appointed to form a Sub-Committee of Cabinet'. The secretary of cabinet was responsible for convening sub-committees and ensuring that the prime minister was informed of all decisions made by them. There was no suggestion that the secretary of cabinet should be anyone but a minister.

The rules largely regularised existing practice. By 1929 there was a clear system that provided submissions and a continuing double record of decisions, one on the submission by Bruce and a second as part of the consolidated list prepared by the cabinet secretary. Often the decisions were quite detailed. The cabinet considered a whole range of proposals for consideration by the premier's conference in 1929. The original list included 36 topics. Cabinet approved some items and deleted others; then a further eight were added in Bruce's handwriting. Regular meetings and detailed decisions provided a rhythm that reflected Bruce's tidy approach to governing.

That tidiness disliked any interruption to due process. In 1929 a cabinet document on the governing arrangements for the Australian Capital Territory (ACT) was leaked to the *Canberra Times*, whose editor, A.T. Shakespeare, duly ran a story. A police investigation followed; for once, it might have been successful. The police found a copy of the cabinet submission in the house of a member of the staff of the Prime Minister's Department, while nominally looking for a heater taken home without authority! The attorney-general, Latham, argued in an apoplectic submission to cabinet that the public servant should be prosecuted. Eventually no action was taken.

But tidiness did not mean political wisdom. The Bruce government was to fall on an attempt to divest the federal government of most industrial powers. The proposal received extensive cabinet attention. It first came to cabinet in June and then was discussed at three further meetings, including being referred to its own cabinet sub-committee. In two of those cabinet meetings, it was the primary topic of only two items on the agenda. Introduced under the name of attorney-general Latham, it had the prime minister's support. But before it passed, a vengeful Hughes orchestrated a defeat in committee. Bruce, insulted, asked for a dissolution when he could have merely reversed the decision. His pride was offended. In the ensuing election, he not only lost government but also his own seat.

Scullin, cabinet in retreat and a caucus in revolt

In the Bruce government, cabinet seemed to have spent little time concerned with the support it would get from the parliamentary party. It was largely taken for granted, unadvisedly so in the last resort. In the Scullin government, from the first month, the Labor caucus was a principal point of concern. Managing caucus became a continuing nightmare. It was a matter of history and of contemporary pressure. At the last caucus meeting held when the party was in government Hughes had walked out with his supporters. Caucus was determined that this time the party would decide what was done and the cabinet would obey. Added to the internal tensions were the economic times. The onset of the depression had been combined with trouble on the waterfront and a lockout on the coalfields. Labor had been given a mandate to govern, but it was in a minority in the Senate and had no idea how to tackle the rising unemployment. Orthodox solutions required the cutting of government expenditure and the hurting even more of those who had elected them.

The process was not helped by the immediate decision to abolish the cabinet secretariat, presumably because it was seen as an invention of Bruce. Instead, ministers reported to cabinet on the range of issues that they wanted discussed and kept their own records, some in detail, others more skimpily. A set of records was kept by a cabinet 'secretary', Arthur Blakeley, the minister for Home Affairs, although there is no record of him being appointed to that position. Blakeley's accounts at least provide some indication of the meetings held and the ministers present from the formation of the government until the fight over the Premiers' Plan to reduce expenditure as a means of ameliorating the Depression in June 1931. Thereafter the last seen of the minutes for the final six months of the government was in a trunk in the office of the Leader of the Opposition.

The records were far from complete. Some meetings have no minutes attached, even though there are references elsewhere to decisions taken then. More often there are incomplete sentences, dates and appointees left out, and conclusions undetermined. Blakeley was however meticulous in recording the decisions made in his own portfolio, details which he used to demand action from other departments. Perhaps typical of the uncertainty caused by this lack of procedure was a note Blakeley sent to a colleague in March 1930 about an item he had brought to cabinet:

> I am under the impression that Cabinet considered this application but decided not to grant a subsidy. I should be glad if you would kindly advise me if any decision of Cabinet has been recorded in connection with this matter.

Public servants, too, found the processes frustrating. In that constant striving for control of expenditure, the Treasury wrote to the secretary of the Prime Minister's Department:

> No decision appears to have been issued to departments regarding the decision of Cabinet that all matters involving

expenditure be referred to the Treasury for examination and report before being submitted for the consideration of cabinet.

A letter from the prime minister was needed and the treasurer (former Queensland premier Ted Theodore) had talked to him about it. Such a decision, too, did not appear in any of the existing minutes. No wonder that cabinet decided in May that 'at every Cabinet meeting minutes of previous meeting be read'. It does not seem to have improved their quality, even though they had to be formally endorsed at the next meeting by the prime minister.

In June 1930 the Prime Minister's Department tried to reinstate the cabinet secretariat, under the guise of a proposal to reduce overlap by moving control of the Public Service Board from the Prime Minister's Department to the Treasury. As part of the exercise a secretariat would be created to receive submissions and ensure that they had been referred to Treasury and its comments were available. The secretariat would also 'examine all Cabinet recommendations in the light of Governmental activities as a whole and make further suggestions to Cabinet where it appears that such Cabinet recommendations conflict with other phases of Governmental work and involve overlapping as between departments'. The prime minister was unimpressed. Acting on advice that seemed mainly concerned with the excessive power to be given to Treasury, and never mentioning the cabinet secretariat, he rejected the proposal with the often-used excuse that it would 'only complicate the present form of administration without achieving any desirable results'.

Lack of any administrative support for cabinet must have exacerbated an institution that was always under stress, with the party making demands that cabinet was unable to meet. The contest for the ministry itself created tensions. Two leading candidates – one of them John Curtin – were defeated. The cabinet was made up of radicals and conservatives in uneasy conjunction. Two former state premiers, Ted Theodore from Queensland, and the newly elected Joe Lyons from Tasmania, were totally unalike in their approach. No one else had ministerial experience.

At its first meeting cabinet noted 'an understanding arrived at in regard to position of Minister in caucus Meetings'. It was quickly put to the test; a backbencher wanted to attack the government for its failure to act on the coal lockout and raised the issue in caucus on 3 December. Cabinet met on 4 December to decide how to react; no decision was recorded. It was preparing its stand for the adjourned caucus meeting of 5 December where the ministers sought to deflect the angry backbench. They were unsuccessful. That incident provided a preview of the way in which cabinet's agenda was often to be driven by the need to determine where it stood on items to be introduced by caucus.

Cabinet met regularly. Sometimes it voted. It was split, 5–5, in March 1930 over whether cabinet should select the delegate to an International Labour Organisation (ILO) conference. On another occasion when there was a tie, it decided to leave the prime minister to make the decision, informed by the opinions expressed in cabinet. In February cabinet spent a meeting considering the resolutions of the ALP conference in New South Wales (NSW) that were critical of what it saw as a lack of action, relying on the *Labor Daily* for its information.

Quickly cabinet and caucus began to meet in tandem, with cabinet deciding what stand it would take in the face of constant criticism. On 8 May first cabinet, then caucus, discussed the strife caused by the Bruce government's demand that waterside workers take out licences. Scullin declared that 'Cabinet had discussed the question: but had not come to a decision'. He brought the whole question to caucus for full consideration and a decision. It took three meetings and caucus still came to no agreement on what to do. On 21 May cabinet discussed a motion to be debated in caucus later that day that £20 million be made available for public works. The pattern continued. Cabinet managed to amend the motion to convene a meeting between the leading ministers and caucus representatives. With only a two-week break in April, caucus met weekly, sometimes two or three times a week, from March to August. The meetings were invariably long, critical and contested.

Then in August the prime minister decided he had to visit Britain. Originally, Theodore was to act as prime minister, but a week after his appointment was announced to cabinet Theodore was forced to resign when scandal about his activities as Queensland premier became too embarrassing to ignore. Instead, James Fenton, a much less decisive figure, was made acting prime minister in Scullin's absence. It was a poor choice for neither Fenton nor his principal supporter in cabinet, acting treasurer Joe Lyons, were able to cope with the wave of resentment that was about to break.

Before Scullin left for England, Sir Robert Gibson, the custodian of orthodox finance and the bête noire of the Labor left, was reappointed as chair of the Commonwealth Bank, which then had central bank responsibilities. Scullin had promised to let the caucus discuss the appointment; he did not. Then cabinet met at Scullin's home in Richmond where it decided:

> That we agree the Budget should be balanced this year and that the position will be watched carefully and that the steps will be taken, at the earliest moment, necessary to adjust the position by in the first place reductions in expenditure and any adjustment of taxation required should be made so as not to encroach upon the states' fields of taxation.

It was not the approach that most of the caucus wanted, but the ministers were committed. On 5 September Gibson attended cabinet and 'explained the financial position of Australia'. Cabinet ended the meeting by endorsing the pledge made to the prime minister at his house.

Ministers were divided. On 1 October in cabinet, 'Mr Beasley brought up the matter of refusal of Treasury to allow him to see the Niemeyer file. After discussion and explanations it was decided that the acting treasurer [Lyons] explain the proposal for balancing the budget'. Sir Otto Niemeyer, an official of the Bank of England, was examining Australia's economic performance; his recommendations were expected to be conservative.

At the next caucus meeting, on 27 October, the lack of support for the leading members of cabinet was clear. The acting treasurer explained the government's financial proposals. Then Beasley, using caucus to try to achieve what he could not do in cabinet, moved a motion condemning the Niemeyer proposals to cut government expenditure; it was carried. The subsequent debate on the cabinet's financial proposals lasted for the next four days, for over 30 hours, as caucus first debated and then rejected the cabinet's proposals in favour of a scheme of credit expansion developed by Theodore. The amendment was carried by 26 votes to 14. At the next caucus meeting a telegram of support from Scullin for the minority was read out but it did not ameliorate the opposition to cabinet. Lyons proposed a renewal of loans. His proposal was rejected: cabinet was instructed to meet the directors of the Commonwealth Bank and give them directions on meeting the loan. That amendment was passed 22 to 16. Two ministers voted against the cabinet. Fenton and Lyons informed cabinet they 'would consider their position'.

In fact Fenton and Lyons ignored the resolution. Cabinet met at 9 a.m. on 12 November and decided that 'the party should not precipitate a crisis while the prime minister and his two ministers were absent'. It reported to caucus at 11 a.m. The loan was converted in the usual manner on the advice of Scullin. When caucus members proposed to reaffirm their motion, they were persuaded to adjourn the issue until the prime minister's return.

But cabinet was on the run and for the next month caucus and cabinet tic-tacked, meeting one after the other. Caucus members attended cabinet to discuss the gold bonus and the fellmongering industry. As the acting prime minister, Fenton, told a meeting of caucus:

> Cabinet was sitting discussing Gold Bonus, fellmongering Industry and other questions which Caucus had decided upon. On behalf of the Govt. he asked the party to adjourn this meeting until tomorrow when they would be in a position to place certain proposal before members.

In these months there was no doubt who called the tune. Scullin was sometimes consulted but his opinions were by no means authoritative. Cabinet was quite happy to ignore his wishes.

The most obvious case was appointments to the High Court. In January 1930 cabinet had decided to make no appointment to fill a vacancy and instead proposed to reduce the number of judges from seven to six. On 11 December, on the recommendation of the acting attorney-general, cabinet determined that 'the matter of filling the vacancies on the High Court bench be held over until a full meeting of the Cabinet in deference to the wishes of the prime minister Mr Scullin and other absent ministers'. Since Scullin and the attorney-general were still at sea and only five ministers were present it was a reasonable position. The next week, cabinet agreed to appoint Evatt and McTiernan to the Bench, reportedly on the instruction of caucus (although there is no mention of the motion in the caucus minutes). The acting attorney-general had pushed the issue there. Thus, despite the prime minister's explicit disapproval, cabinet followed caucus's instructions. It was the end of only one nightmare.

Another began when Scullin returned. On 23 January he chaired his first cabinet meeting in five months. A number of decisions were made, including appointment of the Chief Justice, Sir Frank Gavan Duffy. The crucial question was whether Theodore should be reinstated. Scullin wanted him back in cabinet; other ministers objected. In cabinet Scullin sought the opinion of ministers on 'the proposed reinstatement of Mr Theodore'. But cabinet did not make a decision. That was to be decided by caucus in a meeting that lasted from 11 a.m. to 11.30 p.m. Lyons tried to trigger a spill of all cabinet positions, but lost. After long debate, caucus decided to reinstate Theodore, by 24 votes to 19. The ministers were badly divided; the minority included Fenton, Lyons and Anstey. By the next cabinet, on 31 January, Lyons and Fenton had resigned. A month later a spill was accepted; three ministers lost their position and discontented members followed Lyons into Opposition ranks. Two weeks later a second split occurred. NSW Premier Jack Lang had advocated repudiation of debts owed to Britain. Eddie Ward had won a by-election supporting Lang's platform, and in opposition to the federal government's proposals. After cabinet and the caucus agreed that Eddie Ward could not be a member of caucus, several other Langites departed for federal caucus to establish a NSW Labor splinter group led by Beasley.

The following months were dominated by the negotiations between the Commonwealth and state governments that led to the Premiers' Plan and the threats that the Lang government in NSW would repudiate its debts. Cabinet seemed to be on the edge of activities, useful for statements of intent but little involved in detail that was run by Scullin and, mostly, Theodore. On 30 March cabinet resolved that the Commonwealth government would be responsible for interest payments due by the NSW government and that it would take action under the Financial Agreement to recover the amount from NSW. In May, with the prime minister and treasurer absent, the acting chair told cabinet that the government:

> ... had no intention of agreeing to any cuts in pensions without consulting the party and the Cabinet. There was a general expression of opinion that when Mr Brennan the chair for the meeting rang the prime minister, he should be informed, pending receipt of fuller information that the feeling of Cabinet was adverse to reductions in pensions and that the basic wage in the Commonwealth Public Service should not be interfered with.

On Saturday 6 June cabinet met in Melbourne where the state premiers were negotiating the plan. Scullin and Theodore explained the tentative proposals. Scullin was keen to lock in his ministers. Cabinet

> ... after hearing the explanations as to the proposed plan, and the inevitable default at the middle of the next month, if nothing is done, supported the prime minister and the treasurer in the general plan explained by them although they regretted the necessity for such economies, especially the necessity to interfere with pensions.

Against the comment were the signatures of nine ministers. These were individual commitments, not merely hiding behind a veil of collective responsibility. One minister, C. Culley, had left the meeting after three hours and before the expressions of opinion were given. Another,

E.J. Holloway, said he could not accept the proposals to cut pensions and lower public service salaries. Both had been leading trades hall officials before their election to parliament.

At 10.30 a.m. on 11 June cabinet met to consider the proposals to be put before the party and it was agreed to consider Holloway's position later in the day. At 11 a.m. the caucus met and, apart from a break from 1 p.m. to 4 p.m., debated until 10.25 p.m. that evening and from 10 a.m. till 3.45 p.m. the next day. In that initial break cabinet had a hurried meeting:

> Mr Holloway's position was discussed, and it was agreed that as a compromise Mr Holloway be allowed to vote against the Government proposals in preference to resigning his position in the Cabinet.

Collective responsibility had, it seemed, already been under strain, with the prime minister reminding ministers they should attend divisions in the House and even with a decision in May that 'members of Cabinet should support unanimously tariff items as moved by minister'. Now it was relaxed entirely.

But to no avail. Caucus rejected a proposal to call for a dissolution of parliament and approved the premiers' plan by 26 votes to 13. Holloway and Culley resigned. The government, lacking a majority in the House of Representatives, awaited the execution that would occur when Beasley's rebel group joined the Opposition, now led by Lyons, to bring the government down. It happened on 25 November. On 19 December the government was decimated at the polls. Lyons won such a majority that for the next three years he was able to form a government without the support of the Country party.

Why was the Scullin government so chaotic? The contemporary chronicler, Warren Denning, provides a number of suggestions: the lack of control of the Senate, the absence of alternative policy options, the hard times, the failure of nerve that stopped the government from engineering an early double dissolution, the feeling that any Labor government was better than the alternative. But he notes two in particular. The caucus included extremes of opinion that had nothing in common except the title of Labor, so that Theodore and Lyons would never agree on a means to tackle the crisis. Above all, there was a lack of leadership. Scullin could talk but not act. When the crisis worsened he insisted on going overseas. With Theodore sidelined, Fenton and Lyons had neither the personality nor the policy flexibility to deal with a rampant caucus. Denning ponders whether it might have been different with the aggressive Theodore as prime minister, as he would never have permitted the criticism and lack of discipline from cabinet, and would have been harder than Scullin on caucus. As it was, cabinet often ignored Scullin; he was unwilling to act without debate that was invariably divisive and indecisive. Cabinet and caucus may have debated everything, but the resulting indecision provided no advertisement for the qualities of cabinet government.

Lyons and Menzies

The first decision of the Lyons government, on 6 January 1932, was to re-establish a Cabinet Secretariat, and require that an agenda and explanatory memoranda be circulated in advance. Lyons's private secretary and an official from the prime minister's department were to be responsible for the documentation. The secretariat was not meant to have any policy input. Nor does it seem it had the capacity to maintain any central record that would allow any oversight of the implementation of the cabinet's decisions. A letter, similar in format to that circulated five years earlier (when the cabinet secretariat was first formally created), was sent to all ministers.

Cabinet met frequently: seven times that January, and 11 times in February as the cabinet came to grips with its challenges. It had a break in mid-year with only five meetings in June and July and then another rush. There were 14 meetings in August, sometimes every day in a week for budget formulation. And there were another 13 in November. In all, there were 88 meetings, mostly in Canberra, but 16 in Melbourne and one in Sydney. The pattern continued in the following years. The cabinet might meet in different months, but the frequency did not decline. There were another 87 meetings in 1933 and 79 in 1934, an election year.

At some meetings there were a number of decisions; at others cabinet recorded nothing but a general discussion of the political situation. Six cabinets in 1934 were dedicated to broad debate, one of them lasting from 10 a.m. to 11 p.m.!

The secretary of cabinet, Major C.W.C. Marr, was minister of health in addition to his secretarial responsibilities. In each agenda he circulated a number for each item (which ran through from '1 Cabinet Secretariat' onwards), a subject, and a note of any document provided to form 'the basis of discussion'. The meeting of 5 February 1932, for instance, listed 32 items and seven on a deferred list. All but two items were accompanied by memoranda. Of the seven deferred items, five were under consideration by cabinet sub-committees, every one of which had a different membership. The sub-committees reported back to cabinet at later meetings; they were *ad hoc* committees *par excellence*. In addition, committees might take up really important issues. One committee developed and recommended to cabinet a defence policy that was duly approved.

When cabinet met, the prime minister could add items to the list. Lyons ticked off the items as they were discussed, or noted that they were deferred. Marr then wrote the minutes and circulated them to ministers. Sometimes the public servants queried the precise wording. When the Secretary of the Department of the Interior was awarded a salary of £1300, the Treasury wanted to ensure that the caveat '(subject to reduction under the Financial Emergency Act)' was added, suggesting it was in accordance with the Cabinet's decision. It was so added.

What constituted a memorandum for cabinet depended on the whim of ministers. It could be a cable from London, a lengthy historical analysis of strike action, eventually leading to a suggestion for action, a report of a conversation with members of the Chamber of Manufactures, or a request for the purchase of buses for Canberra. Sometimes the memorandum might ask cabinet to endorse a line of action; at other times it just provided a background to which ministers could speak.

The range of items could be extensive but on occasion cabinet might have one item only. On 30 April the minutes record:

> Cabinet had before it a suggestion, embodied in a letter to the prime minister from Mr J.D. Stevenson owner of Stevenson's Service Station of Goulburn, that a secret ballot should be taken as a condition precedent to the hearings of industrial disputes. This proposal, it was pointed out in a memorandum submitted by the Attorney-General's Department, would involve an amendment of the Commonwealth Conciliation and Arbitration Act.
>
> Cabinet decided that the matter should be referred to the Acting Attorney-General for report.

It was the only item that day, generated by a letter from a citizen and with a comment from the public service.

There was little common approach. Take this apocalyptic opening of a memorandum in 1937:

> We are faced with a situation which demands serious thinking and courageous action. What is the greatest problem of nations

> today? We are faced with world unrest which is causing great anxiety; we have fierce economic wars between countries; we have the piling up of armaments; and behind all these we have the separation of peoples into political camps of the most extreme kinds.

Was this dire memorandum opener a demand for rearmament or a new diplomatic initiative? No. Billy Hughes was merely asking cabinet to approve the provision of milk for school children in his brief stint as minister for health.

Cabinet was provided each year with an extensive brief on the budget from the treasurer, R.G. Casey. In 1935–36 Casey forecast an annual surplus of £377 000 in a budget revenue of £75 352 000. With an accumulated deficit of £17 216 000, he asked:

> In the budget of 1933–34 the prime minister who was also the treasurer, in referring to the surplus for the two preceding years of £4,860,000, stated that, in normal circumstances, this sum should be devoted to the reduction of the deficit, but in view of the great need that existed to relieve the burdens of the people, he proposed to use it for this purpose. He added, however, that 'in the near future, as soon as circumstances permit, it will be necessary to take steps to deal with the accumulated deficit ... it might be claimed that the time has arrived to deal with the accumulated deficit. There is no doubt as to what the normal procedure should be, but it is for Cabinet to decide whether the surplus should be applied in reduction of the deficit, or whether it should be taken to meet Budget expenditure in 1935–36.

Cabinet, in this and other budgets, was asked to decide the strategy, on the assumption that full 'cuts' to department bids were achieved.

Much of the formal paraphernalia of a cabinet system was there. Whether it worked was more in doubt. Sir Maurice Hankey, the father of cabinet processes in Britain, visited Australia in late 1934, nominally on holiday but in fact to review the defence arrangements. He thought cabinet procedure 'is evidently very loose and rambling'.

> There is a nominal agenda paper, but they don't stick to it and wander all over the place ... Casey [then treasurer] gets exasperated at the waste of time. Menzies, entering the Commonwealth Cabinet for the first time, was appalled and contrasted the procedure unfavourably with that of Victoria. He asked a lot of details as to how we conduct cabinet business, as did other ministers.

Hankey found his work frustrated by the process of cabinet-making after the election and 'by the relaxed attitude of Australian public servants who knock off work religiously at 5pm and they don't go to [the] office on Saturdays. I could have done a lot more but for the incessant functions, parties, public holidays etc.'

Lyons' first cabinet ought to have been the easiest to manage because his victory in 1931 had been so striking that he did not have to include the Country Party in the cabinet. Everyone there was from the United Australia Party (UAP). Nevertheless it seemed accident-prone. James Fenton, his old colleague in strife from the Scullin days, left in December 1932. As he wrote, 'for reasons given at Cabinet last night I hereby tender my resignation as a Minister'. Fenton wanted, Lyons told the Governor-General, to vote as he chose on detailed tariff items and could only do so as a backbencher.

Ministers were able to set terms for acceptance of office. Walter Massy Greene was ill in 1932 and told the prime minister he would not be able to do much for the next three months. Senator Sir Harry Lawson set three conditions for accepting office:

(a) that in the event of my being unable to give reasonable attention to business interests on account of public duties, I shall be free to retire without any suggestion of disloyalty or desertion;
(b) that you will facilitate the discharge of the duties entrusted to me so that I shall be able to give reasonable attention to business affairs;
(c) that the question of status, prestige and the duties to be entrusted to me shall be left to your unfettered discretion (subject to consultation with me).

Then he went on to insist on future promotion:

As you are only able to offer me a subordinate position, I think there should be a promise of consideration of my claims for office if opportunity should occur and I desire appointment.

Lawson then wrote a postscript assuming his conditions would be met and asking whether he needed to go to Canberra before parliament met. He was sworn in a week later. Not many prime ministers would have accepted such conditional commitment. It is no surprise that he only lasted a year as a junior minister.

An unusual feature was the appointment of ministers who were effectively posted overseas. The former prime minister, Stanley Bruce, had been re-elected in 1931, but he was appointed initially as assistant treasurer, then as minister without portfolio and finally as 'minister without portfolio, London'. In effect he was the government's representative there and regularly sent suggestions for action to cabinet. After a year in London he resigned. Lyons accepted his resignation with the comment: 'The members of the Government are in agreement as to the importance of the maintenance of collective Cabinet responsibility. Your indefinite continuance in London as Resident minister would, of course, involve a departure from that principle'. In fact Bruce had suggested that formula as a means to allow him to shift from minister to High Commissioner, a position he held until 1945 (the fourth and last former prime minister to go to London). His new standing as a government official did not obviously restrict his ability to send policy proposals to cabinet; in 1938, for instance, he proposed that Australia should take 30 000 refugees. Used to writing for cabinet, he even provided a press release for the prime minister when the decision was announced. He still acted as cabinet colleague, not as an adviser. But then, as a successful and still confident former prime minister, he was in an unusual relationship with the ministers, many of whom he had once led.

Nevertheless the experiment with overseas ministers was effectively continued after the 1934 election. Sir Henry Gullett was appointed minister without portfolio directing trade negotiations; he spent much of his time overseas, reporting to cabinet by cable and seeking instructions. There were running debates on issues such as the imposition of sanctions after Italy invaded Abyssinia. Eventually, in March 1937, his views clashed so dramatically with the perceptions in Canberra that he resigned.

When overseas, like all prime ministers, Lyons wanted to be kept in touch. In 1937 he sent drafts of words that he wanted to add to a submission on the 40-hour week. Negotiations went to and fro, with a degree of frustration on the part of the prime minister. Finally, the acting prime minister cabled: 'can you arrange to telephone us in Cabinet Canberra tomorrow Friday between 5 p.m. and 6 p.m. Australian time. Conference telephone facilities now installed in Cabinet room.' Lyons duly made that call to benefit from the modern technology. When he did not receive his summary of decisions, the head of his department, Frank Strahan, cabled that: 'no summary of important Cabinet decisions received in respect of this week's meeting. P.M. would be glad to receive'. It was quickly sent.

Lyons never had the authority to drive cabinet. Hankey had observed that Latham:

> ... ruled Lyons with a rod of iron. Rather a hard man and above all a realist he was a constant check on Lyons' sentimentalism. But Latham, who is poor but extravagant, has retired to the bar to make some money and no-one has yet quite taken his place. For this role Mr. Menzies, the leading figure at the Bar apart from Latham, is generally cast ... Menzies is regarded in inner circles as the coming man ... He is, according to British standards, rather a rough diamond; very contemptuous of soft and soppy policies, but a good fellow at bottom and quite fearless of responsibility.

From 1937 the impending war began to dominate much of the discussion and the requirements to concentrate on its potential brought gradual change to the format and running of cabinet. Cabinet committees were far from new. At times they had contained junior ministers who dealt with a series of individual cases, operating within guidelines. More often they were created, in large numbers, to consider a particular item and then report back to cabinet with recommendations for action. In the 1930s a few committees began to have a continuing existence; in 1938 the treaties sub-committee of cabinet brought proposals to cabinet on treaties with Eire and Switzerland. It does not appear that they had the authority to make decisions on behalf of cabinet.

In November 1937 cabinet created a standing committee for defence. Its membership consisted of the prime minister, treasurer, ministers of defence and external affairs, the leader of the Country party and the deputy leader of the UAP. Its membership was both based on portfolio and political weight. It had the authority to make final decisions. After a meeting at the Lodge in August 1938, a list of decisions were circulated for action. In November it approved the development of a recruitment drive. It also formalised the delegation of authority and looked forward to the way a war might be run. Sir Maurice Hankey, Secretary to the British Cabinet, had reported on Australian Defence preparedness in 1934. A continuing interchange with Britain led to a proposition, approved by cabinet in March 1938, for the preparation of a war cabinet, if hostilities occurred. The submission included Australian proposals, with observations from Hankey attached. It began:

> In view of the size of the Cabinet in Australia, it would be important for quick decisions and the vigorous prosecution of the war policy that a war cabinet should be constituted. As the Council for Defence is a purely advisory body, it could be transformed by creating the War Cabinet from the ministers on the panel of the Council.

The chiefs of staff would advise; the secretary of defence, by virtue of his position as secretary of the council of defence, would be secretary of the war cabinet; the department of defence would be divided into four, each with their own ministers, and with the prime minister as minister for defence coordination. Cabinet approved the basic organisation in March 1938; further details were accepted in September. The decision spelt out the arrangements for political and military controls and contrasted its proposals with those that had applied in Britain in the 1914–18 conflict.

In November 1938 Lyons's leadership came under challenge. It was confirmed at a stormy party meeting on 2 November, but there was talk there of a need for a change. Lyons then reshuffled his cabinet, primarily to remove an inefficient minister for defence. He also announced that there would be an executive committee of cabinet consisting of six ministers. A day later, T.W. White, the minister for trade and customs, resigned in protest. It was not, as Lyons pointed out to parliament, that he opposed the idea of an inner group. He was offended that he was not a member of it. He need not have worried, as the inner group never actually met. Its nominal creation was, however, indicative of a broader discontent with the way that cabinet was working. In early 1939 two cabinet committees were created, with ministers divided between them. They pre-digested the less significant issues and made recommendations to cabinet, which seems to have accepted them *en bloc* during March. The system did not outlive Lyons.

In March 1939, too, Lyons was planning to create a stronger cabinet secretariat in his department that would include an official as notetaker in the cabinet room, following the practice in Britain. The proposal was leaked in the press on the day that Cabinet was due to discuss it, and, in part for that reason, ministers were not inclined to agree.

Cabinet was seriously divided, with doubts about Lyons's continued leadership. In November 1938, in a speech that was taken to be critical of the leadership of Lyons, Menzies raised the tension by claiming that democracies needed inspiring leadership; even though he denied that Lyons was the target, the speech infuriated many of his colleagues. Strikes at Port Kembla also raised the temperature. In February 1939 Lyons invited Bruce to return as prime minister, although the invitation seems to have disappeared a day later. Whether there was an agreement that Lyons would move over and allow Bruce to assume the prime ministership may be disputed. At different times a number of Lyons' cantankerous crew hoped they might supplant him, but no efforts were made. They could get no agreement among themselves.

After the 1934 election Lyons had lost his majority. He made an offer of coalition to the Country party that was rejected as inadequate. When he tried to adjourn the House to allow members to watch the Melbourne Cup, Page announced he would oppose the motion. Lyons needed the Country party. Even though some of Lyons' colleagues argued that he should continue with a UAP minority government, he offered better terms and Page now accepted. By February and March 1939 the coalition cabinet finally broke over the issue of the introduction of a scheme of national insurance. Menzies and the treasurer wanted it; the Country party opposed the proposal. Cabinet met in Melbourne and Hobart, with almost all the time, five or six hours a day, spent in the discussion of the scheme. The party room debated the matter at length. Finally, cabinet agreed to defer the scheme, effectively giving in to the pressure from the Country party. The issue seemed to be what they would accept and on 20 March Menzies resigned in protest. No sooner was that crisis temporarily put off than the international situation deteriorated. Cabinet then spent four of the next ten days agonising over its reaction to the German annexation of Czechoslovakia.

A week later an exhausted Lyons had a heart attack and died in office. Page was sworn in as prime minister until the UAP elected a leader. Page announced the Country party would not serve under Menzies. There were further attempts to persuade Bruce to return, but he wanted to be anointed as head of a national non-party government, a proposition never likely to be acceptable to Labor. Four candidates addressed the UAP party meeting before Menzies was elected, narrowly defeating the ancient Billy Hughes on the third ballot. Page stuck to his refusal to serve under Menzies who then had to form a cabinet from his own party and survive for the next 11 months as a minority in parliament.

Looming war dictated the cabinet agenda. On 23 June cabinet 'proceeded to discuss at considerable length the question of the policy of the defence of the country and in particular the necessity for a standing army'. On 28 June it appointed standing committees for defence and finance. It returned to the question of a permanent defence force in August. After listening to the inspector-general of the defence force, it decided, after meeting day and night, the cost of a permanent force would be too high. As war drew closer, time became more limited. On 28 August the prime minister reported he had cabled a response to Britain, 'after discussions with ministers available in Melbourne'. On 29 August, reacting to a Royal Navy request for readiness, the cabinet decided not to send a cruiser, as requested, to the Mediterranean. The prime minister read the British government's reply 'as far as it was decoded at 12.20'. The last sections were read after lunch. Once war began the value of Bruce in London became apparent. He had access to members of the British war cabinet and, day by day, the cabinet received reports on what was happening and a range of possible scenarios.

On 26 September cabinet formally changed the structure of its decision-making:

> **Direction of the War**
> It was agreed that the War Cabinet, which should include such ministers as the prime minister may direct, together with such ministers as from time to time were coopted, should deal with all matters in relation to the conduct of the war other than matters of major policy. Matters of major policy should be determined by the full Cabinet.

A month later the prime minister told cabinet that he wanted to establish an economic committee in addition to the war cabinet.

Not everything went to the war cabinet. When asked by Britain to comment on the war aims, the prime minister read to cabinet 'a cable in reply which he had despatched, without consultation with members of the cabinet, over the weekend as there was no opportunity to consult ministers'. There was a long discussion before the cable was finally approved.

Throughout 1940 cabinet was meeting 10 or 12 times a month. The items decided were often domestic and of lesser significance. It spent two days in April examining the budget proposals, usually approving decisions made by the economic committee. When cabinet considered the appointment of a trade commissioner in Tokyo, it asked the British government whether it would have a problem with such a move. Cabinet, contemplating war with Japan, agreed: 'we do not consider a settlement of the Sino–Japanese war would be beneficial'. It proposed to ask the United Kingdom parliament to pass an act to allow the federal parliament to 'postpone the life of parliament, should it be deemed necessary'. Otherwise the details went to the war cabinet and economic committee. Cabinet was becoming the fall-back forum.

Nor was it working well. In 1940 the secretary to cabinet was the minister for the interior, the Country party's H.K. Nock. He used to list the decisions briefly and send them to Frank Strahan, secretary of the prime minister's department. On one occasion, to Strahan's embarrassment, there was no available typist and he had to write them out in full by hand. After the 1940 election, T.J. Collins took over as secretary and the situation deteriorated further. Sometimes Collins provided no notes to Strahan, who had to learn from departments what had happened. On 3 December Collins just wrote that 'the whole discussion by the Cabinet was on the budget and possible compromises'. Collins advised the Secretary of the Army that cabinet had made a decision on wet canteens and sent him a press cutting that, he stated, 'correctly states the decision of Cabinet'. On 11 December Collins sent six decisions of cabinet; Strahan collected the rest, and there were a large number, from other departments. In March Collins told Strahan that the 'other discussions of Cabinet relating to matters bringing about no precise decision to be recorded'. Sometimes important items were just left off. When cabinet decided to appoint a minister to China, Strahan noted:

> Copy of the minute prepared by the Department of External Affairs (suggesting cablegram to High Commissioner's office in London, received from Private Secretary to the prime minister marked "approved, afternoon of 2/5/41").

The system was reverting to that of the first 20 years when ministers idiosyncratically recorded the cabinet outcomes.

When Menzies returned from Britain in May 1941 he had attended meetings of the war cabinet there and talked to Hankey. Doubtless Strahan also emphasised the shortcomings of relying on a not very competent minister at such a difficult time. In the war cabinet, too, secretary of Defence Coordination Fred Shedden had become accepted as the attending secretary. Combined, the arguments were strong for a resuscitation of the Lyons 1939 proposal for a cabinet secretariat. On 15 July Strahan sent a memo to ministers:

Cabinet Arrangements

Cabinet will in future function as-
    (a) Full Cabinet
    (b) War Cabinet
    (c) Economic and Industrial Committee of Cabinet.

The War Cabinet will operate as previously.
    The following details relate to the Full Cabinet and the Economic and Industrial Committee of Cabinet.
    The Full Cabinet will discuss matters which cannot adequately be dealt with by either of the other sections of Cabinet, as well as subjects referred to it by them.

> Mr. Fadden will be the Chairman of the Economic and Industrial Committee of Cabinet.
>
> Meetings of the full cabinet will be notified by the prime minister and in the case of the Economic and Industrial Committee by the Chairman, through the Secretary of Cabinet (Mr. F. Strahan).
>
> Professor Copland will be Economic Consultant to the prime minister. He will attend meetings of the Economic and Industrial Committee when necessary and will act as liaison between the prime minister and that body.
>
> Notification of the subjects to be listed for discussion, together with supporting papers, should be sent to the Secretary to Cabinet. Ministers are asked particularly that such information should be forwarded in sufficient time to enable the necessary action to be taken by the Secretariat and to permit the prime minister (or, in his absence, the Chairman of the Economic and Industrial Committee) to indicate which subjects should be dealt with by each Cabinet body.
>
> The Secretary to Cabinet will prepare an agenda paper and submit it to the prime minister for approval and will take a note of decisions on matters raised in Cabinet.
>
> In the case of the Economic and Industrial Committee, Minutes of Proceedings will be submitted to the chairman for approval and initialling before being sent to the prime minister.
>
> The Secretary to Cabinet will convey to ministers and departments concerned a notification of decisions arrived at in full cabinet and in the Economic and Industrial Committee.
>
> The Secretary has been instructed by the prime minister to take any steps necessary to ensure the "follow up" action involved in decisions by full cabinet for the Economic and Industrial Committee of cabinet.

Menzies wrote to Artie Fadden, deputy prime minister and treasurer, to explain how he saw the system working. All agenda items, except those of the war cabinet, went to the secretary and either the prime minister or Fadden (if the prime minister was not on the spot) who would decide which items went to full cabinet, which to the economic committee and 'which should be left for administrative decision by the Minister concerned'. Menzies told Fadden:

> The Economic Committee will be a committee of decision and action in just the same way as the War Cabinet. But, just as I will reserve from the War Cabinet questions of high principle for decision by the Full Cabinet, so I will expect you to exercise

> similar discretion in the case of matters coming before the Economic Committee.
>
> As each of us will be relieved under this arrangement from a certain amount of Cabinet work which he now attends to, I am anticipating that we shall be able to maintain fairly regular personal contact, which will facilitate the organisation of business generally. In any event, the secretary to the Cabinet will be attached to my Department, and if I see any matter passing through on which I would like to have a word myself, it will be quite simple to get in touch with you.

As in Britain the prime minister would thus run the war and leave his deputies to take control on the domestic front.

The changes set the basis for a new system. Committees were standing and had the powers of decision. An official would now sit in with responsibility for maintaining an account of what occurred, notifying departments and where necessary following up action. Even if these letters can be seen as a development of the cabinet system, building on earlier precedents, they were to prove dramatic in their effects.

But Menzies as prime minister was not to benefit immediately. Strahan first took the minutes on 17 July, noting general discussions on the budget and the eastern situation. Then cabinet again collapsed. The portents had not been good. Backbenchers had been openly demanding Menzies' removal for months. On return from Britain Menzies had appointed an additional five ministers, so that almost half the UAP caucus were in the ministry. On 28 July there was a bitter party meeting in which Menzies was confirmed as leader, once again an indication that the need for any such vote of confidence was a clear sign of the lack of it. On 8 August the prime minister began cabinet by complaining about stories in the press and 'referred also to the corporate responsibility of the Cabinet', another sign that all was not well. On 12 August cabinet meetings were interspersed with the prime minister meeting with Curtin and Scullin, on behalf of the Labor Opposition, as Menzies sought again to form a national all-party government. Labor refused. On 19 August cabinet discussed whether there should be permanent dominion representation on the British war cabinet. Menzies thought he should visit London to ensure representation. Ministers thought it essential for national welfare but they were not certain it should be Menzies. Such a move required Labor support and that was not forthcoming. On 21 August, Strahan noted:

> A full meeting of the Full Cabinet was called for 9 p.m. on Thursday evening (21/8/41) but no decisions were recorded. Political matters were discussed.

Again the next day the same cryptic note was made. That might be described as understatement, as these were two of the most dramatic cabinets ever held. The meetings openly discussed the future of the government and the tenure of the prime minister. Several UAP cabinet ministers, including Spender, Hughes and Holt, said that new leadership was required. They joined the Country party ministers in proposing that Fadden take over. Although some colleagues remained loyal, the defection of so many of his own party made it hard for Menzies to continue with such a divided cabinet. When the UAP met on 28 August Menzies declared he would resign. Then a combined party meeting elected Fadden unopposed.

Full cabinet under Fadden met five times in September to discuss the budget, and once to discuss accusations about secret funds. (Strahan kept a record, but then noted separately: 'Notes of the full Cabinet 23rd September 11 A.M. held by Mr. Strahan'. The word 'Political' was added by hand and represented the sum total of the minutes.) Thereafter cabinet only discussed the last rites of the government. The two independents who held the balance of power decided to vote with Labor against the budget and thus force a change of government, with John Curtin as prime minister.

5   FIGHTING WAR AND MANAGING MAVERICKS: 1941–49

Labor came to office in October 1941 just before Japan entered the war. It had to adapt to difficult conditions with little experience. Only one minister, the deputy prime minister, Frank Forde, had been a minister for the whole of the Scullin government. Three others had been in office briefly: before the March 1931 split in the case of Beasley, and after it for Chifley and Holloway. Scullin himself acted as an unofficial adviser, working from a small office close to the prime minister. As a minority government, Labor had to rely on the support of two independents in the House, though they proved reliable. Nor did it have a majority in the Senate.

Curtin welcomed ministers with a reminder of their responsibilities:

> The Prime Minister spoke generally with regard to Ministerial and Cabinet responsibility. Each Minister would be responsible for his own administration. In coming to any decision a Minister would conform to the Government's general policy. Some matters naturally would require Cabinet consideration and it was assumed that Ministers would take action accordingly in accordance with the recognised procedure.

Curtin nominally started with one advantage. Before the ministers were elected, his predecessor as a Labor prime minister, James Scullin, moved in caucus that 'the Prime Minister be empowered to remove a minister if at any time it was deemed desirable or/and necessary'. It was a power that was never used by Curtin or Chifley, despite provocation. It did allow Curtin to suspend Ward during the 'Brisbane line' imbroglio in 1943.

Ministers and the party

Almost immediately the question arose of whether ministers were bound by collective responsibility in cabinet. In discussion of the budget:

> The question of Cabinet responsibility was referred to particularly as to the freedom to be accorded Ministers to express their opinions in Party meetings. The general idea was explained by the Prime Minister and the necessity for cabinet solidarity emphasised.

Almost immediately the reason for such a ruling emerged. Throughout October cabinet discussed the budget in detail, settling on a pension of 23/6d. When the budget proposals were put to the caucus, a motion raising the amount to 25/- was passed. Later that day caucus reconvened and rescinded that original proposal. The recision was moved by the prime minister and seconded by the deputy prime minister. It was agreed that the pension would be raised at some time in the next year. It was. But clearly there was also a determination by Curtin that cabinet was not going to jump at every caucus whim.

At the next cabinet, on 4 November, in a statement in which the frustration showed through:

> The Prime Minister explained that repeatedly Ministers are required to yield something so that common ground may be arrived at. Statements should not be made by Ministers at variance with Cabinet majority decisions. It was realised that frequently newspapers took statements from their context and distorted them. It was necessary generally that a common ground be found for all matters of policy. Naturally there would be differences in Departments and among Ministers. These problems should be brought by Ministers themselves to the Prime Minister when they could be discussed and decisions to all could be arrived at.
>
> With regard to pensions, no figure had been fixed in the platform of the Party. Sometimes pledges had to be made by leaders of parties but these were read in concert with other principles adopted by the party. Patience is required to bring them all to consummation.
>
> The Prime Minister elaborated this theme by reference to the obligations and rights of the Government and Ministers generally.

Not all ministers accepted this restriction, but at the time Curtin was adamant.

Curtin was well aware of the sensitivities of the party. He had been a backbencher during the Scullin government and knew what could go wrong. He had made his name as an anti-conscriptionist during the 1914–18 war. Consequently, he knew that sudden changes to established party policy had to be managed with care. In 1942 he believed that restricting the use of the militia to Australian territory was too limited and wanted to expand the sphere in which they could be sent. Militia regiments had served heroically on the Kokoda track, but that was seen as part of Australia. Conscious of the problems of gaining cabinet or caucus support for an amendment of the party platform, he took it straight to a national Labor Conference in November 1942. He had not consulted cabinet. Several ministers, as delegates to the conference, opposed the prime minister there. That conference decided to send the motion back to the state branches for decision.

After his initial speech to the conference, Curtin took the proposal to cabinet. There 'a discussion took place with regard to this matter and the Prime Minister outlined the proposal that was placed before the ALP Conference'. Cabinet endorsed it. At the next meeting of caucus, on 9 December, the reaction was stormier. Curtin read the statement he proposed to read to parliament. Arthur Calwell, always antagonistic and still a backbencher, moved that the party was 'opposed to any proposals for the conscription of Australian Manhood for overseas service as being fundamentally the same in principle as those which the Labor movement rejected in 1916'. Curtin ruled the motion out of order, on the grounds that the conference was the only body competent to deal with the issue. Calwell moved that the ruling be disagreed with. His motion of dissent was defeated 37 to 13 with Ward breaking cabinet ranks. When Curtin's statement was debated in parliament, Labor voted solidly against an amendment, but only after a bitter caucus meeting on 11 December and a near brawl there. Indeed, Calwell had seconded the amendment in the House of Representatives and Ward had publicly supported it.

Curtin persuaded four of the six branches to agree and in a further conference in January 1943 his proposal was accepted. Later that month he brought a submission to cabinet spelling out the details of the proposal; the militia would not be used north of the equator and only within the boundaries of the area declared to be the south-west Pacific region. He pointed out that the decision of the conference was now the policy of Labor; its introduction was just a question of timing.

The bitterness rankled. In March 1943 Curtin and Calwell clashed in caucus. He had called Calwell 'the hero of 100 sham fights'. Calwell retorted that, the way Curtin was going, he would 'finish up on the other side leading a National Government'. Curtin withdrew from caucus and sent a letter to his deputy, Forde, then in the chair, inviting the party to 'disassociate itself from the accusation or appoint another leader'. Calwell retracted and the caucus voted a unanimous vote of confidence in the leader.

On some occasions a minister wanted to send an issue to caucus, but his colleagues did not agree. In October 1942, when the Nazi invasion of the Union of Soviet Socialist Republics (USSR) brought it into the war, cabinet considered lifting the ban on the Communist party. 'One minister wanted to submit the question to the party. This suggestion did not find general acceptance'. In January 1945 there were lengthy debates over six days as cabinet considered the Commonwealth Bank bill and a bill to regulate trading banks. 'Cabinet did accept the suggestion that the recommendations in the Agendum be not decided but that the matter be referred to caucus for decision'. In the first case it never came to caucus. However, treasurer Chifley brought the Bank bills there for consideration. The debate lasted from 19 to 21 February. Amendments to the bills, including a proposal that the government nationalise the trading banks, were lost. Calwell and Ward, both then ministers, moved in caucus amendments to the bills that had been approved by cabinet. They were not averse to restarting a battle in caucus that they had lost in cabinet.

Prime ministers took caucus seriously. Curtin chaired most of the meetings while he was prime minister, until he fell ill in 1945 when the task fell to Forde or Chifley. Chifley chaired *every* caucus meeting of his prime ministership, from July 1945 until the government's defeat in December 1949; he regarded the task as important to the running of a Labor government.

He, too, knew the Labor party well and understood how to use the various forums to best advantage. The campaign to gain approval for Australia's signing of the Bretton Woods agreement that established the World Bank and the International Monetary Fund (IMF) provides an example of a political craftsman. Initially cabinet was nervous about the whole development of international financial organisations; they were too suspicious of money power and international capitalism. In January 1944 a sub-committee had been appointed to consider the plans for economic reconstruction. In June the cabinet chose not to send a minister, as initially proposed, to the original Bretton Woods meeting, but an official delegation of Professor L.G. Melville, Fred Wheeler and Arthur Tange (the latter two became powerful mandarins in later years). The delegation reported back to cabinet in September that year. Cabinet deferred any decision to join until the United States and the United Kingdom had defined their attitudes.

In September 1945 cabinet agreed to consider the plans. In January 1946 the prime minister brought the issue to cabinet:

> At the conclusion of the debate the Prime Minister intimated that if the recommendations contained in the Agendum were rejected the proposals would be re-submitted at a suitable time.
>
> The following motion was placed before the Cabinet and lost: – "that cabinet recommend to the Parliamentary Party that the Bretton Woods proposals be approved and that the necessary action be taken to obtain Parliamentary concurrence".
>
> Cabinet approved that Members of Caucus be informed to the effect that the Bretton Woods proposals are to be further considered at a future date.

This is the *only* occasion when the Cabinet records identify a motion that was put and lost, let alone a motion formally put by the prime minister; but it was not often that the prime minister failed to win so clearly.

Chifley did not bring the proposals back until after the 1946 election, although Ward had openly opposed them in public. On 19 November 1946 cabinet had another debate. Melville and Wheeler attended the meeting 'to advise generally on the fund, i.e. the risks and benefits associated with Australia's participation'. The cabinet decided:

> That Australia will join the International Monetary Fund and the International Bank for Reconstruction, but at the same time makes clear to Britain, the United States and other interested countries, that the Australian Government regards the fund and the bank and the International Trade Organisation as being clearly linked, and that the Government will review the question of continuing Australian membership of the fund and the bank when the outcome of the International Trade Organisation discussions is known.

Several ministers, led by Holloway, Ward and Calwell, opposed the motion.

On 27 November the prime minister moved in caucus for authority to ratify the Bretton Woods agreement. The debate was adjourned till the next day. That evening Chifley addressed the federal executive and, by seven votes to five, gained endorsement for Australia to be a signatory. At the caucus the next day, he read out the Executive resolution and the rule that gave the executive authority; the debate continued. Before the caucus reconvened the ministers who opposed Bretton Woods asked in cabinet where they stood. The prime minister gave a ruling:

> When a Cabinet decision is reached it should be supported by Ministers but there is no inflexible rule in this regard. The action of ministers is left to their own personal honour, i.e. a technical right exists for the Minister to disagree with the ruling of Cabinet.

Ministers expressed different interpretations. Holloway suggested:

> ... that the parliamentary party is supreme and has a right to direct the policy of the Government. Accordingly, Ministers had an individual right to put their personal views to the party.

That view at least had party history on its side.

A second view, expressed by Ward, was that 'in matters of individual importance a discretion existed for the Minister to oppose a decision of Cabinet and the Party' as long as, he argued, they were not covered by the policy determined by Conference. That opposed all the traditions of collective responsibility. The pragmatic John Dedman, minister for Post-War Reconstruction, suggested that 'if a particular matter was so vital to an individual minister he could resign from Cabinet and oppose the matter in the party; at the same time standing for re-election to the position rendered vacant by his resignation.' (The views were noted in the Cabinet Minutes, the identities of the speakers noted 20 years later by Dedman.)

Chifley's ruling provided at best a very relaxed view; he was more concerned with maintaining party unity than constitutional nicety. Caucus ignored the recommendations of cabinet and executive and proposed, by 29 to 26, that the matter be referred to a special conference. Six ministers voted with the majority against the prime minister. Chifley persuaded three of the state executives to oppose the calling of a special conference, so the issue came back to cabinet on 28 February. That meeting had a busy agenda that discussed a wide range of increases in pensions and changes to income tax provisions. Then, without circulating any supporting memorandum, the prime minister brought the proposal up again and 'Cabinet approved that a recommendation be made to the Parliamentary Labor Party that Parliament be asked to ratify the Bretton Woods Agreement'. This time caucus agreed by 33 votes to 24. Six ministers could still be found in opposition. When the bill was put to the vote in the House of Representatives, Ward abstained, another re-interpretation of the concept of collective responsibility.

For Curtin and Chifley the party had to be managed. They had learnt the lessons of history. If it meant living with the shenanigans of Calwell and Ward, with ministers opposing them in caucus and in special conferences, that stress could be survived. Maintaining party support in general was a central requirement for continued governing.

The operations of cabinet

Cabinet during the period had three components that made up the cabinet system. War cabinet made decisions about the war and the use of the fighting services. The Production Executive, presided over by the treasurer, dealt with economic and financial matters that ensured the continuance of the war effort. Full cabinet (sometimes spelt with a capital F) dealt with other matters of policy, or in effect whatever the prime minister wanted discussed there. To an extent full cabinet became a forum for the occasional significant political decision: on conscription, banking, Bretton Woods and the budget, but much less for the daily running of government. Table 5.1 shows the frequency of meetings of cabinet and caucus.

TABLE 5.1 Labor at war: cabinet and caucus meetings

Year	Full cabinet meetings (more than a day)	Caucus meetings
1941 (3 months)	11 (3)	8
1942	16 (2)	12
1943	17 (1)	16
1944	21 (2)	18
1945	24 (12)	19
1946	25 (8)	15
1947	18 (2)	16
1948	23	20
1949	26	15

Creation of the war cabinet changed the role of full cabinet. Horner has noted that:

> ... it was intended that the War Cabinet would become the executive sub-committee of the Full Cabinet, but as the war progressed the reverse tended to take place. The main decisions concerning the conduct of the war were taken in the War Cabinet and the Full Cabinet was left with more peripheral issues.

In terms of the war that was clearly true. The war cabinet met more often and discussed more issues. It operated from September 1939 to January 1946. According to its own records it met 355 times in those 6 1/2 years – an average of just over one a week. It dealt with 3998 items (on average 50 a week) and recorded 4645 minutes. It determined the great issues of the war: such as the commitment of troops and the determination to bring the Australian Imperial Force (AIF) back to Australia, and some of the semi-domestic problems such as the organisation of manpower. The war cabinet acted as a *de facto* inner cabinet; it included the principal ministers and Curtin was able to exclude those with whom he was less comfortable, particularly Ward and Calwell.

In December 1942, after its first year, the Production Executive reported it had transferred between 400 000 and 500 000 people from civilian to war uses. It made almost 200 decisions on all areas of activity from simplification of clothing (including elimination of waistcoats and shortening of shirt tails) to rationalisation of shovels and pastry-cooking, restrictions on domestic servants and prohibition of non-essential production.

The war cabinet was not only able to direct the war, it also created new standards for organisation and professionalism necessary to execute the decisions made there. Backed by a team from defence, Shedden provided detailed and accurate minutes. 'Documentation, thy name is Shedden', quipped Menzies. It also provided a model for the Production Executive, supported in its turn by Giles Chippindall, head of the department of War Organisation of Industry. There were considerable logistic problems in an era where travelling from Melbourne to Canberra took a long time. Menzies often held the war cabinet in Melbourne because the Service departments were located there and he lived there too. Full cabinet symbolically usually met in Canberra. Curtin, being from Perth, lived in the Lodge in Canberra and therefore held the majority of war cabinets there. The officials were constantly on the move from their departmental base to their political masters.

Officials had to serve more than their elected masters. In October 1940, after the election had stripped Menzies of his parliamentary majority and the Labor Party showed no interest in joining a national government, Menzies created the advisory war council. It provided a forum where four, later five, members of the Opposition could be briefed on the progress of the war. The Labor party was divided on whether it should force Menzies out and the advisory war council provided an alternative. Only when the Menzies government imploded was Curtin prepared to take over.

Curtin retained the advisory war council that met 174 times in five years before being disbanded in August 1945. Its role had become less significant after the 1943 election had given Curtin a clear majority, but meetings could still be tense. The Service Chiefs were often vigorously cross-questioned by opposition leaders, particularly by Hughes who had mellowed little with age. It became so aggressive that in September 1942 at the height of Kokoda, Blamey [Chief of Defence Staff] asked Curtin to give some thought for the difficult position of the Service chiefs. Initially they were to attend occasionally to provide details.

> These meetings, from the point of view of the Heads of Services have become a weekly inquisition. Apart from the time absorbed, the necessary mental effort of seeking information on all subjects in order to be on guard on all points against a battery of cross examination diverts the attention of the heads of services from many urgent problems to a great extent. A great deal of time is taken up in addition to the time taken in travelling to and fro, to the detriment of their normal duties, which are unavoidably performed under pressure under war conditions. Moreover a political atmosphere is sometimes imparted to the proceedings in which the Services should have no interest.
>
> I beg to suggest most respectfully that the responsibility of the heads of Services should be limited to responsibility to the Government. There are constantly in touch with their Ministers and with the Minister for Defence. I would submit most earnestly that heads of Service should not be required to render account to any other body than the Government itself.

The plea had little impact. Political imperatives took precedence over military convenience, for the time being at least.

The three units — full cabinet, the war cabinet and the advisory war cabinet — were part of a system. Items were from the beginning sent from one to another. War cabinet passed the issue of manpower planning to full cabinet. Full cabinet in turn, after the *Prince of Wales* and *Repulse* were sunk in December 1941,

> Authorises the War Cabinet to take immediate steps for the total mobilisation of all resources — human and material — of Australia on a Commonwealth-wide basis in order that the defence of Australia may be provided for.

Issues thus bounced form one forum to another. Several cabinet subcommittees were also established, as items needed greater attention. Alternatively, issues were sent to a couple of ministers to provide a common view on coal, rural employment, compensation for internees, medical research, a Roosevelt memorial, the table of precedence, standardised railway gauges and secondary industry, to name but some of the committees appointed in 1944 and 1945.

At times ministers could get frustrated with the loquacity of their colleagues. In 1944, while Curtin was in Britain, cabinet agreed that 'intrusion on the typed agenda should not be allowed unless matters were of urgent importance', only to invalidate their resolution by agreeing that of course 'in any event the Presiding Minister of the Cabinet should determine as to the order in which subjects would be dealt with'. There is no evidence that thereafter fewer items were brought without submission. In 1945, amid a long debate on the bank bills, cabinet decided that each minister be allowed to 'only speak once until all have spoken'. There is no evidence that such a resolution was put into effect. Chifley tried to insist on greater notice for ministers. In late 1945 he pleaded that, to expedite cabinet business, 'all agenda should be in the hands of the Secretary of Cabinet at least (4) four clear days before each meeting' to give ministers time to study the subjects. In 1947 he stressed the need for 'prior consultation between ministers before matters were brought to cabinet'. Too little consideration, too many disputes in cabinet, must have been on his mind.

By Crisp's account, the organisation of the cabinet secretariat remained rudimentary before 1949. Before 1945 the war cabinet with its careful support team hid the deficiency. After 1945 it did not matter because Chifley was also treasurer and he used his officials there for policy support. Only in 1949, when Chifley was contemplating giving up the Treasury and dismantling the Department of Post-War Reconstruction if he won the 1949 election did he consider bolstering the capacity of the Prime Minister's Department. He appointed Allen Brown as secretary when Strahan retired after 15 years in the post and began to review the structure and purpose of the department.

Fortunately for the historian, despite the limited support, the minutes taken by Frank Strahan from 1941 to about 1945 were often full and detailed. They not only include the decisions but also the comments of ministers. If the contributions of all the ministers are not always identified during debates, the prime minister and often ministers speaking on their own items are. It is thus possible to get a flavour of the debate and the issues that were raised. After 1945 the minutes became more cryptic, often little more than a note of decision. At times the secretary noted that items were discussed 'exhaustively' with a degree of weariness that unfortunately excluded any continuing summary of views.

The prime minister would often use full cabinet to encourage his ministers. In May 1942, the 'manner in which party questions would require to be subordinated to these national problems was emphasised by the prime minister'. In August 1942, when the threat was greatest, he:

> Urged ministers to endeavour to inspire their departments with enthusiasm and to see the executive drove ahead to a complete war effort.

Cabinet went into considerable detail as it sought to introduce an 'austerity' campaign in August 1942. The prime minister brought a series of proposals to cabinet under his austerity regime. Cabinet decreed that 'meals provided at hostels, cafes etc be limited to not more than three courses'; and that there was a need 'to restrict to the greatest possible minimum the space given ... to all phases of sport'. It did not reach the proposal that 'employers to be told to remove bans on girls going without stockings at work'. Cabinet kept bemoaning the level of beer consumption, but accepted it was difficult to reduce because 'returned AIF men and Americans were responsible for the large consumption'. They deserved it.

Before the 1943 election the prime minister told the cabinet 'what he had in mind in connection to the elections' and circulated the policy speech at the last cabinet before the poll. After the election he went through the issues that would have to be considered to maintain a balanced war effort. In October 1943 he warned that there would be:

> ... a long Cabinet meeting in November so that Ministers could discuss generally and at length proposals for new legislation etc which would be necessary to carry out Government policy (eg Commonwealth powers).

He asked ministers to send to him or to discuss with him any ideas they had with regard to legislation etc.

This approach would in later years be regarded as a strategic cabinet, looking at the directions for the government in the next year.

The minutes were kept by Strahan in the full cabinet, and by the secretary of the department of defence, Shedden, in the war cabinet. Strahan would follow up with a memo to the minister reminding him of the decision of cabinet. Occasionally these decisions were challenged by ministers. Usually he started the note with: 'I am instructed to write ...'. On occasion, when writing to the treasurer (Chifley) after a cabinet meeting chaired by the prime minister (Chifley), he would start 'For the purpose of record ...'. When a minister was absent he would write to the secretary of the department, telling him the outcome of the cabinet debate and asking him to draw it to the attention of the minister.

Full cabinet still debated big issues at length. The budget was brought for analysis. The treasurer circulated a memorandum at the beginning of the meeting, but then collected it at the end. Several days could be spent on income tax or other fundraising proposals.

Industrial strife on the coalfields was a constant thorn in government plans. Curtin was annoyed that, as a protected profession, the miners were prone to strike and threatened to withdraw their special status or to call them up. Ward blamed the employers. There was little sympathy between these two Labor stalwarts, even if Curtin tolerated Ward as one of the burdens a Labor prime minister had to bear. After the ministers had been elected, Curtin told Ward that he had not voted for him. Ward retorted: 'I know that Jack, the only reason I didn't vote against you was because you were not opposed'. In the conscription debate, Ward had attacked Curtin as a person who was 'putting young men into the slaughterhouse although thirty years ago you wouldn't go yourself'.

On one occasion, in November 1942, the interchange led to a situation that Curtin must have enjoyed. In the first half of the meeting conscription had been discussed, with Curtin under attack from Ward. When cabinet reconvened, Ward complained that he had been called 'The Man who Makes Trouble' in the *Daily Telegraph*. The newspaper claimed that he was 'personally and deliberately responsible for the fact that the most vital of war industries is constantly interrupted'. It was, declared Ward, an attack on the whole ministry. Curtin and Doc Evatt, attorney-general and former High Court Justice, were having none of it. Their lack of support was tangible and understandable after all they had put up with from Ward. Curtin:

> ... suggested that although the statements were untrue they might not be regarded by the legal fraternity as libellous. The Minister for Labour and National Service did undertake the tour of the coalfields and had accepted the task of establishing peace in the coal industry. In these circumstances it might be claimed that these offensive words were fair comment.

> The Attorney-General outlined the legal position; he considered the attack was vicious and unfair. He suggested however that one could never rely on a verdict even though the law seemed clear. If the matter came to a legal action it would be for the jury to decide, but very often it did not give a verdict on a strict legal interpretation. If malice could be shown then of course an action would lie.

Seldom has 'support' been so two-sided.

There was no correlation between the significance of an issue and the length of cabinet's deliberations. In 1945 the banking bills received careful attention. Cabinet debated the details of the legislation over several meetings, taking it clause by clause. The meeting, spread over five days, produced 35 pages of summarised debate and decisions. By contrast the decision to nationalise the banks was taken late in a meeting, without submission on the recommendation of the prime minister. The time and intensity of the debate varied from one circumstance to another.

Cabinet could be the arena where ministerial ambitions clashed. Dedman and Ward, working in overlapping areas, fought constantly, the former with the sympathy of his leaders and the latter without. Dedman was the driving force behind the Production Executive, created by Curtin in October 1941. The original proposal had been put to Menzies by Shedden in July that year; the purpose was to organise the economy within the boundaries set by the war cabinet. In the political chaos nothing was done. Shedden proposed the idea again to Curtin, this time successfully. Dedman was keen that the Production Executive had a standing similar to that of the war cabinet. Curtin would not agree. He told Dedman that the Production Executive was a meeting of ministers, not a cabinet committee. (It was not clear what the difference was and later in the war it was sometimes referred to as a cabinet committee.) When Dedman tried to extend its terms of reference, Curtin changed the draft to emphasise that the Production Executive worked within the guidelines set by the war cabinet.

In July 1942 Ward took a detailed submission to cabinet to propose planning for post-war reconstruction. The submission showed the skill and foresight of his secretary, Roland Wilson. It noted the minister had talked to the prime minister and proposed the creation of a small cabinet committee to oversee the process. Dedman wrote to the prime minister suggesting that it would be more appropriate for the Production Executive to serve as that committee as all the relevant ministers were already involved.

Curtin responded that he noted his suggestion and seemed to agree; 'I think that this might be the best arrangement'. By the cabinet of 3 August he had changed his mind again and cabinet agreed to create the small cabinet committee initially proposed. In January 1943 Dedman proposed that the Production Executive should become the economic cabinet; cabinet did not agree. In 1945 the ambitious Dedman asked his officials to consider if the Commonwealth could get into education. As later minister of post-war reconstruction after the war ended he was able to exercise his talents and energy with the close support of Chifley.

Cabinet considered a range of appointments. All heads of departments and a number of diplomatic appointments came to it. They were not all accepted readily. When trade unionist Dr Lloyd Ross was considered for a position as deputy in the Department of Post-war Reconstruction, cabinet considered the suggestion; both 'the merits and disadvantages of Dr Lloyd Ross were fully gone into'. The extension of Bruce's tenure as High Commissioner in London, the decision to post ministers Beasley and Makin to diplomatic positions, a replacement for Roland Wilson at secretary of the department of Labour and National Service in 1945, all came to cabinet.

Prime ministers are naturally in a special position, but their powers sometimes come under challenge. In November 1943, Ward complained that he had read of the appointment of the King's brother, the Duke of Gloucester, as Governor-General in the press:

> He said that it had been embarrassing to him as a Minister to get the news of the appointment from the press. He asked two questions:-
> (1) Why had not all Ministers been advised; and
> (2) Was not such an appointment in opposition to the accepted policy of the Labor movement.

Curtin defended his prerogative and personal duty to advise the King. Ward complained at length, in a speech that canvassed White Australia and cabinet leaks, that cabinet should have been consulted. Calwell agreed that the prime minister had the right to make some policy decisions without cabinet approval, but the public would believe that cabinet has acquiesced in the appointment and so the party should have been consulted. 'He would like an assurance that Cabinet would be consulted and would thus have corporate responsibility.' Evatt thought it 'was a mistake to endeavour to lay down general rules as to the power of the prime minister. He referred to the recent dissolution and to the return of the AIF. He took it that the prime minister did not mean that in every such case it would be a matter of his own determination.'

While the deputy prime minister agreed that the powers of the prime minister should be left undefined, another minister (unnamed by the secretary) thought the difficulties in getting 'heads of organisations to carry out the government's wishes ... would be accentuated if people thought that certain Ministers were not being taken into the Government's confidence. He thought the authority of all Ministers should be maintained. Decisions of major importance should be made only after discussion by all Ministers.' The discussion came to no resolution but emphasised how little trust some Labor ministers had in the power of prime ministers and why they needed to be treated with care. Labor prime ministers had more problems with a cabinet that was elected and harder to dismiss than their Liberal counterparts did.

There were ways in which prime ministers were still able to influence the directions of their governments. Sometimes cabinet was content to allow the prime ministers to make the decisions. The Brisbane Line controversy exploded with the claim that the Menzies government had considered abandoning northern Australia if faced by a Japanese invasion. Ward accused the former government just before the 1943 election, crying conspiracy and claiming documents had been stolen. Cabinet left it to the prime minister to defuse the issue; he suspended Ward while a royal commission examined the charges and found no evidence. In 1945, when issues of peace treaties were under discussion, it was agreed that 'the prime minister would endeavour when it was not possible to consult Full Cabinet — to interpret accurately the Government's wishes and intentions'.

Even when issues came to cabinet, prime ministers knew how to manage their colleagues. The minutes of the early Labor years are full enough to illustrate where the prime minister was able to steer the debate. The meeting of 3 August 1942, at the depth of the worst time of the war, can provide an example. The sitting date of parliament was set and after an exchange of views the dates for daylight saving were settled. The prime minister was authorised to meet the AWU and Australian Council of Trade Unions (ACTU) to discuss their attendance at a conference of trade unions from Britain and the dominions, with a commitment that the government would provide the transport. Then the prime minister spoke at length about government publicity. He set the terms of the discussion but deferred any decision. The prime minister described what he had done in his austerity campaign. He saw sport as a great distraction and complained that the waterside workers and miners were disinclined to work at weekends. 'War could not be waged without ruthlessness.' He intervened later in the debate and ended by encouraging ministers to drive their departments 'to a complete war effort'.

He then set out the government position on profit limitation, regretting that the proposals they had accepted could not be applied. Cabinet agreed. The treasurer led on the next items: taxation on overseas film companies and an entertainments tax. The treasurer and prime minister then briefed cabinet on the financial position, with the prime minister announcing that later in the month cabinet would consider how the extra funds would be raised. At the end of a long discussion on the creation of a mortgage bank for rural reconstruction, the prime minister was cool on the proposal, arguing it was a peace-time idea; cabinet nonetheless agreed to introduce a bill. On a proposal for an Australian food council, the prime minister summarised by saying immediate action was needed, he praised the ministers for their 'excellent job' and drew the attention of the Production Executive to any major proposals going to the council. Cabinet agreed. On the appointment of a commonwealth railways commissioner the prime minister 'read a précis of his file'. He then explained the background of the proposal for a small cabinet committee on planning for reconstruction. On the issue of extracting rubber from New Guinea, the prime minister talked about the shipping problems and said 'a decision could not be reached at the moment'. He intimated that he would 'take the submission on this subject to Brisbane and discuss it with General MacArthur [American military Supremo in the Pacific]'. He said nothing on wheat stabilisation, but, a reformed alcoholic, he had strong views and was active in the discussion of problems with the control of liquor. Ministers agreed that drinking had increased:

> The prime minister explained that it had been reported to him that the quantity of beer consumed instead of being less (as was the intention and decision of Cabinet) was greater. The press had come to him from time to time with alarming statements and had asked him to issue on behalf of the Government a statement. This had caused him to ask the Minister for a report as to the true facts of the matter.

He drew the attention of cabinet to the drinking figures. Cabinet then looked at means of control. Throughout the meetings the prime minister could either set the terms of discussion with an opening statement, sum up in a form that became the decision or interpolate where it was appropriate. There was no doubt that the prime minister could control the meeting.

There is one account of the way that Chifley ran his cabinet worth quoting at length. Crisp had worked closely with Chifley and in 1949 had been briefly appointed director-general of Post-war Reconstruction before he left for a chair at the Canberra University College. He wrote from experience:

At Cabinet meetings, Chifley was careful to give everyone the opportunity to express a view. He was skilful at inviting and drawing out views which would buttress his own. He was patient and persuasive in working, before and during Cabinet meetings, to get adopted what he thought right. If need be he would throw into the scales all his great personal charm, and in the occasional crisis invoke the full measure of loyalty and affection he commanded. Officials who attended Cabinet committee meetings frequently had to master a private smile as they watched him deploying the resources at his command. After a long discussion conducted somewhat formally in terms of 'Mr Minister', he would at the critical moment turn with a smiling intimacy to a reluctant colleague and say: 'Well, Reggie (or Jack, or whatever the name might be), what do you think about this now?' Or with an amiable and disarming grin he would bring about the complete collapse of a splendid rationalisation. When, for instance, a colleague delivered a most righteous onslaught on big residential flat projects ('If you could see the things that happen in flats in my area, you wouldn't support this. They destroy family life, they are incentives to immorality'), Chifley quietly interposed: 'With their white collar tenants they're not too good for the local Labor Member politically, either, are they, Dick?' ... Other Ministers might be as energetic as he, one or two might have been in some sense his intellectual superior, but none combined at once his range of mastery and his massive stability. Part of Chifley's strength came from the fact that he never reached any decision lightly or easily, though he was capable of delivering it promptly. His acuteness of mind enabled him to cut right through to the essence of the issues and to sum up essentials and conclusions in two or three forceful sentences. As one of his closest Ministerial colleagues has explained it: 'When he had reached a decision you could sometimes object to his reasoning, but the care and deliberation with which he had proceeded were beyond question. He was willing to have you demonstrate his error. He would listen carefully and rake you with questions. If your demonstration stood up to scrutiny he would concede gracefully, for in those circumstances his firmness never went, as his critics sometimes claimed, to the point of pigheadedness.' And on the rare occasions when a decision of Cabinet was not all he desired, he nevertheless loyally accepted and applied it.

Chifley's prime ministerial style led to great personal support and affection. He was personally liked even though politically unsuccessful, losing as he did the election of 1949. John Dedman, close to both of them as a minister, said that Curtin was the most able Labor prime minister but Chifley the most loved. It is a telling contrast.

On 12 December 1949 the Secretary of Cabinet summoned ministers to a final cabinet meeting. The government had been defeated. The filed telegram noted: 'The Secretary did not attend the meeting'. It was Chifley's farewell. No records were kept.

6 AN EMPEROR AND THREE PALE SHADOWS: 1949–72

In 1949 Allen Brown, secretary of the Prime Minister's Department, proposed to Chifley that the capacity of the department to advise on policy matters should be bolstered. Chifley had remained treasurer while he was prime minister and had relied heavily on his officials there for policy support. But if he won the election in 1949 he was considering giving up the additional burden. He would therefore need, as prime minister, a department that could provide the advice to which he was accustomed. The Department of Post-war Reconstruction was to be abolished and the economic section, with its highly qualified and vigorous staff, transferred to the Prime Minister's Department. At the time the department had little capacity beyond the servicing of the cabinet system, and that system seems to have declined after the pressures of war had receded.

Not much had been achieved when Menzies took power in December 1949. The prime minister chose to take no additional portfolio; he relied on his ministers, his own experience and, of course, his department. He was thus able to build on the plans that Chifley and Brown had put in place.

In one respect the insights into Menzies' cabinet are unique. In July 1950 Allen Brown began to keep cabinet notebooks that recorded the discussion in the cabinet room. The purpose of the notebooks was not to provide a verbatim record, but to act as an *aide memoire* for the secretary from which decisions of cabinet could be constructed after the meeting. If, as often happened, there was no debate in cabinet, a submission would be noted and ticked off; the minister's proposals were approved. Where the debate was extensive, so were the notes. They included the whole range of comments, from the political and the technical, from lengthy perorations to one-liners and asides. They illustrate the frustrations, the anxieties and the motives of the ministers there. A few people spoke more readily, more forcefully, than their colleagues.

The notebooks are covered by a 50-year, rather than a 30-year rule. Only the first five years, from 1950 to 1955 are available so far. As the years roll out we may be able to see more of the debate inside cabinet. At the moment those years are the only direct contemporary insight we have to the cabinet table and the mode of decision-making that took place there. Even while accepting that these are not full accounts of everything that was said, the notebooks provide a richness that whets the appetite. This chapter accordingly loiters more on the first years of the Menzies government than might otherwise be justified because of the immediacy of the debate that can be explored there. Such accounts are essentially partial; they describe how the cabinet saw issues, what it regarded as significant. The picture from cabinet is never rounded, or even necessarily accurate.

The structure of cabinet

All ministers were sent a handbook that described the cabinet system and the place of ministers within it. The handbook developed earlier primers of behaviour and took the lessons from earlier regimes. In this respect Menzies benefited from the experimentation in, and developments under, the Labor governments, though doubtless Brown would have pushed for these changes regardless of who won the 1949 election. The handbook explained the 'General Functions of Cabinet' as follows:

> Cabinet Government rests on the need to reconcile two principles of our constitution-
> (a) Ministerial responsibility; and
> (b) Collective responsibility.
>
> Each Minister in charge of a Department is responsible to parliament for the administration of his department along lines which command the support of his colleagues.
>
> In addition, all Ministers are collectively responsible for the Government's policy and must share in formulating it.
>
> The system of Cabinet Government, therefore, is the instrument by which practical effect is given to this principle of collective responsibility of Ministers who are separately responsible to parliament for the administration of their own Departments.
>
> Cabinet meetings are essentially meetings of Ministers. The Secretary of Cabinet is present to record the decisions.

The handbook then set out the procedures for the preparation and lodgement of submissions. It exhorted ministers to discuss proposals with Treasury (as by that means 'Cabinet business is facilitated') and with other interested ministers. Decisions would be sent to ministers 'who are themselves responsible for taking action thereon'.

The handbook also noted the role of cabinet committees 'to help Cabinet take decisions on Government policy smoothly and quickly, in sure knowledge of all facts'. It stated:

> The mass of business engaging the collective responsibility of the Government is too great to be handled by a single body, and Cabinet Committees can relieve the burden falling on Cabinet in the following way:
> (a) They can dispose finally of a number of problems of minor importance, acting in Cabinet's name and by virtue of the powers delegated to Cabinet.
> (b) On problems which are of such importance that they must in any event come to Cabinet, or which are technical and intricate in nature, a Committee can shorten Cabinet discussion, by preliminary examination, which focuses the attention on the main issues.
>
> Membership of a Committee may help a small group of Ministers to acquire in spheres of policy related to their own a detailed working knowledge which will add strength and cohesion to the administration. This system not only relieves the pressure on the Cabinet itself but also lightens the collective work of Ministers generally.

There were two types of committees. Standing committees provided a means of handling minor issues that arrived regularly and could be settled within existing policy. *Ad hoc* committees looked at specific questions. There were 18 standing and 26 *ad hoc* committees identified.

In effect the handbook set out the guidelines for the way that a cabinet system should work. It laid out the principles underlying a cabinet and the ways in which decisions should be made at different levels. It explained the role of committees of different types. The handbook was in this regard a seminal work. With variations, all that has been done in future copies of the cabinet handbooks is an elaboration of these ideas.

Yet even such good intentions did not work effectively. After the government was re-elected in May 1951 Menzies appealed to his ministers to try harder to make the system work.

> He urged ministers to decide matters for themselves within the limits of ministerial responsibility and within Cabinet policy already laid down rather than to bring matters before Cabinet. He proposed to use Cabinet committees again but he would treat none of the existing committees as still existing. He would appoint committees for matters of great moment as they emerged – eg defence policy, economic policy. He would have other matters considered by a few ministers brought together for that purpose. He asked ministers to help him shorten Cabinet meetings by making themselves familiar with Cabinet papers before the meetings and by speaking briefly. He proposed a general rule to call on the Minister bringing forward a matter to explain it briefly and then to call on ministers to speak to it as necessary. Submissions were to be in the Secretary's hands three clear days at least before meetings except in the case of submissions declared by the prime minister to be urgent. He would send out on the day before the meeting a notice listing the business which would be taken the next day.

By implication the problems of the first term in office were clear. Too many cabinet committees were ineffective. Ministers talked too much; at least it is clear that some were indeed garrulous. Ministers did not read their papers and come prepared to contribute. Again these were the standard problems that so often plague a cabinet system seeking to provide a sense of collective knowledge and purpose on a group of busy ministers of varying quality.

Another re-election brought another experiment. In 1954 Menzies established only two committees: the prime minister's committee and the general administrative committee. The former had all the senior ministers and was designed to tackle the big issues; 'matters in which new questions of policy require continued study and discussion'. The other was to deal with 'matters of administration and matters which require application of principles which have been already adopted'. The press immediately (and accurately) described them, using cricket analogy, as the first and the second eleven. In response to a minister asking if issues discussed in the prime minister's committee would come to full cabinet, Brown argued that:

> It now seems clear that Menzies' general intention is that the committee should not carry out its discussions to the point of arriving at decisions on specific issues – that these should be taken by full Cabinet but that the Cabinet will have the benefit of knowing that the policy issues have been gone into in some detail by its senior members and that they favour a line tending in a particular direction.

Menzies emphasised the same view:

> Where the matter is of political importance the decision will be taken to Cabinet ... when this emerges into action that is for cabinet. We mustn't put half the Cabinet in the position of not knowing.

As Lee notes, 'it would have taken a brave minister to challenge the collective insight of the likes of Menzies, Fadden, McEwen and McBride'. It is difficult to imagine that any decision made there would ever be overturned by a coterie of junior ministers. But there was a nominal process that recognised the superiority of full cabinet.

That structure did not work either. In 1955 Brown was again complaining that:

> ... rather than adhering to the principle of operating mainly by standing committees and setting up *ad hoc* committees only as an exception, we have tended to discard Standing Committees and change to *Ad Hoc* Committees as a normal practice. This has stifled the development of strong and efficient Committees, and with a flood of numerous *Ad Hoc* committees, the Committee system is regarded by Ministers as a nuisance.

Over the last six years almost 140 *ad hoc* committees had been created.

Finally, Menzies bit the bullet and in January 1956 created a cabinet that was distinct from the whole ministry.

> In order to secure more concentration of discussion and expedition of decision on policy matters, the size of the Cabinet is being reduced to 12. I have decided to adopt something like the United Kingdom system of having a cabinet which includes certain Ministers and of having other Ministers, not in Cabinet, who will be responsible for the administration of their own departments. Ministers not in Cabinet will be invited to attend and to participate whenever matters affecting their own department are under Cabinet consideration. I will also have the right to invite to a Cabinet discussion any non-Cabinet Minister who has special knowledge or experience on the particular under consideration.

It was an historic break with tradition; but unlike Britain he did not introduce different tiers of ministers or the notion of senior and junior ministers that existed there. Section 64 of the Constitution referred to the appointment of ministers 'to administer' departments of state. The belief was that under the Constitution all ministers had to have their own departments to administer. When the Morshead report into defence organisation argued that there should be a single senior minister, and a number of junior ministers in a single defence portfolio, the prime minister sought legal advice on the interpretation of the Constitution. He was warned that if ministers did not have their own departments all their actions would possibly be invalid, although there was some diversity among the opinions provided. Menzies did not take the risk and retained an umbrella defence department and a series of junior departments whose ministers were not in cabinet.

Support and attendance of officials

Officials both supported and, to a degree unusual in later cabinets, attended and even debated issues in cabinet. In August 1950 the Commonwealth Statistician and economic adviser to the treasurer, Roland Wilson, went to cabinet with Nugget Coombs (Chairman of the Commonwealth Bank) and economist Douglas Copland. They gave their views on the best economic strategy. Then Wilson gave his forthright perspective:

> I agree with Coombs on the analysis and largely with Copland's ideas on what to do about it ... But you are not a war time government and therefore you have no controls. All you can do is exhort the private investors and make it expensive for them ... I wonder whether you could not have made a bigger effort to induce business to call off investment.

On other occasions Wilson interacted with ministers in lengthy debates. Cabinet gave weight, even deference, to his views. Wilson argued and became involved in discussion. On 18 March 1953 the prime minister said:

> ... tell me Wilson, Why can't we say – this looks like the picture. What we have to do is so & so. We are examining this. We will so far as we can bear down on non dollar non sterling. We don't know what this will bring. Wilson, we can say that & shall do so.

When defence issues were discussed – and that was often in such internationally fraught times – the chiefs of staff attended cabinet regularly. On 4 December 1951 they were there from 10.30 a.m. to 5.05 p.m. Others could be invited too. On 12 June 1953 Mt Lyell mining representatives (associated with the mine in Tasmania) were allowed to address cabinet; after they left, officials were asked to comment on the case they had put.

At other times the notebooks provide a means for Brown to remind himself what he needed to do after the meeting, or what other officials in attendance had promised to do. So Alan Watt, secretary of external affairs asked on 25 August 1950: 'Shall I dig out latest statement. Brown: Yes'. Or he noted on 5 December 1950:'{Remind PM about this}'.

Brown briefed the prime minister on a range of items coming to cabinet in reference to both procedural and tactical issues. Thus Brown wrote on 4 August 1951:

> Shedden has asked that the paper be circulated at the meeting and collected afterwards. I do not see that any useful purpose can be served by discussion of any of them at this stage.

And on a draft submission from the minister for trade and customs in November 1951, Brown advised:

> I have some doubts about the proposal. Wants three public servants and 3 industry to examine the facts. The shipowners and the government have not got even within arms length of each other. How can a group of public servants negotiate such a deal on behalf of the government? How can anyone negotiate when the parties are so far apart?

Cabinet committees, too, often included both ministers and supporting officials. On 1 October 1950 a cabinet committee on US wool proposals had four ministers and six public servants; the committee of defence forces in December 1951 has six ministers and the chiefs of staff; and on the Glen Davis mine, there were four ministers and six officials. Where records are available, they indicate that both sides participated fully in debate, even if only ministers were responsible for decisions.

Brown was responsible for writing up the decisions of cabinet. He would sometimes check with colleagues, once sending a draft to the secretary of the department for air to ensure that the section on the deployment of the air force was sensible. Ministers could object, and occasionally did so. If there was an irresolvable issue Brown might resort to the prime minister as referee:

> Up to the time you left I had awarded the points in every round to those who were questioning the need for any sort of contract between the government and Alcan. Your own statement towards the end was that as we are not going to lend dollars the present proposal was dead ... But a little later it was said that if there was to be a new proposition we ought to give Alcan an idea

> of the terms we want, instead of leaving it to them to put up their idea. Mr Beale said to this: 'Right. I'll talk to them and I'll say: "no dollar loan. A long term contract up to 20 years, 10,000 tons till 1954 and 7,500 tons thereafter".' The discussion was left at that.
>
> My impression is that except for the last development, the Cabinet had not accepted the need for a long term contract ... But in view of the last few comments, Mr Beale has some justification for saying in his letter to me that we are to go out after a long term contract. I see quite a difference between Mr Beale and me. I think he is right if we are to take the last few minutes at its face value. Otherwise I think I am right.

In March 1952 Brown tried out a draft of extended cabinet minutes that followed the British model of summarising, but not attributing, opinions. The only official records were still to be the minutes; his proposal for fuller minutes was not taken up by the prime minister. In any case the drafts were austere and measured when compared to the sometimes racy accounts to be found in Brown's cabinet notebook.

The department, too, was bolstered in its advisory capacity. Brown wanted to combine the economic policy section inherited from post-war reconstruction with the cabinet secretariat. The chair of the Public Service Board was sceptical, both of the proposal and of the skills of economists. He responded to Brown:

> ... economics is not an exact science or if it is our principal economists have not yet been able to agree on points of exactitude. A variety of counsel therefore seems to be inevitable at final points of consideration.

He asked whether that consolidated skill should be in the Prime Minister's Department or Treasury. Brown denied any overlap was envisaged. It was to be a recurring theme as the Prime Minister's Department fought with the Public Service Board for more senior staff.

Brown recognised the need for constant Treasury advice on government business. In October 1951 the staff of the Prime Minister's Department were told by a cabinet officer:

> Would you therefore make sure that the Ty department is given a copy of every Cab or committee decision (except where specifically instructed to the contrary). Since dept consultation with them may not take place, it is imp[ortant] that they receive their copy as soon as possible after a decision has been authorised.

Brown also ensured that the cabinet program reflected the prime minister's desires. So in October 1951 Brown wrote to the Treasury: 'PM wants a lengthy cabinet to consider the broader aspects of policy which it has not been possible to deal with during the Parliamentary Session. PM wants papers on Trade balance, sterling dollar, land tax'.

The debates and the arguments: Politics in the raw

Up to 1952 three subjects dominated the Menzies cabinet discussions: (1) communists and the activities in the unions; (2) appreciation of the Australian currency (the pound); and (3) foreign affairs, with war in Korea, the expectation of crisis in the Middle East, the emerging Vietnam crisis, and the control of defence expenditure and equipment. The first topic illustrates the degree to which cabinet constantly considered party political issues and consequences, the second illustrates coalition tensions, while the third shows cabinet acting as a sounding board for the prime minister.

Cabinet is an intensely political forum where partisan advantage underpins debate, and is sometimes absolutely explicit. The battle against communism in the unions was to be the central political strand for cabinet and the vehicle for embarrassing the Opposition. As soon as the government won office, it decided to ban the Communist party, with a bill referred to variously as 'the como bill' or the 'red bill'. When the High Court declared the legislation unconstitutional, the government sought a referendum to gain the necessary powers. All the time it considered how its strategy might also undermine the Labor party. Without a majority in the Senate after the 1949 election, the government wanted to trigger a double dissolution that could (and in May 1951 did) give it control of both Houses.

The strategy was set on 11 September:

> PM: I propose to introduce the red-bill early – and give it a 2 days guillotine in the Reps & get it into the Senate immediately. They will have to decide on whether or not they throw out the budget.

Ministers were spoiling for a fight. On 25 September:

> McLeay: Can we not postpone the budget and concentrate on the como bill? Within a week they may be split in two.

If ministers were keen, Menzies remained calculating. On 10 October:

> Spicer: We should move that the Como bill take precedence over the Prices Bill. Discuss it at some length indicating that we are prepared to stop when they are ready to go on with the Como bill.

> PM: No, let us be normal – let us have two or three crisp speakers. Take every opportunity of showing: 1. That they are dodging the como bill 2. That they are taking its business out of the hands of the govt.

Menzies argued he would place the budget on business paper 'after the como bill and new Bank bill'. But he was determined to maintain the initiative in planning the double dissolution. On 12 March 1951:

> Holt: why not an agreed double dissolution?
>
> PM: No we must be the people who want an election.
>
> PM: should introduce this bill as a part of the Como attack.

After the High Court decision to declare the bill unconstitutional:

> PM: We will get it in the house and under guillotine the Secret Ballot bill and we will then have the Labour Party hold up the Com bill. Evatt argued for coms and the party is split ... On the double dissolution – banking bill can be put at the top of the list. We can force them to vote against it.

In 1952 and 1953 the cabinet debated the presence of communists in the public service and whether to change the Public Service Bill to allow the board to refuse appointments on grounds of security; it eventually decided not to.

The political calculations and their electoral consequences touched all areas. When there was a proposal to introduce television gradually across the country, Page complained on 11–12 November 1952:

> Should we not defer this. We have to win 2 small states. Under this scheme both of these states have a very low priority.

On another occasion in the prime minister's committee, national service and ballots was discussed. In the summary, Menzies defined the preferred tactics in getting the people used to the idea that national servicemen might be used overseas: 'We must decide what our actual commitment is to be. When we know we should tell the people the measure of the commitment. Then when the people have got used to this we will have to tell them that national service training [has been changed] into national service in the area'.

The Petrov affair saw cabinet discussing political tactics. In the middle of a cabinet meeting on 13 April 1954 Menzies dropped a bombshell:

> A few days ago Petroff [sic] 3rd Sec left the service and came to Security Service claimed political asylum & claimed to make avail-

able documents illustrating methods of espionage. He has masses of documents –MVD man himself received instructions, concentrate on E[xternal] A[ffairs], what were their habits etc, given reports on individuals in Australia, code names used. We will notify Embassy at noon today that he is seeking political asylum. The documents also contain the names of a number of people who would embarrass our opponents. Should we announce this. Should we issue a Royal commission ... The Commission cannot sit and make its decision before the poll. It will be a slow job – will take 2 to 4 months. It would not be fair to publish names in the first documents without proceeding with the changes. I think that I should tell the house of the facts but mention no names.

A debate ensued on the best tactics, with the conclusion that a commission should be appointed and then adjourned. A suggestion that Evatt's concurrence be gained was opposed. On 19 April cabinet decided that 'if Mrs Petrov asked for political asylum she should be granted it ... The air co[mpany] can refuse to take her on if drugged or if put on by violence'.

When the interim report came down in October cabinet could afford to be judicious and wait for the Opposition to pull itself apart. Menzies said the report 'should not be made a political argument ... that should be left to the opposition. ...If there is a debate we must conduct it on our side with restraint and dignity.'

Appreciation and the economy: Preserving the coalition

The standing of the Australian pound remained the most divisive issue to face the cabinet. The Country party opposed any appreciation of the pound; Liberal ministers thought it essential. From the beginning Menzies argued, on 11 September, that 'On appreciation: The public will respond better to vigour than to inertia'.

But the Country party was not prepared to accept any such action and declared it threatened the continuance of the coalition. In August 1950, McEwen had challenged the interpretation of economic circumstances and argued:

> It is said we are now in galloping inflation. This is only a declaration and we have not enough facts. This would have a most serious effect on the govt ... Out of 33 seats 18 in Vic are practically unsinkable for one party or the other – the rest change hands by how tomato growers, poultry raisers etc vote ... We did lose a

> govt in 1940 election by doing the resp[onsible] thing on wheat. You may do something which is objectively the right thing but we may lose the govt.
>
> PM: Why not excise?
>
> McEwen: your proposal is expropriation and this is novel particularly from our side of politics.

Later McEwen returned to the issue, with the support of his party leader, Arthur Fadden:

> McEwen: The people must be told that part of the price of these things is inflation ... we have a real cabinet problem to be resolved and I am prepared to move. It is also a practical problem of first magnitude. What would the party say if we do it? It is also an election problem: appreciation. Done alone I am sure we would lose an election on that – we would lose country seats. Do this bold wool scheme & I think that many wool growers would vote against us.
>
> Fadden: I am not convinced this appreciation will have all the merits that are claimed ... I am sure that one man only in the party room would support it and I doubt whether you can get it through your party. We can't stay in the Cabinet & stay in the Country party if we agree with appreciation.

By 12 September the tensions between the parties were palpable. Liberals were demanding action but, with the Country party adamant, Menzies declared:

> If we are an agreeing Cab[inet] there is no use in pursuing the matter.
>
> White [Minister for Air and Civil Aviation]: We sometimes take decisions on very slender majority, why not now?
>
> Fadden: Even if app[reciation] had all the virtues claimed for it, you can be certain that we will be sent to the country on the budget. None of its advantages would then be apparent but all its disadvantages would be obvious. The Country Party would not win a country seat. The opp[osition] would introduce socialisation and would inflate. In the aggregate you can't possibly inflate. We can't stay in Cabinet and in the C[ountry] P[arty] too if we inflate appreciate. [sic]
>
> PM: The division of opinion is about 8 to 7. At least 7 are against. I am not prepared to accept a decision on such an important matter on such a majority. Let us turn to wool.

The prime minister was not prepared to push on an important issue where the cabinet was so clearly divided. Obviously, if cabinet cannot agree when its members are nominally on the same political side, the country itself will be more heavily divided.

The decision to impose a wool tax instead brought on political problems. On 25 September:

> PM: I have been told by my own party just what they think about the wool tax. There has been at least one meeting of members. I get the impression that we may have a first class argument in cabinet [party room?].
>
> Holt: We meet the parties tomorrow. Everyone knows that we have rejected appreciation & are in favour of a tax on wool. It would be politically disastrous now to revert to appreciation ... we mustn't let the public think we can't make up our mind.

If that took the item out of discussion for a time, the proponents of appreciation returned to the issue at the beginning of 1951. On 22 February they took a vote but still made no decision:

> Holt: Our party assumed that this would be reconsidered this year.
>
> PM: On the politics. If the public think we are only talking we will be destroyed.
>
> Casey: This is a tragedy and marks the end of this govt and of the Aus economy. The Maj[ority] of this composite cab[inet] is for app[reciation].
>
> Spender: Altho[ugh] a maj[ority] is in favour, we are told it wld wreck the govt. Why should not the parties decide it by maj[ority]?
>
> Con: Fadden, McEwen O'Sullivan, McLeay, Anthony, Cooper, Lyons, McBride
>
> Pro: Menzies, Spender, Casey, White, Holt, Spicer, Francis, Beale, Spooner.

The vote was thus 9–8 with two absent. But still no decision to appreciate was taken. The vote, with only Liberals in favour, but with a combination of Liberals from the small states and Country ministers against, merely illustrated again the divisions in the cabinet.

In July 1951, after the election, the prime minister tried again:

> If this severe budget and the works cut do not produce a marked effect on price I hope we will all agree we must try appreciation – let prices rise without restraint.
>
> Casey: We have been discussing this matter for 15 months ... it has always had a majority for it but we have not done it ... If nec[essary] we then approach appreciation with a predisposition in favour of it.

McEwen once again launched an attack on the proposal but this time his party leader was more cryptic. Fadden just noted: 'I acc[ept] the view as expressed by the PM'. The coalition survived.

It was not the only issue when Liberal and Country parties were clearly divided. A budget debate on the level of defence spending and international aid elicited different perspectives. McEwen argued on defence that the priorities were wrong: 'The contribution of another division by us is microscopic in comparison with the same effort spent in developing the country'.

In a debate on an increase demanded by the external affairs minister, Casey, in the amount spent on foreign aid, Fadden argued that 'charity begins at home'. McEwen said that he 'had never been impressed that this has been of any defence significance. Spender [the previous minister for external affairs who had introduced the Colombo Plan] bought the dearest headlines in history. Nehru is no closer to us'. Menzies was conciliatory: 'I have never been enthusiastic about the "Spender" plan. But you can't go in and then get out. I am a sceptic to shell out for Palestine relief. The UN is always busy-bodying about. But for the Colombo plan we are in loco parentis'. The minister eventually had to settle for less than he wanted (the treasurer wanted no increase at all). He did so with poor grace. Menzies had to keep the cabinet forces in balance.

When he finally resigned, Menzies asserted that maintaining the coalition was his greatest achievement. Given how strained relations had been in the 1930s, it could not at first be taken for granted. There were to be a series of tense moments in the next decade: over Australia's attitude to Britain joining the common market (leading to the resignation of a junior Liberal at the insistence of McEwen), fights over electoral redistributions and currency valuations, and finally McEwen's refusal to serve under McMahon if he were elected leader in 1968. The continuance of the coalition, until it was taken for granted, was founded on Menzies' management of cabinet in the early tense days.

Foreign policy, defence policy and defence spending

On 25 August 1950 Menzies returned from overseas to report to cabinet on the crisis in the Middle East and Australia's position. The terms he used have been almost universal in decision on Australian foreign policy:

> We are largely in a world at war. USA has a large body of opinion which favours instantaneous atomic bombing of USSR if war breaks out. We are pretending that Korea is a UN operation. But we would not be in unless US were in, and we are in because they are in it. What are the real dangers, who are our real friends. But on a political basis we have been pretending that everything is based on the UN ... This is the broad picture as I see it and if there is some grievous error in it would you please let me know.

In response to answers he responded, *inter alia*:

> Many people say the bomb is the only thing.
> The large no of bombs is probably sufficient.

There were still differing views of where Australia's interests lay, even while the Korean war was raging:

> McEwen: The Russians as orientals can take no account of time. We cannot hold armaments for so long ... We should examine just how candid we can be with our own people ... We will not be bogged down in Asia. Aus's role is to fight with Britain in Europe and the Middle East.

Times could change perspectives. On 6 April 1954, discussing a telegram from the US, cabinet held a frantic debate on what might happen if Dien Bien Phu were to fall in Vietnam. How much assistance should be offered to the United States, to what degree should we use the United Nations? 'Let us try not to disclose our hand before the election', begged McEwen. Menzies did not want 'to exaggerate the ANZUS aspect. We are not being called on to fulfil an obligation under ANZUS'. Another minister was 'terrified by the implications of this. We cannot insist on protecting a country for our own security even with the US because that involves getting rid of the UN. The UN supports self-govt.' External affairs minister Casey thought 'you would get a majority tho' a slender one for action against the Viet Minh in Indochina' and not to respond would 'morally harm ANZUS'. Cabinet left action to the prime minister.

In June 1954 cabinet again discussed what attitude Australia should take to the growing crisis in Vietnam. Although some ministers argued simply that Australia's future was tied to the US, Menzies was at that time more sceptical of the value of commitment there:

> We are being asked to participate in a forlorn hope. Let us concentrate on what is left. Siam, Burma etc. Let us organise behind this. The US approach is unreal except on the assumption that they intend to provoke a global atomic war while they have atom superiority. There are profound differences. Are we going to participate in a war in which the rest of the Br[itish] C[ommon]/W[ealth] is out – except perhaps New Zealand? The US are not incapable of unreality. The State department and the Pentagon do not always agree. US sees intervention in S.E.Asia as stopping Coms in relation to Japan & Pacific. We are entitled to know two things before deciding.
>
> 1. What is their immediate military objective? If US forces are to be token only they will be no use. I think it is time that they were told it is damn silly.
> 2. What is the political objective? Suppose we inflict military defeat on the V[iet] M[inh]. You still have the political future of I[ndo]C[hina].
>
> V[iet] N[am] has been promised or given self-government. We are propping up French military power. So the political objective is to see that the French leave. The Coms. come again and they collect in peace what they failed to do in war. This is worse than Korea ...
> Yes. Let us save what we can of southern Asia; we went into Korea because it was a UN war. There was no quarrel in Aust. with this. How can we justify a war which will fail, merely to keep in with the US.

The comments were prescient. At the end of the long debate that covered several hours, Menzies decided: 'I will dictate a memo tomorrow'. Foreign policy was discussed and the action to be taken was often disputed. Yet, invariably after lengthy debate, decision was left in the hands of the prime minister.

When time was limited prime ministers could exercise due authority. In 1950 the external affairs minister, Percy Spender, discovered that Britain was about to commit troops to Korea. Determined that Australia not be seen as being dragged in by the tail, he wanted to announce Australia's commitment first. Menzies was at sea, between Britain and New York. Spender pulled the acting prime minister out of a political meeting. Fadden was worried what the 'Big Fellow' would think. Spender insisted he could not delay. Left with the decision by a reluctant Fadden, he released a statement announcing that Australia would respond positively to the United Nations appeal.

> The nature and extent of the forces will be determined after the conclusion of discussions which the prime minister will have in the United States.

Menzies was only told of the commitment when Spender contacted him on trans-ocean phone. Spender noted:

> He was obviously put out. He said little; and in the circumstances I could not say much, but even over the distance of some 12,000 miles, I was aware of the sourness in his voice.

Prime ministers do not appreciate their countries going to war without their being told first. But when he landed he spoke with fervour of the preparedness of Australia to assist in the common cause with the United Nations and the United States.

On another occasion, on 20 May 1953 during a crisis over Egypt, acting prime minister Fadden refers to 'possibility of urgent developments and to possibility of his need[in]g to act in a hurry, Cab authority to act after consulting such Cab members as appropriate'. The rhythms of cabinet did not always suit the rush of foreign affairs.

More frustrating to cabinet was the Defence department. Year after year, cabinet felt that it could neither push Defence into action, nor control its spending. Menzies showed both irritation and frustration that, try as it did, the cabinet seemed to have no impact. He wanted to explain to the public why defence expenditure was needed. On 13 September 1950 he said:

> I am to give broadcasts & I want them to contain a clear statement of what the defence forces are for, their rates of pay and conditions of service ... In the first I want to tell the story of the nature of the danger & then the need for more armed services.

He was not sure what the real answers were. In 4 December 1950 cabinet discussed the government buying a range of planes, Vampires, Meteors or Mustangs. Menzies complained:

> It looks as though we will always be manufacturing planes that we don't propose to use ... if our role is now to be combat and not reconnaissance, should we not be told ... I would like the Chiefs of Staff to be asked if this is purely a Korean proposition or whether they would recommend apart from that. If the second then Cabinet approves it.
>
> Beale: I would like aircraft production looked at generally.
>
> PM: You had better get in touch with Chiefs of Staff.

And later:

> PM: We have an extensive building programme but we don't build anything we want. I have no confidence in their recommendations. Jones [RAAF chief] contributes nothing. Rowell [Army chief] is disappointment.

Menzies felt there was always a problem of squaring the government's economic policy with its alarmist foreign policy warnings. First, on 1 March 1951:

> PM: So far there is nothing on the economic side to compare with the startling ann[ouncements] on the defence side. Can we leave the public feeling that we don't really mean it. We must talk a language that they understand – tell them they have to pay for it.

Then again on 15 October:

> If we say anything on this it is to be something which stiffens action against the Egyptians. We also say the Middle East is vital. But we are making no commitments – it doesn't add up ... less we say about the ME the better. But it is an absurd position for A/a [Australia] which of all the C/W [Commonwealth] Govts is the most likely to put troops in.

On 25 September 1951 cabinet discussed the number of troops to be committed to Korea. It decided to double them. After the decision was made, advice came from the Defence Council recommending against any increase. The PM was angry:

> Defence recommendation leaves me cold. Everything is impossible till we say it has to be done. We should double our contribution.
>
> McBride [Defence Minister]: Suggest we get [Sydney] Rowell [Army Chief] up here – tell him our desire & say we must have recruiting.

> PM: Cabinet decision clear – we don't need to bring the Chiefs of Staff here on this but the Ministers concerned should convey the decision to them & discuss with them the means of putting them into effect.

But time and again there were problems. On 18 March 1952 Menzies declared:

> I want to say something about Defence. It is a mess – impossible in terms of finance and also materials in the time. We have an impossible procedure – the cabinet c[ommit]tee is not competent to decide.

On 15 August 1953 McEwen complained, too:

> All the defence exp[enditure] has ceased to be a full cabinet business and has become a committee business and in substance a Defence department business ... We shld accept proven designs (of aircraft). We should not be trying to build half a dozen types of aircraft. I think we should have full Cabinet criticism of this.
>
> PM: We are deciding something that is scandalous. We approved £380,000 on trainers. It is now £3 1/4 m. The additional expenditure is completely unauthorised by Cabinet. We should say this is our ceiling and that is where we stick. I would like to know how this has all happened. Millions have been muddled away.

Earlier in that year, on 23 June, the treasurer and his officials had an informal meeting with the defence minister in which they tried to work out how to limit the demands for military spending. It was not a cabinet committee, but Bunting kept notes. Roland Wilson, head of Treasury at the time, insisted that 'we in T[reasur]y cannot say what is nec[essar]y & what is not ... but need the savings.' Defence minister McBride expounded on how to handle the services, which he had proved incapable of doing. 'If they think there is any manoeuvrability they will be eloquent in putting their case. But if costing is firm they don't put things up.' It was a plea for help. Wilson tried to summarise the meeting: 'The job today is to determine the issues for Cab to consider ... I think they are ...'. McBride was accommodating: 'we will accept whatever Cab thinks nec[essary]'. Fadden just said: 'Well, I wanted to have this yarn with you in advance'. That afternoon a cabinet committee, consisting of four ministers and Wilson and Bunting, met to discuss defence estimates formally.

Politics, budgets and complaints

Budgets were always a constant organisational problem. Cabinet would meet for two or three days to debate the estimates. There was always a question of strategy; how to ensure that the debate could be completed in time and yet let ministers have adequate involvement. Even for the prime minister there could be problems in gaining support. In 1962 there was a note for file:

> The Secretary has said that in future Budgets, we need to do what we can to see that University estimates do not come up for discussion early in the proceedings. In that situation it is extremely difficult for the prime minister to give strong support to the Universities in the face of attack from the treasurer.
>
> We cannot expect to influence the Treasury to list Universities down the line, but certainly should do nothing to promote the item in the list. What we can do is to suggest to the prime minister, if the agenda makes this necessary, that when the item comes up, he ask for the paper to be taken later. He will then be in a better position to judge whether he should make strong representations in favour of the Universities.
>
> This problem arises simply because experience has shown that first come can be worst served.

More often there was a fight about the influence that the Treasury should have. Treasury preferred to circulate the key papers at the last minute and would collect them at the end of the meeting. The numbers of papers were growing: in 1957 there were 64 papers, totalling 499 pages. Cabinet spent approximately 25 hours working its way through them. Thereafter the numbers of papers tended to increase.

But when McMahon, as treasurer, hinted that the demand for agreement and clearance ('co-operation perhaps in particular with the Treasury') be a condition for submission to budget cabinet, Holt, by then prime minister, responded:

> I would not want to see the eligibility of topics for cabinet too narrowly drawn and I think we would do well to continue the well-established practice of access to Cabinet, but, of course, with clearances at Ministerial level when Cabinet so requests.

There was to be no limit to ministers' ability to introduce submissions, but the move reflected the constant effort by Treasury to get any bids agreed before cabinet met.

Sometimes issues only went to cabinet at the last moment. The point is illustrated on 18 February 1952: 'The P.M. mentioned the press statement about test of atomic weapon'. It was the first that many ministers, including the responsible minister for supply, had heard about the negotiations for nuclear testing programs to be held on Australian soil.

Other issues showed the interplay between politics and policy. When two ANU (Australian National University) academics wanted to attend a conference in China, several ministers wanted to stop them going by refusing them passports. 'You can't', said McMahon on 19 August 1952:

> The C[ommunist] P[arty] is a lawful org[anisation]. We are not at war with China. Unless we declare the party an unlawful party under the Crimes Act we should not take this action. It is an arbitrary act of government.
> PM: I have had discussions with VC and D/G of Security. It is not easy. Some academic freedom must be maintained. You should not examine political views of appointees. I agree.

A year later, in September 1953 McMahon stuck to his views:

> We should not introduce arbitrary methods. If we let them go we know whom we have to watch.
> McE[wen]: We should not let people go to China, the enemy's country.

On immigration, ministers were opinionated and concerned. The minister, Holt, in December 1950 discussed the problems of attracting migrants. 'The north Italian was a good type but the S[outh] Italian was not'. More problematically, on 18 July 1951:

> The migration which is accepted politically is not the best economically. Politically we would like British migrants – economically it is wasteful. You need 5 beds for every British worker – the only countries where I can get large numbers of single persons are Germans and Italians.

When considering whether to allow the migration of the Japanese wives of Australian servicemen, one minister opposed the proposal, but relented when told the decision would only affect 12 people. Cabinet decided: 'Agree to, but no statement to be made'.

Federalism and fiscal relations were then, as later, significant issues, particularly control over tax. In 1950:

> PM: The central problem was responsibility. Not one of the states wants the power to tax. There are two advantages: 1. The perfect answer to all agitation. 2. They can engage in an orgy of hatred against the C/W. I threw out a hint some form of tax might go back to them.

Again, on 4 July 1952, with the discussion of the uniform tax system:

> Casey: Our main obj[ective] is to stop the insults of the states.
> McM: Proposal is nec[essary] to maintain the fed[eral] system.
> PM: I never had any doubt about the principle that he who spends shld raise the money. But there are practical problems.

At times Brown recorded whimsical comments purposely without attribution. On 5 May 1952:

> UNESCO is an organisation for bogus intellectuals ... and for the study of the influence of sex at high altitudes.

Cabinet might make decisions but it would often provide an opinion to support the prime minister. On 11 June 1952 it asked: 'That the cabinet's strong views be graphically conveyed to the PM'. When there was a debate on import restrictions in July 1953, the prime minister was in London. In cabinet the process ran as follows:

> ... first qu[estion] is whether Cab agrees with Ctee's decision. General chorus-yes & we shld tell the PM full Cab confirms.

Then there were the political calculations that cabinet had to make. On the creation of a parliamentary standing committee on foreign affairs in October 1951 cabinet was concerned to ensure 'the manner by which the Ctee's work could effectively be limited to the matters referred to it by the Minister'.

Cabinet could be a venue for ministers to complain about central agencies. In March 1952 Spooner complained about the dominance of the treasury:

> I will not accept a[n] allocation of imports by Customs, T[reasur]y. The admin within the Ty is not as it should be. It is intolerant of other departments' views and will not approach them ... The constructive departments must have some say in the allocation of imports. The Treasury and the C/W [Commonwealth] bank dominate the capital issues as well.

Cabinet made decisions concerning public service appointments. In discussing the appointment of Arthur Tange in a capacity as permanent head of the external affairs department, the question was raised as to whether cabinet could make such an appointment for a specific time period. The resulting decision was negative. In October 1953, 'App[ointmen]t P[erma- nent] H[ead] of E[xternal] A[ffairs], Cabinet insisted there could be no appt for a term of years'. The debate took 45 minutes; it was summarised in a line. The appointee indeed stayed for nearly 11 years this time.

The prime minister made requests of Cabinet:

> I want a statement of the 6 things that must be done urgently if we are to get more coal. I want it within 24 hrs.

He could also direct debate:

> We should first direct our attention to the problem of reducing expenditure as our problem is not that of insufficient income. Treasurer wld you direct your attention to that.

He could welcome visitors to cabinet meetings. In the two months, September and October 1953, for instance, they included Duncan Sandys, British Minister of Supply, Lord Cherwell from Britain and the Vice-President of the United States, Richard Nixon.

Imposing the rules

Cabinet decisions were not often taken by vote. Apart from the vote on currency appreciation mentioned earlier, cabinet voted on 28 May 1951 for or against the Minister's recommendation on commutation of the execution of a Japanese war criminal. The numbers were 9–8 in support of the minister. On 20 August 1951 there was another vote on an agenda item, 10–7 this time. But the evidence is that voting was rare. The standard practice is that prime ministers decide the mood of the meeting as they see fit.

More often the counting was informal. In one committee the chair, Spicer, breezily comments: 'Numbers against you, Howard [Beale]; we will reject the offer'.

The notebooks give an insight into the way, and the level, that debate was developed. There was a constant to and fro, with ministers becoming involved at different times. Occasionally the debate was willing, with ministers disputing with the prime minister. If some ministers echoed their leader, others, and particularly Country party ministers, had fundamental differences of opinion. Whether that vigorous debate continued into the last years of the Menzies reign is questioned by observers; the ministers of his own generation were replaced by a younger cohort that was more in awe of the long-serving prime minister. He was reputedly less patient with views he did not accept. On two issues, the relaxation of the White Australia policy and the removal of the marriage bar for female public servants, his colleagues and senior public servants waited for his departure. As soon as he was gone, both were pushed through. In the earlier debates there is some support for the judgment of Hasluck, in cabinet after 1951, whose view is that Menzies dominated not because he was domineering or authoritarian but because he was the best man around the table. Menzies was indeed both a tactician and an able chair who knew when to allow cabinet to talk and when (as with Petrov and atomic testing) to tell them only at the end of the show.

The successors

Menzies' successors never managed cabinet as successfully. They maintained his cabinet system but seldom had the capacity both to dominate and involve that had allowed Menzies to oversee the cabinet. Each successor had a different philosophy; none was effective. Holt has been a long-time acolyte, treasurer and assured successor. He won the position unopposed but was never able to replace his master. He believed:

> Leadership can take various forms. There is the type of leadership which is so far out in front of the team that there is a danger of lack of cooperation, lack of warmth and some loss of effectiveness. There is the leadership which can lead but, at the same time, be close enough to the team to be part of it and be on the basis of friendly cooperation. I will make that my technique of leadership.

But that may have been Holt's problem. He wanted to get on with colleagues. Perhaps as a consequence he failed to give leadership on the affairs associated with the sinking of the HMAS *Voyager* in 1964 and the scandal of the VIP planes of 1966. Menzies' assessment of Holt's leadership certainly reflects Holt's desire for approval and its subsequent implications for his period as leader. Menzies, commenting on Holt, stated, 'his besetting sin' was 'that he wanted everyone to love him ... the result was he had made a muck of everything in his second year ... it was a dreadful performance. Dreadful'.

In 1966 Holt allowed cabinet to discuss the issue of whether the cabinet should be elected. The Country party quickly opted out; McEwen stating that Country party appointments would be made by the leader. Thereafter the debate continued only among the Liberal ministers. They decided 'that the elective system would lead to disruption in the party and in the Cabinet, and thus would weaken rather than strengthen the government, that it would reduce the prime minister's authority unacceptably; and that in general it could not be regarded as wise practice'. The prime minister would express these opinions as personal views in the party room and colleagues would support him as necessary. That summed him up.

Gorton as prime minister from 1968 to 1971 took a different view. Prime ministers should lead:

> The prime minister now or in the future is not to be chairman of the committee so that a majority vote in the committee says what's going to be done. He should put to the cabinet or the committee what he believes ought to be done, and if he believes strongly enough that it ought to be done, then it must be done.

Gorton's most dramatic step was to split the cabinet office and the Prime Minister's Department; he had been unimpressed by the advice given by Bunting and, besides, wanted to make Lenox Hewitt (chairman of the Universities Commission) his principal adviser. Unable to remove Bunting entirely, he chose to make Bunting head of a cabinet office while installing Hewitt as head of a separate Prime Minister's Department. The public explanation was pure spin:

> ... the servicing of Cabinet has hitherto been a part of the functions of the Prime Minister's Department and the Secretary of the Department also had the role of Secretary to the Cabinet. Cabinet pressures have been steadily increasing because of the diversity and complexity of Government action in the Federal sphere, and must be expected to continue to do so. At the same time, the other demands on the Department have risen steadily, and these will continue to do so.
>
> In the Government's view, the time has now come when these two major activities should be separated if each is to receive the necessary attention and control required for the full conduct of the Government's business.

In fact the split meant that the secretary of his department had to rely on the prime minister or the cabinet secretary to appreciate what cabinet had decided. When McMahon became prime minister he wanted to be rid of Hewitt. So he declared the division 'inefficient'.

> I want the Cabinet Secretariat and the Prime Minister's Department to act as a clearing house and to be able to co-ordinate the staff work so that when it comes to Cabinet we can be assured we have cleared away all that is unnecessary and get down to work on what is critically important for a Cabinet decision.

Gorton lived up to his statement of intent to lead as prime minister. He and McEwen fought Treasury over the establishment of the Industry Development Corporation. One account suggested that most of cabinet was opposed but 'recalled Gorton simply announcing cabinet's acceptance'. McEwen was shown the draft decision by Bunting and wanted the endorsement more clear-cut. Even though Gorton recalled saying that cabinet had agreed 'in principle', he had the words deleted at McEwen's request. Bunting also cleared a decision on constitutional responsibility between the Commonwealth and the states for seas and submerged lands. Cabinet, he noted, had decided 'the Commonwealth was under no obligation to inform the states in advance of the course it proposed to take and that it should not do so'. Bunting asked whether Gorton's recollection of the decision was so stark. Gorton said he had understood the cabinet position correctly. Gorton upset colleagues and Liberal premiers. It was not that cabinet did not still meet regularly; it met on 61 days in 1968 and 35 in 1969 before the election. Rather, what mattered was the way that Gorton treated his colleagues and their opinions.

These decisions reflected the way that Gorton worked. Opinions on his ability to run cabinet varied. Doug Anthony, his deputy at the end, described him as a prime minister who was a good chairman of cabinet, did his homework thoroughly, wrote incisive comments on his cabinet submissions and would win the support of Cabinet 'by force of well-prepared arguments and not because he insisted on having his own way'. Another minister thought 'cabinet meetings so ill-disciplined they reminded him of a tennis club'. He certainly provoked opposition and was constantly undermined by the supporters of McMahon. Eventually a revolt, precipitated by Fraser's resignation, brought him down.

But lessons of leadership and coherence were not absorbed by his successor, McMahon, who had neither the aptitude for the task nor the trust of his colleagues. His cabinet colleague, Paul Hasluck, thought McMahon 'disloyal, devious, dishonest, untrustworthy, petty, cowardly' (and that was written before McMahon became prime minister).

> He was disloyal and could not be trusted and he worked for his own advancement by trying to destroy the reputation of his rivals.

He gave away Cabinet secrets, sometimes out of vanity and sometimes corruptly in order to buy favours for himself from the press or to injure his colleagues. He was an habitual liar and a man who lied by calculation about other people and about himself. He worked against Menzies, against Holt, against McEwen and against Gorton.

McMahon started his term by emphasising that it was the function of the prime minister:

> To ensure that leadership is given; that there is effective co-ordination, through the cabinet machinery and by individual consultation, of the activities of ministers, each of whom has full responsibility and accountability to parliament; and that, through the cabinet machinery and in other ways, the ever-changing problems of Government are given full attention and co-ordinated and speedy resolution. These are the central functions of the prime minister as leader of the Government.

Such a perspective contrasts with his comments during the 1972 election campaign. Asked what he had learnt as prime minister, McMahon replied:

> I have learnt a lot. I have learnt first of all the fact that I now must make more decisions than I had the intention of making when I first became the prime minister. I wanted to be head of a team. I wanted to delegate the authority to the relevant Ministers responsible for the Departments.
> Question: What went wrong with that principle?
> Prime minister: I couldn't get the work done quickly enough and I found frequently that the political approaches to it were not as good as I thought they should be. So from September last year, I gradually started to change, and I have been changing a little more quickly as the days have gone by.

Most of his colleagues had learnt that Hasluck was right. The contrast between McMahon's comments on leadership sums up the difference and the disasters of his undistinguished prime ministership.

What went wrong after 1966 and the resignation of Menzies? The Liberal decline emphasised that more than good process was required for effective government, and that leadership was not just about rules. The division, internal opposition, and individual ambitions that were let loose upon Menzies' exit show that, even if good systems have been devised, they cannot save for a government in decline.

7 DASHED HOPES: 1972-75

The election of a Labor government in 1972 brought an immediate change to the style, rhetoric and scope of government activity. Labor took office with no recent experience of government and, it turned out, few procedures for learning, or even recalling and adapting the methods used in the immediate post-war years. From an early stage its cabinet arrangements attracted vociferous and often contradictory complaints and suggestions for change.

Labor elected a ministry of 27 sitting as an undivided cabinet. The size of cabinet had been determined before the election, and the decision to sit as one was reputedly carried in caucus by one vote. Twenty-seven portfolios meant 27 jobs; none of the shadow executive wanted to miss out. So Labor reshuffled the pack, abolished 18 departments, recreated others and ended with 27 portfolios, a number that had grown incrementally under the coalition government.

In electing cabinet, caucus gave preference to seniority. In the first ballot all the former Opposition executive were elected. They then chose the remainder of the cabinet. Although at the outset most of the members Whitlam preferred for cabinet were elected, he had to modify his proposed administrative arrangements to create jobs for those actually elected. Responsibility for the environment was separated from urban and regional development and health from social security. Two planned departments became four. Several other departments, including one or two of doubtful significance, were established to create jobs without much responsibility for those who he saw as potential duds. Although caucus had no effective say in the actual allocation of ministerial positions, its choices limited the scope within which Whitlam had to work.

Formally, Labor's arrangements allowed the prime minister to reallocate portfolios from time to time, but in practice reshuffles were hard to carry out. Senior ministers resented being shifted, and in any case the choice of replacements was limited to those already in the ministry. Unless vacancies occurred through resignations or electoral defeat, there was no room for new members. Nor did the party take the opportunity of the re-election of the ministry after the 1974 election. Caucus re-elected all ministers except the one who had been defeated at the polls. This was not simply an example of caucus myopia. Ministers constituted the largest single bloc in caucus, and reportedly one of them successfully put it to the remainder that they should support one another. Caucus' system of voting assisted this move. Unless supporters of change in the ministry could agree on whom they would promote to it, their votes were likely to be dispersed ineffectively among a large number of ministerial aspirants. For these reasons movements for a 'spill', especially in 1975 when the composition of cabinet was discussed incessantly, were also frustrated. Over the three years Labor was in office, the five new elected ministers entered cabinet as a result of single vacancies.

In the two cases where these arose from resignations from parliament as well as from cabinet (Murphy and Barnard), the political costs for the government were especially heavy, leading to the loss of a Senate position to a 'political neuter' and a disastrous by-election defeat. The removal of Cairns after his earlier demotion and the resignation of Connor, both senior ministers whose support had been important to Whitlam early in the life of the government, were also costly. Whitlam's sacking of Cairns after he had misled parliament showed that in an extreme case a Labor prime minister could dismiss a minister. But the dismissal required ratification by caucus who had in effect to choose between the prime minister and the disgraced minister. It is doubtful whether caucus would have accepted the removal of ministers merely because of prime ministerial dissatisfaction with ministerial performance.

From the beginning there were misgivings about the size of cabinet, and as the government ran deeper into trouble, proposals for setting up an inner cabinet received considerable attention. The prime minister himself supported the idea and said publicly that a cabinet of half the size would be twice as good. The logistical difficulties of a gathering of 27 ministers were obvious. The cabinet was far larger than the size regarded as convenient for decision-making. Moreover, the large tail in the ministry suggested that cabinet as constituted was not the place for full and frank discussion of critical policy issues.

In 1975 a report by the caucus committee recommended the establishment of an inner cabinet of 12. After the election of the four parliamentary leaders, it proposed caucus would elect a further eight members of cabinet and then the rest of the ministry. However, after extensive discussion, caucus referred the report back for further consideration. Although Whitlam's endorsement of the proposal was supported by the treasurer, Bill Hayden, a number of ministers opposed it. Before the proposal could be taken further the government fell.

The creation of an inner cabinet in the Menzies tradition may not have overcome Labor's problems. It did not mesh well with established caucus practices. Two problems were immediately apparent. First, an elected inner cabinet would add further rigidity to an already highly constrained set of arrangements. While within an elected cabinet of 27 ministers there was only limited scope for shuffling portfolios, in a cabinet of 12, those who failed as ministers would be even harder to shift. Some of the most disappointing ministers in Whitlam's cabinet were among those elected to the ministry in the first dozen, both in 1972 and 1974. Second, a Labor minister outside cabinet would be tempted not only to take decisions on his own and pre-empt cabinet discussions, but to appeal to caucus if he thought cabinet had not considered his case adequately. In caucus discussions during 1975 this consideration was used as a persuasive argument against the rationalisation proposals then put forward. Arrangements that proved satisfactory for Menzies could well cause more trouble than they were worth for a Labor government. The Hawke government was to prove these arguments wrong, but primarily because the experience of the large Whitlam cabinet had been seen to be so dysfunctional.

Standing committees

More important than debate about creating an inner cabinet was the evolution in thinking under Whitlam about systems of cabinet committees. Although slow and uneven, by the time the government was dismissed the elements of an effective committee system were beginning to emerge. The importance of a system of committees for a large and busy cabinet had been recognised by Whitlam before he took office. From the outset, Labor used cabinet committees more extensively and more openly than the coalition. But the experience showed the ease with which apparently admirable arrangements could fall into disuse. Ministers had not only to be convinced of the usefulness and fairness of a committee system, but also to find time for committee meetings in schedules of work that were already overcrowded. The longer parliamentary sitting times introduced by Labor combined with meetings of full cabinet, caucus, and caucus committees presented ministers with punishing rounds of meetings each week.

The Whitlam cabinet began work with a system of five standing committees. These arrangements followed proposals developed by Dr Peter Wilenski (who, when Labor gained office, became Whitlam's principal private secretary). Wilenski's intention was to establish a framework 'which [would] facilitate logical ministerial consideration (if ministers wish[ed] to exercise their powers) of all major recommendations, alternatives to them, and their side-effects on other policy areas'. His ideas drew explicitly on the federal Canadian experience under Pierre Trudeau. He proposed standing committees in all policy areas, routing all cabinet business through committees, participation in decision-making by all ministers, regular meetings, and the establishment, where appropriate, of coordinating committees. At a press conference the prime minister described the proposed system in the following terms:

> The procedure will be that when submissions for cabinet come to me from ministers I will send them to the relevant committee. The committee will hopefully make a recommendation on them. They will then be listed on the cabinet agenda and the recommendation also listed, and unless anybody wants it debated further the recommendation will become the cabinet decision ... The members of the committee are under an obligation to attend the meetings of the committee but any other minister will be entitled to attend and hopefully will do so when the documents indicate his department is involved.

The intention was to avoid overcrowding cabinet's agenda without excluding any minister with a valid interest in business before a particular committee. Wilenski recognised that the proposals had disadvantages as well as advantages; he listed problems of competing demands on ministerial time, the possibilities of a slowing down of decision-making and of excessive public service influence on committee deliberations, and the risk of obvious divergences of view between ministers and their senior public servants. He emphasised that how the system would work would depend on how ministers saw it:

Whether the system works is finally up to ministers. It is unlikely (after the first month or two) that all ministers will wish to attend all meetings, which would clog up the system. The greater danger is that they may give the committees a decreasing amount of attention – but of course any cabinet has the right to decide what control it wishes to have over policy and what aspects they wish to pass to the Public Service.

During 1973 the arrangements worked reasonably well; however, after the election in May 1974, the system withered. From mid-1974 *ad hoc* committees became much more important than they had previously been. In the 16 months before June 1974 they met 47 times and made 29 decisions; in the year from June 1974 to May 1975 they met 62 times and made 117 decisions. From mid-1974 only the legislation committee among the standing committees continued to have an active and effective life. Although the decline of the other standing committees was decisive, it was never the subject of cabinet discussion and none of the committees was ever formally disbanded.

Many reasons may be given for the withering of the committee system. First, items did not go to a committee unless the prime minister referred them. When explaining the system, Whitlam had made that clear. At his own discretion and without giving reasons he was able to control the flow of business to committees. After the 1974 election he preferred other vehicles. Within days he summoned five ministers and a small number of public servants and other advisers to the prime minister's house in Sydney. The subject was inflation, which during the election campaign Whitlam had recognised belatedly as a central issue facing the government. In a few hours the issues were thrashed out; ministers had the advantage of immediate and collective access to different strands of advice. The meeting cut through the more long-winded processes entailed by the committee/full cabinet approach and included only those people whom the prime minister thought had a real contribution to make. Although other ministers were furious, it was clear that the prime minister regarded the format of the meeting as one to be repeated.

Second, when the standing committees were set up there was a failure to integrate the aims of the system with operating requirements, especially with the demanding timetable of expanded parliamentary sittings. At the outset cabinet decided that neither it nor its committees would meet while parliament was sitting. When other commitments of ministers were taken into account (including cabinet meetings) the remaining diary space left little time for committee meetings.

Third, the arrangements were cumbersome. Although discussions in the committees did clear the way for dispatch of cabinet business, committees could not take substantive decisions; their recommendations were endorsed as a matter of routine unless a minister raised a specific objection. But when a well-attended committee made a decision (attendances could be as large as 19), there was a strong desire to make an announcement as soon as possible. This led to the stratagem of declaring that those present constituted a cabinet and could endorse it forthwith. The press of business in 1973 and early 1974 made the arrangements especially hard to operate.

Fourth, there was no general administrative committee to relieve the cabinet workload. One estimate of the proportion of non-controversial submissions (which could possibly have been dispatched by a general administrative committee) suggested that these included 35–40 per cent of all submissions. A later estimate suggested that a general administrative committee could well have dealt with between 50 per cent and 70 per cent of all submissions.

Two important aspects of Wilenski's proposals were not taken up in the initial committee arrangements. First, he had advocated a priorities or coordinating committee modelled on the Priorities and Planning Committee of the Canadian federal cabinet which, according to an official source, gave 'a sense of direction to the cabinet in assisting to develop an overall set of priorities and a plan of action to guide the work of the Cabinet and of the government as a whole'. Wilenski wanted it to deal 'with long-term issues and not those requiring immediate political action'; it was not intended to be an inner cabinet. He observed that the Canadian committee was chaired by the prime minister and that attendance was restricted. However, there were practical difficulties in putting Wilenski's plan into action. These difficulties attracted more attention than any benefit the committee would provide. The priorities and planning committee looked more and more like (and effectively was) an inner cabinet.

There was a second proposal not taken up in initial committee arrangements. Wilenski advocated more direct discussions between ministers and public servants so that before items reached full cabinet, ministers would have increased opportunities to explore wider ranges of options and information. He did not propose that public servants would speak in full cabinet. He wanted ministers to take an interest in matters that were often resolved in interdepartmental committees. But, as he recognised, ministers might not want to do this, and public servants might be embarrassed by the disclosure of differences between them or they might dominate discussions.

Despite Wilenski's prodding, the Whitlam cabinet did not face the issue squarely. From an early stage ministers were happy to hand over difficult matters to interdepartmental committees. Although frustrated by the unwillingness of departments, notably the Treasury, to canvass different options, ministers were unwilling themselves to go out and search for options among public servants. Part of the attraction to the prime minister and his staff of the Sydney meeting mentioned above was that it showed what ministers would do to absorb 'the conflicting and normally unrepresented noise which emerges within departments on major policy matters'.

Once having shied away from, or failed to recognise, the need for some kind of priorities committee (whether to deal with long-term or short-term issues) and for collective ministerial opportunities for seeking and sifting different streams of public service advice, the government found it hard to reach systematic conclusions about what to try next.

Ad hoc committees

During 1975 a small number of *ad hoc* committees paralleled by committees of officials assumed increasing importance in the working of cabinet. These were the Expenditure Review Committee (ERC), Resources Committee, and Australian State Regional Relations Committee (ASRRC). They were *ad hoc* committees with a continuing existence, and their formation was publicly announced. In many respects they behaved like standing committees but were not given this label or status.

Beyond these committees there were committees of a more truly *ad hoc* nature that usually had a short life. Their existence was rarely made public and their work was regarded as part of the domestic relations of the government. As with previous governments, there was resistance even to saying how many of these committees there were at any one time. The range of work they addressed included coordination and the resolution of differences, making allocations within specified guidelines, and special tasks that generally did not require sustained committee activity. In all cases their work was far more specific than that of the original standing committees.

Of the three *ad hoc* committees that came to prominence in 1975, the ERC was the most important. Its members included the prime minister; the treasurer; and the ministers for social security, labour and immigration, and urban and regional development. In the course of the year Hayden, when he became treasurer, and Jim McClelland, as minister for labour and immigration, combined their formal and influential positions on the committee with informal roles as the prime minister's closest ministerial confidants on economic policy. The committee was set up by cabinet in January 1975 when the government had decided that its earlier open-handed approach to public expenditure could no longer be maintained. The committee was to examine all proposals for expenditure both during and outside the budget round. In announcing the formation of the committee, Whitlam outlined its functions in the following terms:

> The committee will ensure that the Government is kept fully informed of the economic and budgetary implications of all its programs, and of the effects of new programs which it might consider.
> Any new expenditure proposals which are brought forward outside the budget decision-making framework would be considered by the committee established by Cabinet.
> The Government has decided that there ought to be a general presumption against further increases of Government expenditure. Any such increase must meet the criteria adopted by Cabinet.

The working of the committee conferred considerable influence on a small number of selected ministers. If it rejected a proposal for expenditure, the prime minister tended not to list the item for full cabinet unless the minister concerned persisted. In a time of expenditure restraint, that was rare. Committee decisions effectively became cabinet decisions.

The composition of the committee ensured that some senior ministers from spending departments participated fully in and supported the cuts imposed. The committee's deliberations were supported by an officials committee drawn from the departments of ministers on the committee. These officials worked as a task group rather than as departmental representatives. However, like their ministers, they were not entirely free from departmental considerations. Officials did not meet together with ministers, but the chairman of the officials group (an officer of the department of the prime minister and cabinet) attended ministerial meetings to assist with recording decisions. Ministers not involved in the committee's work did not attend, even to explain their own proposals. Had restraining expenditure seemed less important, the committee's authority could soon have come under sustained challenge.

The creation of the ERC was a limited but definite step towards establishment within cabinet of a group that could give detailed attention to priorities. The committee's focus on expenditure was specialised, but this was one of the most important matters on which the government had to make decisions in 1975. Determining where and to what extent cuts would be made gave the committee enormous scope for influencing the shape of government activity.

The *ad hoc* committees had been developed to meet a variety of needs. Their functions included coordination of policy, resolution of particular policy problems, review of expenditure, and several special tasks. Their formation indicated the discovery of a need for a more efficient means of drawing together threads of business; cabinet thus began to establish a three-tier cabinet structure, in which cabinet, cabinet committees and officials' committees each reinforced one another.

But the new structures also had some potentially divisive implications. The capacity of the Resources Committee to make decisions without reference to full cabinet, and the *de facto* power of the ERC to prevent new proposals being put on the cabinet agenda, meant that power was concentrated in the hands of a few ministers. Perhaps this was a logical consequence of the size of cabinet and the mediocrity of many of its lesser members. The elitist system might not have been acceptable to cabinet as a whole or to caucus in the longer term, but after the forced election in 1974 the government always was operating in an atmosphere of crisis. The need to align talent with problems was an important step that showed an increasing sophistication. But it was all too late.

Whitlam as prime minister

Whitlam had a superb memory and worked hard. His main interests were in the fields of foreign affairs, urban development, and legal and constitutional matters; he understood little about economics and often left the running in this area to others.

His own personality restricted his use of the resources at his command. He tended to make snap judgments, to act hastily without any concern for the victims of his sudden wrath and biting sarcasm. Occasionally his partial or incomplete appreciation of situations and individuals meant that in party terms his was a brittle leadership, sometimes constructive and magnificent in conception, but often erratic. His tendency to surround himself with groups of ministers in favour and to act on advice from a broad range of sources without consulting cabinet meant that he did not always retain the full confidence of his colleagues and was restrained by the limits to their tolerance. Further, the public service, and more specifically the Department of Prime Minister and Cabinet (PM&C), had at first only a limited capacity to respond, and Whitlam had difficulty in obtaining alternative options in economic affairs from those presented by the Treasury. In caucus, too, Whitlam used his position of prestige to bully his supporters into line. He tended to assert his position and demand support, rather than arrange consensus in the style of Chifley.

The major resource Whitlam wielded was his capacity to shape and direct the business of cabinet. He could decide what came to cabinet, how meetings were run, and, if controversy developed, what decisions were taken. The following matters are often seen as business for cabinet:

1. Major policy issues
2. Proposals involving employment or large expenditures
3. Proposals requiring legislation or amendments to legislation
4. Proposals having a considerable impact on relations between the federal, state and local levels of government
5. Senior appointments, including appointments to the first division of the public service and to statutory bodies.

These topics provide general guidelines rather than binding rules. There are instances from several of these categories where business was not taken to cabinet.

The form of the submissions, the supporting information, and the degree of consultation with other interested parties, laid down in a paper circulated by the prime minister, did not vary much from the coalition governments that preceded or followed it. The Treasury had to be consulted about financial implications, involved departments had to be consulted, a particular format had to be adopted, and the submission had to be lodged with PM&C a prescribed time before the cabinet meeting; usually either three or ten days. Decisions were seldom taken without prior circulation of a submission, except for senior appointments or matters that the prime minister chose to raise himself.

The lodging and circulation of a submission did not ensure that it would be listed; nor did listing necessarily mean that the item would be discussed. These matters were decided by the prime minister alone. He could also decide that a circulated submission should be withdrawn. Ministers could use a variety of official or political connections to try to persuade the prime minister to bypass the rules in extraordinary cases, but ministers' appreciation of this process varied as did their skill and success in using it.

The prime minister took advice on the ordering of cabinet business from the secretary or other officers of PM&C, and from his own staff. However, responsibility for decisions remained firmly his own.

Some ministers wanted prime ministerial discretion in cabinet agenda-setting modified by the formation of an agenda committee of ministers. No prime minister would willingly share this power. The power not to list submissions was the power to defer deliberation of matters that ran against prime ministerial preferences, but which might yet gain majority support in cabinet. These same ministers also proposed that the prime minister need not necessarily be chairman of cabinet, but the chairmanship of cabinet carries too many resources for any prime minister to accept its loss. Cabinet meetings were always chaired by the prime minister. His choice of speakers could be crucial, especially when ministers often had a limited capacity to be provided with an effective brief on the submissions of other colleagues. Often Whitlam preferred to ask for objections to a proposal rather than for a directly constructive discussion of it. In most cabinets opposition from the treasurer, with support from the prime minister for his stand, is enough to ensure the failure of a submission. But Whitlam often failed to support Crean, particularly in 1973 and 1974, which led in part to the temporary eclipse of his department, the Treasury.

Records of the decisions of cabinet were taken by officers of PM&C. Following a cabinet meeting, officers wrote up decisions as quickly as possible. Where recording officers, after consultation with each other, were still in doubt about the terms of a decision, they could consult relevant ministers and other people concerned. In cases where issues were confused they still had to produce something that looked as if cabinet had made an implementable decision. Post-cabinet consultations could involve the prime minister and several ministers and heads of departments. Officers writing decisions could consult ministers orally or produce a draft decision or 'forward copy' for comment and possible amendment. Knowledge of this process varied both among ministers and among departments, and extensive post-cabinet consultations were rare. The inclusion in submissions of draft decisions significantly reduced earlier problems of consulting ministers and officials to make sure that the actual language used in decisions was correct.

The prime minister's authority here was decisive. Decisions were circulated before the prime minister had seen them, but if there was any argument about a decision he would have the final say. However, the prime minister did not usually instruct recording officers. Once a decision was circulated it could not be varied without a new submission; however, amendments of a limited and technical nature could be made. Records of decisions were certified as correct by the senior officer of the cabinet division of PM&C present at the meeting.

The Whitlam cabinet: An overview

The most notable feature of the Whitlam cabinet was its lack of coherence. All cabinets must suffer from this problem to some extent, but this one seemed to have more problems than most precisely because it was trying to effect major change at great speed. At no stage was there an attempt, or even apparently an expressed desire, for cabinet to take a clear view of where the government was going. The pace was always too hectic. As a result, obvious overlap and a lack of coordination were the features most often remarked upon, as policy at times seemed to lurch from crisis to crisis.

That organisational disharmony was exacerbated by the international economic crisis caused by inflation and the oil shock. Familiar diagnoses were no longer viable. All governments had problems in the 1970s. In addition, Whitlam had to face a constantly hostile Senate.

Cabinet simply had difficulty organising itself. Because everyone wanted a voice in full cabinet, the workload of cabinet was not reduced by the establishment of a successful set of cabinet committees until it was too late. There was little coherent debate about the organisation of the public service. Its relations with the Treasury were considered unsatisfactory, but the government never developed a constant and alternative source of economic advice. When attention finally explored possible improvements, the turbulent political and economic conditions, leading to the dismissal in November 1975, made such concerns irrelevant.

If Whitlam's cabinet did not work well, he must take much of the blame. While Whitlam was without doubt the government's greatest asset, he was also one of its greatest problems. He was often not willing to work to ensure smooth relations with caucus or to orchestrate the deliberations of cabinet. At the same time, as a Labor prime minister, he could be outvoted in cabinet or have his decisions overruled by caucus. He had to work within a structure that depended on consultation, among a group of ministers who had no ingrained tradition of consultation. Whitlam alone had the capacity to make the system work; he rarely put his mind to it.

A cabinet is not self-stabilising; and the Whitlam cabinet was less so than most. Ministers and the prime minister had often divergent ambitions which led to a lack of coherence at the centre, particularly when the traditional coordinators of policy, the Treasury and PM&C, temporarily lacked influence. Caucus was a constant irritant to the prime minister, with ministers (and even once the prime minister) appealing cabinet decisions to that higher court in Labor theory. If never as destructive as in Scullin's days, the caucus was never as controlled or well-managed as it was to be under Hawke. Certainly, ministers had to account to one another, but cabinet became a battleground precisely because many ministers were concerned only with their own portfolios. The prime minister alone could provide coherence; too often Whitlam failed to do so, and the inevitable failings of any cabinet became even more marked.

8 WORKING ALL HOURS: 1976–83

Fraser came into government publicly committed to the institution of cabinet and the processes of cabinet government. He had condemned Gorton in 1971 for bypassing cabinet, whereas Fraser argued in favour of it as an important institution, with use of proper procedures being essential for good government. Thus the centrality of cabinet was to Fraser more than a mere constitutional necessity; it had been publicly and constantly pronounced as an article of faith. Under his leadership cabinet met regularly and considered the critical issues. It was also politically convenient: Fraser understood the value of collective action, the advantages of drawing his ministers into decisions and the strength of cabinet commitment. He even extended the formal cabinet structures to include many consultations that under earlier prime ministers had been undertaken on an informal basis in the PMO.

Consultation and control are not by any means mutually exclusive. Prime ministers do not have to choose between collective or individual styles of decision-making. It is as possible to dominate through consulting cabinet as through ignoring it, perhaps even more so. It is more time-consuming, but it may also be more effective. Cabinet discussion has political advantages as well as policy benefits. Fraser's use of cabinet illustrates how he was able to maximise his influence without bypassing the cabinet.

Setting the arrangements

Fraser determined the schedule of cabinet meetings, the particular arena (either full cabinet or a cabinet committee) where a submission would be taken and the agenda for each such meeting. The way this process was adjusted illustrates Fraser's style of running government and the power it gave him.

The cabinet agenda for each week was gradually put together in the ten days before the meetings. PM&C maintained a record of submissions outstanding and sent a proposed schedule of meetings and agenda to the prime minister the week before they were due to be held. Full cabinets met at a standard time in the cabinet room in Parliament House – usually Tuesday mornings; the additional committee meetings would be fitted around parliamentary sittings and the timetables of busy and senior ministers. Occasionally, as an exercise in public relations, cabinet would meet in other capital cities.

The submissions were listed on the agenda according to the seniority of the ministers presenting them. It was the only sensible way of organising material. Officials in PM&C were not in a position to decide that one submission was more important than another; and the political costs would be high for a prime minister labelling them as of greater or lesser significance. So although a review of cabinet procedures in 1981 proposed that items be listed in order of importance, that plan was never implemented. The prime minister did not have to take the submissions in the order listed, and often did not. The submissions were required to be lodged with the Cabinet Office ten days before the minister wanted them discussed. Only the prime minister could waive the rule and permit quicker listing; ministers therefore had to approach him to ask for special consideration. Two sets of examples illustrate the way the choices were made. Each proposed schedule included the week's cabinet and committees. For instance, on 11 September 1978, PM&C proposed:

Tuesday 19 September	Legislation committee	9.00
	Cabinet	10.00
	(7 items)	
Wednesday 20 September	General Administrative	4.15
	(2 items)	
Thursday 21 September	Machinery of Government	2.30
	(4 items)	
	then Intelligence and Security	
	(2 items)	
	then Monetary Policy	

Two weeks later on 29 September PM&C proposed:

Monday 9 October	*Ad hoc* (Industrial Relations	2.30)
	Ad hoc (Parliament House	5.00)
	Cabinet	8.00
Tuesday 10 October	Legislation committee	9.00
	Cabinet	9.30
	Machinery of Government then Monetary Policy and	
	Ad hoc (Uranium)	4.15
Wednesday 11 October	General Administrative	4 15
Thursday 12 October	Reserved for *ad hoc* committees	

Each schedule therefore included standing and *ad hoc* committees that ran on, one after the other, until the business was completed. The details were liable to change. As crises emerged, or if the business was not completed, the meetings would be reconvened in the afternoon or the late evening.

Each proposed timetable was accompanied by a list of the submissions and a set of letters from ministers asking for special treatment. Then the negotiations between Fraser and his ministers began. For instance, one minister wanted to waive the ten-day rule to allow a report on study leave at universities to be considered quickly, arguing that the prime minister had asked him to bring it to cabinet. On PM&C's advice, Fraser said no.

Fraser always had to take account of a range of pressures. The interests of senior ministers were important. Anthony, in particular, had the right to ask for special treatment. In April 1982, for instance, he asked that submissions on environmental protection in the Northern Territory and on gas subsidies be postponed as he was away. The prime minister agreed but then forgot and cabinet made decisions. Anthony complained that they did not take into account key interests. The prime minister resubmitted the decisions for reconsideration. As PM&C secretary Sir Geoffrey Yeend noted to the officials of the Cabinet Office, the prime minister overlooked – and Yeend did not remind him (because no one had reminded Yeend) – Anthony's request to be present.

The ten-day rule was there for the convenience of ministers; whether the prime minister chose to apply it was a matter of judgment. Fraser generally went through the list provided by PM&C, annotating with 'if possible', 'forget it', 'hold', 'Thursday', or 'not if it can be reasonably avoided'.

Sometimes he seemed to be searching for excuses to justify decisions to bring items on promptly. In January 1982 PM&C noted that Fraser had wanted a good reason to waive the rule for a submission on Olympic coverage. It indicated that as a deadline was approaching, the item had to be dealt with quickly.

At times Fraser became frustrated when submissions were too long or were lodged late and then he tried to tighten up the system. In July 1979 he told Yeend that the Cabinet Office had all the necessary authority to send submissions back to departments. On 27 June 1980 he wrote:

> The handling of papers for this week's cabinet was unsatisfactory, to say the least. Given the size of the Business List and the fact that it included many items which had to be considered for the Premiers' Conference this week, it was unacceptable to have papers and briefing notes coming in over the weekend and on Monday. This comment applies also to the *Ad Hoc* Committee (Budget) Decisions which required confirmation before the Premiers' Conference.
>
> I am writing to all Ministers who have breached the 10-day rule for lodgement of Cabinet Submissions. In addition, I want you to make clear to Departmental Heads in a very firm and direct manner that such extensive breaches of the 10-day rule are not to occur again immediately before next year's Premiers' Conference, or indeed before any Cabinet.

Fraser had to guard the system to an extent to allow other ministers the opportunity to read the submissions. A waiving of the ten-day rule was not a defeat for PM&C; it was one of the routes available to have items considered by cabinet.

A similar approach was taken to under-the-line items – items considered without any formal submission being circulated in advance. Ministers often requested permission to bring urgent items forward. On some occasions they were accepted. Under-the-line items at a meeting in April 1982 included the terms of reference for a consultant's review on the selling of shares in TAA (Trans-Australia Airlines), support for Britain over the Falklands, and the funding of Aboriginal sacred sites. A month later cabinet discussed polling laws in the Australian Capital Territory (ACT), allowances for High Court judges, the upgrading of Launceston airport (relevant as a Tasmanian election was being held) and a parliamentary motion by a Western Australian backbencher on waterfront labour. Other requests were rejected; when the attorney-general wanted to discuss legal aid, he was told to wait until the submission he had been asked to bring forward was ready. Appointments were always taken under-the-line; they had to be cleared with the prime minister and with the senior minister of the state from which the appointee came before they were brought to cabinet. At times there might be a considerable number; the meeting of 8 December 1981 decided 33 positions, including membership of the National Gallery, the Electoral Commission and the executive of CSIRO. No appointment was considered by cabinet until Fraser had agreed to the listing. He had an absolute veto.

This attention to detail was time-consuming, but vital to Fraser because of the information it provided and the control it gave him. He was not prepared to give it up. The initial draft of the report on cabinet procedures in 1978, written by Yeend, proposed that the powers to determine the agenda might be delegated to the deputy leader of the Liberal party. It was not a serious suggestion and was intended as a gesture towards Lynch, because control over the agenda cannot easily be delegated. Only the prime minister can decide what should or should not be discussed. Says Fraser:

> Every prime minister is going to say 'no' to that proposal; it's an important part of keeping in touch with ministers and it's an important part of knowing what's going on. If you delegated the job to somebody else the day would come when you went into cabinet not having read the papers beforehand and not knowing what was on the list.

As a senior official commented:

> Lynch would have liked to have been chairman of cabinet, rather like the chairman of caucus. Purely on the grounds of cabinet administration, we were never keen on that because it was just a fifth wheel on the coach. If we thought for one moment that the decisions of the chairman of cabinet or the minister in charge of the cabinet agenda would automatically be endorsed by the prime minister, that would be fine. But they wouldn't be. You'd settle it with one and then have to go to the other.

Yet this control over the agenda was not used by Fraser to prevent a minister putting an item on the agenda. No minister recalls problems with having items listed; Fraser had experienced problems himself when a junior minister and was determined that the situation would not be repeated:

> If a minister wanted the submission before cabinet, in my view he had a right to have it before cabinet and not some months or even weeks after the submission was in the list. In at least one administration I was in, if the prime minister didn't like the submission, he just didn't list it; it just never got discussed. That is a hopeless way to run a government. So I just made up my mind, however much I like or dislike the submission, it will get on, it will get discussed and a decision will be taken on it.

Nevertheless, on the occasions when he was consulted before a minister put an item on the agenda or when he saw a submission, Fraser might ask that more work be done before it was deemed ready for cabinet discussion. In June 1980, for instance, he complained that the draft cabinet submission on contingency planning for vital services affected by strikes was inadequate. It did not advance the debate beyond the request for an interdepartmental committee report made 13 months beforehand. Fraser spelt out a series of analyses he wanted completed and demanded a second report within two months. There was no point in wasting the time of cabinet with submissions that would not lead anywhere.

Indeed, far from items not being listed, the more common complaint was that too much was put on the agenda. Much of the excess was generated by ministers. Some of the pressure was created by budget expenditure cuts that were always based on cabinet, not simply departmental, consideration. Many items were listed in response to requests by Fraser, who may have wanted to get proper discussion of a problem.

Occasionally, Fraser sought broader discussions of the political situation. In April 1977 he asked ministers to identify the more complex matters that were facing the country and sought submissions that could be considered by cabinet. He asked Anthony to prepare papers on energy and minerals questions, putting the Australian situation into an international perspective and relating the different parts of the problem. The discussions on these broad papers later led to some specific proposals.

Meetings of the full ministry were sometimes held without a fixed agenda; the debate could range widely. In February 1979 the ministry had noted the decision for an Australian contribution to the Namibia peacekeeping force; discussed the importance of parliament as a forum for the presentation and explanation of government policies; received a report on the prime minister's overseas trips and examined other issues such as the economy, technological change, the Indo-China conflict and refugees. In August the discussion concentrated on government procedures; it confirmed, for instance, the need for revenue matters to be discussed by a small group of ministers (thus legitimising existing practice) and reviewed parliamentary tactics. In May 1981 the ministry agreed to discuss policy and program priorities. That was the essence of meetings of the full ministry – general issues about the performance of the governments, assessments of policy areas but few specific decisions. The ministry meetings were to create a sense of involvement. It was part of a process of trying to maintain some direction and coherence, even if too general in its debates to go far.

The prime minister determined which non-cabinet ministers were able to attend cabinet meetings. Fraser rejected the practice in earlier coalition governments by which non-cabinet ministers were shuffled in and out of the room as their submissions were taken. In March 1976 he agreed to a suggestion from Sinclair that co-opted ministers should be allowed to attend from the beginning of each cabinet meeting, instead of being called in for the one item for which they were co-opted. 'You were always able to attend meetings if you could find out when they were on', said one junior minister. Cabinet meetings usually consisted of many more than just the cabinet ministers; outer ministers often attended and officials were called in to explain options and submissions.

Meetings could also come to authoritative conclusions without decisions being recorded. On 5 November 1977 a group of cabinet ministers decided to proceed with the establishment of an ethnic television service, but agreed that there would be no formal decision. Action was to be authorised by a record of the meeting. But, as the secretary to cabinet noted, it was still a meeting within the cabinet system. Even if not included in the official register of cabinet decisions, the record of the meeting was simply a cabinet decision in another form. The commitment to the ethnic television service was made in the policy speech on 21 November and included in the Governor-General's speech on 21 February 1978.

Yet these occasions were exceptions: rare examples of the ultimate flexibility of the cabinet system. Fraser attributed great importance to the form of cabinet and the value of the collectivity. He regarded the process of cabinet decision as necessary, desirable and, above all, proper. Many papers were annotated with the comment 'To Cabinet' scrawled across them. Cabinet was to be the forum for discussion, even where it might be possible for action to be taken alone. The consequence of this level of consultation was a massive workload. Cabinet met so often that ministers complained they spent too much time 'in the bunker'.

Running cabinet

Although Fraser was relaxed about attendance, outside the formal schedule his organisation of cabinet was not always considerate. Committee meetings might be suddenly called, and adjourned meetings reconvened at little or no notice. His private secretary recalls:

> Ministers were irritated at being summoned at a moment's notice. He would call together a cabinet or cabinet committee and adjourn it to 10.00 o'clock and then suddenly decide to start at 9.00 o'clock. They resented it. He lost goodwill because of the demands on ministers' time.

As a minister put it: 'there were always so many meetings going on and you were being summoned to this and that, you were never quite sure which meeting you were at!' Sometimes Fraser would be late for cabinet, leaving 12 or so important people sitting there grumbling. Running the timetable to suit the prime minister might be the chairman's prerogative, but it was not the best way to maintain cohesion or obtain the best contribution from its members.

The sheer statistics of the number of meetings held, submissions or memoranda lodged and decisions taken with or without a formal submission are impressive. The Fraser cabinet took about 19 350 decisions. Some were important; others were not. Between 180 (in 1982) and 224 (in 1981) appointments came to cabinet for approval in any one year, a total of 836 positions between 1979 and the end of the government. It had 2446 meetings; many were held in sequence, one after the other. Some items came back to cabinet time and again. Between September 1977, when cabinet first considered a proposal from Kerry Packer to explore the prospects for a satellite, and October 1982, when it made its final decision, AUSSAT was considered by cabinet or one of its committees on 31 separate occasions, as ministers gradually dealt with the technical details. Uranium was discussed at eight different meetings in July and August 1977 alone. This was either because the problems were intrinsically insoluble, or because they were so complicated that it needed several bites before ministers were able to understand the issues fully. Issues reach cabinet because they are complex; to take decisions at the first opportunity may be promoting expedition above understanding, and thereby ceding authority to the technicians. Nevertheless, for all the caveats with all the extenuating excuses, the amount of business undertaken by the Fraser government was immense.

Another indicator of the work is the time spent in meetings. May to July were the budget months during the Fraser government in which ministers were the hardest worked and the statistics include budget committees where only four or five ministers were present. Yet important decisions can only be taken by senior ministers, so the weight fell disproportionately on a few individuals. Further, for every hour spent in cabinet some time needs to be used for preparation: reading the documents, being briefed about the issues. So in May 1979, when there were on average two and a half meetings every day, and three and a half hours every day – or 27 hours a week – were actually spent in meetings, the total load on those senior ministers was staggering, particularly when all the other functions of ministers – parliamentary, party and departmental – were added. 'In the bunker' was an apt phrase (see Table 8.1).

TABLE 8.1 Time spent in meetings – selected months from the Fraser cabinet

Month	Meetings	Hours
May 1978	63	85
June 1978	35	48
July 1978	43	98.42
January 1979	8	23.52
May 1979	78	107.36
June 1979	37	49
July 1979	51	67.58

SOURCE: Weller 1989

In a search to reduce the workload, two reviews of cabinet procedures, in 1978 and 1981, were instituted. The first review by Yeend and his deputy, Mike Codd, examined the prospects of changing the rules on what came to cabinet, lengthening the ten-day rule, possibly altering the question time procedures to put questions on set days for each minister, increasing spending discretion for ministers and linking senior and junior ministers in the administration of departments. A wide range of statistics documented the heavy workload. They showed, among other things, how many submissions dealt with appointments, and how many with items that cost less than half a million dollars.

Several ways to reduce the volume of business were suggested: that there be a prescribed expenditure level below which the minister for finance had authority to decide; that minor legislative matters go straight to the

Legislation committee of cabinet; that the prime minister be assisted by another minister in cabinet procedures (Fraser put a line through that idea); that matters be settled as far as possible by correspondence. Ministers welcomed the discussion of items under the line, but felt that substantial policy proposals should still be made through submission. They also wanted to have strategic meetings without considering specific submissions, and a small 'leadership committee'.

The review made the following recommendations:

- all under-the-line items be cleared in advance with the prime minister
- appointments be cleared with senior ministers from the relevant state
- the minister for finance be allowed to approve expenditure on a program of not more than $500 000 in each of three years
- that ministry meetings be held more often
- a 'leadership' committee be established, consisting of the leader and deputy leader of each coalition party, and the leader of the government in the Senate.

Fraser rejected two suggestions that business lists and a list of cabinet submissions be circulated to permanent heads. This refusal was part of a desire to keep items as secret as possible.

Cabinet considered the report in December 1978. Fraser made clear that its discussions were not intended to lead to decisions, as it was his prerogative to determine which of the recommendations would be adopted. He demanded tighter control by the Cabinet Office of the flow of cabinet papers.

In January he selected the title 'co-ordination committee' in preference to leadership committee. The minister for finance was allowed to approve items up to $1 500 000 over three years and was to provide quarterly reports of approvals granted. Lynch could talk to ministers about the flow of cabinet papers (but not the specific agendas). Fraser vetoed the principle of allowing assisting ministers to attend cabinet committees as replacements for the substantive ministers. As Fraser reminded his ministry, in the last resort it was the ministers themselves who had to make the cabinet work effectively.

A second review in 1981 again emphasised the need for ministers to take decisions on their own and for submissions to be better digested. On 1 December 1981 cabinet merely reiterated the need to keep items away from cabinet, suggested that items that breached the ten-day rule be listed at the end of the agenda and that items be listed in order of priority for discussion. It also proposed that under-the-line items be taken at the end of the meetings. It seems that these reviews made little difference. The problem was not in the procedures – although changes could help – but in the pressure from above and below to have issues discussed by cabinet. Fraser saw cabinet discussion as necessary; the ministers thought them a useful self-protection. The workload stayed high.

Arenas for discussion: The committee system

If Fraser did not keep items off the agenda, he did decide where they would be discussed: in full cabinet or in a cabinet committee. There were two types of cabinet committee: standing committees that dealt with the regular business of government and *ad hoc* committees that were established for specified purposes. Some standing committees met more often than others. The economic committee, seen initially as the crucial forum for government strategy, only met 14 times in the first two years before it was abolished. Fraser explained that, as most of the important decisions on the economy were taken in cabinet, the committee was not needed. The Legislation committee, responsible for vetting the final drafts of legislation before their presentation to parliament, met 127 times in the same period. Others, such as the social welfare or the machinery of government committees, met rarely. Their authority to make final decisions depended on the importance of the issue. The social welfare committee was able to make final decisions, but they had to be cleared with the prime minister before being issued.

Ad hoc committees were established with particular terms of reference to consider troublesome or difficult issues such as uranium, AUSSAT and the new Parliament House. The Review of Commonwealth Functions (known as the Razor Gang) was one of several *ad hoc* committees that undertook the detailed consideration of budget estimates or government activities. These committees sometimes thrashed out options and then brought recommendations for action to cabinet. A few had the authority to make final decisions. Fraser decided all the terms of reference and the membership. Between July 1977 and July 1979, for instance, 1220 of the 6400 recorded cabinet decisions were made by *ad hoc* committees: 590 by budget committees; 136 by the Uranium committee that took any new policy issue to cabinet; 25 by the committee on the Williams report on education; 29 by the Crawford Industry Report committee; 33 by the New Parliament House committee. The range of subjects was broad.

Three standing committees were of particular importance. Foreign affairs and defence, and its later offshoot, the intelligence and security committee, made decisions on many issues of broad significance in relation to Africa, policy towards the great powers, defence procurement and Australia's role overseas. Its decisions were often not circulated to other ministers in cabinet. The monetary policy committee and the wages committee were created in 1977 to replace the economic committee. The monetary policy committee was responsible for issues that had traditionally been kept isolated in Treasury, or had been finally decided by the prime minister and the treasurer. It brought crucial economic decisions (on, for example, interest and exchange rates) into the cabinet arena, so that departments other than Treasury became involved in advice on economic policy. The Reserve Bank became more influential; so did PM&C. Thus Treasury's pre-eminence over economic information and advice was diminished and, as a PM&C official put it, Treasury was forced to become part of the normal advisory framework.

The most significant committee, at least from the point of view of cabinet control and political decision-making, was the co-ordination committee, created in 1979 after the 1978 cabinet review. Where the co-ordination committee differed from the others was in its lack of a clear functional role. It had precursors in an informal committee of the party leaders that had been convened initially to consider the 1977 electoral redistribution and in the planning and co-ordination committee established in 1976 but which rarely met. The co-ordination committee's terms of reference stated that it should 'consider overall government strategy and priorities, and to deal with matters referred to it by the prime minister'. In other words, it could discuss anything Fraser chose to take to it.

There was nothing sinister in the existence of a small inner group. All prime ministers are likely to be surrounded by a group of advisers and ministers whom they find compatible; these meetings are often labelled kitchen cabinets and have no official status. Fraser took many of those activities out of the PMO and into the cabinet system. That meant that decisions had a formal weight. As a senior official explained:

> Co-ordination committee was a testing ground for him to discuss a broad range of political issues and tactics. Not everything in Co-ordination needed a decision. Most prime ministers have that sort of sounding board. Few of them have given it the designation of a cabinet committee.

The membership of the co-ordination committee was initially only the leaders of the Liberal and the National parties in the House of Representatives, and the government leader in the Senate. But others were co-opted, depending on whom Fraser trusted and what was being discussed. In September 1979, when Sinclair resigned after being charged in a NSW court, Nixon was appointed as the second National party minister on the committee. Nixon's advice was highly regarded. When Sinclair returned to office in 1980, Nixon received a formal letter stating that Sinclair would rejoin the co-ordination committee in Nixon's place. But Fraser added a personal note saying that he had agreed that Nixon be co-opted for all co-ordination committee meetings until the election. In March 1980 Fraser and Lynch discussed the membership of the committee. While they decided to keep the official membership at five, Fraser instructed that Nixon be co-opted on most occasions and for most matters; he wanted the department to find the odd occasion when Nixon was not co-opted for the sake of appearances. The impression of a small membership was thus to be retained, but Fraser saw it as important that Nixon's advice continue to be available. During the 1980–83 parliament, as the committee became more involved in economic matters, Howard (treasurer) and Guilfoyle (minister of finance) were often co-opted as well.

The co-ordination committee discussed a range of subjects. Some were political: the parliamentary program, four-year terms and whether the speaker should be independent. Others were tactical: should ministers be allowed to appeal against decisions of a budget committee or against the imposition of a level of staff ceilings? Some were previews of items that came to cabinet: they were tossed around to guess their impact before being taken to full cabinet for discussion. Fraser stated: 'If I was unsure how an issue should be handled, I might discuss it with the co-ordination committee and then it would be decided by cabinet'. Gradually the co-ordination committee became the body responsible for revenue decisions (traditionally the province of a small inner group). In May 1979 it previewed the revenue options before the May statement. In August 1980 the co-ordination committee spent two meetings looking at the priorities for government business in the next six months. The ministry then endorsed the report, the day after the second of the committee meetings. On 18 September 1980 it discussed proposals for the electoral policy speech, with Fraser annotating each idea. The co-ordination committee examined all the main budget papers in July 1981 before their consideration by cabinet and housing interest rates before the housing package of 1982. Its agenda gave the impression of a wide-ranging committee that looked at anything that was significant or immediately topical.

The free-flowing style of the committee meant that the formal agenda bore no relation to what was discussed. The committee could start with a preliminary discussion of the budget and then roll on to other issues for which the responsible minister was not present. The committee became the place where the political agenda was exposed (often on the basis of flimsy information). It set priorities, commissioned work, developed options and ideas, and made a preliminary review of the political problems of the day. In November 1980 it asked for policy reviews on the length of parliamentary terms; Commonwealth–State financial relations; income or indirect taxes; north–south relations; Radio Australia; the Makarrata (a proposed treaty between Aboriginal and White Australians); Agent Orange (the herbicide defoliant used in the Vietnam War containing dioxins that allegedly cause health harms); nuclear safeguards; and poverty. Its influence could be wide-ranging. The meetings kept senior ministers informed about the prime minister's timetable and thinking.

Fraser liked small meetings of this type. A colleague recalls: 'he was at his best arguing a proposition around a table – that was probably his greatest strength – his knowledge, his strength, the authority of the position'. Partly as a consequence of its exclusive and privileged membership, the co-ordination committee led to resentment among other ministers. When Andrew Peacock, long-time rival of Fraser, resigned in 1981, he claimed that the co-ordination committee had been superimposed over the cabinet and its other committees; that when it discussed issues the responsible ministers were often not present, and that:

> ... it was in fact an extension of the prime minister's well-known lobbying of ministers before issues are brought to cabinet ... when cabinet meets a significant number of ministers have already determined many matters concerning government strategy; In some cases, policy matters may have been decided. The decision of cabinet is a foregone conclusion and so collective wisdom of cabinet is aborted.

He objected that ministers were 'dismissed from the cabinet room' so the co-ordination committee could meet. He argued that the co-ordination committee 'is not just a kitchen cabinet; it is a formal structure crushing the cabinet system'.

Peacock's charges were denied by his colleagues in the debate that followed his resignation. The committee took up a wide range of issues for political reasons and for matters of convenience. Some of this may have been a cabinet preview, but not all was. One official described the committee as 'Fraser talking, us taking down decisions'. When the committee did make decisions, its members appreciated that they were expected to throw their weight behind those views and stick to them in cabinet. When it operated as an 'inner cabinet', it was the first of an expanding group of concentric circles. If the committee, consisting of the strongest ministers, had committed itself, Fraser had fewer qualms about asserting his views in cabinet as he knew that the leading ministers agreed.

The co-ordination committee, like all other committees, was a 'partial' cabinet. It included only a few ministers, had terms of reference (very general in this case) and the authority to make decisions that bound all other members of cabinet. Fraser used his committees extensively. That was necessary to get through the load of business; a committee structure is a vital part of a modem cabinet system. It also allowed the forum for discussion to be carefully chosen, with a select membership. Important decisions were taken by foreign affairs and defence, by the monetary policy and by the co-ordination committee, decisions that determined foreign policy, defence purchases, interest rates, wages policy and so on. Every one of these had the weight of a decision taken by full cabinet. Committees were an essential part of that system, a part that Fraser used with skill to get the business done.

Running the cabinet

Fraser went to cabinet well prepared. PM&C gave him a brief on every submission and he sometimes went through the agenda with his staff to assist in clarifying his thoughts. He not only knew what problems were likely to be involved, but what their possible consequences were. He believed that cabinet should not take a decision if he had not considered fully any likely implication:

> The prime minister has to be in a position in cabinet to know whether the decision that has been made is a sensible one or not. If a prime minister is not in that position, he is falling behind in his own work load. That doesn't mean to say you have got a violent interest in the subject yourself; it just means, if a decision of some importance is to be made, you want to know enough about it to be satisfied from your own knowledge that it is a sensible decision.

He therefore needed to give thought to every proposal to know that all questions had been asked and adequately answered.

He also ensured that as far as possible the important ministers understood issues. At times he asked his minister for finance to take a careful look at a proposal, fearing that the responsible minister did not understand all that was involved. On other occasions Fraser asked the attorney-general to raise difficult legal questions in cabinet. Lobbying in the coalition cabinet was strictly forbidden, but prime ministerial consultation was regarded as fairly usual. Lynch 'liked to know what my view was on any important issue he was taking to cabinet, which meant we discussed the issues right along the line', remembers Fraser. The Treasury also recalls that Lynch only argued 'until he got a whiff of the prime minister's direction'. Some ministers would preview an important item with the prime minister before the meeting. Fraser wanted to know the details and the means by which the political problem would be handled. He would say, 'What you are doing I think is great, but we'll look at it when it's lodged!' However supportive, he would wait for briefs from PM&C and Treasury. Ministers argued that Fraser was never committed to the point where you could enter cabinet and say, 'I've got the prime minister locked into a submission!'

Prime ministers need to have a broad appreciation of the directions cabinet is taking. Fraser could often guess on which side his colleagues would fall without having to discuss the specific items with them. Dealing with ministers on a regular basis meant that he had a fair estimate of who would support the leader and who would support the particular solutions. He stated:

> Henry Bolte used to say, 'don't let anything go into cabinet unless you know how you want it to come out. You've got to know the decision that's made is safe and will work'. That was good advice. I'd quite often not know how the numbers were going to go. But because I did a bit of work on the submission and I'd got briefed I wasn't all that often on the losing side in a cabinet discussion. If you're arguing with a bunch of people who are basically fairly pragmatic, if you've done your homework, you're likely to be on the winning side in an argument, not always, but more often than not.

On important topics, these calculations would be essential.

Fraser chaired all cabinet meetings in a very active fashion. The atmosphere was formal. He was called 'Prime Minister' by his ministers. On many items the discussion was brusque. If Fraser thought an item was of little significance, he was inclined to push it through fast, without encouraging much discussion. If an issue was cut and dried, he would lead cabinet to a quick conclusion — and some ministers wanted to talk. If an agenda was of 20 items, only two would be of substance where proper argument should be developed. For the 18 he seemed dominant; to get a quick conclusion he might go straight to the recommendations. It was not that he cared much what the result was, but time was needed for the more sensitive or substantial issues. Indeed, on these minor items he might lose interest in the discussion. A colleague recalled:

> When ministers were putting a case, he'd turn aside, talk to other people and appear not to be listening. He was never known as a charming man and a lot thought he was rude. But it was not a calculated rudeness. His mind was working on so many areas he appeared rude when what he was doing was thinking about something entirely different and concentrating on that. Yet for ministers to be talking to the back of his head while he talked to Doug Anthony was not encouraging.

When items of importance or of interest to Fraser were discussed, the atmosphere could become charged with tension. The cabinet spent much of its time on issues that were politically sensitive. Under-the-line items were taken first; for instance, a report on negotiations with the ACTU might lead to a broad hour-long discussion (or, less seriously, there might be a comment on the previous evening's episode of *Yes Minister*.) On occasion under-the-line items led to discussions so lengthy that the substantive submissions were barely reached. Fraser's own interventions in a discussion were unpredictable, although, given his contribution on every item, he talked in total far more than any other minister. So much so that ministers and officials thought he was too interventionist to be seen as a good chairman (although cabinet is scarcely a normal committee). If he felt strongly, he might state his views early and explain why he held them; in a sense such a statement could be regarded as a challenge to other ministers to back him or not. Some ministers were always inclined to support the prime minister, but it was dangerous to assume that every question or statement was an accurate reflection of his views, because the process of cabinet was more a process of interrogation than formal debate. Fraser 'wanted to make sure that cabinet was fully exposed to the issues before taking a decision and I didn't want senior ministers to be jumped'. One minister complained that he was never given the opportunity to develop a case; as soon as he started to speak 'you had these questions rolling down the aisles like a bowling alley; if you let yourself be intimidated by that and went away speechless, it was your own fault'. So the process was tough – and as brief as possible. It was a busy forum for making decisions, not an area for the judicious exposition of all the issues. Some ministers were treated more gently than others. Fraser was inclined to push and probe those whom he believed eventually might become senior; those who were never going to make it and had difficulty ever answering a question were treated more gently.

The process of questioning sometimes led to ministers feeling they had a great victory. An official claimed:

> If Fraser put his view early, ministers often thought he was decided because he'd come out with a challenge. But he was simply going on with the questioning style. If satisfied at the end, he would be happy to go along with the minister's submission. And the minister might think he had a stunning victory.

It was often dangerous to accept Fraser's view precisely because he might just be floating ideas. If his first hypothesis was accepted too quiescently, it just might not have had sufficient scrutiny. Ministers did change their views after Fraser spoke. In itself that is not surprising; ministers are meant to be influenced by the discussions they hear around the table. One minister changed his opinions so often he was known as 'Mr 180 degrees' and lost all influence. The weight of ministers was important too; if Fraser, Anthony and Lynch were united, opposition was unlikely. There was a clear pecking order in cabinet. Fraser's terse style – it was easy to tell if he was relaxed or not about an issue – led to charges that he bullied cabinet. His aggressive approach made it an easy charge to make. Even a close colleague like Nixon agrees in part: 'He tried to bully me as I opposed him at times. He would swing on me in cabinet with an angry look and say "What are you up to? What are you going crook about?"' But he never excluded a minister who wanted to speak. No minister recalls being prevented from speaking, although many thought some colleagues were often too scared to speak. A typical comment was: 'I was never stopped from saying something I wanted to say, either to him or to the cabinet. Never'.

Ministers were never certain how a submission would be received. Those who had duly consulted everyone before bringing a submission to cabinet may have been annoyed when they were questioned rather than given a soft ride; but that was always the way the cabinet process worked. The fact that departments and their ministers had agreed with the recommendation was no guarantee of cabinet approval; problems that had not been recognised before could easily be identified in cabinet.

Summarising the discussion and announcing the decision were the prime minister's prerogatives. He could draw together the strands of the discussion, weigh the voices or postpone debate. His colleagues thought he was always ready to defer an item if he was not getting his own way. A minister recalls he would get ministers to withdraw submissions on the most curious pretexts, and ministers would do so rather than have the submissions rejected substantially. Ministers would talk to the prime minister after the meeting and the submission would come back in a different form – and with a greater chance of success. One tactic was to ask for further information or another paper; it was, an official recalls, an alternative to saying we haven't reached a decision. This procedure was a useful tactic when Fraser was not gaining support.

Decisions were reached in several ways. Votes were not taken in the direct sense of a formal motion, but Fraser sometimes went round the table, asking ministers where they stood. It was not always easy to get views; sometimes he had to drag colleagues into expressing them. Fraser recalls:

> I can remember one very senior minister; I tried to get him to give a view. He said; 'On the one hand, this; on the other hand, that!' I said: 'Yes, but look, the numbers are evenly divided and it's an important issue. I would like to know, if you have got to make a decision, where you would come out.' 'On the one hand, this; on the other hand, that.' It took me about fourteen minutes to actually find out which side of the ground he was going to hit. I really struggled to make a minister give a view. If somebody said 'Look, I just haven't got a view', I can't have it, that's not doing your job. You have to have a view and to help in reaching a collective view.

Even when Fraser went round the table, his counting was often regarded as suspect. Nixon was reputed to have asked 'which way' when the prime minister stated one result. Killen grumbled that he must have counted the notetakers. There were also 'eight–six decisions', as they were called, which occurred when, on the basis of the views expressed, Fraser had stated, as the clear cabinet decision, the view of the minority – with which he agreed. But few were prepared to contest summaries of this type; most acknowledged such results were rare.

Numbers were often not in themselves enough. Fraser wanted more than a bare majority because of the importance of collective commitment. When everyone who wanted to speak had had a turn and there was a clear majority, cabinet would not pursue it further. If ministers were badly divided, then a decision might not stick and they all had to live with it and defend it. Fraser preferred to delay such decisions until there was greater support. He had a good notion of what could be pushed through and what needed to be reconsidered. He had to balance particular decisions against future cabinet cohesion. On important issues, therefore, a badly divided cabinet meant that the issue was likely to come back again and again. A widely held view was:

> He would persist. If he had a group of people against him in cabinet, he wouldn't just use the numbers, he would keep arguing; he would put it aside and come back to it at another meeting; then he would tend to try and get alliances together.

When cabinet was divided, the process of making a decision was interminable. Even when consensus was achieved, it could be at the cost of innumerable meetings. Unwilling to have a badly divided cabinet, Fraser wanted to win the argument. At the very least he wanted acquiescence; he would have preferred agreement. When ministers disagreed and fought, the discussions went on and on. But if the issue was sensitive, Fraser would seldom close it off. 'He would do it by exhaustion; he knew what he wanted, but if he didn't have his colleagues on side, he kept them locked up until they caved in', said one cabinet official with only slight poetic licence.

There are also good political reasons for bringing things to cabinet. As one observer commented, the prime minister has got to make the right decision for the country's sake, for the party's sake and in the end for his own sake. 'The hard facts of political life are that if the prime minister keeps getting rolled, his authority becomes weakened and that of the party becomes weakened and he'll fail rapidly.' Fraser was unable to recall any occasion where he cared and lost. Prime ministers have to live with and sell cabinet decisions. If they want something badly enough, most cabinet ministers are prepared to live with it. A senior official explained:

> If prime ministers felt strongly, given their sense of politics, the decisions were likely to be supported by most of their colleagues. Even when senior ministers felt uneasy, in the end they gave their support because they felt, I think rightly, that the prime minister has got to sink or swim as the political leader of the government. In that sense, prime ministers do get their way.

Ministers do not argue but have good will.

> A prime minister has got a certain amount of room to move. He can take an unpopular stance on a limited number of issues. If he does it too much, he will exhaust his political capital.

However, Fraser was often not prepared to use that power; he did not end debates by announcing where the government would stand. One minister 'can't ever remember Malcolm saying: That is that and I brook no argument. He wouldn't override a cabinet majority against him; he would just wear it down because he wanted people with him.' At the end of a debate, some ministers did not know whether they had won or not, or what they had won.

Decisions were written up by the Cabinet Office and often had to be extracted from the debate, since they were not based on formal motions. If the recommendations in the submission were accepted, they could be rephrased as a decision. If amendments were made, the Cabinet Office had to develop a coherent and consistent conclusion. One official, only half-jokingly, commented, 'we record the decision ministers would have reached, if they had time to read their briefs and discuss the submissions at length'. Sometimes clauses not mentioned were added to make the decision logical. If any ministers objected the decisions could be reviewed.

Fraser could vet decisions before their circulation. For instance, in October 1977 he wrote to Yeend, then under-secretary of PM&C:

> You will be aware of my concern with the cabinet decision on Seas and Submerged Lands. I think it might be desirable if important cabinet decisions were not circulated without coming to me for clearance ... I would be glad if you could examine the idea.

But that right was seldom exercised. When the Cabinet Office prepared a brief for Fraser after Peacock's resignation, it noted that only three or four times a year had the prime minister asked to clear decisions before circulation and that was usually when a decision was based on a discussion in cabinet rather than a submission.

In theory decisions were circulated to all ministers. In practice the distribution was often far more limited. Each decision had attached to it a list of ministers or officials to whom it should be sent. Often, for routine or non-controversial issues, that circulation list would include all ministers.

Some were far more limited. When the budget *ad hoc* committee or the Review of Commonwealth Functions (RCF) committee made decisions, they were usually circulated only to members of the committee. Some of their decisions later came to the cabinet for ratification or endorsement, but, when proposals were rejected by these committees, the other members of cabinet were never informed. When issues were under discussion, interim decisions might only be given to a limited number of people. In February 1981 cabinet was considering the introduction of an indirect tax.

When Industry Minister Phillip Lynch returned from overseas in the middle of the debate and asked for a briefing on the progress of the proposal, he was told by his department:

> We have no idea at this stage what decisions, if any, cabinet might have taken on these various submissions in your absence abroad; access to the decisions has been limited to Mr Anthony, the prime minister and Mr Howard [treasurer].

Overview

Fraser always regarded cabinet as central to his government. He appreciated the political value of collective decisions. Former ministers point out that his speeches were always 'the government has decided' or 'cabinet has decided', it was never 'I have'. 'He would often emphasise that 'cabinet was unanimous'. He insisted that cabinet discuss and decide; every significant issue went to cabinet, sometimes time and again.

Yet even consultation created problems. The workload of cabinet was large; the schedule was wearing. Ministers argued that the cost of consultations and meetings 'in the bunker' was government by exhaustion, with too many decisions made at late hours by tired ministers. Two reviews of cabinet procedures emphasised the need to reduce the workload of cabinet. It never happened.

Why? Partly because the growing interrelatedness of government business meant that there were more disputes to settle. Partly because ministers were rather too keen to bring items to cabinet, determined that they would get the collective support of cabinet, but also because items were considered at length. The repetition was an indication both of a search for certainty and of caution. Fraser 'roared like a lion but was pretty much a kitten in decision-making', said an official.

Fraser's imperatives kept cabinet busy too. His insistence that cabinet was the proper forum for decisions meant that he constantly demanded that submissions be prepared. He was less prepared than other leaders to determine issues outside the cabinet forum. Collective discussion gave power and legitimacy to decisions, at the cost of long hours. The process of exhaustive gaining consensus, or at least acquiescence, was seldom easy.

Insistence on consulting cabinet, combined with Fraser's impatience, put great pressure on ministers, pressure that made them tired and thus probably led to mistakes. It was not seen as necessary. One official noted: 'The moment Malcolm went away, you could almost feel everybody breathe a sigh of relief'. Doug Anthony's style was more relaxed, less interventionist and less impatient; cabinet meetings had a totally different atmosphere. Cabinet meetings tend to discuss sensitive issues; Fraser's determination to take all things there increased the difficulties cabinet must systematically face.

Fraser's style was not easy to cope with for those who lacked confidence. To be met with an aggressive range of questions prevented any free-ranging discussion; it may well have foreclosed options as debate concentrated on particular alternatives rather than divergent options or general perceptions. In part that is a natural consequence of any cabinet striving for solutions, but it was probably exacerbated in this instance by the prime minister's personality and the fact that some ministers were not prepared to argue. At times, too, Fraser's drive to win arguments – not always so difficult against weaker ministers – might have meant that views were not expressed adequately. Strong ministers may have performed even better in the demanding atmosphere. If some thrived, others suffered.

Too much time, too many papers, too much consultation, too much interference in ministerial or departmental affairs: these are the readiest complaints. They are clearly accurate in that the cabinet was in constant session, but in each case a counter-argument can be launched. Cabinet ought to be involved; papers are needed for information; ministers complain if they are not consulted. Every cabinet has its share of weaker ministers and the prime minister needs to protect the government from their mistakes. It is a constant search for balance within the cabinet system. There are, claimed a senior official, 'institutional things that weigh against an efficient system. You can't even talk about an efficient system of government in the boardroom sense.' The contrary pressures remain too strong. Less consultation may have led to fewer meetings but more complaints about lack of discussion and too much prime ministerial direction. It was probably the combination of the cabinet system and Fraser's style of running it that created some of the tension.

The activity of the Fraser cabinet indicates some of the dilemmas of cabinet government, and particularly for the prime minister. He or she needs to maintain some overview of what the government is doing, but how much detail is required for that to be achieved? Political sensitivity or crisis can often be found in the aberrant detail. Fraser believed that he had to understand the detail to achieve the breadth of vision and cabinet therefore became deeply involved in many detailed discussions. That is part of the problem of collective responsibility. It was interpreted to mean that, as appropriate, ministers should be involved and often should express a view, even where their knowledge and interest might be limited. Uninterested ministers may well be loath to cross prime ministers on issues important to them and their support could be crucial even if uninformed.

Under Fraser, government was indeed collective; cabinet was involved in all the important issues. But the collective purpose was imposed by the leader, the only person able to stretch across the whole government in an active way. Everything went to cabinet; everything important was decided collectively; everyone was consulted – frequently and exhaustively. The cabinet process was used; the cabinet form adopted. Even decisions normally taken in the PMO were brought within the cabinet system. Yet Fraser was still able to run the system. His retort that: 'Just because I consulted, it doesn't mean I didn't dominate' is illustrative. He used the levers of power through consultation and cabinet discussion. His success depended on the willingness and capacity of his colleagues to argue and sustain a case. Because Fraser's capacity was greater, his view prevailed most often.

9 CONTRASTING STYLES: 1983–96

Hawke and Keating governed for 13 years in the longest period of continuous Labor rule in Australian history. They are examined here as one government, although in practice their styles were conspicuously different. Hawke was a thorough and careful chair, good with paperwork, and concerned that cabinet reach sensible decisions. Keating was mercurial, interested in some issues, disengaged from others. In some ways he was elected because he was different from Hawke whose impetus seemed to have run its course as his government, riven from inside and under siege from without, stalled in 1990. They provide a contrast, showing how styles could differ within a single government.

The Labor party was well prepared for government. Before 1983 the party had been presented with the example of Whitlam's government as a model of how cabinet should not be run. Cabinet had been poorly organised and ineffective as a forum for decision-making. The leading members of the party were determined not to follow that route. A working party had considered the problems of governing before the 1980 election and produced a taskforce report that was then endorsed by caucus. Another taskforce was convened in 1981, and by September 1982 it had produced a further and more detailed report that covered a range of topics, including the appointment of permanent heads and the control of statutory authorities. Although the later report was published and discussed by the party executive, it had not been endorsed by caucus when the snap election of March 1983 was called.

Both task forces made recommendations about the size and working of the cabinet. Although it had become part of the demonology of the

Whitlam administration that the size of cabinet had been one of its main problems, neither report argued for a division of ministers into an inner cabinet and an outer ministry. Both reports argued:

> ... that – provided an effective system of Cabinet committees is developed to relieve the full Cabinet's workload – there is no reason why Cabinet business could not be effectively and expeditiously conducted by meetings of the full ministry and that meetings of the full ministry are highly desirable when major policy or strategy matters have to be resolved.

The reports recommended 'the Cabinet to consist of all ministers with no "inner" or "outer" divisions'. Both reports thought too many problems would be caused by such a division and they sought instead to establish a priorities and planning committee of cabinet that would act as a *de facto* inner cabinet.

A group of senior shadow ministers (not including Hawke) decided in November 1982 that a division of ministers was nevertheless essential for effective decision-making. When Hawke became leader, he launched *Labour and the Quality of Government*, which was based on the report; it made no comment on whether all ministers should be included in cabinet. Hawke then announced on the hustings that an inner cabinet would be created, and this was endorsed at the first meeting of caucus. It could scarcely do anything else.

The original cabinet had 13 members, but as a result of an oversight the minister for defence was excluded. He was added and the minister for finance shifted out. Inevitably the latter had to attend almost all meetings and in mid-1983 he was officially added to the cabinet. By the 1984 election, cabinet had grown to 15. After the election, primarily as a response to left-wing demands for greater representation, cabinet size was further increased. In order to retain some balance between the factions, two new ministers (one left-wing, one right-wing) were added. Cabinet then had 17 members.

Did this size make proceedings unwieldy? Apparently not, partly because some ministers were often away and there were usually only 12 or 13 at all but the most crucial meetings; partly because most decisions were taken in committee and lengthy discussions were held there. Cabinet acted as a forum for endorsing committee recommendations. Outer ministers were co-opted to meetings for a range of reasons: responsibility for an item, as minister assisting, as representative in the other chamber or because of state interests in an item; their attendance was controlled more rigidly than it had been under earlier governments. But it was also because cabinet was seen as to some extent playing a representative role and it was therefore important that the range of views held by the factions be expressed there.

The Labor party's factional system became institutionalised under the Hawke government. The three factions – left, centre left and right – organised the numbers in the caucus and, whenever a vacancy in the ministry occurred, negotiated between themselves to determine whose turn it was for promotion. The faction system had the effect of channelling ideological differences so that, where opposition to government decision occurred, it could be contained in private. One consequence was that each faction had recognised leaders in cabinet, where their factional importance gave them a weight not otherwise justified by their portfolio. Factional representation in cabinet has been a way of reducing opposition within the party and enhancing consensus.

The members of cabinet were selected by the four parliamentary leaders: initially Hawke, Lionel Bowen, John Button and Don Grimes. Their selection did not depend on a precise number of votes obtained in the caucus ballot. The committee of leaders also had the capacity to remove a minister if there was due cause, although that power was never used. The decision to give them this power was taken by the caucus executive in November 1982 and did not emerge from the task force's reports. For ministers to be sacked, they had not merely to be proved inefficient, but to have transgressed in some way against proper behaviour.

The structure of cabinet was changed dramatically in July 1987. The number of departments was reduced to 16. Until that date it had been assumed that, in the terms of section 64 of the Australian Constitution, every minister had to have a separate department 'to administer'. Some skeletal departments, containing only two or three staff, had been created to circumvent this problem. But the solicitor-general advised that more than one minister could be appointed to one department and this advice led to a total restructuring of the federal administration.

Sixteen departments were created, with veterans' affairs being a part of a larger grouping. Cabinet then consisted of the 16 senior 'portfolio' ministers and (for a few months) Senator Ryan as special minister for state. Thirteen non-portfolio ministers were appointed; each was allocated specified responsibility within a larger department. Some of their titles, such as minister for resources or minister for consumer affairs, were not reflected in the names of departments. Non-portfolio ministers were comparable to junior ministers in the British system of government; they were in theory answerable to their seniors and did not usually hold cabinet rank.

Since all areas of the administration were represented in the cabinet, it became much easier to organise. Non-portfolio ministers would be co-opted only if they had specific portfolio interests. Portfolio ministers were required to carry the arguments for the whole portfolio in cabinet debate. The distinction between ministers became more distinct. Divisions of opinion could now be settled within departments, rather than coming to cabinet as a dispute between departments. Cabinet could therefore in theory be slightly removed from some areas of policy development.

The intention of the consolidation of departments was to reduce the number of meetings and decisions that cabinet must take. The figures for cabinet business reflect the changes (see Table 9.1).

TABLE 9.1 Activity in the Hawke cabinet

Meetings					Papers	Decisions Committee	Cabinet
	Min.	Cab.	Comm.	Total			
March–June 1983	6	19	99	124	422	198	595
1983-84	7	68	257	332	1137	1251	1430
1984–85	5	54	140	199	1406	1202	1430
1985–86	8	57	156	221	1040	690	871
1986–87	4	52	154	210	879	1035	718
1987–88	5	41	148	194	889	830	817

After the hectic activity of the earlier years, there was a reduction in the number of meetings and, compared to 1986–87, in total decisions. The figures for 1987–88 were particularly significant because they refer to the first year of the mega-departments. The objective that far less material be brought to cabinet was gradually being fulfilled; the cabinet agenda then contained only seven to ten items. Ministers were able to concentrate on the most important issues, those of such political significance that they could be decided only by the most senior ministers.

At the same time, procedures were developed to ensure that ministers were not surprised by items coming to cabinet. In the first years, under-the-line items (items discussed without a written submission) could be raised only with the approval of the prime minister. Whereas under Fraser under-the-line items had been taken first so that long debate left no time for consideration of the formal submissions; the cabinet office persuaded Hawke to take them after formal business. By 1988 the cabinet office had in addition developed the practice of circulating in advance a list of items that were to be discussed under-the-line. Ministers had the opportunity to give the general area some thought. If one criterion for sensible decision-making is the ability to be prepared for discussion, the procedures of the Hawke cabinet were constantly pushing in that direction.

Ministry meetings and strategy

Separation of the cabinet and the ministry in 1983 led to certain problems. First, some ministers were not involved in the making of any formal decisions, for unless an item was to be reconsidered in cabinet, there was no need to co-opt the ministers who had been involved in developing the initial committee recommendation. This led at a very early stage to some dissatisfaction among the junior ministers who wanted to be more heavily involved. Second, the 'inner' and 'outer' distinction raised the question of the function and regularity of meetings of the full ministry.

The latter were to some extent meant to be strategic. The government's policy paper, *Reforming the Australian Public Service*, claimed that the government would hold 'an annual ministerial meeting to ... review national prospects and Government operations and priorities' along the lines of the Chequers weekends in Britain, or the Meach Lake gatherings in Canada. The first was held at Kirribilli House in February 1984 and the main outcome was a committee to examine the relationship between cabinet and the outer ministers, and between ministers and caucus. This committee developed a set of guidelines that became known as the Kirribilli rules.

A second strategy meeting was held during the early stages of the budget deliberations in 1985. No further meetings of this type seem to have been held, partly because ministers were not convinced that anything useful was emerging out of them. After that, the prime ministers held a few informal, or only slightly structured, meetings that have included the parliamentary leaders, the faction bosses and the caucus committee chairmen, and at which they considered the general political situation.

There were only seven meetings of the full ministry in the July 1983–June 1984 period, compared with 68 meetings of cabinet and 257 of its committees. Ministry meetings did not appear to have found a role that was distinct and necessary, yet separate, from that of cabinet or its committees.

In the Keating government there were a number of general debates about the political situation, which sometimes rambled. Blewett recalls a couple of them in 1992:

> 23 June: Cabinet opened with a gloomy three-and-a-half hour discussion of the state of the nation. Pessimism stalked the room and it was perhaps the most despairing cabinet meeting I have attended.
>
> 14 July: We then had another of our general discussions. (Duffy, who had the temerity to suggest that nothing came of 'these general waffles', was pounced on by both Keating and Dawkins who repudiated his assertion with concrete examples of actions deriving from cabinet waffles.)

Cabinet committees

The 1982 taskforce laid down a sophisticated procedure for managing cabinet business through a system of committees that owed much to Canadian precedents. The taskforce proposed that three co-ordinating committees and five functional committees be established. Co-ordinating committees ranged across all the government's activities; functional committees dealt with particular policy areas. As a result of the creation of the inner cabinet, there was no priorities and planning committee; a legislation committee, earlier seen as a sub-committee of the parliamentary business committee, was formed. The third co-ordinating committee, on expenditure review, turned out to be a crucial arena for governing.

In the early years the functional committees were retained, with one exception: the industry and infrastructure committee was split into two. There were therefore six functional committees: economic policy; industry; infrastructure; social policy; legal and administration; and defence and external relations. After the 1984 election, the infrastructure committee was abolished and a security committee was given separate status. There was also a sub-committee on industrial restructuring and a committee for the National Crimes Authority. The prime minister was *ex officio* chairman of all committees except the one for legislation, but each had a nominated alternative. The prime minister determined the membership; it was usually settled on the basis of portfolio, although Hayden, the foreign minister, was on the economic committee, a consequence of his experience as treasurer and status as former leader.

Before any business reached cabinet, it was meant to be considered by the relevant functional committee, which had as members all the ministers who were likely to have a portfolio interest in the topic. The committee made a recommendation to the cabinet (called a 'blue' because it was recorded on blue paper), but it was not regarded as final until it was later endorsed by the cabinet – and recorded on white paper. Cabinet accepted the majority of the committee recommendations without amendment. On occasion there was a challenge to the wisdom of the decision, or some clarification of technical items or some additional information provided, but these cases were rare. More often ministers went to cabinet with a folder of committee decisions that were taken under the agenda item 'endorsements' and they were read through by the prime minister and dealt with in about ten minutes.

Because ministers were initially involved in the creation of the system of cabinet rules and committees, and were conscious of their value, in the early years they were often guardians of the process. The importance of abiding by procedures established by cabinet had been impressed on the minds of the party leaders by bitter experience. The rules gave to ministers the advantage of predictability. While the prime minister was formally responsible for the workings of cabinet, other ministers intervened if one of their colleagues wanted to short-circuit the system. For instance, the *Cabinet Handbook* required that submissions be lodged with the cabinet office ten days before they were considered by the cabinet or a committee. The prime minister was fairly strict in applying the rule. But when ministers asked if they could bring an item on more quickly, their colleagues also asked two questions: why should it not go to the relevant committee, and why was it so urgent? Most of those attempts failed, since ministers did not satisfy the first point. Further, when ministers expressed dissatisfaction with a cabinet decision, they were reminded that 'it was decided by the rules'.

This broad commitment to process was remarkably well maintained for the first four years of Labor's time in office. Ministers were prepared to wait for the recommendations of committees to be ratified by cabinet and there were only a limited number of leaks about government intentions.

The cabinet agenda and the precise committee in which submissions were to be considered were still formally determined by the prime minister, but given the effective use of cabinet committees the system became almost automatic and the power to refuse listing used infrequently. Sometimes the agenda consisted of only three items: endorsement of committee decisions, appointments, and under-the-line items (including parliamentary tactics).

Some changes had to be made to the procedures, primarily as a consequence of the pressures of time. There were only so many hours in the day for the senior ministers whose involvement was crucial for strategic decisions. Hawke was nominally the chairman of all the functional committees and, since the substantial arguments and decisions occurred there, often attended their meetings. This increased the problems of scheduling them and was often the most important constraint on the number of meetings that could be held.

Much of the business done by cabinet was concerned with micropolitics: approving expenditure on new policy items, changes to existing policies or agreeing to options where ministers wanted the comfort of a collective decision. The choice facing the managers of the cabinet's business was either to delegate these decisions to the individual minister or to allow committees to work through them as a clearing house for cabinet and as an information exchange. As the submissions were often contested, the second was really the only practical option. In those cases the system can only work if ministers are prepared to abide by the rules and if they do not want every battle lost in committee re-fought in the full cabinet. Labor ministers were prepared to live with the system and as a result it probably worked better than any previous one. In particular, the prime minister resisted the temptation to bypass standing committees by creating a series of *ad hoc* committees; the establishment of the *ad hoc* committee on tax is notable because it is exceptional.

The 1987 reorganisation led to a different approach. Since every area of government was now represented in cabinet by a portfolio minister, there was less danger of important views being ignored or forgotten. Less important items no longer needed to come to cabinet; they were to be settled within the portfolio. So there was a distinction drawn between items that were politically significant and those that were routine. Important business was to go directly to cabinet; other submissions went to a general administrative committee where they could be expeditiously considered. Three standing committees – on parliamentary business, expenditure review and legislation – dealt with those issues that cut across portfolios. The security committee covered sensitive issues. Three other committees, called policy development committees, were created to consider particularly intransigent problems that needed constant analysis and review: public service reform, structural adjustment, and social and family policy. They were to develop options and act as working parties. The structural adjustment committee was the most significant as it teased out the implications of microeconomic reform; the public service reform committee barely ever met. Cabinet endorsement of committee decisions was normally a formal process that did not include the re-opening of discussions. The streamlining of the process of cabinet committees, in addition to the reduced number of departments, was quite effective.

Initially, such priorities as were set came from the ERC. It gave ministers financial targets for their portfolio in the May 1985 mini-budget exercise and a series of suggestions as to how these targets could be met; they were designed by the Department of Finance and were drawn up with cost-cutting in mind. ERC targets did not necessarily reflect the cabinet's priorities nor were they designed in those terms. Some ministers thought that as a result they did not follow the directions that the cabinet had chosen (for example, the emphasis to be achieved in the problems of youth). There was therefore some dissatisfaction with the process, even if no alternative schemes were suggested.

The ERC was always significant. The committee was important because it not only included the senior ministers of the Department of Finance and Treasury, but also a number of spending ministers. Officials could attend and on invitation debate with ministers. Those with spending proposals would attend, supported by their officials, and be interviewed. Unsuccessful ministers sometimes sought to blame finance officials, but ministers took the decisions. As Walsh's account illustrates, the exchanges could be rugged. Decisions were generally final. Only one minister appealed to cabinet against an ERC decision – successfully in that case. It did not create a precedent. The ERC was seen as the core of government policy development. Keating chose to cut back the numbers, in theory to increase his own control. But unlike Hawke who frequently chaired the ERC, Keating rarely attended and left the details to his treasurers and finance ministers.

Even then there could be frustrations. Neal Blewett's *Cabinet Diary* is in a sense a constant search for the site of real power within government. Even after he was appointed to the ERC, he did not find there his elusive power location. He gave an example of the process of decision-making. On 6 August 1992 Blewett settled a number of issues in the PMO:

> Gathered in the PM's office were Willis and Dawkins, the PM and an array of key personal and public service officials ... Many of these people have more influence than us ministers. ... My whole experience of ERC confirms my belief that the closer one

> gets to what one thinks is power the more it seems to recede. I have always assumed the critical committee of the government is the ERC; now it is obvious that members of the ERC, apart from the treasurer and the Finance minister, are second-class citizens. None of these second-class participants knows the full extent of the outlays and revenue side, nor do they participate in all the numerous side deals made in the margins of the Committee, and therefore one can never know precisely what the overall balance is ... this shows the inadequacy of the structure; even on the ERC one is never fully clear about the framework within which the budget is being constructed.

Blewett's observation was probably always true and always will be. Final decisions, even in the most collective of governments (as Hawke's was, but Keating's was probably not), require eventual decisions by a few crucial and powerful people. Ministers are often concerned that their influence may be hijacked both by bureaucrats and senior ministerial advisers. Power can never be fully shared.

Collective responsibility and cabinet policy

Appeals to collective responsibility remained common. Yet in the context of the Hawke government, what does the convention mean? The answer was still: whatever the prime minister has decided it should mean. In the Whitlam government the ministers defeated in cabinet were able to appeal to caucus, nominally the final court of appeal in the Labor system of government. The caucus taskforce in 1982 acknowledged that. It considered whether cabinet solidarity should be applied as rigidly to caucus as to the general public and concluded it should not:

> Our grounds ... are that it is inconsistent with the Caucus sovereignty principle embodied in the rules and – perhaps most importantly – is not likely to be thought necessary by anyone if a satisfactory system of progressive Cabinet–Caucus consultation is *in fact implemented.*

The decision to create the inner cabinet changed the situation. At its first meeting it was argued that if the smaller cabinet were to achieve the objective of greater cohesion and discipline, then solidarity had to be maintained by all cabinet ministers all the time. Cabinet ministers were therefore required to defend and vote for cabinet decisions in caucus.

The definition of collective responsibility was then changed by political necessity. Stewart West, Minister for Immigration and Ethnic Affairs, resigned from cabinet because he did not support the government's policy on uranium, but he wanted to remain a member of the ministry. Hawke agreed to the compromise. There was therefore a need to bring the definition of constitutional theory into line with actual practice. So the cabinet office rewrote the principle. The *Cabinet Handbook* declared that non-cabinet ministers were not prevented from debating cabinet decisions in caucus in accordance with their personal views.

Ministers were only bound by cabinet collective responsibility for those decisions for which they were co-opted. Everyone was bound to defend cabinet decisions in public. This relaxed definition of collective responsibility was after 1987 extended to non-cabinet ministers who could debate in caucus cabinet decisions 'in areas apart from their portfolio'.

The consequence of the application of collective responsibility to caucus debate and the development of the faction system was a decline in the influence of caucus. Where divisions between the ministry and the party occurred, they were negotiated between the ministers and faction leaders. There was therefore a reduction in the involvement of caucus as a whole in policymaking. The rambunctious caucus of the Whitlam government was replaced by a carefully controlled exchange of views.

Collective responsibility was also relaxed at national conferences of the Labor Party, where ministers took their factional alignments into disputes about the direction of government policy to the conference floor and argued fiercely about the effectiveness of existing policy. But as conferences became more representative, so they were more fully managed. There were no policy surprises as, in a reversal of traditional Labor theory, party policy was brought into line with government policy.

Constitutional conventions are no more than guidelines to be moulded to circumstances. Maintaining solidarity was simply a good political tactic, but had to be fitted to political realities. The Labor government retained an uneasy co-existence between the concepts of caucus supremacy and collective responsibility. Both doctrines were refined and redefined by political circumstances. Neither could be regarded as absolutes. In both cases what worked became the preferred interpretation and what worked was what was best able to accommodate the pressures created by the faction system.

Prime ministers would constantly plead with ministers to maintain their silence about cabinet activities. Thus when Keating was sworn in, Blewett records that he:

> ... made an eloquent plea for cabinet secrecy. Typically quiet delivery – one strains to hear – quite unlike the Hawke hectoring. The impact of the economic statement will be gravely undermined if details are leaked beforehand. Characterising cabinet solidarity as the essence of our system, the PM appealed for the containment of cabinet discussions. He claimed that cabinet had maintained a good record through the 1980s but deteriorated in the 1990s. He wryly acknowledged that some might argue he is now demanding something that by its very breach had contributed to the destabilising of Hawke, but he urged that the divisions of the past be put behind us.

Others problems were created by the 1987 reshuffle. The division into ministerial tiers raised additional issues. Were non-portfolio ministers expected to tow the line in cabinet with any prearranged policy determined by the group of ministers within a portfolio? Keating, as treasurer, once mocked proposals from Simon Crean for industry assistance. He preferred to do a deal with the senior minister, John Button. So he argued in cabinet that the problem was that:

> ... Simon's not the minister. I mean, we need to have a bit of order. We can't go dropping in proposals in someone else's portfolio. I'm not opposed to helping industry ... But to go around nominating industries, which don't now exist, and being nominated by a minister who is not the Minister, well, it takes the cake.
>
> 'It got a bit heated then', Keating concluded. 'They don't like it getting heated – but it's always like this'.

Cabinet had two fraught debates on whether gays could serve in the military. The first time, the minister, Robert Ray, committed his junior minister, Gordon Bilney, to the official Defence department line, early in the debate. The second time:

> Bilney then came in; his courageous opposition to his boss was a rare, possibly unique, event in ministerial relations over the decade.

Later Blewett records:

> Saw Bilney, who had apparently been castigated by Ray for not supporting the ministry line on gays. Difficult: are junior ministers bound to their seniors on such questions?

The answer to Blewett's question, epitomised by the Ray–Bilney exchange, was never entirely clear.

The prime minister and the working of the cabinet

Hawke was accepted as an excellent chairman. His skills were honed when he was president of the ACTU and had little institutional authority to bolster his position. At trade union meetings, he had only his personality and his skills to support his chairmanship. As prime minister he could have used the several powers of the position to make himself particularly strong in cabinet; but his style led to a different type of cabinet leadership.

His skill was to focus the cabinet debate on essentials and to keep it there. The sponsoring minister opened the discussion; Hawke might then make a comment or directly throw it open to debate. He asked those opposing a proposal whether their objections were due to political or technical difficulties or just to general unease. He listened and worked on the last standing among those opposed until he could reasonably sum up a consensus. He seldom tried to push a decision against a clear view or to sum up his way when a majority were opposed to him. He would avoid pushing ministers into a corner from which they could not escape without embarrassment.

When some prime ministers state their views in cabinet early in a debate, it tends to stifle, if not pre-empt, discussion. Not many ministers were prepared to take on a Thatcher or a Fraser after a determined position had been stated. With Hawke, ministers felt less restricted. One minister acknowledged that, if Hawke were clearly opposed to a proposal, it would be 'harder to win'. Harder, but not impossible or even unusual. Nor was there any suggestion that because the prime minister had stated a view, the debate should end. Hawke's opinions were given great weight, but were not regarded as revealed truth. It is true that on big decisions he was invariably supported by the senior ministers and their views combined would be given precedence; in his turn he generally helped Keating hold the economic line, more certainly when Keating was actually present. But most of the time, since he had been prepared to listen to the views of others, he could be persuaded to change his position.

Hawke therefore played a less dominant role in cabinet than either of his two predecessors. In part this is because of the restrictions that always apply to a Labor prime minister. The Labor party gives less automatic authority to its leader than its conservative opponents; its elected ministers had their power base in the organised factions and therefore did not rely on the prime minister for their existing or future positions. Consultation and collective action are part of the party's tradition.

But in this case, there was also more to it. Hawke was always meticulously briefed on the details of any policy submission, even if he did not always display the knowledge or seem too concerned. He had a general desire for a more cohesive and cooperative society, but there were few specific policy objectives to which he was committed. As long as the general direction of a submission seemed to be right (that is, did not clash with or undermine the Accord or some other principle seen as basic), and as long as it could be sold to the public and would not have obviously unfavourable electoral consequences, Hawke was prepared to leave the recommendations to his colleagues. This meant that some ministers were particularly influential in policy development, both in specific portfolios and in cabinet generally. The other leading figure was Keating as treasurer and faction leader. Leading ministers had at least as much influence on general policy directions as the prime minister. Further, the faction system often determined outcomes in advance.

Hawke was concerned as much, and at times more, with the process of decision-making as he was with the particular outcomes. Generally he was concerned to conciliate, to identify the points of difference and then to reach an agreement. He wanted to ensure that the process was predictable, that ministers were not taken by surprise, and that all the available information was there to assist the process of discussion and decision.

Indeed, this desire for agreement also extended to trying to ensure that there was a consensus about the way things were decided. Procedures were not handed down from above but were discussed. Agreement was sought. This approach explains the predictability and continuity of cabinet procedures under Hawke's leadership. Perhaps this sprang both from his industrial relations background, where conciliation is the point of the exercise and everything else is open to negotiation, and from his personality which attempted to include others in the processes of decision-making.

But not always. As with all prime ministers, there were times when Hawke took decisions outside the cabinet arena and tried to manipulate processes to that end. Some of these decisions were important. The 1987 restructuring of the cabinet and creation of mega-departments was made without widespread discussion. Although the administrative arrangements order has always been the responsibility of the prime minister, this dramatic step was unexpected. The launch of the special premiers conferences in 1990 was another example. Hawke was conscious of the limitations on his capacity to manipulate or ignore cabinet. After cabinet had made decisions about the allocation of channels on the domestic television satellite, Hawke came under pressure from the media proprietors to give them a better deal. He wanted to change the decision, but was not prepared to go back to cabinet because he was not confident he had the numbers. As long as the minister insisted that the cabinet decision be upheld, and Hawke would not try to reverse it there, the prime minister could not change the policy. One observer commented that the 'rules' had replaced the 'senior boys' as the most important factor in cabinet decision-making.

The treasurer, too, was important, both institutionally and personally. A Keating adviser noted:

> A strong minister with an independent support base can avoid, delay or obstruct the development in his portfolio of policies he does not like, even if the prime minister supports them. He can encourage and sometimes advance into cabinet policies to which the prime minister is opposed ... Only the treasurer can bring forward a cabinet submission on the budget or on general economic policy, and by and large all decisions on spending, taxing, and legislative change must be made in and endorsed by cabinet. A successful treasurer needs the support or at worst the neutrality of the prime minister, whose authority in cabinet is signified by his control over the listing of submissions and the agenda of the meeting. But no economic policy can be helped or hindered without the active cooperation of the treasurer.

Most decisions in the Hawke government were therefore collective. For the Labor government that may be fortunate. Many of the politically troublesome decisions were made by Hawke on the run: the holding of the Combe–Ivanov inquiry, the length of the 1984 election campaign, the tax summit, the MX missile commitment, for instance. These were all personal decisions, some made publicly and without consultation. While they might have been exceptional, it seems likely that they would have met opposition if considered by cabinet. Many ministers preferred collective decision-making because, whatever respect they may have had for Hawke's cabinet chairmanship and his ability to sell the government to the public, they had doubts about his political judgment.

Keating saw the role of prime minister and cabinet chairman differently:

> 'I don't like aimless meetings where I sit mum trying to let a consensus develop for fear of showing my hand. That I reject as a style of leadership', he said in a clear swipe at his predecessor's habit of letting Cabinet meetings run for hours while everyone had their say.

But he did not always manage the process well. His adviser, John Edwards, has noted that Keating:

> Had never been a punctual, meticulous person. Some of the requirements of the new job annoyed him. It was important that he be on time for cabinet, for example, because he chaired it and it couldn't begin without him. But he was often late, and often changed the meeting times. In his mind, he was putting substance before procedure. In the minds of his ministers he was simply disorganised.

When he wanted, Keating could get his own way. Once the prime minister had spoken forcefully, observers believed, then the debate was over ('It was his creation and his authority is utterly dominant' wrote a journalist). But in other instances he did not seem to care. Edwards again:

> In his approach to government, except on the issues of pay television and aviation policy, where he was a relentless busybody, he did not often second-guess his ministers. The One Nation statement embraced many of the areas of government, but after it was delivered responsibility went back to ministers and their departments. As a cabinet chairman he elicited all views and as prime minister rarely attacked other ministers during Cabinet meetings in the way he had as treasurer.

Like any prime minister, he could run issues himself. On the republic Kitney claimed:

> So far only a handful of senior ministers are privy to the details of the republic plan and Mr Keating will not take it to Cabinet until just before he releases it. Mr Keating wrote in long hand much of the Cabinet Submission which has been circulated to members of the Cabinet sub-committee on the republic in sealed envelopes and which were returned to Mr Keating after the subcommittee meetings.

Keating pre-empted cabinet on Aboriginal land rights, in effect challenging ministers to take him on. They did not want to. When he announced the break-up and sale of the airports authority, he did not tell cabinet 'irrespective of the fact that the scheme flies in the face of existing party policy'. He and his treasurer only told cabinet about tax increases and the decision to sell the Commonwealth Bank in the hours before they were announced to parliament. The problems occurred when he was uninterested, when he did not want to talk to some of his ministers who bored him, the times when he gave the impression to his advisers that he did not seem to want the job he had always coveted.

Conclusions

The Hawke cabinet should be, in some respects, the delight of constitutional theorists. If its eccentric interpretation of the convention of collective responsibility was excluded, it more readily fitted models of Westminster cabinets than many of its predecessors. It worked as a cabinet, with collective decision-making, established and predictable procedures, and the development of a consensus. It ran into problems where, outside the cabinet system, disputes between the factions led to the public image of a divided government.

Further, Hawke in cabinet fits the norm of what many commentators would like to argue is a proper job description for a prime minister. He acted as chairman, publicist, troubleshooter and, at times, guardian of the central strategy of government (that is, the Accord). He was personally involved in detail in only a few areas of policy. Hawke's personality and the political fortunes of the government both allowed this style to develop. Blewett summed it up:

> Some commentators have seen this formal picture of the Cabinet under Hawke as an almost ideal prime ministerial/cabinet relationship. Yet the picture needs qualification. At the heart of government there were a group of hard men, who along with the prime minister provided the engine room of government. They were mostly members of the Expenditure Review Committee, the most powerful committee in the government; it was a kind of inner cabinet, possessed of superior knowledge, which vetted all expenditure and prepared the Budget ...
>
> Hawke's style of management was characterised by a prime ministerial concentration on a few major strategic concerns, while leaving vast swathes of governmental policy making to individual ministers ... Ministers were generally on a light rein, neither the prime minister nor his department seeking to involve themselves in policy making, provided it was not an area in which the prime minister was intimately involved or that was central to the government's survival.

In discussion with foreign affairs minister Gareth Evans, Blewett noted:

> We agreed that Hawke's combination of talents was unique: a passion for bureaucracy and an amazing populist appeal – a physical rather than an intellectual charisma, visceral rather than mental. Usually the bureaucratic politician lacks charisma and the charismatic is normally sloppy and accident-prone. Not so Hawke. His bureaucratic application contrasted strongly with the ebullient, if often infuriating, idealism of Whitlam and with Keating, who has a real disdain for bureaucracy and bureaucrats, a fact reflected in the confusion surrounding governmental processes at the moment. Evans sees this as an intellectual failure, for Gareth's passion for order is offended by the slipshod approach of the PM to the political process. I disagreed.

Cabinet structures remained in place because of widespread ministerial commitment to them; at least, if the decisions of the government were seen to be wrong, no-one was blaming the cabinet structures in the early Hawke years. The system allowed discussion and calculated decision.

Effective cabinet procedures do not in themselves make governments successful. Nor can it be argued that there is only one set of arrangements that could be adopted; obviously there is a variety of possible packages that could make the machinery of government work smoothly. But, given the stresses of decision-making in modern government, exacerbated in the case of the Labor government by the activities of the institutionalised faction system, it can be argued that a predictable, consultative cabinet of Hawke was a necessary component of a successful Labor government – necessary, but by itself not sufficient.

10 DISCIPLINE AND CONTROL: 1996–2006

Howard came to office determined to avoid the errors of the last coalition government. His experience of office under Fraser had made him sceptical of the frenetic pace. He wanted to ensure that the cabinet was able to combine the political and the policy perspectives, and to maintain control of the public agenda. Indeed, 'controlled' is a good description of cabinet in his time as prime minister. Cabinet has usually remained united, leak proof and on-song. The ministers reveal few divisions (except of the timing of any succession) in terms of personalities or message. Howard can be both dominant and collective, locking in support through collective debate in cabinet or its surrounds.

Howard has behaved with an ever-increasing sureness as he has grown into the role. By 2006 he was, like Menzies in his later years, a generation older, and infinitely more experienced, than most of his ministerial colleagues. Like Menzies, too, he had been written off, but doggedly fought on until the party returned in appreciation of the value of his experience. In government he was often courageous: fighting an election on the goods and services tax (GST) when the traditional orthodoxy was that no-one could win advocating a new tax; joining the coalition of the willing in Iraq in 2002–03, even though the polls suggested that public opinion opposed such a move. He could equally be cynically opportunistic, squeezing maximum political benefit from Tampa and the children overboard stories.

It is hard to provide clear descriptions of current practices under the Howard government. Governments are often defined by their ends, by the last sight that they provide. Invariably it is a government, or at least a prime minister, in defeat. Further, we do not yet have any inside accounts of the government by former ministers or advisers that provide a portrait of the Howard cabinet in action. That is not surprising, partly because traditionally Liberal ministers have been less inclined to write memoirs, but also because party loyalty may restrain any wish they have to tell that story. Indeed little, by the press or anyone else, has been written of the way that the Howard cabinet is run. What is available suggests that, underpinning his government's record of success, lay a highly professional government: well led, well managed, tight and controlled.

Making cabinets

Howard selected his cabinet with some caution. There were few initial surprises, and reshuffles were undertaken only rarely and then not radically. His principal lieutenants, the treasurer and the minister for foreign affairs, were still there after ten years in government. But gradual change can bring extensive renewal over a decade; only four cabinet ministers survived that first decade, and one of them, Amanda Vanstone, had done a stint in the outer ministry before she was restored to cabinet. Almost no senior cabinet ministers were axed without a soft landing, either directly into a diplomatic post or after a short period away from parliament. When they left voluntarily (perhaps often after encouragement), it was to retirement from parliament; none were left to smoulder on the backbench.

Usually cabinet ministers served an apprenticeship in the outer ministry. There the rules were different. The successful were later promoted; some seemed to be stuck at that level; others failed and were dumped to the backbenches, with a great future lost behind them. The latter were little more than an itch; usually they were quiet. One or two, notably Brendon Nelson and Kay Patterson, were put straight into cabinet, from where one eventually was elevated through promotion while the other exited into retirement. Such a jump straight into cabinet was rare; in 2006 the two star recruits, Andrew Robb and Malcolm Turnbull, were required to earn their promotion by starting as parliamentary secretaries.

Just after his election Howard released a set of guidelines on ministerial conduct. The product of work that had been undertaken in PM&C, they contained some stringent requirements both in respect to personal behaviour and private interest. In the first three years of his government, several ministers were found to be in breach of the guidelines, either because of share holdings or because they were seen to have rorted the system of ministerial travel expenses. Howard secured their resignations. The initial impression was of a government in constant crisis. Thereafter Howard chose to tough out any ministerial crisis; the cost of a few days of heightened awareness of ministerial shortcomings is far less than a remembered record for ministerial instability. According to Paul Kelly:

> Howard's working rule of ministerial responsibility ... is that ministers, in effect are responsible not to the parliament or to the party but to the prime minister. The test Howard applies or rationalises is that of ministerial responsibility to the people with the prime minister interpreting the public will.
>
> In practice Howard is loath to remove a minister for policy or administrative reasons, a judgment dictated by his political experience. The upshot is that Howard's working rule is that ministers should go only 'if they are directly responsible for significant failings or mistakes or if their continued presence in the government is damaging'.

That approach is reflected in the attitude to ministerial responsibility that has developed. Ministers are responsible only if they know about a problem. When there were critical reports about the administration of the Department of Immigration and Ethnic Affairs, both the incumbent minister, and the minister from the time under criticism, simply declared they had no intention of resigning. The former minister did not know about the problems and the incumbent was seeking to fix them. Neither believed that they could reasonably have known about the detailed incidents. The prime minister agreed; they stayed. Kelly suggests that 'a literal reading of this example – that ministers cannot be held to account for decisions that are made by their officials – would suggest that Australia has completed a precise reversal of the classical theory that ministers are responsible for their departments'. Yet there is nothing new or surprising in the ministerial reactions; they just followed 100 years of precedent.

Two problems associated with cabinet were in effect continuing. The first was leadership succession. The treasurer and Liberal party deputy, Peter Costello, wanted to be prime minister and, like Keating before him, thought that he should have his turn. Howard, like Hawke, enjoyed the job, believed he was doing it well and had no intention of giving it up while he thought he could still win elections. Unlike Hawke, Howard's poll ratings stayed high and few doubted that Howard could win again if he chose. He stated that he would re-think after his 65th birthday; well before then, he announced he would stay on 'as long as the party wanted him to'. Unlike Keating, Costello did not have the support on the backbench to take the position by force, nor was he prepared to destabilise the government by launching a doomed challenge as a first step to a later triumph. Consequently, there may be a number of Costello supporters on the backbench waiting for a change of leadership and the chance of a ministry. They may hope that the hand-over will be soon and smooth, but they have never had the numbers in the party room.

The second enduring cabinet 'issue' was maintaining the coalition. The National party was losing numbers. In the decade of the Howard government it had three leaders and had to repel the Pauline Hanson insurgency in its territory. None of the leaders had the clout or public weight of a McEwen or an Anthony. There seemed to be little difference between the parties in policy terms, although the National party retained the capacity to pork barrel through its regional portfolio. When a National senator switched sides in 2006, the prime minister was able to justify, through the brute force of the arithmetic, his decision to strip one ministry from the Nationals. Noisy, and very occasionally rebellious, National senators held the balance of power in the Senate and thus a capacity to hold the government to ransom, but within cabinet, the Liberals appear to dominate. There were none of the battles of the early 1950s to threaten the coalition. It has remained strong under Howard's direction.

Preparing for cabinet

The rules of cabinet under Howard have broadly continued the pattern of previous years. One initiative was the development of a computer system on which cabinet submissions were prepared and circulated. 'CABNET' allows drafts to be circulated on the secure ministerial communications network that links all departments and ministers' offices. While submissions are in draft, the network is also used to collect coordination comments or reactions from other departments. The cover sheet has to be filled within a template. It is not expandable, so those drafting the submission have to keep to the prescribed limits for the covering summary information because they cannot add further words. Automation through CABNET has thus provided a neat mechanical means of disciplining departments without any overt exercise of authority that had earlier been necessary.

The cabinet secretariat has also had some success under Howard, with the support of the PMO, in enforcing rules in length and content that apply to submissions and their attachments (even if the latter can still be large). Submissions have a number of impact statements that have to be included: on regions, small business and families. While ministers can access the draft, only the cabinet office can circulate the official submission and thus include it on the list of final documents ready for cabinet discussion. Before that occurs there has to be agreement with the Department of Finance; on the rare occasion when there is no agreement, finance's figures are included in the submission. This is perhaps the strongest instance of the cabinet office continuing to ensure, on traditional terms, that the 'facts' are agreed to, to avoid fights in cabinet on those details and to identify the important issues that ministers had to decide.

Howard made two crucial appointments immediately. As secretary to his department he chose Max Moore-Wilton, a no-nonsense public servant with a brutal reputation, reflected in his nickname of Max the Axe. Howard also appointed a cabinet secretary who was explicitly partisan. The appointee worked from the PMO in parliament house, with an office just outside the cabinet room, and was meant to provide a political input. In effect he took over some responsibilities in the cabinet suite from the former head of the PMO and some from the secretary of the PM&C. Much of the planning of the agenda is determined by the cabinet secretary; he can decide when the submissions are ready for discussion by cabinet and if the facts are suitably agreed. As necessary, he can deal with ministers, while the secretary of the PM&C interacts with departmental secretaries. The cabinet secretary provides both a political and a policy focus; he can also brief the PMO on the cabinet outcomes.

As every cabinet before it, the Howard government sought a way of restricting the items that came to cabinet to those that needed attention. In 2002 Howard introduced a ten-day submission process. Submissions that by the rules required cabinet approval but were unlikely to be contentious were, with his approval, circulated to ministers. Those ministers with an interest could negotiate with the sponsoring minister and meet some agreed outcome. These submissions often tended to deal with more technical issues. As long as everyone was satisfied, the submissions under this procedure were then approved in a bunch at the next cabinet. There were seldom any problems and up to 20 per cent of the business could be dealt with this way. The process did allow a greater focus. Whereas previously it had been difficult to forecast precisely what would create debate, and therefore ministers had to be prepared to discuss everything on the agenda, now, with the less controversial matters managed under the ten-day rules, most submissions on the agenda would generate debate.

Under-the-line items became more formal. They might not require a full submission, but could be circulated in advance on CABNET. What is included is up to the cabinet secretary who consults with the prime minister as necessary. Ministers deal with the cabinet secretary, rather than the prime minister, and thus do not clutter his diary. The rushed nature of such items still leaves some concern that all the implications are not always explored.

A cabinet agenda typically includes 20 to 30 appointments, two to three under-the-line items and eight submissions. Cabinet meets usually three times a month, about 30 to 35 times a year. Cabinet ministers are instructed that cabinet takes priority over all other functions; non-cabinet ministers may be co-opted for discussion of any item they bring forward themselves and for items in which they have a direct portfolio interest. Officials occasionally attend to provide information that the cabinet needs, but this is uncommon, occurring three or four times a year.

There are two officials operating as notetakers in cabinet, in addition to the cabinet secretary. They are the head of the cabinet division secretariat and one person from the functional division of the PM&C. The latter writes the first draft of a decision if cabinet varies the recommendations of the minister in the submission. The cabinet secretary signs off for circulation. The secretary of the department attends and particularly takes notes of those issues that need action; he can also involve himself in the drafting of minutes to the extent he considers necessary in any case. Ninety per cent of decisions are circulated within 24 hours through the CABNET system; it is rare for a decision not to be released in less than 48 hours. Decisions routinely go to all ministers; they may be restricted to cabinet and on a rare occasion to action ministers only.

Use of committees

Part of the business of the Howard cabinet is dealt with through three principal committees: the national security committee (NSC), the expenditure review committee (ERC) and the parliamentary business committee. In all three of these there is extensive interaction between ministers and officials, as also happens in the other committees occasionally used by Howard for cabinet consideration of specific issues, such as the implementation of the GST and the development of an energy statement.

Two of the three principal committees serve to keep large volumes of routine, but important business under ministerial control – yet away from the main cabinet. The parliamentary business committee plans the parliamentary timetable and oversees the passage of legislation. The parliamentary secretary to the prime minister usually represents him there.

The ERC carried on the procedures established under earlier governments for detailed formulation of budget spending measures. Although serviced as a cabinet committee by the staff of the PM&C, its agenda papers, Department of Finance 'greens', summarise and comment on ministers' spending proposals and sometimes propose where cuts in expenditure are possible. At the ERC, officials can contribute to discussion, although it is clear that the final say lies with ministers.

The most interesting and new committee has been the NSC, sometimes referred to as Howard's pride and joy. He has called it 'the most effective whole of government arrangement with which I've been associated as prime minister'. It has given him 'a much stronger grip on the details of defence and security policy' and, in effect, is a mini-cabinet that deals with national security policy. Except on rare occasions where Howard may wish to have a full cabinet discussion of an issue before the NSC, the committee's decisions stand on their own as cabinet decisions, unlike those of the ERC, which are referred to a 'budget cabinet' meeting for final discussion and ratification.

Most cabinets had a committee for security and intelligence, and for foreign affairs. Howard collected these issues into the one powerful committee of senior ministers and included discussion of defence, security, intelligence and a number of foreign affairs issues. Senior officials – the chief of defence force, secretaries of defence, prime minister and cabinet, foreign affairs, the head of the Office of National Assessments and ASIO – will attend all meetings; the ministers sit on one side of the table, the officials on the other. The heads of the Australian Federal Police, Department of Finance and other organisations will attend as required. The proceedings are informal; all contribute and officials do not have to wait to be asked if they have something to say. If there is a crisis, the NSC meets as often as required. During the East Timor peacekeeping operation and the initial stages of the Iraq War, it would generally meet daily and often more than once a day.

The NSC is serviced by an officials committee, the Secretaries Committee on National Security (SCONS), consisting of the heads of departments and agencies who attend the NSC and a few other agency heads. The role of the officials committee is to ensure that potential items are ready for discussion by ministers. It meets monthly to process submissions before they go to the NSC for decision.

The Howard government often managed other sensitive issues through taskforces that gather for the issue and are then disbanded. At the higher end of this activity there may be direct interaction with cabinet. Thus there was a taskforce on 'welfare to work' that prepared a report for cabinet consideration and then disbanded. Officials were seconded to the PM&C where they were required to forget for the time being their departmental affiliations and interests. A taskforce on indigenous affairs oversee initiatives and the formulation of budget bids for the ERC in this area, reporting periodically to a ministerial committee rather than cabinet.

Politics and strategic planning

The Howard cabinet has a range of mechanisms for trying to get above the daily grind. Howard was conscious of the problems faced by the Fraser government as it felt overwhelmed by an avalanche of paper. He meets the leadership group of senior ministers almost on a daily basis to discuss political issues, but this group does not vet cabinet business. Each cabinet meeting begins with a political discussion, held in the absence of notetakers. How long it lasts depends on the issues and the prime minister.

Each November there will be a meeting of the prime minister, deputy prime minister, treasurer and minister for finance, called in the budget process 'the senior ministers' meeting', to discuss likely priorities for the government. They are likely to determine the priorities for the budget and to provide parameters for the ERC's deliberations. They will ration budget bids and narrow the range of items to be pursued.

Since 2002 cabinet aimed to have an annual strategy meeting; it can be held as part of a two-day meeting, with the second day taken up by a routine meeting of cabinet. The purpose is to 'consider the major strategic issues facing the government in the medium and long term context'. These meetings do not consider formal submissions, although there may be background papers provided. There are occasional presentations, sometimes in PowerPoint, to address substantial topics such as the treasurer's intergenerational report and the deputy prime minister on transport infrastructure. In July 2002 cabinet endorsed nine 'strategic priorities', which were then announced by the prime minister.

Outsiders such as the chief of defence force or governor of the Reserve Bank may be brought in to address the cabinet on specialised topics. The purpose is to allow full and open discussions without being restricted by the format and demands of specific decision-making. No policy decisions are made there, but cabinet may decide to commission work. The cabinet secretary, as a partisan appointment, may be there throughout, and the secretary of the PM&C for policy-oriented discussions. The three meetings a year of the ministry seem to be more to encourage the troops than to make significant decisions, but they do provide a forum for discussion of the broad political approach and position of the government. PM&C officials do not attend these meetings, but the cabinet secretary does.

All these discussions are reflected in the charter letters that Howard sends to his ministers after they are appointed. The letters, which follow a practice initiated by Hawke after the 1987 move to the system of senior and junior portfolios, set out the prime minister's expectations of the ministers, both of them as individuals and as ministers. The letter would emphasise the electoral commitments, list the prime minister's priorities, explain what should be accomplished, and delineate the demarcation between senior and junior ministers. The 2004 letter emphasised the need for whole-of-government activity to achieve the government's objectives. Ministers take the letters seriously and respond with their plans of action. But so far there is little follow-up. It is possible that the charter letters will become annual events, with ministers required to report progress each year against the previous charter letter.

Running cabinet

Howard entered cabinet determined to 'run a proper cabinet system'. As Kelly describes it:

> The process is formalised and disciplined; meetings are scheduled well ahead. Howard, unlike Keating, is punctual and starts on time. Unlike Fraser, he doesn't call cabinet at short notice or late at night, nor prolong debate to physical exhaustion. Howard is civil; he rarely personalises issues or abuses people. Howard has a business-like approach. He wants people to have their say, but he doesn't want ministers imprisoned in the cabinet room.

Since 2002 Howard has provided time at the beginning of each cabinet meeting 'specifically to consider broader strategic issues'. That discussion may be brief, perhaps no more than ten minutes, but it adds to the pressure for consideration of the formal agenda. Some critics have suggested that strategy often 'descends into a discussion of the polls and a rumination on how the government is "travelling"'. Notetakers will be absent from this part of the cabinet; but the cabinet secretary usually stays in the room.

Meetings last usually from two to four hours from 10 a.m. to 12.30 p.m., or from 4 p.m. to 7 p.m. There are rarely marathon sessions; if a meeting lasts longer, the prime minister is likely to reschedule the items. Yet, even though the system is designed to keep less significant business away from cabinet, there is a still a relentlessness, and almost inevitability, about the demands for discussion and decision.

Non-portfolio ministers stay in the cabinet only for the item in which they have an interest. If they bring an item, there is a preference that cabinet ministers have agreed with it in advance. When the chemistry between senior and junior ministers works, the process can be smooth. Where the two do not get on, or where they work across parties, the senior minister may become nervous. But since the prime minister gets irritated when the two do not talk, the onus is on them not to show their differences in cabinet.

The cabinet secretariat prepares anticipatory minutes in advance of the meeting, based on the minister's recommendations. If cabinet's decision diverged from them, the junior notetaker will write the initial decision, with the cabinet secretary signing off on the final version. He can, if wanted, clear it with the prime minister, but that is not often required. Ninety per cent of decisions are circulated within 24 hours.

Support for the prime minister and cabinet

Howard believes that a multiple supply of contested advice is useful.

> Ministers obtain advice from within their own offices, government initiated reviews and inquiries and, in increasingly sophisticated ways, external sources such as interest groups, industry bodies and lobbyists. This is a positive and healthy development.

The prime minister now gets support from three sources: his department, his office and the new cabinet secretary.

The cabinet policy unit (CPU), based in the PMO, not in the department, and headed by the cabinet secretary, is charged, *inter alia*, with:

* retaining a clear strategic focus to cabinet's work
* settling lesser order issues between ministers in a way that is transparent and only requires cabinet discussion where there is disagreement
* consulting departments in the development of papers for cabinet's consideration
* avoiding disputes about facts or opinions that have not been analysed prior to going to cabinet
* ensuring the cabinet's decisions are carried through expeditiously and effectively.

A former cabinet secretary argued that its purpose was 'to really strengthen the capacity of cabinet to identify where the long-term strategic challenges were for Australia and where were the areas where we wanted to really focus our effort'. That required a 'very structured, formal organised system for looking at long-term issues' if they were not to get lost in the daily rush. The Unit is however small and is designed for thinking, not daily management.

The department of prime minister and cabinet continues to maintain both a policy initiation and a coordinating role. Its structure reflects the main policy arenas of government: security, economic, social policy and international relations. It continues to be seen as the route to the top for ambitious public servants. It services government and its committees. Workloads up to 2004/05 are provided in Table 10.1. The large jump in NSC business coincided with the Iraq War.

TABLE 10.1   PM&C workloads

Activity	2001–02	2002–03	2003–04	2004–05
Briefings	3000	4000	3000	6200
Cabinet meetings (including committees)	48	71	70	57
Cabinet submissions (decisions)	315	440	379	302
NSC/SCNS meetings	28	64	32	22
NSC/SCNS documents	174	250	206	150

PM&C also leads initiatives to drive whole-of-government solutions; several secretaries have spent a term in the PM&C as deputies; grooming these officials for future roles is one, but only one, of the reasons for their selection there in the first place. The meetings of secretaries are held more often than in earlier decades and with greater expectations of some common initiatives.

In late 2003 the secretary of the PM&C, with the prime minister's support, created the cabinet implementation unit within the non-partisan cabinet secretariat (in contrast to the CPU) in his department. With up to ten staff, its role is to oversee implementation of cabinet's decisions. Based on the United Kingdom cabinet delivery unit, it is tasked with both ensuring strategic planing and a retrospective function to monitor and report on delivery. It relies on reports from departments, which it checks with the policy divisions of the PM&C and uses a 'traffic light' warning system to report against agreed milestones. It can also review existing areas of policy 'to inform government of the extent to which policies or programs have been delivered as intended, and distil essential lessons from the implementation approach adopted'.

The cabinet implementation unit works on the basis that cabinet can act as a 'governing board with regular reports on organisational performance'. It provides quarterly reports initially to the prime minister, but these are then distributed to cabinet ministers for consideration at the next available cabinet meeting. Cabinet can discuss problems identified with implementation. The unit may also choose to look closely at items that appear problematic, both to expedite corrective action and to draw out lessons from their implementation. As many as eight to ten items per quarter may attract that sort of attention.

The third unit supporting Howard and beefed up by him was the PMO, which now has 37 staff (up from 23 for Fraser, and 30 under Keating). As well as other political and policy development activities, the PMO assists the prime minister to prepare for cabinet, working with ministers and advisers on those policy and political aspects that are of concern to him. The core personnel in the PMO have remained fairly stable for much of Howard's term of office. His chief of staff, Arthur Sinodonis, has been there for Howard's whole term of office, initially as an economic adviser. Others have served for long periods; a fact that suggests a degree of satisfaction among those who work for him there. Howard appointed a parliamentary secretary to assist with cabinet and legislative business.

Combined, the staff of the PMO have an extensive capacity to brief the prime minister or access necessary material. Sometimes, as a big issue is beginning to emerge, they may develop a PowerPoint presentation so that, over a lengthy meeting of 90 minutes, they can make him aware of all the ramifications that will have to be managed. The prime minister will distinguish between the expectations he has of his political advisers and officials.

Howard as prime minister

Howard's dominance of the political scene is not based on an absence of cabinet discussion of big topics. He has several advantages that help give him control. He has served in cabinet longer than any colleague and has greater experience of those issues that recur. As prime minister for more than a decade, he can feel comfortable; there is none of the nervousness of the early year or so. He is interested in maintaining oversight of the delivery of services and that requires knowledge of what is going on. He is also interested in whole-of-government solutions that have to be driven from the centre. Add to these ideas the pressure created by additional demands for security and it is easy to see why so much is controlled from the PMO.

Howard does not, however, seek to do it all. His belief in the constant campaign means that he is constantly listening, constantly arguing. Cabinet discussions are suffused with political calculations; ministers have their say and may run their own empires. Senior ministers are frequently consulted. But eventually, working through cabinet, tying in his colleagues, Howard can set the direction and the tone of policy. He criticised the Fraser cabinet because it was too concerned with policy outcomes and did not pay attention to the political consequences. Howard has sought to redress that balance. He runs a tight and effective government through cabinet and collective processes.

PART 2

THE CABINET SYSTEM

11 CABINET, PARTY AND PARLIAMENT: THE THREADS OF ACCOUNTABILITY

Cabinet government is party government. Where the Constitution is vague or silent, parties fill the void. Cabinets are based on the continued support of the party in the House of Representatives. Ministers hold their position by virtue of their membership of parliament that in turn depends on their party nominations. Cabinet is, in practice if not in constitutional theory, accountable to the meeting of the parliamentary party. The MPs in Australia elect the party leader, and hence the prime minister, and can, if circumstances are dire, remove the leader speedily, if rarely without trauma.

Constitutionally, Australia may have a system of responsible government. In practice that system has better been described as responsible party government. Ministers are more accountable to the prime minister and to the party than to the parliament. Collective responsibility is as much a convention of political survival as of constitutional necessity. Bagehot's 'buckle that binds' ties the cabinet to the party, far more directly than to the parliament.

This chapter puts the institution of cabinet within the political context of party and parliament. It seeks to show how the foundations of the cabinet system rely on the ability of parties to recruit MPs capable of holding ministerial office and how the discipline of the party provides the cohesion that allows decisions made in cabinet to receive support outside. The chapter sets the principles of ministerial and collective responsibility within the reality of practical politics. It contrasts that understanding with those who see in the principles more fundamental constitutional truths.

Electing and dismissing leaders

Prime ministers hold office because they are party leaders. Party leaders are elected by their parliamentary peers: by the members of the Labor caucus or Liberal parliamentary party. That tradition was established by the time of federation. Watson was elected in 1901, Deakin by the newly combined parties in 1909. Cook beat a disappointed Sir John Forrest for the Liberal leadership when Deakin retired in 1913. Those three contests, all conducted in opposition, set the precedent. The transition in leadership is rarely uncontested, and even then usually after considerable behind-the-scenes negotiation.

Usually, prime ministers leave office after the defeat of their party at the polls. They resign and propose that the successful leader of the opposition be asked to form a government. If the three caretaker prime ministers, installed after the death of the incumbent while the party elected a new leader, are excluded, altogether there have been ten changes of prime minister *without* the defeat of the reigning party, from 1903 to 1991. Three were caused by death (1939 – Lyons; 1945 – Curtin; 1967 – Holt). Only three of the others could be described as choice, where the prime minister decided to stand down (1903 – Barton; 1915 – Fisher; 1966 – Menzies). The other four prime ministerial changes (1923 – Hughes; 1941 – Menzies; 1971 – Gorton; 1991 – Hawke) were brought about by party revolt or coalition pressure.

On nine occasions (1915, 1923, 1939, 1941, 1945, 1966, 1968, 1971 and 1991) the party knew that, in choosing a leader, either to a vacancy or by deposing an incumbent, they were choosing a prime minister. Sometimes the contest was tough. In 1939, after Lyons's death, four candidates addressed the UAP meeting. Each candidate spoke for 30 minutes, before Menzies was elected to the leadership and thus the prime minister's position. In 1945 Chifley easily beat Evatt and Forde after Curtin died. In 1966 there was a long, hard-fought battle between Hasluck and Gorton when Holt drowned; in that case the leader of the Country party had vetoed the appointment of McMahon. In so doing he followed the example of Page who declared in 1939 that the Country party would not serve under Menzies. The UAP ignored him and elected Menzies anyway, leading to a minority government until the Country party in turn dumped Page as leader and re-entered a coalition. In 1971 McMahon won a sudden ballot after the prime minister had been voted out by the party room. In 1991 Keating defeated Hawke for the leadership and the prime ministership in the second round six months after his initial challenge. By contrast, on the only three occasions when the prime minister resigned as a matter of choice, their successors were chosen without a contest. Deakin followed Barton. In 1916 Hughes was elected leader unopposed, as was Holt in 1966. They were the obvious candidates. The governor-generals commissioned whoever the largest party chose.

There is a reverse side to the ability to choose a leader. Those who elect can also dismiss. As long as the eligible constituency remains limited to the parliamentary party and there are no rules that prevent a 'spill' of the leadership occurring when the members wish, prime ministers are always on notice. In Australia those conditions still apply. That power of dismissal has been used on occasion. Gorton was challenged in the party room after he had won the 1969 election and again 15 months later. On the second occasion the vote was a tie; he then declared he was using his casting vote against himself and resigned the leadership and the prime ministership. He did not stand for the leadership, though perversely he was elected as deputy leader. Whether he has a casting vote was not clear, and no-one was prepared to ask. He could barely have continued in office with half the party against him.

In 1982 Fraser was challenged by Peacock and managed to win by a margin of two to one. Hawke was twice challenged by Keating; the first time Hawke won two-thirds of the vote, but the instability continued. Six months later Keating won narrowly. For a challenger, a narrow win was enough and the regime changed. No-one ever talked about going back.

Coalitions can create problems for prime ministers, too. In 1923 the Country party refused to enter a coalition under Hughes. Hughes almost certainly would have maintained control of the Nationalist vote if he had retained an overall parliamentary majority. Eventually, after extensive negotiations the Nationalists conceded and Bruce followed Hughes as leader and prime minister. When Page tried again in 1939 to exercise the veto, the UAP preferred to go into minority government. In 1941 two factions demanded Menzies' departure: Country party ministers and a group of dissident UAP members. Menzies had lengthy discussion in cabinet, initially with all the ministers and then only with those from the UAP. When it was obvious that his support was limited, even among ministers from his own party, he announced his resignation to the party room. The joint parties then elected Fadden as prime minister.

All these shenanigans were intra-party, or at least intra-coalition. They were the sign of broad discontent with the state of the leadership. Whenever a prime minister has to seek a vote of confidence or a confirmation of his leadership, he is clearly in trouble. The only occasion when there was a change of party without a change in the status of prime minister was in 1916 when Hughes, faced with a vote of no-confidence that would have surely been passed, led half his caucus out of the Labor party to form a National Labor minority government. It lasted only a few months with the support of the Opposition before Hughes and Opposition leader Cook combined to form the Nationalist Party and returned with a clear majority. In that case Hughes had the commission to form a government and was able to advise the Governor-General that he should be invited to re-constitute his government without Labor ministers who had stuck with the party.

Only two prime ministers have held the party leadership, lost it, and then staged a revival to reach the top. That requires determination, self-confidence and staying power. The two are Menzies, who was dumped in 1941 as prime minister and then as party leader, and then reconstructed the Liberal party after 1944; and John Howard, who contested one election as opposition leader and saw three other candidates become party leader before the Liberals turned back to him. Menzies is the only prime minister since 1915 to have two separate terms as prime minister. It may be no coincidence Menzies and Howard are also the two longest serving prime ministers. As a general rule, politics is unforgiving of failure, or even the likelihood of failure.

Cabinet's relations with prime ministers are crucial to the way that it is organised. The cabinet contains the prime minister's successors, even rivals. If a core of ministers believes that the prime minister should go, as they did in 1941, 1971 and 1991, then the prime minister is quickly undermined. The prime minister knows that the potential sanction of sacking the disloyal is hard to exercise, for they will be on the backbenches where they can conspire without limit to bring on a spill of positions. As a result, prime ministers generally like to keep their main rivals close and restricted in what they can say by imposing collective responsibility and the limitations of a ministerial portfolio. Cabinet therefore has to be respected as a group, or dominated by force of personality. Cabinet cannot be ignored because a prime minister who loses the support of ministers is vulnerable to a spill in the party room. There is no need for formal notice for a spill; although whenever one is planned, everyone usually knows.

So, too, prime ministers must pay attention to the party and the party meetings; they are electors of prime ministers and they know it. Prime ministers and their ministers are accountable to their parliamentary party for their performance. Party meetings thus have a special significance. Prime ministers know it and usually behave accordingly.

Who are the ministers?

All ministers are members of a party and elected under that banner. By 1901 parties had taken sufficient hold on the electorate that few independents were elected and none of them have been included in the cabinet. With the single exception of the inclusion of Higgins as attorney-general in the Watson government, no Labor cabinet has included anyone not elected for the Labor party. In non-Labor politics there have been a variety of coalitions, with Nationalists and with the Country party, but again independents were not selected.

The first Australian cabinet had just nine ministers, two of whom were without portfolio. By the end of World War 1, there were ten; again two of them had no departmental responsibility. In 1939 there were 11 ministers with departments, and a further five appointed to assist nominated ministers. War increased individual ministerial responsibilities. Defence was divided into three services departments (navy, army and air) and new departments were created for areas such as munitions, aircraft production, war organisation of industry and home security. By the fall of the Menzies government in 1941 there were 19 ministers.

After Menzies split the ministry into cabinet and non-cabinet ministers, cabinet only contained 12 ministers, with ten outside the cabinet in 1956. That number has gradually increased. The balance between the two types of ministers changed from time to time. The Whitlam government abolished the distinction, with all its 27 ministers in cabinet, but the experience there proved how unworkable such a body was for good decision-making. Instead, the distinction allowed a gradual growth of outer ministers, even if for a time there was a perceived need to create skeleton departments such as the department of the special trade representative or the vice-president of the executive council, because of the belief that to satisfy the Constitution every minister had to have a department to 'administer'.

The change in constitutional interpretation in 1987 released the prime minister from that institutional straitjacket. Hawke was advised that more than one minister could be appointed to administer the same department, as long as the terms of appointment did not declare that one was in charge of the other. That problem was solved by the development of 'charter letters', in which the prime minister spelt out the expectations he had of each minister. The letters explained which minister was in charge and what the lines of accountability were. It would also delineate the precise duties of the non-portfolio ministers. Portfolio ministers were in cabinet and were expected to represent the whole portfolio for which they were responsible. The development of tiers of ministers allowed the number to increase without visible political pain. Of course, for the prime minister, the growth in ministerial positions increased the available patronage and also provided a number of soft positions for the loyal, but not massively talented, ministers who would never reach cabinet rank.

The Australian Constitution allows ministers who are not yet members of parliament to be sworn in as ministers, as long as they gain a seat within three months. That clause has only been used once since 1901, when John Gorton was shifting from the Senate to the House of Representatives. He remained prime minister while he was running for election. On occasion, newly elected members may go straight into the cabinet or ministry: Lyons in 1929, Menzies in 1934, Crean in 1990, Fahey in 1996; in each case they already had had distinguished careers in state politics or the labour movement. In the first two cases, the transfer from one forum to the other was accepted on condition of advancement. Ministers must first have proved themselves within the party: first to win pre-selection for a seat and then the seat itself, and usually thereafter within the parliament. Party recognition is the prerequisite to office.

In the Labor party, the caucus (the parliamentary Labor party) elects the ministers. Watson was given a free hand in 1904 but even then he consulted with his senior colleagues. In 1906 the Labor interstate conference determined that all future Labor cabinets would be elected. Watson strongly objected, believing that the resolution indicated a lack of trust in the leader. Nevertheless, the principle was accepted. As a consequence, all Labor prime ministers have had to live with ministers that they would not have chosen, if given a free hand.

Labor ministry elections were not always predictable. While prime ministers may have their preferences, they did not always prevail. Hughes asked caucus to elect only one minister to replace Fisher after he had been elected to the prime ministership unopposed. Caucus still decided to spill all the positions, with the newly elected (and those defeated) becoming a constant source of bitterness and discontent in the next year. Scullin did not have all his supporters chosen in 1929, with Curtin missing out, the last man eliminated. Curtin himself had to accept Calwell when he was elected in 1943, despite longstanding antagonisms and accusations of apostasy earlier that year. Whitlam could not get his preferred minister for Aboriginal affairs into the ministry in 1972, even with the political prestige of being the first

Labor prime minister in 23 years. After the development of the national factions in the 1980s, there was less unpredictability in the process. Without factional agreement no member would reach the ministry. That control over votes did allow Hawke to send back the list of potential nominees provided by the faction leaders in 1990 and demand a more balanced and representative selection, even if the general shape of the ministry, the distribution between factions, was not entirely in his hands.

As a consequence, all Labor prime ministers must live with a range of cabinet members that they would prefer were not there and without those who might be their preferences. Fisher was constantly driven mad by the presence and style of King O'Malley. Curtin had to tolerate Calwell and Ward. So did Chifley, but Chifley was better able to manage the animosities. Prime ministers retained the right to distribute portfolios, and were able to determine which ministers were on cabinet committees. In the later ministries they determined which were the portfolio ministers in cabinet and which were non-portfolio and assistant ministers. As already noted, Hawke once sent the faction leaders back to reconsider their choices. Only the deputy prime minister, in that position by virtue of caucus election to the deputy party leadership, had a formal choice of portfolio (though some ex-leaders such as Hayden were accommodated too).

Further, Labor prime ministers cannot readily sack ministerial failures. Since they did not elect them, they cannot so readily dispense with those ministers who prove not to be up to the task. Where Labor prime ministers may try, the decision may always be open to review by the caucus. Yet Labor prime ministers need the support of caucus. Nor are there opportunities for prime ministers to organise substantial reshuffles without a spill. The spill in 1931 provided an opportunity for a prime minister to organise against some of his main critics; Scullin successfully opposed the re-election of Anstey and Daly.

At the suggestion of Scullin, caucus gave Curtin the power to remove ministers; it was a power that neither he nor Chifley used, although Curtin was able to stand Ward aside during the inquiry into the Brisbane Line accusations. Chifley went to great lengths to accommodate Ward's erratic behaviour, rather than push for his removal. There was not a single change to the Labor cabinet between 1946 and 1949.

In 1975 Whitlam did sack two ministers, Cairns and Connor. In each case caucus endorsed his decision in an effective 'them or me' challenge. Whitlam was prepared to sack Cameron when Cameron refused to accept a new portfolio in a reshuffle, using section 64 of the Constitution to withdraw his commission. Cameron acquiesced, but that too would have required caucus endorsement.

When Hawke became prime minister, he received the authority from caucus to sack ministers in consultation with the other three parliamentary leaders. That is, he had to mobilise a degree of support before he could act. Over the next decade a number of ministers resigned, usually because they were accident-prone. Several were dropped by their factions in the post-election spills, but none had to be fired by the prime minister just because they were not up to the task. Sometimes prime ministers would push ministers in trouble to resign. Labor prime ministers had to work with very stable cabinets and, where necessary, organise around the confrontational and the incompetent.

In coalition ministries, prime ministers both choose the ministers and allocate the jobs. There are of course a number of restrictions. Some ministers have to represent the government in the Senate; initially it was only one, but with the spread of responsibilities that number has grown. Each state requires some representation and there is likely to be some balance between the larger states. It may be possible to ignore Tasmania for a time, but not the others. Placating state interests does not mean that every state will be represented in cabinet, but one minister at least will be in the ministry. So selection is a jigsaw: balancing the powerful, the states, the Senate and the coalition. Sometimes the leader of the Country/National party would choose their own ministers, at others the prime minister would make the choices in consultation with the leader of the minor party.

For Liberal prime ministers the calculation is slightly different when it comes to removing ministers. There is little tradition in Australia for retired senior ministers or party leaders to sit on the backbench as elder statesmen. When their ministerial career is over they tend to leave parliament and seek a diplomatic posting or remunerative position in the private sector. Prime ministers prefer that arrangement, too. They do not want senior rivals plotting behind them. Both Peacock in 1981–82, and Keating in 1991, used their time on the backbenches after their resignations to act as a focus for discontent and for plotting the next leadership challenge.

In a small parliament there is a danger in leaving out those who thought they should be in. For all those satisfied by promotion, there are the disappointed who think they have a better case than those chosen. Sometimes the discontented can solidify around a challenger. If the prime minister will not select the disaffected, then their ambitions may require them to tie their fortunes to the next in line; internal opposition may be caused by thwarted ambition as well as dislike of the incumbent. Enemies on the backbench could be dangerous if they had leadership ambition or if they thought they had a future only under a different leader. When Gorton dumped Howson in 1968 he made a bitter enemy whose diaries show that his only interest thereafter was to undermine Gorton, and to conspire in his overthrow.

Accountability to party meetings

Party meetings are the gatekeepers to office and the sentinels protecting and scrutinising cabinet. They are the forums for extensive party debate about policies and legislation. Prime ministers take them seriously. They will usually attend if they can and they will listen to the debate. The people at party meetings elected them and can remove them.

In the Labor party it goes further than that. Under Labor's theory of representation, caucus makes the decisions and cabinet acts as the executive. Caucus is the superior body and its decisions are meant to be binding. In turn, caucus is bound to act within the constraints of policy determined by the national conference. Caucus may determine the priorities within the program and the timing of the changes, but should not act contrary to it. In the Labor governments before the 1980s, caucus often insisted on its authority, with the effect of making governing difficult.

In the 1914–16 Labor government, caucus was constantly critical of the priorities of the government in prosecuting the war and the restrictions created by the War Precautions Act. Then, reflecting the labour movement outside parliament, a substantial proportion of Labor members opposed conscription. Members of parliament had split loyalties: to the government they supported and to their state branch. State branches controlled the party preselection and thus the political futures of MPs within the Labor party. In this instance, faced with irreconcilable opposition within the caucus, the prime minister led his supporters out of the party room. The problem with the principle of caucus control was that caucus only met while parliament was in session. Hughes had delayed the final party split because caucus had barely ever met in the previous year. For ministers, the absence of caucus as a vehicle for criticism was doubtless a blessing.

In 1929 to 1931 caucus became so dominant that cabinet often acted in reaction to demands from the backbench. While Theodore was stood down as a minister, caucus even became the source of constructive ideas. Caucus and cabinet tic-tacked, meeting one after the other to determine what was acceptable; the weakness of the cabinet was obvious. In the 1940s prime ministers twice went outside the caucus to get approval, in one case from the national conference or in the other from the federal executive, both bodies that could instruct caucus to accept policy proposals. Curtin persuaded the national conference to approve of conscription for service in the areas north of Australia. Chifley both persuaded the executive to approve of Australia signing the Bretton Woods Agreement and then ensured that requests to call a national conference to review the proposal were defeated. In each case the prime minister was uncertain that he could get the support within caucus for proposals that he felt necessary. Aware of the tragic consequences of a caucus and cabinet in open warfare, they chose to use other forums to bring the party behind them. Their actions were an indication of the power of caucus in Labor. Curtin and Chifley were always attentive to caucus. Chifley chaired *every* meeting of caucus in the four and a half years that he was prime minister; it was not a responsibility to be delegated.

Whitlam chose to hand the chairing of caucus to an elected backbencher. He still attended regularly and on occasion ministers who had lost in cabinet chose to re-run the issue in caucus, hoping thereby to overrule the cabinet decision. Even Whitlam was prepared to appeal to caucus when he lost in cabinet. By contrast the Hawke–Keating cabinet applied the principle of collective responsibility, and was thus far more disciplined. In addition, a formalised faction system meant that the factions met separately and determined their position in advance of caucus. Faction leaders would negotiate both appointees and policy positions, so there was less unpredictability. In essence its leading figures had seen the problems of the Whitlam government and were determined that they would not be repeated.

At times the Hawke and Keating governments were prepared to espouse policies, such as the export of uranium to France and the privatisation of Qantas and the Commonwealth Bank, that were actually contrary to the national conference decisions; they were prepared later to bring party policy into line with government policy. A disciplined caucus, when compared to earlier practices, made cabinet government easier. Caucus, as the accounts of Labor governments illustrated, was a constant factor with which Labor cabinets had to contend.

Nevertheless there was an expectation that caucus committees would examine legislation, that ministers would attend and answer questions, and that the views of party members would be taken into account. By 1996 caucus would no longer really be seen as cabinet's master, as it had believed itself to be in the earlier Labor governments, but nor could it be entirely ignored.

By contrast the Liberal party and its predecessors worked by a different code. The external organisation could not direct the parliamentary party. In turn the parliamentary party could not instruct cabinet. It could advise, warn and be consulted. However, they did meet regularly when parliament was in session. In recent governments its committees could review legislation and request changes. They could insist that proposals reflect their views. Ministers would answer questions. This attendance meant that debates on policy could take place within the comparative privacy of the party room. Thereafter, members were expected to abide by the government line and vote solidly in public.

At different times party meetings have played crucial roles in determining the policy and leadership of the government. Opposition within the party to Menzies, over a long period, finally broke his first leadership in 1941. Gorton's principal opponents were in the party room in 1969 to 1971; the Howson diaries attest both to their bitterness and their persistence in seeking to undermine him, even with the final result that the Liberal government was fatally wounded by their internal divisions. There is little that prime ministers can do to discipline backbenchers with no hope of any ministerial future under their leadership. If, on the other hand, they retain their standing in the eyes of backbenchers and provide the expectation of continued success, as Howard has done, then there is nothing to fear from a party room that credits the prime minister with their very presence. A contender must just wait for circumstances to change, or the prime minister to decide to retire (so far, a rare phenomenon).

Usually Liberals and Country/National members participate as one in the joint party meetings. When the leadership is at stake they will meet separately. They have made decisions on legislation and on the future of governments. Prime ministers may appeal to the party if cabinet is divided. They know that, in the last resort, if they cannot keep the party happy, their tenure is limited.

Cabinet and parliament

Yet this political reality is covered by a series of constitutional principles that direct attention away from the party to the parliament. Governments are constitutionally responsible to parliament. In the House of Representatives, governments can usually rely on the discipline of their parties. In the first nine years after federation, five governments fell when, in a three-party house, the party that held the balance of power withdrew support from the government. It occurred three times in 1904–05, and then twice in 1908–09 as the non-Labor parties realigned into a single force. These were *party* decisions, not individual mavericks changing sides.

Since then only three governments have fallen by parliamentary vote. In 1929 a backbench revolt engineered by Hughes brought down the Bruce government; Bruce called an election and lost government and his seat. In 1931 the Labor government had fractured and lost its majority; eventually all its enemies combined to vote it out. In 1941 two independents switched their votes to remove the Fadden government and install Curtin and Labor in office. Since 1941 there have been no significant *parliamentary* revolts within a governing party. Discipline now appears more total than in the first 50 years. Public dissension is discouraged. The fights, and there have been many, have been kept within the party room.

The government controlled the Senate for most of the initial 80 years. Only in 1913–14, 1929–31, 1950–51 and 1972–75 was the Senate clearly in the hands of an Opposition that was obstructive and determined to thwart the cabinet. That was for eight of the first 80 years. In those periods, cabinet had to find alternative ways of delivering policies if it could not pass its legislation. Scullin used to issue regulations that the Senate then disallowed, so they were re-promulgated and then disallowed again, time after time. Whitlam stockpiled bills in the hope that they could be passed in a later joint sitting; ironically it was the 36 bills rejected by the Senate opposition that allowed Fraser to ask for, and receive, a double dissolution in 1975, even though it was his party that had defeated the bills in the Senate. In 1914 and 1951 the government enthusiastically sought to create the conditions for a double dissolution and went to the polls. Cook lost both houses in 1914; Menzies won both in 1951. In 1974 Whitlam was prepared to accept a challenge and called an election; in 1975 he had to be sacked before an election was called. Only in 1931 was there no double dissolution, primarily because the government was too scared to call one, even in the first months of its term when momentum was on its side. Thereafter they were faced only with total defeat. Opposition-controlled Senates always made governing difficult.

In the 1950s and 1960s the Liberal–Country governments had to rely on Democratic Labor Party (DLP) senators. Since the DLP was primarily an anti-Labor party, the government's existence was not in doubt. From 1981 to 2005 no government held a majority and therefore successive governments had to negotiate legislation through minority parties in the Senate. At times, as in 1993, ministers had even to negotiate the details of the budget. Bills for native title and for the goods and services tax (GST) had to be modified as a means of ensuring they passed; they were usually negotiated with the minor parties that held the balance of power. Other bills were never passed; some may have been introduced for symbolic purposes, to show how obstructionist the Senate could be. Governments invariably had a war chest of items that had been presented twice and that were available as triggers for double dissolutions. In practice they seldom pulled the trigger because of the benefits that minor parties gained from a double dissolution.

From 1 July 2005 the coalition government had gained a majority in the Senate. In the 1960s the occasional senator voted against their party, but never to the extent of destroying government legislation. In 1976 a group opposed a small item, the removal of funeral benefits, and stopped the measure, the only time the Senate revolted in the Fraser government. It is likely that the Senate will only occasionally act as a hurdle that cabinet has had to consider for the next few years.

Cabinet therefore answers to parliament, but is not in any real or detailed sense accountable to parliament for its actions if the party numbers hold. And they do. If the Senate chooses to censure a minister, and it occasionally has, ministers shrug and continue in their post. It is only a constitutional formality. Performance in parliament matters for reputation, for symbolism, for public image. Ministers' reputations can be undermined in the opinion of their party colleagues if they cannot answer questions and ward off criticism there. But parliament is not much of a restraint on the choices that cabinet makes; its power is at best latent. It can wound and damage; it can undermine a reputation. Ministers may cease to rise – and eventually leave politics after a parliamentary hammering. Party politics ensures that the execution is seldom immediate as that would give too much credit to the Opposition. This is reflected in an account of the way that the doctrines of collective and individual ministerial responsibility have been interpreted and applied in respect to cabinet government.

Collective responsibility

Conventions of behaviour are always contested. Lacking legal force they can either be described as principles that must be followed or practical wisdom that offers guidance. If the first description is followed, then the regular reinterpretation of the conventions to provide greater flexibility (and thereby to avoid responsibility) represents a constant decline in political standards. Those who argue in favour of conventions being principles to be followed fit the category of those who were described by Richard French as 'theorists'. These theorists define the standards and compare behaviour against it, almost always to the detriment of practice. Often there is an implied reference to days (usually not precisely dated) when more principled politics were pursued. If the latter view of conventions is taken, a group of 'pragmatists' (again French's term) suggest they incorporate practical wisdom and offer guidance. Pragmatists ask how the conventions affect the actual process of governing.

The problem with the first approach is that there is no clear definition that can be applied. The term 'convention' is bandied around in political debate primarily for political effect; none of the Opposition critics would accept in government the standards to which they would like to hold ministers while they are still in Opposition. It is easier to understand cabinet behaviour if the realist 'pragmatist' approach is accepted, for analysis does not degenerate into imprecise nostalgia and despair for the quality of modern politics (which in my view is no more or less principled than Australian politics ever was). In reality, conventions have always been available for use as an exercise of power. Collective responsibility *is* necessary for government, but as a political imperative; it is dressed as constitutional convention that conceals its force as a rule of political prudence. As history has shown, how it is interpreted and enforced is a matter of calculation, not law.

In 1901 Quick and Garran wrote:

> The principle of the corporate unity and solidarity of the Cabinet requires that the Cabinet should have the one harmonious policy, both in administration and in legislation; that the advice tendered by the Cabinet to the Crown should be unanimous and consistent; that the Cabinet should stand or fall together. The Cabinet as a whole is responsible for the advice and conduct of each of its members. If any member seriously dissents from the opinion and policy approved by the majority of his colleagues it is his duty as a man of honour to resign.

Quick and Garran were referring to practices established in colonial governments which were transferred without comment to the new national level. As a principle it was accepted from the beginning as part of the government's practice. In 1903 the cabinet was split on the Conciliation and

Arbitration bill, with Forrest and Kingston the two main protagonists. The bill was debated over several meetings until eventually Kingston found himself in a minority and resigned.

In the 1920s and 1930s such resignations seemed quite frequent. Lyons and Fenton resigned from the Scullin cabinet in protest at the reinstatement of Theodore. Later that year Holloway and Culley were unable to accept the Premiers' Plan, even though cabinet had explicitly decided to relax the principle of collective responsibility to allow Holloway to voice his opposition. In 1934 Fenton disagreed with the government's tariff policy, in 1936 Gullett fell out over trade treaties and in 1938 White objected to a cabinet reshuffle (primarily because he was not in the announced inner cabinet). In 1939, most famously, Menzies resigned when cabinet buckled to the demands of the Country party and deferred the national insurance plan (although some saw the decision as more evidence of Menzies' determination to displace Lyons as prime minister). Sometimes these resignations may have indeed been over an unwillingness to accept government policy; on other occasions they may have been a useful excuse to camouflage more personal political divisions.

But *when* a disagreement turned into a crisis depended often on how it was managed. Chifley allowed Ward to be a critic in caucus; even a public absence from the vote on Bretton Woods in parliament brought no censure. Ward rampant in cabinet was less damaging than a crisis created by his sacking, since that would make him a Labor martyr. Several ministers used the floor of a Labor national conference to attack, and vote against, the Bretton Woods proposals. Ministers moved motions in caucus to overturn cabinet decisions. For Chifley, collective responsibility was flexible enough to allow such party dissent.

In 1962 Les Bury, minister for air but a former Treasury and IMF economist, stated that the fears being expressed over the impact of Britain entering the common market were 'greatly exaggerated'. He repeated the statement twice. It was contrary to the line being run by Menzies and, even more so, by McEwen who argued that Bury 'was publicly undercutting Australia's negotiating strength'. The violent reaction of the Country party leader may have had an impact, because after two meetings with Menzies, Bury resigned. The prime minister declared that the principle of collective responsibility was:

> Supremely important when a government is engaged in advocating the legitimate interests of Australia in a series of negotia-

tions which we have repeatedly declared to be the most important of our time. I cannot allow a state of affairs to continue in which ... our own Government contains and retains a Minister whose views are not those of the Cabinet.

That requirement never applied to the leader of the Country party. Fadden was quite happy to air his opposition to the appreciation of the dollar in 1951 while cabinet was discussing it. McEwen publicly criticised the Holt cabinet's decision not to follow the devaluation of the pound in 1967; he had missed the cabinet meeting. After heated discussion, Holt ignored the breach of collective solidarity. The political cost of seeking to apply it to the leader of the Country party was too great. It is, after all, a matter of political calculations and convenience, not some immutable physical principle.

Such resignations caused by disagreement over policy have become much less frequent. In 1978 Bob Ellicott resigned from the Fraser government when he disagreed with a cabinet decision that he should take over a private prosecution of former Labor ministers and then withdraw the prosecution. He both disagreed with the decision and disputed the right of the Cabinet to give him, as attorney-general and first law officer, instructions in the matter. By contrast, Fraser's spectacular departure from the Gorton government was entirely about his lack of trust in the prime minister and his way of running government. Twelve years later Peacock borrowed Fraser's own language to throw the same charge at Fraser as prime minister when he in turn resigned from the cabinet. There have been a rash of sackings or resignations over inappropriate behaviour in the Fraser, Hawke and Howard governments. In each case it was the actions of ministers as individuals, not as ministers, that created the conditions that led to their departure. They were cases of personal responsibility.

In 1984 the Labor government adjusted the principle of collective responsibility to suit its own circumstances and convenience. A left-wing minister, Stewart West, opposed a cabinet decision to export uranium. He wanted to resign from the cabinet but not from the ministry. A form of words defining collective responsibility was devised to let him, and the prime minister, off the hook:

> 2.1 The convention of the collective responsibility of Ministers for Government decisions is central to the Cabinet system of government. Cabinet Minutes reflect collective conclusions and are binding on Cabinet Ministers as Government policy both outside the Party and within. This applies also to non-Cabinet

> Ministers co-opted to attend Cabinet meetings, in respect of matters dealt with while they are present.
>
> ...
>
> 2.3 All Ministers are expected to give their support in public debate to decisions of the Government; non-Cabinet Ministers, however, are not prevented from debating in Caucus decisions in areas apart form their portfolios. Caucus decisions are binding on all Ministers.

This interpretation of collective responsibility provided a distinction between cabinet and non-cabinet ministers and thus changed the traditional concept of a government being collectively committed whether or not ministers were involved in the making of the decision. As a consequence, some ministers preferred not to be co-opted to a meeting when they wanted to oppose an item in caucus; they preferred the option of being seen to make a stand before their colleagues than lose in cabinet and be effectively gagged. That said, the freedom of non-cabinet ministers did not become a problem for the government after the strange semi-resignation of West.

The West affair did, however, emphasise the central position of the Labor party doctrine of the nominal supremacy of caucus. Ministers could display their differences in the party but not in public. In the Liberal party the distinction does not arise; ministers are bound by cabinet decisions.

Committees extend the concept for responsibility for decisions in which ministers were not involved. Whereas in the early years committees reported back to cabinet, by the 1940s, under pressure of war, committees were given authority to make decisions on behalf of cabinet, particularly the war cabinet (see Chapter 5). That reality was later extended to foreign affairs, defence and national security committees and to ERCs. At times prime ministers might decide on limited circulation of decisions. The commitment remained: all ministers were collectively responsible, even when they were not aware that a decision had been made.

The other side of the collective coin was a limitation of the range of items on which ministers should speak. The most recent *Cabinet Handbook* states:

> 2.8 Ministers should not make public statements or comment on policy proposals which they are bringing or which are to be brought to cabinet. Promotion in public of a particular line may pre-empt cabinet deliberations. Identification of individual ministers with particular views tends to call into question the collec-

tive basis of agreed outcomes. Each portfolio minister is responsible for direction and public presentation of policy, and other ministers should avoid separate policy stances becoming matters of public debate.

2.9 It is inappropriate for ministers to accept invitations to speak or to comment publicly on matters outside their portfolios in circumstances which may involve disagreement – or which are likely to be construed as amounting to disagreement – with the conduct of another portfolio, without the prior concurrence of the appropriate minister or the prime minister.

For prime ministers faced with serious party rivals it is often better that the latter are in the cabinet and restricted in their capacity to range widely across government policy areas than free on the backbench to comment on anything that is happening. In 1975 Fraser chose to return Don Chipp to the backbench after the caretaker ministry: he eventually left the party and had the public standing to form the Democrats who were able to win the balance of power in the Senate for over 20 years. When Peacock and Keating left their respective cabinets they became the focal point and public face of internal opposition in a way that would have been harder, and certainly less public, had they remained in the cabinet.

Collective responsibility may indeed be the political cornerstone of the cabinet system, but it works because of its flexibility and the capacity of prime ministers to determine the meaning. There is little dispute that the declaration of Lord Salisbury remains nominally applicable: 'For all that passes in Cabinet, each member of it who does not resign is absolutely and irretrievably responsible'. It is just that over the years its application has been moderated, or on rare occasions relaxed, by political necessity. The prime minister alone will determine what it means and when it will be applied. He may well be provided with a range of unsolicited advice from the Opposition and the press, but the final calculation must be, and can only be, his alone.

Ministerial responsibility

Ministers are members of parliament who are appointed 'to administer departments of state' according to section 64 of the Constitution. By implication they are responsible to parliament for the activities of their department. In practice this convention means that they answer questions about their department and, where inadequacies are uncovered, seek to ensure that they are fixed. It does not mean, and never has meant, that ministers should resign if the departments fail in some respect or other. Nor has that happened in Britain or any other Westminster system. Demands for resignation are easy rhetoric, but no more. Snedden, as attorney-general, made the position explicit:

> What of cases where the minister is not personally involved? Responsible, yes, in the sense that he may have to answer and explain *to* parliament, but not absolutely responsible in the sense that he has to answer for (is liable to censure for) everything done under his administration ... There is no absolute vicarious liability on the part of the Minister for the 'sins' of his subordinates. If the Minister is free of personal fault, and could not by reasonable diligence in controlling his department have prevented the mistake, there is no compulsion to resign.

What is important is the way in which ministers interact with their departments, and with the broader public service, and respond to parliamentary examination of their activities.

In December 1998, Howard issued *A Guide on Key Elements of Ministerial Responsibility*, which seeks to define relations with the public service. The guide raises the values enshrined in the *Public Service Act 1999*, notably the provision of frank and comprehensive advice to ministers, and party-political impartiality, as well as emphasises the need for trust:

> Ministers will obtain advice from a range of sources, but primarily from their private office and from their departments. There is clearly no obligation on ministers to accept advice put to them by public servants, but it is important that advice be considered carefully and fairly. It is not for public servants to continue to press their advice beyond the point where their ministers have indicated that the advice, having been fully considered, is not the favoured approach. Public servants should feel free, however, to raise issues for reconsideration if they believe there are emerging problems or additional information which warrant fresh examination.

This account, like the exhortations in sections 2.8 and 2.9 of the handbook quoted above, may be unexceptional; that is how it is meant to work. No one would have demurred 80 years earlier. What is interesting is that, by now, it is considered necessary to write it down.

The *Cabinet Handbook* and the 1998 guide provide an insight into the current state of thinking on the processes of ministerial decision-making and responsibility. So ministers are told that ministerial responsibility:

> Does not mean that ministers bear individual liability for all actions of their departments. Where they neither knew, nor should have known about matters of departmental administration which come under scrutiny it is not unreasonable to expect that the secretary or some other senior officer will take the responsibility.
>
> Ministers do, however, have overall responsibility for the administration of their portfolios and for carriage in the parliament of their accountability obligations arising from that responsibility. They would properly be held to account for matters for which they were personally responsible, or where they were aware of problems but had not acted to rectify them.

Again the guide is merely spelling out the way the doctrine of ministerial responsibility had always worked; in fact, it describes the existing understandings. It also allows the minister to transfer blame to the public servants if anything goes wrong. That is not entirely new either, even if it has become more explicit. One minister learning the ropes said that initially, when he answered a question in parliament, he largely repeated the advice provided by the public service. After an occasion when that advice was wrong and he was severely embarrassed, he ensured that every answer thereafter was prefaced by the words 'I am advised ...' in case the advice was wrong.

Now there is not even a pretence that ministers should cover for public servants. In Senate committees, ministers will not seek to defend officials, even though by convention officials still often protect their ministers. When the Department of Immigration was severely criticised for the failure of its system and the detention or deportation of Australian citizens in 2005, both the current and the former ministers denied any responsibility; both argued that they did not know, so how could they be responsible? The report blamed officials; that was enough, in their view, to absolve ministers, even if the culture of the department, for which the ministers could be held responsible, was under fire too.

The question then is what can, and did, ministers know. Not much, if they do not want to. The inquiry into the Wheat Board's sales to Iraq in 2006 found that numerous cables had been sent to the offices of the prime minister and the ministers for foreign affairs and trade. The minister of foreign affairs once asked for further information. Yet ministers were comfortable with the statements that just because information had reached their office, it did not mean that they had seen warnings. In the past, one of the arguments against the demands to make ministerial staffers accountable to parliament was the assumption that, if staffers knew, ministers knew. That belief can be no longer sustained.

In equity law there is a principle of constructive notice. It arises where someone knows enough that objectively they should have made further inquiries that, had they been made, would have revealed the full facts. It stems from Chancery notions of fiduciary obligation and trusteeship; it basically prevents someone pleading ignorance when they should have done more to become informed. In politics, the reverse is true. Unless it can be proved that ministers had been explicitly informed, they can shuffle off responsibilities, arguing that they *should* have been informed but were not.

Ministers resign only when they have been somehow personally involved. Thus a royal commission decided in 1978 that Senator Withers had committed an 'impropriety' in ringing the chief electoral commissioner about the name of an electorate; John Brown misled parliament in 1987; Ros Kelly, Minister for Arts, Sport, the Environment, Tourism and Territories under the Hawke government, made decisions on funding on a white board that broke proper practice; John Sharp, Minister for Transport and Regional Development under Howard, failed to pursue misuse of travel claims; others had undeclared share holdings.

In these cases ministers are responsible, not really to the parliament, but rather to the prime minister and potentially to the party. The prime minister has to make a decision: is it better to ask for the resignation of the minister as a means of ending the scandal or should he ride out the rough water in the expectation that the tide will turn and the issue will be forgotten? Often prime ministers begin in the first camp of strict application of standards and demand resignations, but end in the second when it is apparent that crises are forgotten whereas resignations are often listed as a sign of government instability. In all cases the calculation is political, not constitutional. Retribution on the ministers can come later, when they can be dropped or reshuffled into less sensitive areas. An immediate reaction admits fault on the part of the minister and, in the adversarial political system, admitting fault may be more damaging than the original error. There is no evidence that prime ministers are rewarded for running a tight ship; rather they are damned for heading one that is accident-prone. Choices are determined by convention, and the prime minister is the judge and jury in the application of the convention. Ministers are responsible first to the prime minister, and only thereafter will they explain to parliament the reasons for the decisions.

Party: The source of legitimacy and the centre of accountability

Cabinet is formally accountable to the parliament. Question time and debate may draw to public attention its failings and misrepresentations; they may uncover its plans and criticise its intentions. That is the core of political warfare: aggressive, partisan and unforgiving. Cabinet ministers must answer to parliament, even if they speak in ambiguous terms. Yet that accountability is essentially rhetorical. Debate does not change minds or alter votes. However reprehensible the behaviour, ministers can be assured that the party majority will line up behind them. In public, the party stands firm.

In the party room accountability is far more real. The party room contains critics and rivals. It chooses the prime minister and can remove him. It can undermine ministers' reputations. It has the right to discuss legislation and suggest change. It would be entirely wrong to suggest that the party room is a *de facto* opposition. The members there support the government and work for its, and their, return. But, between elections it is one forum in which the decisions of government may receive some scrutiny that can bring change. Is it adequate accountability for the constitutional purists who demand the actual supremacy of parliament? Certainly not. But that supremacy never existed either. Accountability to the party is the only immediate means that makes sense under existing practices. That is why prime ministers and ministers take the party room so seriously, and why cabinet and party government are so inextricably intertwined.

12 THE RULES OF CABINET

Rules create norms and expectations. They can structure the way that issues are approached, information collected, debates held and decisions interpreted. Rules allocate power either directly, or through the capacity to interpret and adjudicate. They alter the balance of power and are generally introduced because they work to the interests of some and against those of others. Rules serve several different masters. They allow prime ministers to control the processes of cabinet, and they let officials bring order to a process of central decision-making. Sometimes these imperatives clash; more often they complement one another to advance the political and administrative interests of both parties. A history of the changing rules of cabinet is thus a study of the bureaucratisation of cabinet, seen through the lens of prime ministers and central officials.

Cabinet is an institution, in the sense that it is a forum structured by a series of rules, norms and behaviours that alter over time. The way that a small group of ministers, overseeing the establishment of a fledgling government in 1901, could organise their meetings and affairs, has to be different from the extensive organisation required to manage government in 2006. Inevitably, the story also becomes tangentially a study of the impact of technology: from the typewriter to the Gestetner, from the carbon copy to the computer network. Cabinet systems are designed as much by what can be done as by prime ministerial desire.

This chapter first explores the reasons for which some bureaucracy and rules are needed, then traces the way that the cabinet has become more routinised over a century, and finally explains what the forces were that made it happen. The chapter, then, is meant to answer a series of questions:

- What issues come to cabinet? How should they be presented?
- How are meetings run and decisions reached?
- What support does cabinet need from officials?

The challenges

Ministers are busy people. The demands on their time are constant. Attendance at cabinet may be significant, but ministerial contribution can vary in depth and intensity. Ministers have to fulfil several other roles as well. They act as local members, parliamentarians, government advocates, and as heads of their department. Each of these roles takes time. Then ministers have to prepare for, and attend cabinet. There they are expected to participate in a process of collective decision-making.

The initial challenge for ministers is to be aware of the *implications* of the issues that appear before them, to understand what must be decided and to make an informed decision. Often the reality must fall far below this expectation. There were constant complaints, from prime ministers and from officials, that ministers came to cabinet without reading their papers, that that failure never stopped them contributing to the debate, but that the debate was consequently not always well directed.

The workload of cabinet has at times been so extensive that adequate debate on each item becomes impossible. The reasons for the workload may be both personal and political. Individually, ministers may prefer to get the endorsement of their colleagues for decisions that they want to make; there is protection in numbers. Collectively, ministers may wish to know what their colleagues are doing, particularly in those cases where the decisions may have some impact on their portfolio or their state.

Determining what is significant enough for cabinet consideration, and what criteria should be used, is thus a continuing issue. Prime ministers always maintained the traditional prerogative of determining the agenda of cabinet, acting on the advice of their officials and drawing in later years from the range of departmental submissions that had been lodged. In more recent times, submissions may only be lodged after some indication, with prime ministerial authority, that it is worth having a departmental submission prepared. Prime ministers always had to make the choice of when cabinet was to consider the broad political issues and when they could analyse more pressing problems in depth; when there would be presentations and when cabinet was ready to decide the big issues. In cabinet, prime ministers chair the meeting and determine in which order items are taken, in what terms issues will be debated, how long the discussion may be, whether a decision is taken and what it might be.

The recording and distribution of decisions are vital parts of the cabinet process. Cabinet decisions are the currency of governing. They provide the authority to act; they give recipients bureaucratic legitimacy: what Peter Hennessy for Britain described as 'the power and majesty of the Cabinet minute'. The way the decisions are recorded and the process of follow-up and distribution become important for the smooth running of government and for ensuring, as best it can, that a cabinet's conclusions are translated into action. As the activities of government became more extensive, so the need for bureaucratic support, housed in a cabinet secretariat, became obvious. The development of the cabinet rules is inextricably linked to the development of an efficient secretariat.

The issue of how cabinet sought to understand the policy issues will be discussed in the next chapter. Here I will show how the rules and procedures of cabinet have been constantly altered as cabinet failed to perform adequately.

Guidelines for cabinet and its ministers: Defining the arena

In the first decade of cabinet after federation the prime minister was able to maintain his own records, noting the issues to be considered, arranged by minister in order of seniority. He noted, too, in brief form the outcomes of the discussions. These records were for his own benefit. Ministers were thereafter responsible for informing their departments of the decisions and for ensuring that they were carried out. There was no central repository to check what had been determined. Nor was there evidence that cabinet members circulated any submissions. Rather it seems likely that they spoke to the arguments and content of their cases. But they were a small group, mostly living away from home and of comparatively equal status. They knew how cabinets were meant to work. Expectations were understood.

Only gradually did the idea of an agenda emerge. Then it was a floating agenda, a list of all those items that the ministers had indicated that they wanted to discuss. Again it was organised minister by minister, and there was no assumption that the presence of an item on the agenda list ensured that it would be discussed. That was the choice of the prime minister.

The creation of a Prime Minister's Department in 1911, dedicated to serving the leader in the role as head of government, provided some support to the prime ministers. But although at first papers were often prepared for cabinet, they were not initially circulated. Rather, ministers still spoke to issues, noted the decision, often on the paper before them, and remained responsible for telling their departmental head of the outcome.

The first handbook appeared in 1926 as part of a process of systemising the operations of cabinet. Ministers appointed as secretaries of cabinet had initially been responsible primarily for keeping one version of the decisions. Now there was an attempt to develop some minimal set of rules that prescribed the attendance of ministers and the operation of the support services. The handbook was the outcome of a draft from the department and a final version that contained the amendments made by Bruce as prime minister. That set the tone. In all the sets of rules that developed out of this first draft, the officials provided suggestions to solve continuing dilemmas by seeking to impose routine, predictability and an exchange of information. By contrast, prime ministers were properly concerned with the politics of the process and often were concerned to ensure that the authority remained in the hands of ministers and was not ceded to officials. Rules, however, gave the excuse to refuse ministers wanting to raise items: they were an available excuse.

These alternative perspectives are reflected in Bruce's changes to the initial draft of the handbook. He did not want views attributed to individual ministers in any circumstances: cabinet was to be collective in its outlook. He did not want the Treasury to be given all submissions as a matter of course. That would be up to the prime minister and cabinet. The process by which these rules were developed allowed the prime minister to create the structure *he* wanted. The rules were to be a matter of practice; the prime minister could decide when and if they were to be enforced. The rules thus provide an amalgam of political and administrative logics.

The Scullin government dumped the cabinet secretariat and the application of Bruce's rules, precisely because they had been devised by Bruce; they were the methods of the previous regime that should be discarded with that regime to the junk heap. Yet the Bruce rules had a degree of logic that might have assisted the chaotic cabinet proceedings that characterised the Scullin government, although they could never have alleviated the tensions that broke it. Good procedures can assist good government; they can never be an alternative to good policy if the ideas are not present.

Even after Lyons had re-established the secretariat, there remained a degree of randomness in the way that cabinet worked. The secretariat remained small; it was designed at most to circulate the papers. In 1941 the attendance of the secretary in cabinet marked a new stage in cabinet development. Now minutes were kept and decisions circulated, but there is no evidence that the department provided much more to the prime minister. Since Chifley, prime minister from 1945, was also treasurer he could rely on those officials to give him policy advice on items coming to cabinet.

The creation of the extended cabinet secretariat, proposed by Allen Brown to Chifley and implemented under Menzies, gave increased administrative clout to the Prime Minister's Department. Over the next 50 years there was an incremental growth in the form and rules of cabinet. What had begun as a few pages developed into an extensive cabinet handbook. The skeleton of a system grew sinew and muscle. Menzies sent out letters defining the role of ministers generically; at the first cabinet of each parliament he gave the same lecture to his ministers, encouraging them *inter alia* to listen to the advice of their officials. Since 1987 the prime minister sent out 'charter letters', explaining the government's priorities, and allocating responsibility to senior and junior ministers in the portfolio. In turn, ministers were required to forecast when legislation would be ready and what issues they expected to bring to cabinet. What had begun as letters setting out expectations of ministers developed into these priority-setting charter letters.

As the handbook grew more extensive, so the rules became more public. The *Cabinet Handbook* was published for the first time in the academic journal, *Politics*, in 1981, in breach of copyright but with none of the resounding collapse of the cabinet system forecast by those who argued that cabinet was, and ought to be, protected by secrecy; proponents for secrecy tended to argue that those involved knew how it worked, and those who were not did not need to know. One consequence of publication was that the department argued that, with the handbook now public, there was no reason to pretend it needed to be secret. In 1984 the *Cabinet Handbook* was officially published by the Australian Government Printing Service. In March 2004 the fifth edition, with the latest amendments, became public and is accessible on the Web. The handbook is now only one of a series of publications providing guidelines for ministers and senior officials, and explaining how the system of cabinet government should work. Also on the PM&C website are the *Legislation Handbook*, the *Federal Executive Council Handbook* and the December 1998 edition of *A Guide on Key Elements of Ministerial Responsibility*.

Combined, these documents provide a network of rules, conventions and practices that prescribe how cabinet business should be done. These are the prime minister's rules and guidelines. He determines what should be included and in the last resort only he can police them. The latest *Cabinet Handbook* includes a definition of the cabinet system:

> 1.1 The cabinet is a product of convention and practice. It is not mentioned in the Australian Constitution, and its establishment and procedures are not subject to any legislation. It is for the government of the day, and in particular the prime minister, to determine the shape and structure of the cabinet system and how it is to operate.

The handbook describes the supporting structures, defines the conventions and principles of collective responsibility and canvasses the whole range of cabinet business and procedures. Each handbook has some new items included and others excised as practices develop. The 2004 edition seeks to emphasise cabinet's strategic focus, and explains the new rules for the ten-day submission process for non-contentious items (see Chapter 10) and with explicit demands for consultation between ministers and for the processing of appointments. The handling of cabinet documents, and access to them, is described in detail. Just this account shows how far the handbook has shifted from those early documents of the 1930s and even from the more extensive accounts of the 1950s.

The additional documents to which ministers must refer give detail to those issues that were once decided by prime ministerial instinct and choice. The guide on ministerial responsibility explains the range of ministerial activity: the responsibilities of the portfolio ministers and their relation to junior ministers, the declaration of interests, and the expectations of ministers in cabinet. It sets out standards of ministerial conduct: they include some interesting formulations:

> Ministers must be honest in their public dealings and should not intentionally mislead the parliament. Any misconception caused inadvertently should be corrected at the earliest opportunity.
>
> Ministers should ensure their conduct is defensible, and should consult with the prime minister when in doubt about the propriety of any course of action.

Neither proposition would be disputed. Deliberately misleading parliament has always been regarded as a crime demanding resignation, hence the caution with which ministers often chose their words. Immediate correction to avoid misconceptions when parliament is sitting is indeed essential, but is presented here in a suitably defensive way. The exercise is less about accountability than about avoiding blame.

How far does the bureaucratisation of convention and rules matter? The answer: substantially. In the early years all interpretations were left to the instinct or interest of the prime ministers. That left them scope to be lenient or otherwise. The relations between Watt and Hughes provide evidence of the wide range of ways that the system could be run. Since the rules were not defined and only the prime minister would know all the circumstances, crisis management was more readily left for his decision. The press and Opposition could grumble about his standards but those could not be defined with precision. They could be flexible or rigid, according to choice, and the weight of the ministers with whom they dealt. Whether behaviour was a 'hanging' or resignation offence could never be precise.

Public guidelines provide an open yardstick against which a minister's behaviour can be judged, and every observer can make a judgment. Ministers may be no worse and no better than their predecessors. But, because there are public guidelines, there is a constant search to see if they have been breached. Prime ministers therefore have to defend not only their ministers but their interpretation of their own guidelines. It adds to the pressure and limits the flexibility. It may not necessarily improve performance, just nervousness.

Submissions

In the early years there was no format for cabinet submissions. Anything could be regarded as suitable: a letter from an elector, a cable from a high commissioner, a note from the public service. These documents raised the issues, but no more. Even when they were circulated – it seems in the early 1920s – ministers did not necessarily read them. Some could be lengthy, but did not state clearly what the issues were that the cabinet was being asked to determine. Hence the rules gradually began to determine first, that papers be circulated, then that they be provided in a form that assisted ministers when they had to read them.

By 1950 the handbook began to stipulate the beginnings of a required format for submissions, but still a very limited one. Although it listed the conventions and the details of meetings, the only format requirements were spaces for security clearance and submission number, a title and recommendations. There were no demands about the presentation of material, about the needs for costing, consultations or a discussion of options (although Treasury was constantly seeking to include an obligation for departments to consult with it before the submissions were presented to cabinet). Nor was the length prescribed; some submissions in the 1940 had been a dozen or more pages. Such details were all left to the ministers' discretion. The cabinet secretariat did require that 30 copies were provided for numbering and circulation to ministers.

Section by section the handbooks became more prescriptive. The 1983 handbook spelt out in detail how a submission should be constructed. There had to be a detailed cover sheet that followed a clear format that included details of the submission's purpose, relation to existing policy, sensitivity, urgency, consultation and proposals for handling of any announcements. The purpose of the introduction of a cover sheet was obvious: to assist ministers understand the tenor and implications of every submission, without them having to read them in full. After perusing the cover sheet they could decide whether they wanted to go through the rest of the submission in detail or whether they wanted their department to provide a brief on the submission. Since few probably read all the submissions, it allowed a slightly better informed debate in cabinet.

By 2004 there was a separate Drafter's Guide that was intended to assist senior advisers and officials in preparing cabinet submissions. It explained how they should be structured; what consultations should take place; and gave samples of ideal submissions, cover sheets and even details for audio/visual presentations by ministers to cabinet. Formerly, the Cabinet Office had policed the process. If submissions did not fit the guidelines, the submissions could be sent back. Since submissions came from ministers, not departments, a refusal to lodge a submission could be politically sensitive. Now, with the benefit of technology, the Cabinet Office is to an extent relieved of that role.

There always were space limits on the cover sheet and the submission. The former now has to fit a non-expandable computerised template; the latter had to be contained within 10 pages. However, there was not any restriction on the attachments of additional and supporting data and they could be huge and often contain indigestible technical material.

The process of formalisation and bureaucratisation has continued throughout the century. An initial informal arrangement became described in more and more detail. The very general page (that was almost a blank page and just provided a security number and commanded the official to 'write a submission' with no headings provided) that sufficed in 1950 became a separate and detailed cabinet handbook document by 2004. A random process by which ministers brought items in different forms was replaced by one that required ministers to forecast what items they planned to bring to cabinet in the next session. Preparing a submission for cabinet had become more closely monitored and restricted. Cabinet had become far more rule-bound and bureaucratic.

Getting on the agenda was never the same thing as getting discussed. In the early days when the agenda was a running list of items the prime minister determined what was actually debated. Later the agenda became more precise, decided by the prime minister, usually on the recommendation of his departmental head. It would be circulated in advance. If ministers wanted to raise an issue without circulating a submission, that is 'under the line', they would still have to seek the consent of the prime minister in advance. Such topics could include appointments (that always needed prior approval of the prime minister) or items of sudden significance. Initially, they were introduced without a submission, but more recently even these have required a paper for circulation.

Records and decisions

The precise wording of cabinet submissions and decisions becomes ammunition in departmental clashes. Decisions tell the world what resources are allocated, what policies are to be adopted. Yet cabinet rarely moves formal motions and relies on a summary from the prime minister, if even that.

How did cabinet or those working for it know what had been decided? In the first years there was no perceived need for any central recording of decisions. Prime ministers kept a note in their own record book and ministers were required to inform departments what they were required to do. Gradually a more formal system was developed in which the secretary of the department wrote to the minister confirming the outcome of the cabinet discussion. Even when it was obvious, as when the prime minister was also minister for external affairs, the secretary would end a note 'for the record'. Often the ministers had already told their secretaries. There was still no central repository. Nor was there any capacity to provide follow-up.

The creation of an active secretary of cabinet, often a junior minister who took on the role as an additional responsibility, provided more regular recording of cabinet, even if the understanding of the decision varied from the prime minister to the cabinet secretary. In 1927 a formal cabinet secretariat was established, but, as the prime minister emphasised, it had no policy responsibilities and was only created to ensure the smooth circulation of cabinet papers. That arrangement might have worked as long as the minister as secretary performed his responsibilities conscientiously; not all were effective.

In 1941, faced with an incompetent minister who simply did not record many of cabinet's decisions, and as a result of the pressures of war and Menzies' positive impression of the cabinet system in the United Kingdom, the system finally changed. The war cabinet had created the precedent; the secretary of defence, an admirer of Hankey, copied the British system when he recorded the decisions there. So Menzies decided that the secretary of the Prime Minister's Department should attend cabinet as a recorder of decisions. Some of the minutes the secretary kept were initially quite full. By the end of the 1940s they provided only the bare bones of the decision. Cabinet had been loath to provide any record of the opinions of ministers. Indeed, since then the formal cabinet records include only the agenda papers, the submissions and the decisions. On one occasion Allen Brown proposed a slightly fuller minute, summarising but not attributing the different opinions, and even provided a sample for the prime minister to consider. Neither he nor any of his successors have chosen to take it up. The Australian system has never adopted a process by which minutes include an account of opinions raised in the debates; the only official records are the decisions which ministers must implement.

A minister once described how it worked under Menzies and Bunting:

> Menzies had an extraordinary capacity to synthesize a decision of all the discussion with which everyone would agree. I've seen him time and time again say not a word; considerable discussion would ensue. When he thought it had gone far enough, he just ... well, it would become apparent he was about to speak. He didn't tap the table or anything, it just became apparent and he'd say, 'Well, I think what we've agreed to is ...' and then you'd see Jack Bunting writing like fury, and they'd get a decision down and then you'd get people who had appeared to have been taking opposite view saying, 'yes, that's what we've agreed to'.

Perhaps Menzies' standing in these later cabinets, surrounded by ministers of less experience, gave finality to the conclusions.

Bunting, in asking for a second official to attend cabinet as notetaker, gave some idea of the way the system worked:

> For every full day which I spend in the cabinet room, I must spend something like the equivalent time in writing decisions and conferring with Departments, and if necessary with Ministers, about various aspects of decisions. And the fact is, I can seldom lock myself up after a Cabinet meeting to write decisions because of other insistent pressures. In the result, if there is a batch of ten decisions out of Cabinet, I will probably get say five out on the following morning, with the remaining five going in dribs and drabs according to when I can get enough consecutive time to deal with them ... If I had an assistant whose job it was to do a first draft, but with the final vetting left to me, I would be able to give more time to other work and give Ministers and Departments a much quicker service.

Holt agreed. McMahon later approved a third notetaker in cabinet.

Since 1996 four officials have attended cabinet, three of them notetakers. The junior official, often expert in the area, takes the fullest account. The number two notetaker, as the head of the cabinet division in the PM&C, documents more, but has to ensure the free flow of paper as required. The number one notetaker, the secretary to cabinet, as head of the Cabinet Policy Unit and member of the PMO appointed under the *Members of Parliament (Staff) Act*, oversees the process and is responsible for finalising the decisions. The secretary of the PM&C is a constant attendee in cabinet, but is no longer a formal notetaker. Although he may involve himself in drafting minutes, his main role in the cabinet room is to assist the prime minister and afterwards to communicate, where necessary, to other departmental secretaries the flavour of cabinet thinking.

The process of notetaking is now simpler because the decisions that the minister wants are incorporated in the submission as recommendations. Draft decisions are now prepared in advance on the computer system, based on the assumption that the minister's recommendations will be accepted. If there were changes, then the officials will amend the initial draft. There is less reliance on the summing up by the prime minister, except in those cases where the debate has taken the conclusions far away from the initial proposals.

Computerisation has expedited the process of circulation, too. If the minister was successful, decisions can be circulated rapidly the same day.

The responsibility for drafting the decision lies with the cabinet officials, although, sometimes, interested ministers will provide the officials with a draft of what they thought the decision was, or should be. By 1998 the office had a sophisticated tracking system to identify where each numbered submission or cabinet minute had gone.

From 1951 officials have maintained their notes in the cabinet notebooks. These notebooks do not maintain a verbatim record of what was said, or even a full account of proceedings. They are usually the official's version of what ministers say. They are used only for the purpose of writing the decisions. For the notetakers it does not matter what is said; what matters is the relevance of any comments for the eventual decision. As the acting cabinet secretary explained to a court in 1993:

> The contents of Cabinet notebooks are not intended to be an authoritative record of cabinet discussions. Cabinet minutes are the only official record of an outcome. Since the sole purpose of the notes in the notebooks is to enable the notetakers to reach agreement as to the terms of the outcomes reached at the Cabinet meeting, none of the notebooks, nor the three notebooks together, contain a verbatim transcript of the Cabinet discussions. Thus a note might be made of what one minister said, but no note of what others said. Also the order of notes does not necessarily reflect the order of the discussions ... The style of different notetakers as to what and how much is recorded vary considerably. Some use recognised shorthand scripts and others their own form of abbreviations. Some use longhand.

The message is clear. There may be notebooks but they are, at best, idiosyncratic. The first ones, written by cabinet secretary Allen Brown in 1951, provide full accounts of some debates in the early Menzies governments. They were for his own use to facilitate the writing of decisions and they were not documents that the prime minister or any other minister would have any cause to edit. They had to be accurate to serve their original, indeed their only, purpose. As such they can be trusted as a source as much as most other material. They remain, however, partial accounts. Later notebooks remain idiosyncratic, but there is now a greater number of them for each discussion. So they must still be treated with caution for anything beyond their original purpose; they will *not* provide a full account of cabinet proceedings.

There is an interesting aside. In the 1990s the Northern Land Council sought discovery of the 113 notebooks to provide evidence that is had been unfairly dealt with in the passing of the *Land Rights Act* 1976. Although a judge initially decided in its favour, on appeal the High Court finally held that the opening of this form of cabinet record was not in the public interest and protected cabinet's privacy.

At the same time cabinet itself considered what access should be granted to the notebooks. Leading officials, and a number of senior ministers, thought it best that the notebooks were destroyed once their initial objective had been fulfilled. Fortunately, at both official and ministerial level, history had its defenders. In cabinet, as Neal Blewett records, the historians had their way over the book burners, even if the consequence was legislation that prevented access to the notebooks for 50, rather than the normal, 30 years. Later notebooks may not be as useful, but they will produce more insight than we would have without them. As the section on the Menzies government, the only period for which the notebooks are available, shows the notebooks can at times tell us something about how cabinet works.

Notebooks are part of a growing range of facilities to assist the running of the cabinet system. Everything is now networked and computerised to track where each submission is, who has which copy, and what the decisions are. The system is fast; decisions are usually circulated the same day as the cabinet meeting or the day after. There is little that is *ad hoc* or random in the *procedures* that underpin the contemporary cabinet process.

Circulation of decisions was a matter for the prime minister. Once a system was developed decisions were usually circulated to ministers, but not to departments; ministers could decide if they wanted their department to brief them. Occasionally prime ministers would restrict the ministers who received copies. Howard routinely circulates decisions to all ministers, but may sometimes restrict circulation of some submissions and minutes of decisions to cabinet ministers only. In rare cases, circulation is restricted even more tightly. Committee decisions are far more restricted. Decisions of the ERC and NSC of cabinet are likely to go only to committee members, and ministers who have sponsored the relevant proposals.

Support for the cabinet process

The supporting secretariat to cabinet grew gradually. It can be seen in two forms: the formal cabinet secretariat that runs the cabinet process, and the broader structures that support the decision-making process and the ability to provide the prime minister with a capacity to view each submission with a whole-of-government perspective.

The cabinet secretariat barely existed in the first 25 years, with ministers introducing their papers in cabinet and with little need to circulate papers in advance. In 1927, with the move of the government to Canberra, the first secretariat was created. Its remit was to be responsible for the circulation of the papers, and not to provide any policy input. Nor did it have the responsibility to follow up cabinet decisions or to retain any central record of decisions. Scullin abolished the secretariat, as an invention of Bruce. It was rapidly reinstated by Lyons when he became prime minister. Although the secretary of the Prime Minister's Department, Frank Strahan, began to sit in cabinet after 1941 to keep the minutes and draft the decisions, he did not seek to strengthen the secretariat. Only in 1949, in the twilight of the Chifley government, was thought given to providing a broader capacity to the secretariat, in anticipation of Chifley giving up the Treasury if the government was re-elected. If he were prime minister alone he would want a policy capacity in his own department that had not been seen as necessary when he could receive Treasury briefings.

The 1949 reorganisation brought to the secretariat a number of talented staff from the Department of Post-War Reconstruction who had economic expertise to provide clout for the department. The functional divisions of the department developed knowledge across the range of government activities that enabled comment on cabinet submissions. Over the years department staff developed the practice of providing brief notes to the prime minister on the policy issues that were contained in these submissions, suggesting options and ways of dealing with the material.

By the 1960s Bunting had his finger in all parts of the administration, prodding here, pushing there. The Prime Minister's Department became more activist under Hewitt and a powerhouse under Carmody and Yeend, as they sought to provide the all-encompassing service that Fraser demanded – in that it reflected its masters. The department was interested in whatever the prime minister wanted it to be interested in. Where he demanded answers it sought them out. If he wanted the capacity to provide a running critique on, and alternatives to, the Treasury's economic advice, the department was expected to provide it. The economic division, with forceful heads, became a powerful player in the debate on policy alternatives. From being seen as a backwater (which it really after 1949 never was, even if it liked to be seen as only that) it became a substantial bureaucratic and policy player. A stint in the department became a useful prop for a potential secretary to be; the prime minister could see the official in action.

In 1979 Geoff Yeend, secretary of the Department of Prime Minister and Cabinet, argued that the department was never merely the post box of legend, and explained how it sought to work with departments:

> Coordination requires consultation. I try to insist that in any advising we do there is full consultation with the department concerned. It is a standing instruction in PM&C that before putting notes to the prime minister on cabinet submissions or to the Chairman of Cabinet committees if the prime minister is not chairing them, there is consultation. And on any point on which we take a different line from a proposing department, that department has to be aware of it. There is a practical reason for this. It is not our business to have ministers surprised in the cabinet room with questions they have not anticipated or be faced in the cabinet room with propositions they have not considered.

Yeend asserted it was not the role of the department to take over the responsibilities of other departments, but suggested:

> Within this view of our role as a coordinating agency, there is plenty of scope for us to develop ideas, discuss them with appropriate departments and agencies, intervene in the consideration of issues and put views to the prime minister and other ministers. We do not feel inhibited in what some might interpret as the role of second opinion. Our branches have built up an understanding of policy issues and an expertise in coordination; our officers are sought out for their advice and assistance.

The PM&C could act as the host of taskforces that drove the prime minister's agenda. The flexibility of the department was its great asset. In addition to servicing the prime minister's responsibilities as head of government and chair of cabinet, it could be re-fashioned at will to provide support to his interests, those areas of policy where he wanted to get personally involved. The department was powerful when the prime minister was most interested. It derived its authority from his personality and office.

From the 1960s prime ministers received advice on all cabinet submissions. Under Fraser they followed a standard format:

> It began with a specific recommendation, suggesting support for the proposal, no support or support on certain conditions. It then summarised the background and listed the issues that had to be decided. Briefs were usually contained on one page and almost never took more than three.

The Fraser cabinet briefs thus concentrated on the more significant issues. They were for the prime minister alone and were not sent to the ministers introducing the submission.

The brief provided the prime minister with the advantage that he was well informed on all items. But then, as he was the chair of cabinet, it was important that the difficult issues were identified and discussed. Only the treasurer was likely to be as well briefed. The prime minister had special interests in making the cabinet work effectively. The department, and more recently the PMO, was designed to provide that support.

The causes and consequences of bureaucratisation

Did the changes matter? One observer thought they have made a substantial difference. Sir John Bunting, cabinet secretary for over 15 years under five different prime ministers, argued that between the Menzies and Fraser periods government changed from ministerial government to cabinet government. In the Menzies period:

> ... the minister was supreme, and he ran his own department. That did not prevent him talking to colleagues, talking to the prime minister, going to cabinet. All these things were available and were used, but they were used as adjuncts and not as controls or discipline over the minister. In other words, the minister used cabinet. Now, when a minister announces that he has a policy initiative in mind and will be taking it to cabinet, he is forgetting that in his field he is the authority, the highest authority. He yields that to cabinet. He puts himself in the part of applicant or supplicant. The cabinet is using him.

The picture Bunting presents may be tinged with nostalgia; it does not gel with much of the account here of cabinet in the early years. But it is interesting to see why he thinks these changes have happened. Bunting ascribes the changes to two principal factors: rules and briefing. He admits there is a growing complexity of government:

> But the fact is that the new rules stated that matters coming under a wide range of headings had to be brought to cabinet. There was a compulsion, whereas earlier there were no written rules and few conventional rules. It was very largely in the minister's hands or the minister and the prime minister's hands. It was also understood that the cabinet workload had to be kept

down to certain levels. For instance, to go back to Menzies (and leaving out the Budget Cabinets, which were a special case) the understood number of submissions for a cabinet meeting was five and the frequency of meetings was once a week.

The second reason explaining change from ministerial to cabinet government, Bunting contended, was the practice of the department providing the prime minister with a brief, covering both the content of the submission as well as raising such new principles as the department saw fit. When Menzies was briefed he used the department's advice merely as part of the general store of knowledge that he applied to his consideration of issues. But Holt and his successors were 'apt to say: "I shall read you the Prime Minister's Department note"'. Other ministers then sought briefs from their own departments; ministers began to ask for the views of the department early in the debate. Bunting concluded that 'in terms of preserving ministerial as against cabinet government they may well have been a minus'.

Rules and practices then made ministers more conscious of the collective interest. Note that Bunting does not propose cabinet changed in terms of an increase in prime ministerial power, but in a shift from ministerial to cabinet government.

There were other reasons equally persuasive. The federal government formerly housed a number of departments that delivered services: the Postmaster-General; Works, Shipping and Transport; Civil Aviation; Repatriation; and Customs. They were unlikely to bring many items to cabinet. Many of those services have been hived off to statutory authorities. They have been replaced by more portfolio-crossing issues of the environment, international affairs, and macroeconomic management. These types of issues require greater consultation and collaboration. The developing rules reflect most of all the need for a single whole-of-government perspective – and a consistent media presence.

A further interpretation is to see the changes as a sign of the increasing professionalisation of politics. For officials, the demands of an increasing workload and the need for better advice resulted in better systems to provide the support for cabinet decision-making. If it was often random, even chaotic, in the early years, gradually, partly by trial and error, partly in response to perceived failings, a sophisticated cabinet system has been developed. Contemporary processes ensure that cabinet runs smoothly, its papers arrive for consideration after proper preparation, and accurate decisions are circulated expeditiously.

Ministers, too, have become more professional in their demands for better process and for the management of the issues they must decide. The rules were partly designed for ministerial convenience, to provide them with timely and accurate information to allow them to appreciate the issues they must decide. The formats, structure of submissions, the requirements for consultation and costing can help interested ministers. They can provide a foundation for good decision-making.

13 MAKING POLICY IN CABINET

Cabinet is responsible for the final decision of government in a variety of areas. It will determine expenditure, finalise proposed legislation, settle political tactics, or decide on courses of action. Not all decisions will be effectively taken in cabinet. Some will be reactive, others pre-digested in the PMO and brought to cabinet for endorsement. Many cabinet decisions may be merely routine, determining the next date of meeting, approving a parliamentary schedule, noting a statement by ministers or the prime minister. A calculation of how often cabinet met or how many decisions it made may become nothing more than an indicator of busy-ness, and of activity. It does not assume that everything matters.

Despite all these caveats cabinet remains one place where most of the time the most senior ministers meet to discuss the most pressing problems facing government and, indeed, the nation. Even if, as the next chapter explores, prime ministers may keep to themselves and a small number of select colleagues a number of vital issues, cabinet in Australia, more than in a number of comparable countries, has remained the forum for debating big issues.

The question then is the capacity of cabinet to reach informed and sensible decisions in the time and with the information available to it. The problems are self-evident: a lack of time, an aversion to excessive reading, the need to react to external forces, the complexity of issues that defy simple definition and the range of possible solutions. There is no simple answer to these problems. The history of cabinet is peppered with experiments to find better ways of working. The creation of committees, the holding of strategic meetings, the dedication of long periods of time to particular issues and the attempts to limit the 'big' issues that come to cabinet are all presented as solutions. Given the number of reviews and reforms of cabinet, these all follow diagnoses of the 'cabinet overwork' syndrome in one form or another. The implication is that there should be a 'best way' of organising cabinet.

Yet there is no one 'best way'. The problems are still endemic: how to best inform cabinet when the time of prime ministers and their senior colleagues is the scarcest commodity in Canberra; how to present data in a form that is easy to absorb and to the point; how to present sensible options; how to manage debates; and how to ensure that cabinet's decisions are implemented. Reforms invariably move away from any particular status quo to try new methods because the status quo is unacceptable. Reforms proposed are essentially structural, because in effect that is all that can be advised. Better procedures, sending the less significant elsewhere, greater notice so ministers can consider items in depth, more strategic analysis: these all make sense and all have been proposed (often several times). At least they are plausible, but they may be presented because for the reviewers it is not possible to tell prime ministers to stop interfering in ministerial portfolios or to tell ministers to work harder at cabinet business (even if these really are the problems and public servants might like to say these things). Constitutional purists argue that prime ministers should hold the ring and not run policies themselves. Prime ministers, practical to the core, do what they think is necessary or what they choose to do.

Political calculations will also determine what works well. Some cabinets work better than others because of the personalities involved, because of the strength of leadership, or the common purpose. Other cabinets may be undermined by internal divisions or external forces; in those cases procedures cannot solve more basic political problems. At other times ministers may want to avoid making a decision. Procedures – disguised as a search for better coordination, for instance – can mask indecisiveness.

Here we will explore the opportunities given to cabinet to master issues. We will ask if the ministers had the time through the regularity of meetings, through the appointment of committees, through their access to a group of officials, to absorb briefs and debate them adequately.

There must be two caveats. First, cabinet is a committee of politicians, not a court of law. It has no obligation to ensure that all sides of an issue are canvassed. Its role is to combine the political and the administrative, to decide what should be done with as much expedition as possible. There is therefore no correlation between the intrinsic importance of an issue and the time that the cabinet might spend in discussing it. Ministers may all agree and approve a submission without debate. Alternatively, an item that may appear administratively trivial has a political importance that demands careful attention. Re-election is a legitimate, and ever-present, objective. Seeking political advantage is endemic and also legitimate. The political suitability of appointments will often be a factor in decisions. Confounding the Opposition will always be a potential calculation (for example, the constant references to the 'como bill' in the early Menzies cabinet).

It is hard to be sure by what criteria 'good' policy should be judged. Invariably, when issues are contested, both sides of the argument will have some valid points to make. Is a good policy, then, one which unites the cabinet by providing a compromise, or one that provides political advantage, economic prudence or administrative viability? Does it unsettle the Opposition? Cabinet is important because it needs to bring all these perspectives, in different degrees, to bear on an issue. It is easy to get out of balance. In 1990 Howard argued that the Fraser government was so concerned to get the policy right that it failed to take adequate account of the political ramifications. The tenor of his comment suggests Howard would not fall into the same error.

Ministers come to cabinet with a common party background, but representing different portfolios. Disagreement is, in a sense, institutionalised. Treasurers arrive in cabinet armed with rigorous advice from their department on the financial feasibility of submissions. Their colleagues are briefed from other, often incompatible, perspectives. They are expected to fight their corner; successful ministers are often seen as those who get their proposals accepted, not those who buckle too readily to the central demands for economy. Yet ministers have to come to some common agreement and are all collectively responsible for the decisions they take. Ministers may not agree with the outcome, but they must eventually acquiesce. So we should not expect too much or assume that all that is needed for good decisions are smooth procedures.

The second perennial issue associated with cabinet has been called the 'collective problem': how to ensure that a diverse group of people are adequately briefed to make sensible contributions to the debate. What are the options? Should there be a common appreciation of the problem, provided by some central body? Should each minister be briefed on all issues by their own department, even if the health department may have no expertise in, for instance, defence? There is always the danger of debate from the basis of extensive ignorance, except the prime minister and treasurer, both of whom may be well versed in the intricacies of the submission because their departments brief them on everything significant. Bruce, for instance, was well aware that many of his ministers argued from a basis of ignorance or prejudice. He did not worry, as he did not let their uninformed views influence the outcome, but appreciated the political value of cabinet's perception that it was involved in decisions.

To explore the ways in which cabinet sought to create the conditions for informed decision-making, this chapter will examine:

- the regularity of meetings and the degree to which the meetings were dedicated to the lengthy discussion of a single topic
- the use of committees either to digest extensive material before bringing their conclusions to cabinet for approval, to reduce the workload of cabinet as a whole, or to take responsibility for the final determination of significant areas of policy
- efforts to provide a service to the cabinet as a whole
- the interaction with expert officials to assist the ministers in either committees or in the full cabinet
- the attempts to make cabinet strategic in its considerations of where the government was going.

Implicit in this analysis is the degree to which cabinet as a collective decision-making body still survives. Much of the debate on prime ministerial government, particularly in Canada and the United Kingdom, assumes that cabinet is no longer the focus for hard decisions (if it ever was). Evidence on how cabinet sought to make policy, and the opportunities it had, can go some way to answering these questions raised by British and Canadian experience.

The frequency of meeting

To decide, cabinet must usually meet. For most of its history, cabinet met on a regular basis. Geography played its part. For the first half of the century cabinet ministers travelled to and from Melbourne or Canberra by train. Getting back to the electorate every weekend was neither feasible nor desirable. When parliament was not meeting, cabinet would meet for several days in succession, particularly when they were considering a budget. In the early years they were more a group of colleagues, many of whom had been state premiers, who would work together and then socialise in the evening.

Thereafter the cabinet met with consistent rhythms. At the beginning of the year, or when a new government was formed, there tended to be a series of meetings over a week or so. Then the government settled into weekly meetings, particularly when parliament was sitting. During parliamentary recess, and particularly in July while the budget details were formulated, cabinet might meet every day of a week. Sometimes it met for a few hours only, but often cabinet would meet throughout the day with three or more sessions interrupted only by meal times.

Between 1939 and 1945 the frequency of full cabinet meetings declined because the crucial decisions were being taken in war cabinet or in the production executive; this period remains the only time that there was extensive delegation to committees for final decisions. But war and threat was exceptional. After the war ended the full cabinet reverted to its central position.

The frequency of cabinet meetings, and the number of submissions that came to it, are noted in Appendix 1. These are the official figures – available only for some years. There is no equivalent for an earlier period, although we could count the meetings from the records that survived. The regularity of meetings is not necessarily a sign of influence, but given the busy schedules of ministers it is a useful proxy of opportunity. If agenda are often lengthy and the time spent in cabinet extensive, then those meetings provide the opportunity for debate. The figures may be misleading. In years when there were more than 350 meetings of cabinet or its committees, several meetings could be held on the same day, sometimes one after another. Ministers could be unsure whether they were required to stay or leave as one committee metamorphosed into another. Nor have the statistics always been published in the same form, or at all in the early years. So numbers must be treated with some care. Nevertheless, there is a distinction between the frenetic meetings under Fraser and the record of the Howard government where the number and length of full cabinet meetings has declined to around 30 meetings a year, sometimes for a couple of hours only. Howard was burned by Fraser's practices and wanted a more strategic focus. Far more was to be determined by bilateral discussion and cabinet would only consider those issues that could not be settled within an extended cabinet system.

Some meetings were deliberately dedicated to difficult topics where cabinet spend day after day debating the possibilities. The first was conciliation and arbitration in 1902, a long saga held over at least six meetings where it was the only item discussed. The process could only be completed when the resignation of Kingston in 1903 removed the final objections. Other lengthy debates over a number of meetings took place on arbitration again in 1929 (leading to the fall of the Bruce government), on national insurance in 1939, on Bretton Woods under Chifley, on uranium in the Fraser government, and on GST before the 1985 tax summit and again in 1998 before Howard presented the people with a GST before the election. More recently, cabinet spent a full day meeting on infrastructure, sustainability and the intergenerational report. These topics were all difficult, both technically and politically. Prime ministers allowed the cabinet to discuss at length. Sometimes debate might allow the working out of animosities; Chifley was determined to accept Bretton Woods but party issues required the long analysis. Uranium and the GST were complex; by returning to the issue over several meetings ministers were more likely to absorb the detail, understand the implications and consequently make more informed decisions. Repetition and reconsideration provides access to the able ministers. Menzies debated foreign policy at length, even if cabinet was not required to reach any conclusions.

Budgets were always a matter of detailed concern. From the early years a week of meetings in July went through the estimates, with prime ministers and treasurers seeking expenditure savings. It was a cabinet activity, as the treasurer presented papers describing the economic outlook (and invariably collecting the papers at the end of the meetings as respective treasurers did not trust their colleagues not to leak). Sometimes treasurers wanted direction. More often the papers stated dogmatically what should be done. Then negotiations about individual estimates took place, often in the full cabinet. The cabinet office was constantly looking at ways of doing it better: more time, less papers. But eventually the requirement was the same: getting the agreement of the three or four senior ministers to the pattern of expenditure. In recent years the details of bids has been largely delegated to expenditure review committees, with the final results usually requiring the support of prime ministers. Nevertheless, Australian cabinets have had a constant and direct influence on many of the details of budgets and have done so over a series of days (even if some decisions could be finalised, or even dropped in at the last minute, by the prime minister and treasurer). Cabinet members have not been presented with a *fait accompli* by Treasury, but have been able to argue their case, even if they do not get what they want.

Committees

Committees provide another opportunity to reduce ministerial workloads and digest the information. The first committee for which there is evidence was created in 1903 to consider a number of rural bounties; it remained in existence for a time, because several other issues were referred to it. The committee brought a recommendation to cabinet for approval. Thereafter these *ad hoc* committees were common. During World War 1 a number of issues that dealt with the rights or entitlements of individuals were sent to a committee that contained the two junior ministers without portfolio. Thus the workload of the cabinet as a whole was not cluttered by these cases. The ministers worked within guidelines established by cabinet. During the 1920s and 1930s cabinet often delegated items to committees of two or three people, sometimes at the rate of two or three committees from the same cabinet meeting. At a time when there was no support for ministers and little secretarial assistance, the ministers would meet to decide on a recommendation and then bring it to cabinet.

The need for committees as a means of reducing the workload of cabinet was always appreciated. The best way of achieving this outcome was a matter of constant experimentation. Lyons formed an inner group that never met but led to the resignation of a minister who thought he should be in it. Lyons then tried to split the workload between an A and B committee, but the experiment did not survive his death. Menzies tried different models of committees; they included a prime minister's committee made up of the senior ministers and then a general administrative committee, the first to deal with policy issues and the latter to decide issues within determined cabinet policy. Even then he created far more *ad hoc* committees and sent more business to them than to the standing committees. Eventually he split cabinet into two, into cabinet and non-cabinet ministers, to reduce it to a manageable size. The outer cabinet became a general administrative committee, chaired by a senior minister, and was able to clear those items that were perceived to need approval but not extensive debate.

The experiments continued. As the pressure on cabinet grew, the prime ministers always had to find a balance between the need for cabinet discussion and the need to decide the vital issues adequately. Whitlam came to government with a well-developed scheme of cabinet committees, devised by Peter Wilenski, who was Whitlam's principal private secretary. Whitlam nominated the committee membership, but allowed any minister to attend any meeting of any committee. The economic committee soon became as unwieldy as full cabinet and fell into disuse. The most successful of the Labor committees was the first ERC of 1975, created by the prime minister and with a deliberately restricted membership, as the government tried too late to introduce some discipline into its expenditure plans. It had a tight membership and mission.

Fraser chose to bring more issues into the scope of cabinet proceedings with the creation of a co-ordination committee of senior ministers. All prime ministers consider a range of issues in their own office. These discussions are often informal and consider strategy and political perspectives. Fraser chose to give to some of these meetings formal cabinet status. The strategy had the benefit of allowing a discussion with close colleagues who were also thereby locked into the outcomes. In this way he would use committees to build support for his proposals. He was also prepared to give to some committees the right to make final decisions. The foreign affairs and defence committee was the forum in which he won support for his policy opposing apartheid and South Africa. It was never discussed in a broader cabinet; any questions on the issue were closed off with the comment that the government's policy on that issue was fixed. If the budget committee rejected a proposal, then it was not raised again in cabinet; other ministers may not even have been aware that such a proposal was ever considered. Committees also served an educative function. The proposal for a communications satellite went to an *ad hoc* committee several times both to educate ministers in the new science and to work through the implications before their recommendations were taken to full cabinet for authorisation.

The Hawke government came to office with a clearer commitment to careful analysis because the shape of cabinet had been subject to extensive scrutiny before the party won office. The committee system that emerged was, perhaps for the only time, a consequence of extensive party deliberation. A first cut had been considered before the 1980 election; it was revised and published as *Labor and the Quality of Government* before the 1983 poll. Cabinet ministers were committed to the processes; they would sometimes ask whether the submission under review had been considered by the relevant committee. In addition, the committee system served the political benefit of involving those ministers who were outside cabinet or, after the 1987 reorganisation, were non-portfolio ministers.

Under Labor the most effective committee, often regarded as the locus of real power, was the ERC because the cabinet tried to funnel all resource demands for the year through the one window. It would consider spending proposals, would call minsters to appear to defend their spending bids and determine what funds would be available. ERC decisions were nominally only appealable to cabinet, with the approval of the prime minister rarely given – only one ever was. The ERC had additional advantages: it included some senior spending ministers, or some ministers from the Left, to ensure they understood the pressures on government spending. The ministers on the committee were able to bring their senior officials to the meetings and there they could participate in the debates, ask questions and make contributions. Their active role provided weight to the proceedings. Ministers still made the decisions, but because the officials had the technical expertise the discussion could be more pointed. Not all Labor ministers approved of so tight a process; the 2004 ALP platform promised a 'better budget cabinet process'.

The Howard cabinet continued the ERC in the form it was running under Labor. Howard also created a NSC, which met monthly with its own agreed budget. Senior ministers were supported by an officials committee. At the table both ministers and officials could interact and debate topics readily. It allowed professional and technical expertise to be brought to the meeting and decisions could be made quickly. The NSC is the cabinet innovation of which Howard was reputedly most proud. Apart from these two standing committees, Howard preferred to work through taskforces that examined difficult areas, proposed policy to cabinet and were thereafter disestablished. Each prime minister has their own preferences for the way that problems are tackled.

Advising cabinet as a whole

Cabinet ministers come as individuals, but make decisions as a group. Most ministers are briefed only by their departments. Submissions are sent to them as ministers. If they choose, they may get a comment from their officials if the department has an interest in the topic. Some ministers want more; if they want to say something on all the issues coming up for discussion, they want advice. Not all departments are comfortable, or prepared, to give advice beyond their expertise.

Two or three departments brief ministers on almost everything. The Treasury, and since 1976 the Treasury and the Department of Finance, provide a brief on any submission that may have financial implications; that means pretty well every submission. Since 1950, and sometimes before, the Prime Minister's Department provided a brief to the prime minister on issues coming to cabinet. The brief would provide some background to the issues, explain what was the issue for decision, and might either suggest a procedural recommendation and/or a desirable policy outcome. The brief would usually be contained in one or two pages, designed for rapid review. After Fraser came to power, the department provided even more direct policy advice, to the degree that its influence was often resented by other ministers and departments.

These briefs all emphasised support for prime ministers, primarily for functional reasons as they had to chair the cabinet and know the implications of what was going on – that was a minimal and inescapable role for prime ministers. Key ministers were briefed because they held crucial central portfolios. The briefs they received were not circulated to other ministers, even if at times their departments may have been warned about problems. Officials often wanted to ensure there were 'no surprises', that issues raised by central agencies could be constructively answered. Senior ministers were less willing to cede the advantage that effective briefing gave them in cabinet.

Hence the notion of a collective problem: how does a cabinet allow all ministers to debate with sound knowledge? There was one attempt to develop a brief for all ministers. The Whitlam government established a Priorities Review Staff, modelled on Whitehall's Central Policy Review Staff. The purpose of the unit was to provide detailed strategic analysis of broad problems that could be circulated to all ministers to permit sensible discussions of longer term trends. It never worked effectively, quickly being drawn into the need to provide advice on the daily crises that engulfed the government. Whether the concept was flawed, in that governments are engrossed in the near future, or whether the government was too chaotic to use such advice, may be disputed. The idea has not been tried again in institutional terms.

In the 1970s the British cabinet introduced the concept of strategic retreats; they were to be weekends at Chequers, the prime minister's country residence. Here the cabinet would meet without the usual load of submissions requiring immediate action, but instead could consider the performance of the government as a whole and determine what its strategic directions might be. Ministers were not always impressed. One attendee argued that the broad discussions were all very interesting, but he was glad to get back to the real decisions that were the essence of governing. Strategy was all very well, but how did it help them?

The Hawke government considered strategic retreats where minsters would be able to rise above the daily grind of decisions and consider, for instance, how far the government had progressed in implementing the party platform. There is little evidence that they were held regularly. Keating sometimes opened cabinet with a general debate on the political state of play. Blewett found such meetings frustrating, because there was no outcome but rather a general moaning about the problems. Others argued that once or twice issues emerged from these discussions that proved useful to the government.

Howard has given greater weight to the idea of strategic debate. He appointed a partisan cabinet secretary with a remit to take longer horizons. At times cabinet encourages PowerPoint presentations from ministers who explain some general problem such as the welfare of children or sustainability, and then answer questions. The intention is to bring everyone on board when initiatives are taken. Sometimes cabinet discusses priorities, not with the intention of making decisions, but rather to understand where they might be going. The purpose is to inform cabinet; any actions that emerge from the meeting will come back for later discussion.

Australian cabinets have not always used the language of strategy, but they have tended to hold meetings to discuss the political situation, even if not in a formal sense. General discussions would take place at the beginning or the end of a parliamentary session, one to plan the legislative timetable, others to determine what came next. Prime ministers might ask for broad briefing papers or warn that a cabinet meeting would be lengthy to allow full discussion.

Prime ministers have now developed 'charter letters' to a sophisticated degree. At the beginning of a new parliament, or after a reshuffle of ministers, prime ministers will write to ministers informing them of the principal expectations they have and the main initiatives they expect in the next term. Where there is more than one minister working in a department the charter letters may describe the lines of hierarchy and the distribution of responsibility within the department. The portfolio minister will be the senior officer, but the prime minister might allocate discrete sections of policy to a non-portfolio minister within those parameters. The letters may become annual, with a capacity to act as a measure against which progress can be tested.

There is some question whether the ambition of a generally informed cabinet is even desirable. Submissions are designed to persuade; they inform cabinet with the intention of gaining the cabinet's approval for their proposal. The recommendation is provided in the format that will best achieve their objectives. Briefs question the assumptions, the figures and the objectives. Cabinet is never an even contest. Even if everyone may contribute, some are given greater weight than others. It is a contest, a 'bull ring where everyone has their place and you try not to get knocked off too often', to cite a tough and senior National Party minister.

Officials in cabinet

Officials bring expertise. They know the subjects and the administrative challenges. They can advise what has been tried before, what will work and what can be afforded. That expertise can both be of benefit to the cabinet and a problem as it is difficult to challenge advice if the alternative information is not available.

For policy debate the question then is when, and on what conditions, ought officials be able to bring their expertise to cabinet and what should be the relationship between ministers and officials in cabinet. There is a distinction here between the officials who, after 1940, came to cabinet to take a note of proceedings as a means of writing accurate decisions and those who attended to provide information and even advice.

In wartime, military leaders would attend the war cabinet and advise the ministers on what action should be taken. They also, rather more uncomfortably, had to attend the advisory war cabinet where they could be cross-questioned by leading members of the Opposition. They preferred the situation when they were clearly answerable to the elected government and resented the rough ride given them in the advisory war cabinet by members of the Opposition. Senior service officials, sometimes accompanied by the secretaries of the Departments of Defence and External Affairs, also attended cabinet during the Korean War, although Menzies became frustrated by their reluctance to react enthusiastically to the government's demands for troops. Tension between the ministers and senior chiefs was palpable.

Economic advisers also attended cabinet throughout the 1940s and into the 1950s. Melville, Wheeler and Tange attended to discuss the prospects of the Bretton Woods conference, to which they, and not the ministers, were to be the delegates. On their return they later briefed cabinet on what had occurred there. They explained the implications of the agreements to cabinet when Chifley began to finesse the proposal through the party channels. On the same issue Tange was instructed by Evatt to deputise for him in a cabinet committee:

Tange duly sat in the meeting and, when invited, delivered his minister's views to the meeting ... Chifley, in a characteristic gesture, sat back in his chair, puffed on his pipe, and addressed Tange directly. 'We know what Dr Evatt thinks', he said, 'but what do *you* think?' It was not unprecedented for a prime minister, and especially Chifley, to seek a public servant's personal views, as distinct from those of his minister and department, but to do so in front of a Cabinet Committee placed Tange in a difficult position.

He gave 'a muddled answer, trying to remain loyal to his minister while acknowledging the strength of opposing arguments'.

In the early 1950s the cabinet notebooks show that some advisers, particularly Treasury secretary, Roland Wilson, played an active role in debate. He was at times strident in his criticism of the policies, telling the cabinet both what it should have done and what it could not do. From the recollections of the notebooks, it seemed that he had many ministers in awe of his abilities (a state, I am told, in which he had all public servants of his generation). It is difficult to discover whether officials continued to attend meetings of full cabinet and then expressed their views in the same forthright and, at times, critical way as Wilson.

The tradition over the last decades has been for officials to be called into cabinet where there was a need for expert information; they would provide data and respond to questions, but would not argue with ministers. Before a decision was made, officials would be asked to leave.

That practice has never been true of committees where there is often a combination of two or three ministers accompanied by a number of officials. Again in the early 1950s, where there are records of cabinet committee discussions, officials play a more active role in debate. When Fadden and McBride met to discuss the ways that defence spending could be reined in, secretary to the treasury Roland Wilson took much of the running of the meeting, defining its objectives, and seeking to summarise what had been decided towards the end. Fadden mostly commented that he had wanted an 'informal chat'.

When the Hawke and Keating governments institutionalised the routines of the ERC, officials played an active and constant role interacting with the ministers and proposing options to the spending bids advocated by the spending ministers. Committees were able to make final decisions, so official attendance was not simply about digesting the data before a final recommendation went to cabinet for approval. In Howard's NSC both military and civilian officials will sit at the table and participate in the discussion, even though ministers will still be responsible for decisions.

Ensuring implementation

Implementation of cabinet decisions was the responsibility of ministers. In the early years the ministers themselves informed their departments. Cabinet had no capacity to follow up their decisions to ensure that action had been taken. The initial establishment of the cabinet secretariat made it clear that the body was to have no role in following up decisions. Once the paperwork was concluded, cabinet secretariat interest ended. Later, once the decision was circulated, the PM&C had no role in following it through. It keeps oversight of the decisions, providing through a 'traffic light' system an assessment of progress. It reviews and monitors; it does not instruct. Only more recently has an Implementation Unit been established, to review programs and report regularly to the prime minister and, through him, to cabinet.

Secrecy

Cabinet confers in private. It could not work any other way. The most recent *Cabinet Handbook* declares:

> 2.11 Collective responsibility is supported by the strict confidentiality attaching to Cabinet documents and to discussions in the Cabinet Room. Ministry, Cabinet and Cabinet committees are forums in which ministers, while working towards a collective position, are able to discuss proposals and a variety of options and views with complete freedom. The openness and frankness of discussions in the Cabinet Room are protected by the strict observance of this confidentiality.

No prime minister would dissent. Cabinet can only work effectively if the diverse opinions are not public. As a Secretary of the British cabinet said:

> Ministers will not feel free frankly to discuss and to surrender their personal and departmental preferences to the achievement of a common view, nor can they be expected to abide by a common decision, if they know the stand they have taken and the points they have surrendered will sooner rather than later become public knowledge.

In writing of Canadian cabinet experience, Nicholas d'Ombrain argues that the convention of cabinet secrecy does not protect the decisions of cabinet as much as 'the processes whereby ministers arrive at decisions'.

The principle of cabinet secrecy is easily defensible. Cabinet, after all, was initially a means by which ministers could agree on a common view before they advised the monarch at the Privy Council. They could argue in private, before they presented a single proposal to the king. Hence, the view of Bagehot that cabinet was an 'efficient' part of the Constitution; it worked, because it was the forum for real debate. Demands that cabinet become open miss the point. If cabinet debates were public, the real debates would move elsewhere: to the PMO, to some place where difficult issues could be thrashed out without public consequences for those who lose the argument. Cabinet would become a dignified, not a working, part of the Constitution.

The courts have taken a similar view. There was a request that the cabinet notebooks become 'discoverable' so that applicants could be assured that cabinet gave due attention to their case. A judge initially agreed, but his ruling was overturned on appeal, with the court finding that such access to the notebooks would be contrary to the national interest.

For a long time the procedures of cabinet were treated as a state secret. The existence of cabinet committees was never announced, as to do so might imply that issues determined there were not regarded as important enough to warrant the time of full cabinet. Only gradually, in the last 20 years, has the veil of secrecy been lifted. There have been many leaks as ministers breached the secrecy code, usually for their own benefit. It started under Barton, to his disgust. Leaks were also prevalent during the great crises of the Labor party as ministers competed to tell the public what had been discussed by cabinet and why their leader was wrong. Speculation remains common about who has lost, and who has been overruled by their colleagues. Such detail is seldom publicly confirmed.

A distinction can be made between decisions to leak what cabinet has decided in advance of a formal publication and leaks about the *processes* by which a matter was decided. The former are common, part of the management of the media; the latter are a breach of process even if part of the creation of reputation and standing that are integral to politics. But exhortation is really all that can be done. There is a case for cabinet secrecy, but if ministers breach it the penalties can only be political.

Debates regarding cabinet secrecy were evident, too, in the discussion in the Keating cabinet about the future of the cabinet notebooks. Even though the case brought by the Northern Land Council was lost, cabinet discussed whether the notebooks should be destroyed:

Finally we turned to the issue of destroying the cabinet notebooks, occasioned because they have been called for in a court case on Aboriginal lands rights. Duffy and the philistine Dawkins were in favour of destruction, the latter because the notebooks might be dangerous and the former because, unlike cabinet minutes, the notebooks are only partial accounts – simply the note-takers view of the meeting. I got passionate for once, arguing that all history is based on the reconstruction of essentially partial accounts and that it would be an act of vandalism to destroy the notebooks. Much noise from the book-burners – Duffy, Dawkins, Simmons and Humphreys – but Collins, Evans, Howe and Keating all for preservation. We won. The majority also favoured a 30-year release period identical with other cabinet documents. But Keating took the conservative view and 50 years was adopted.

Presumably after 50 years there would be no one left to care. There is an irony in that the only reason we know about the debate is because Blewett kept a diary, in breach at least of section 2.12 of the latest *Cabinet Handbook* that warns that 'any attempt at publication (eg in memoirs) of contributions made by individual ministers in debate in cabinet, no matter how many years ago the debate took place, would amount to a breach of the personal confidentiality and loyalty owed to Cabinet colleagues'. Some of Blewett's colleagues doubtless would sympathise with that view.

Conclusion: Is the need for coherence and strategy overemphasised?

Does cabinet coherence and consistent briefing matter? Is it essential that some or all ministers understand the full ramifications of policy proposals and therefore make highly informed policy decisions? Certainly, some analysts of cabinet think so in that they advocate 'better' flows of information, more strategic advice and more extensive debate. In effect these analyses argue that cabinet should behave judicially, testing the various options and propositions before concluding what is the best case.

If all ministers are not well informed, then two consequences can follow. First, the debate can be muddled, prejudiced and based on preconceptions of what might or might not be the case. Chaotic cabinets may lead to inconsistent or arbitrary decisions that eventually bring discredit to governments; all the assistance, in procedure or advice, is designed to avoid such a situation. Alternatively, cabinet becomes a forum of debate merely between those who are aware of the issues; often this group may be limited to the prime minister, senior ministers (particularly the treasurer) and the minister proposing. That presents an image of a segmented cabinet, in which a few players, changing from topic to topic, effectively determine what will happen.

Former British minister, Edmund Dell, argued that this inequality of knowledge made collective decision-making a farce; ministers went through the motions of participation rather than contributing anything meaningful to the debate. He proposed instead that a principle of 'collective purpose' be instituted by which the strategic ministers, always including the prime minister, determine policy from field to field. Dell could be described as a technician, concerned with good decisions and good policy. The response, from the Secretary to the British cabinet, was that Dell understated the political, rather than the technical, purposes of cabinet. Involvement of ministers in debate, however incoherent and however limited their contribution, was useful to maintain that sense of commitment that was required for collective decisions.

A senior Liberal commented in the 1980s:

> I find it hard to believe that the good government of a country needs as many cabinet or cabinet committee decisions as it gets. But on the other hand as matters do come before cabinet it is one way of making sure that all ministers understand what is happening and what it is about. It gives the ministers the reassurance of his cabinet colleagues and it is important therefore for the cabinet system and for cabinet solidarity if ministers have been part of the decision.

There is a comment attributed to Chifley, that one man and a dozen fools would govern better than one wise man alone. The cabinet process adds a few extra pairs of eyes to scrutinise the political consequences and predict the likely reactions.

So there was a need to balance participation against information, commitment against policy sophistication. That is not to say that debate in cabinet is not often well informed and sophisticated; it may depend on the personnel and subject. But it is necessary to avoid too technocratic a view of cabinet. The political agenda, to keep cabinet together and the supporters satisfied, may run counter to the technical benefits of particular decisions. No amount of good information will outplay a sense of political urgency or political fear. It is often possible to improve the technical level of cabinet debate, but for ministers that may not be the point. They need to contribute.

14 THE POWER OF PRIME MINISTERS: CABINET AS CONTEST

Cabinet is the centre of political power in Australia and that power is often contested. Within cabinet, prime ministers have traditionally been called *primus inter pares*, the first among equals. They have always been far more than that. Even in the 1898 constitutional conventions, delegates complained of the influence of over-mighty premiers. Consequently, there has been constant, if unsatisfactory, debate about whether cabinet government has become prime ministerial government. The debate has been unsatisfactory because it posits the two concepts as polar alternatives; the first notion seems to argue that everything should go to cabinet and the second that prime ministers do whenever they want to. Neither is, nor could ever be, true.

It is worth asking whether the changing practices of cabinet government have altered the balance between the prime minister, the ministers and the cabinet. This is a three-way, not a two-way analysis. Sir John Bunting, for instance, argued that during the time of Menzies and beyond there was a reduction in the degree of *ministerial* power. As more items were brought to cabinet for consideration, individual responsibility became absorbed by the demands of collective responsibility. Bunting regretted the disappearance of what he saw as strong ministers running their departments.

An alternative view of cabinet change, expressed more often in Britain and Canada than in Australia, is that collective government has been replaced by individual government; that prime ministers have become presidents, able to ride roughshod over the collective opinion of their colleagues. That perspective has thrived for 40 years in Britain, started by the work of John Mackintosh and Richard Crossman. To re-state Mackintosh's original proposition:

> The country [Britain] is governed by a prime minister who leads, coordinates and maintains a series of ministers, all of whom are advised and backed by the Civil Service. Some decisions are taken by the prime minister alone, some in consultation between him and the senior ministers, while others are left to the heads of departments, the cabinet, cabinet committees, or the permanent officials ... There is no single catchphrase that can describe this form of government, but it may be pictured as a cone. The prime minister stands at the apex, supported by and giving power to a widening series of rings of senior ministers, the cabinet, its committees, non-cabinet ministers, and departments. Of these rings, the only one above the level of the Civil Service that has formal existence and acts as a court of appeal for the lower tiers is the cabinet.

Crossman went further, arguing dramatically that 'the post-war epoch has seen the final transformation of cabinet government into prime ministerial government. Under this system the "hyphen which joins, the buckle which fastens" the legislative part of the state to the executive has become one man.'

The problem with such a debate is that it is often fought anecdote by anecdote. One person can point to occasions when prime ministers had their way, others to cases where prime ministers allowed a full debate in cabinet on issues of national importance. Examples of both practices can often be found within the same government. Some leaders do well at times, and then lose the ability to lead. Besides, there are also difficulties in determining exactly what is collective and what is individual. If a prime minister consults colleagues in his office, is it fundamentally different from talking to the same group of ministers in a meeting nominally part of the cabinet system, except that the cabinet meeting may be formally serviced by officials? Strong leaders may well dominate their colleagues. That is almost the recipe for leadership; leaders provide a sense of direction, of strategy and of purpose. Weak leaders may consult because they need to lock in their colleagues before they act. Letting cabinet discuss controversial items at length may be a sign of a floundering prime minister, unable to impose his will on the followers.

Leaders are not the only ones who have an interest in their reputation and standing. For all ministers, cabinet may be vital to their future. Cabinet is a contested forum because of the inevitable differences of interest. In part the tensions are personal. The cabinet is likely to contain the prime minister's successors, with several ministers dreaming of the party leadership and wanting to advance their cause for the time when a vacancy, by choice or force, occurs. Consider the ambitions of Hughes, Menzies, Fraser, Keating and Costello, ministers and leadership aspirants at the same time. Competition between ministers is continuous, both to develop a better national reputation and to impress their cabinet colleagues because they will be the most influential electors when the time arises for leadership succession. Personal antagonisms are endemic.

There is also competition in cabinet between the ideas and plans that appear in submissions. Cabinet tends to deal with those items that cannot be fixed elsewhere and to debate at length those issues when differences of opinion are the most marked. In part the contest is institutionalised by the nature of collective decision-making. There are more plans to spend than available resources to fund them. Treasurers and finance ministers are the institutional enemies of spending; they will argue for restraint because ministers, too, must fight their corner. If the spending ministers do not advocate change or funding for education, primary industry or whatever portfolio they hold, no one else is likely to. Yet these contests have to be restrained because the cabinet must also work as a single unit for the maintenance of government cohesion.

In this environment the prime minister is the rule-maker, referee and judge. It is that combination of functions that allows prime ministers to dominate proceedings. The procedures give greater weight to prime ministers; they already have standing as leaders of their party and the government. They still need to work to retain the support that put them there in the first place.

This chapter will examine the levers of power that prime ministers have and ask to what degree the levers have changed over a century of Australian cabinet government. These levers include the power to:

- utilise the resources available to prime ministers
- have scope for independent action
- control the agenda, proceedings and decisions of cabinet.

At the core of the debate is whether prime ministers can take the support of cabinet for granted, or so control the agenda and processes that, even while nominally consulting their colleagues, the decisions are foreordained.

Prime ministerial resources: Patronage and advice

Prime ministers bestow office. Prime ministers promote. Prime ministers sack. Every minister is conscious of these basic facts of political life. That does not mean that ministers feel constantly insecure in fear of political assassination. It does not mean, either, that prime ministers have a free choice; there are always a range of compromises that must be made to ensure that there is representation from the Senate, the various states, and the factions. In Labor governments caucus elects ministers, although recently the factions have been highly conscious of prime ministers' wishes. As we have seen (see Chapter 11) the selection of ministers link the party and the cabinet.

Prime ministers allocate portfolios and determine who will be promoted. Ministers seek to impress. They are always conscious of the prime minister's views and will take them into account. If the prime minister has strong views about an issue, ministers may acquiesce, rather than fight. In the last resort prime ministers can put items off the agenda or delay their consideration in cabinet if the issues do not have the support.

The tactic does not work all the time. If a prime minister has lost standing, he may find it difficult to impose his views. After the first Keating challenge, in which the majority of cabinet ministers voted for Keating, Hawke's influence was fatally undermined as some ministers withdrew any cooperation and made cabinet impossible to run. Labor ministers who relied on caucus election – several under Scullin and later Ward in the 1940s – could not be disciplined. Party opposition may not be as blatant under non-Labor governments, but can still exist. Menzies and others were discontented with Lyons' lack of leadership. In turn, several ministers, including his protégé Harold Holt, joined the move to unseat Menzies in 1941. McMahon was constantly undermining Gorton, and McMahon in turn received little loyalty from his colleagues once they thought he would lose the 1972 election.

Prime ministers cannot take support for granted, if their standing is low or sometimes if there is an obvious contender who thinks their turn has come and is prepared to use the party to grab the top job. When contenders are in cabinet, prime ministers cannot too obviously use the cabinet against them, although Hughes was prepared to lock in colleagues when Watt challenged his authority in 1920. If they are outside, then cabinet ministers will be ruthlessly corralled to attack and deny the challenger, as Fraser did when Peacock sought to challenge, but as Hawke could not do in 1991 because he no longer had the standing he required.

In cabinet debates prime ministers have more resources at their disposal than any other minister, particularly after PM&C developed a capacity for strategic, and then policy, advice from 1950 on. When it absorbed some of the policy skills from the Department of Post-War Reconstruction it had the capacity to brief the prime minister more broadly and to run with a number of issues. Gradually, the prime minister was provided with a brief on every cabinet submission, providing background, identifying the problems that had to be considered, offering advice on the way that the item should be handled and, later, what the best outcome would be. The briefs may have provided policy prescriptions, but no prime minister relied exclusively on them. Most prime ministers have political nous, the ability to judge individuals and a thread of ruthlessness. They needed those skills to get there in the first place.

The department always has served the cabinet as a unit; if the deputy prime minister or some other minister is appointed to chair a cabinet committee, the department will provide support for that minister. Its responsibility is to keep the cabinet system working. In that sense it has a collective function.

But it is still primarily the Prime Minister's Department. It advises prime ministers on what should come to cabinet and on any other issues meriting prime ministerial attention. It now also has the capacity and resources to take on those responsibilities that are of particular interest to the prime minister. It can incubate new activities; education and Aboriginal affairs began as offices in the Prime Minister's Department. Its staff now are well qualified and it is commonly recognised that a spell there brings officials to the attention of the prime minister and can help their careers. It is a resource for managing the process of government that has had a breadth and clout during the last 30 years that, at its best, is unrivalled in the public service, outside the Treasury.

Added to the power exercised through the Prime Minister's Department is the prerogative of the prime minister to appoint all the heads of departments. In theory, departmental secretaries used to be appointments made on a permanent basis by the Governor-General on the recommendation of the prime minister. Under the *Public Service Act* 1999 the prime minister can now appoint heads of departments for any term up to five years. He can also dismiss them. Secretaries are thus aware that, though they serve their minister, they need to keep an eye on the interests of the government as a whole as reflected in the wishes of the prime minister. Whole-of-government is a mantra of officials to be intoned with feeling.

Since the 1970s prime ministers have also been supported by the creation of a powerful, and expanding, political office. Prime ministers always had a private secretary and sometimes a press secretary. Then their offices took on other functions. The trend started with the addition of a few policy advisers, followed by political tacticians and then the hiring of specialists. The prime minister's political office today has became a source of control and direction, a powerhouse of over 35 operatives and policy advisers with the ability to keep their fingers on the pulse of the party and the cabinet. As Blewett noted, many of them had more influence than 'us ministers'. They have the ability to draw in advice and information, to direct action and to control the management of events.

The media, too, has become more focused on the prime minister. What prime ministers do is likely to be newsworthy. Prime ministers can use the access with skill. Howard prefers to go directly to the electors on talk-back radio where he can get the chosen message across without contest and without his words being interpreted by journalists. The belief that there is a constant campaign assists the prime ministers who can make immediate commitments, where the leader of the Opposition can only issue hopeful promises. The media process has also sped up. Where once Menzies in Washington could tell journalists to wait for comment until he had reported to cabinet and parliament, prime ministers now react immediately and willingly in press conferences.

Combined, patronage, advice, staff and media access give every prime minister resources that provide great advantages. Even if other ministers have the same support at lesser levels, prime ministers can mobilise assets to allow them to operate either individually or through cabinet, always with the assumption that they will constantly and actively be shoring up support as required. For prime ministers the cabinet system is an arena of many sites – full cabinet, committees, meetings of ministers, bilateral discussions with ministers – each of which are forums where decisions can be made.

In asking what prime ministers can do, we can explore what evidence there is for independent action outside cabinet; and ask how they are able to control or direct the activities of cabinet itself.

Scope for independent action

Prime Ministers often act and speak on behalf of their cabinet. Cabinet members then have a choice: they can accept and endorse the actions, or they can dissociate themselves from the prime minister's public statements and actions. Ministers have never followed the latter course; most expect that kind of leadership.

The most obvious occasion for prime ministerial initiative is when prime ministers are overseas, where they can speak on behalf of the country and commit it in discussions with their counterparts. Hughes remains the most striking example. He visited Britain, for long periods leaving the country to either Pearce or Watt as his deputies. He would independently range over a number of issues, not always consistently. Sometimes the first that the cabinet in Melbourne knew of an initiative was through reading a report in a newspaper. Hughes would provide a reaction to President Wilson's Fourteen Points, leaving Watt to expostulate that the cabinet might have something to say on so significant an issue. Hughes had been granted some freedom of action by cabinet before he left and he and his Australian-based colleagues did not disagree on many issues; the one exception was the question of whether the cabinet should be consulted.

Hughes did go through the motions of consulting cabinet when it suited him, at least in part because he wanted to control what was done at home. The telegrams were constant and they illustrated the levels of frustration felt by Watt as he called together his colleagues to give formal standing to Hughes' latest statement. Hughes would react to their comments, sometimes apologetically, sometimes angrily. He played Watt skilfully, but without giving much away. As Watt discovered when he in turn went overseas and wanted some latitude in action, being prime minister provided authority that was not available to mere treasurers. Hughes locked ministers in behind him to frustrate Watt and he gloated as he drove Watt from office.

In the long term Hughes' erratic and selfish behaviour cost him the job. While he retained the uneasy support of his Nationalist ministerial colleagues, the new Country party was not willing to serve under him, preferring the more measured approach of Bruce, a complete contrast in approach, style and ego, but not necessarily any less in control of what was achieved.

But overseas travel by a prime minister could be dangerous if the political support in Australia was not firm. When Scullin went to Britain in 1930, his government collapsed in his absence. Even though he tried to exert the same influence as Hughes by telegram, the cabinet, and even more the caucus, often rejected his advice. His delegates, Fenton and Lyons, were not able to represent him adequately, and by the time he met the party again the caucus was a shambles and the government was doomed. Scullin had been able to represent Australia overseas in discussions about the appointment of an Australian as Governor-General, but little more. Menzies, too, was undermined while he was overseas in 1941; some backbenchers and a number of ministers wanted a change of leader. Menzies may have cut a significant figure in London, but on his return in July he faced crisis after crisis until he was rejected by his party. He resigned rather than fought. Authority is not always sustained by international representation.

Prior to the modern era, travel to Britain or the United States (prime ministers rarely visited anywhere else) took months. Modern travel makes international summitry far easier. Prime ministers can deal with their counterparts and make commitments. But it can produce difficulties. Hawke agreed with Reagan that the United States could test missiles in Australian air space. It needed the faction leaders to smooth over ruffled feathers in the caucus, but they ensured the prime minister was not undermined. Howard can speak frequently to President George W. Bush and may make tentative commitments to send troops in the knowledge that the cabinet will back him. Who else might have been involved in discussions on the Australian commitment of troops to Iraq may not be known, but it is likely that key ministers were in the loop.

Almost all prime ministers love the international stage because there they talk to their equals, and not their rivals. If they make statements, they know they cannot be repudiated. They may be cautious and say that they will take issues back for cabinet discussion, but that ploy may be tactical rather than essential. Overseas, prime ministers speak for their nation. Foreign ministers have become deputy sheriffs, important but playing the supporting role at those international forums or negotiations where prime ministers choose to become personally involved.

How far prime ministers go in taking independent action through international forums is a matter of choice. Fraser promised the president of Zambia that Australia would open a high commission office in his capital. But he wanted to gain cabinet approval. He then asked the secretary of his department to ring the ministers who were members of the foreign affairs and defence committee to seek their approval. One or two wondered if this process was the best way of making decisions, but they backed the prime minister's commitment and the decision was duly recorded as a decision of cabinet, even though cabinet never met on this item. In modern parlance, it could be called a virtual cabinet; the decision was no less final.

Prime ministers may also make commitments at home. They will talk on the radio, speak at gatherings and meet delegations. The promises they make will be duly recorded and staff will follow up to ensure that something happens. Public statements are commitments; careful prime ministers include caveats in much of what they say, providing a dignified exit if the proposals do not work out, as all their words are recorded and can be used against them by the Opposition. In cabinet these public commitments become a means by which prime ministers set the agenda and the direction.

This authority gives prime ministers an ability to operate individually that is effectively untrammelled. Consequently, it is easy to point to occasions where prime ministers have set the tone and the direction of government and/or policy. Hawke announced the tax summit on talk back radio. Keating stated in parliament that if the coalition won the 1993 election the Labor Party would not oppose the GST in the Senate. The statement amazed his colleagues who had not discussed the strategy, but no one was going to object in public. Keating put the republic on the agenda unilaterally; he wanted to create a vision that in his view lifted the national horizon. Howard committed his government to gun control. Even more significantly,

> When he and his government came under heavy attack from business for lack of vision in May 1997 he responded quickly and without reference to senior colleagues, by putting the whole tax question on the agenda; by August a task force was appointed to prepare a report. A year later the government produced the extensive [GST] package ... on which it went to the October 1998 election.

The accepted logic was that no government could win on a new tax. Howard alone made the decisions, committed the government and won. These bold if independent ventures have led observers to comment that they are surprised about the extent to which prime ministers can set the direction and the policy of government. Such comments are naive. There is nothing recent or novel about the independent action of Australian prime ministers.

Prime ministers can also veto their colleagues. At certain times Howard has ruled out initiatives floated by colleagues: vouchers for higher education and abortion reform. 'These issues will not' he declares, 'be introduced in this term'.

The immediate and constant access to the media provides opportunities for commitments on a daily basis. Policies that might once have been announced in parliament, with the public informed through the daily press, now are provided direct to the electors over the airwaves. Photo opportunities and sound bites replace parliamentary statements. 'We will decide who comes to this country and the terms on which they come' was a slogan that encapsulated an election campaign, and was given direct to the media. Prime ministers thus set the direction, with or without the benefit of cabinet debate.

Prime ministers have at different times brought policy speeches to cabinet for discussion, but their content remains the prerogative of the leaders. Prime ministers may consult, but only they eventually decide. Some leaders use this power skilfully as a means of committing a government they later lead. In the Whitlam government the party platform and the 1972 policy speech were known respectively as the old testament and the new testament. If a proposal was in either document, its chances of success in a submission before cabinet were greatly enhanced.

It is also possible to point to the other side of the independent coin. Prime ministers can act independently in areas that interest them, but they still remain concerned to gain cabinet endorsement for most of their actions. There is an institutional need to consult. Cabinet is more than a forum for decision; it also provides collective commitment and support. Prime ministers use that process too when it is regarded as desirable, even if it can often be taken for granted.

Working the cabinet

Prime ministers on many occasions may use cabinet as a means of getting support, maintaining legitimacy or defusing opposition. Prime ministers control the operations and content of cabinet. They determine what is debated there and often the terms of that debate. They nominate the speakers, the length of the discussion and then can determine what the decision of cabinet is. They are the ringmasters.

Prime ministers determine the cabinet agenda; they always did. For a time there was a running agenda; items were added and listed under the name of the minister who submitted the item. Ministers who did not trust the cabinet process took little there in the early years, but as the process became more formal that tactic became less of an option. In those days the prime minister selected those items that he wanted debated. Later a new agenda was developed for each meeting; the secretary of cabinet would propose a number of items that were either there as a matter of timing, urgency or political demand. Prime ministers would then decide whether or not to accept the proposals. It has never been possible to list an item on the cabinet agenda without the approval of the prime minister.

Then there were items that have at different times been seen as items without submission or items below-the-line (of the agenda). All appointments, for instance, have to be cleared with the prime minister before they are brought to cabinet for formal decision-making approval. At times appointments may also have to be run past the senior minister from the state from which they come, to ensure they are politically acceptable. Cabinet may choose not to appoint or at times to replace the nominee with a different name. If items of political urgency need to be debated without any submission being circulated, the prime minister will agree in advance. If cabinet is to have a general discussion on the political situation, or on some pressing item, the prime minister will seek the views of colleagues and decide when enough information has been shared. Some discussions (for example, foreign affairs in the early Menzies cabinet) may be discussed but without any decision; debates are for airing views and options. The prime ministers have been the gatekeepers to cabinet.

In determining what goes to cabinet for debate, prime ministers can also determine what is kept off the agenda, and what they do not want debated. Prime ministers have often avoided debate on their prerogative appointments. Curtin did not seek cabinet endorsement for the appointment of the Duke of Gloucester as Governor-General, an omission that, as ever, brought protests from Eddie Ward. Whitlam only told cabinet of his choice of John Kerr after he had formally adjourned a cabinet meeting; the cries of protest were thus informal and, to him, able to be ignored.

Whitlam avoided any cabinet discussion of foreign policy until the dying days of his government; he saw that area as his personal fiefdom. Fraser would not allow any further debate on Zimbabwe or apartheid after the foreign affairs and defence committee had determined the government stand for the 1976 commonwealth conference. The government had a policy, he told dissenters, and was not going to reconsider the issue. There is in effect no alternative if the prime minister insists, short of open revolt.

Prime ministers, too, decide what cabinet has decided, or when it has decided not to decide. They sum up the discussion, sometimes explicitly, sometimes leaving the debate hanging in a form that allows the secretariat to construct a suitable decision that reflects the prime minister's views. Formal votes in cabinet are rare; even those that can be identified with precision. In the early Menzies years, for example, they were not decisive. Whether the cabinet barely carries a proposal, or whether the prime minister weighs and tests the conclusions, it remains true that any proposal that so badly divides a cabinet that it is pushed to a vote may make a prime minister wary about building policies on such a shifting political foundation. Ministers do not always agree with the outcome of votes anyway. Whitlam's ministers agree he went around the table to get opinions, but were convinced that the numbers he drew from the process were different from theirs. He counted the votes and then fudged the result. They did not challenge the outcomes in cabinet. Did this constitute voting? Bunting thinks not. He argued that 'decisions came more from a sense of the weight of opinion rather than from anything strictly to do with numbers'. The responsible minister and the opinion leaders would get more weight than others.

Labor, with its traditions of equality and voting, still gave more credence to the idea of equality and voting. Bunting recalls one cabinet committee where Chifley was in a minority of two out of eight when the initial discussion was completed. Then, as Chifley described it to Bunting:

> I said with a wink across to the minister, that I knew he still had more to say on the subject, that I had cut him a bit short on his first remarks, and that I felt sure that everybody would like him to have a better go so they could understand the matter fully. The Minister, taking the hint, went through his spiel again, and while I knew we had not turned the corner I did feel we were making progress. So I started another round of discussion myself, and in due course I got the minister going again, and I could sense the resistance collapsing. And after one more round I thought I could risk a vote. And, do you know, the result came out! Six for the Minister and two against! Government by exhaustion.

Managing difficult colleagues was one of Chifley's strengths. He could have declared the result, leaving colleagues disgruntled. He preferred to bring them along.

So did Fraser. He wanted to know what ministers thought; it was their job to have an opinion. If they were opposed he wanted to know why. He would push, cajole and argue, until an agreement was reached with which he was content. If not satisfied he would delay a decision. Prime ministers rarely lose outright when they have a strong view (the Bretton Woods case in 1945 being the only explicit exception recorded in the minutes). But sometimes they may change their opinions in the cabinet after the discussion and sometimes they just do not care and leave it to their ministers to develop and propose policies.

The processes change from one prime minister to another. Some run cabinet in a routine and systematic way; others can be more erratic. Hughes worked with a cavalier insouciance that would never have been possible for the careful and controlled Bruce. Chifley was patient with the appalling behaviour of Ward, who chose to oppose cabinet decisions even in public. Some of Labor's battles, under Whitlam and even Keating, were almost fought in the open. Howard controls the cabinet effectively and maintains its solidarity.

But there should be no assumption that constant routine is necessarily preferable for prime ministers. In 1958 Bunting wrote a memo to the Secretary discussing how budget cabinet could be better organised, to reduce the workload by restricting the number of Treasury background papers and special requests. He feared that:

> These papers either waste time or the Cabinet gallops through them. And galloping, once started, becomes the fashion; they are then apt to gallop when they should work. ... I do not want to pose as a reformer. For one thing there are certain virtues, from the point of view of the Prime Minister and treasurer, for example, in the confusion.

Keeping ministers on edge, a little uncertain, sometimes has its value to a leader. Prime ministers in control can benefit when not everyone else is certain what is being decided. Procedures may be developed for reasons other than clarity of decision-making.

Yet by themselves rules and procedures do not guarantee control. Every prime minister has access to these assets, but not every prime minister is able to use them to advantage. The best means of applying these assets are often intangible. They depend on continuity and maybe a modicum of fear. From the outside, each cabinet submission may be a unique item for discussion; from inside they are merely one of a stream. Ministers are part of a team that must interact over a long period. Few issues are themselves so significant that it is worth creating permanent enmity, so each time ministers must calculate the costs of a fight with their colleagues (and rivals). There is a need to maintain a ministerial team approach for public image.

So, also, must solidarity with the prime minister be calculated and maintained even for the detested rivals who covet the position. If the prime minister has a view on an item, then the ministers must decide whether it is worth a fight, whether they can win and what the costs might be. They may acquiesce, rather than agree, with policies that they do not like but cannot change. Most prime ministers can create in ministers a sense of respect, if not awe, if they are to survive. It is not that ministers constantly fear that they will lose their positions, but rather it is an appreciation that their future lies in the hands of their leader. Consequently, there are in cabinet a number of yes-men, the ballast that will always line up with the leader, regardless of the issue. They may not always be good ministers, but they provide the assenting voices around the table. Asked what would happen if he and his deputy prime minister were on one side and all the others were on another, Fraser laughed and said, 'If Doug and I were in one side, all the others wouldn't be on the other'. Some ministers will always fall into line. Ministers know that prime ministers have long memories.

Cabinet committees are just one forum in which that influence may be exercised. Prime ministers in recent years have determined in which arenas decisions will be made. If they do not chair the meetings of committees themselves, they ensure that a colleague does so in their interests. Where issues are confidential (in the ERC or the NSC, for instance), ministers outside the committee will never know what was discussed. Even then some crucial debates may take place in the PMO, where a select number of ministers, staff and officials determine the final outcomes. In a real political sense it does not matter where the final decisions are made, as long as all the key players are committed.

Relations in cabinet are not simply about powers and prerogatives. They are about personalities, about pecking orders and about the maintenance of power and position. After years working with their leader, ministers accept their leader's judgment, particularly if they seem likely to win the next election. Every Fraser minister would agree that some of their colleagues were scared of Fraser, although all insisted they were not themselves (even the one who followed me to the lift after my interview with him to say; 'you are not going to tell him what I said, are you?'). They were nervous because of Fraser's use of cabinet to cross-examine them on all their proposals as a means of testing the validity of their proposals. Hughes dominated his cabinet by the fierceness, even the viciousness, of his personalty. Yet, to the end his own party's ministers were prepared to stand by him. On issues of interest to him Keating could be very directive, but on others dismissive and bored. Prime ministers are rarely shrinking violets where their own prestige or interests are at stake. They will fight their corner and have the advantage that they act as ringmaster, judge and jury on the proposals before cabinet and on the way that cabinet will be run and organised.

At times the tensions show. Paul Hasluck brilliantly encapsulated the antagonisms of the late Menzies cabinet in *The Chance of Politics*. Labor cabinets were notoriously riven, leading to splits in 1916 and 1931 as different factions battled for their views with little consideration for the government as a whole. Even the Hawke government was eventually split between the personalities of its two giants, leading to a temporary paralysis.

Overall, then, prime ministers have a store of resources that must be applied carefully and constantly replenished. Good judgment, winning electoral ways, effective political instincts, and a reputation for ruthlessness all supplement the formal power of cabinet rules and procedures to allow them to win most of the time. Indeed, given the tenor of the debates about whether prime ministers have excessive power, it is obvious that cabinet government works best when prime ministers are strongest. The Scullin government, the late Lyons years, the Gorton and McMahon interludes, and Hawke's last year were occasions when the prime minister lost authority and political shambles emerged. Menzies, Hawke (initially) and Howard had the strength and reputation to ensure that cabinet pulled together, even if in the latter case Howard's treasurer openly coveted his position.

Cabinet and political support

If powerful prime ministers can so readily get their way, why then do cabinets meet so often? The answer rests on a combination of mutual dependence and political coherence. In part, cabinet is a process of reaching collective, and sometimes consensual, decisions. But to regard cabinet exclusively in those terms is to provide a limited canvas on which it works. Certainly cabinet is an important forum for decision-making, but it may be just one among many. Cabinet may endorse decisions taken elsewhere, legitimise prime ministerial statements or confirm cabinet committee decisions. Yet for prime ministers cabinet serves an essential role in managing the current national and party politics.

The cabinet will include almost all the senior players in the party, so the potential successors to the prime minister sit around the table. Collective responsibility, even with occasional leaks, means that the ministers are publicly committed to government programs. They cannot dissociate themselves from what the government is doing. It is hard for any minister, in expectation of a run for the prime ministership at a later date, to develop an independent image. Since the potential successors who might feel inclined to wrestle the position from their leader are often treasurer, it is even harder to provide a rounded picture of what a new prime ministership might look like. Prime ministers can always ensure that no one minister can gain too public a profile, too many independent successes, or too clear a position. Prime ministers will promote, praise and counterbalance their ambitious colleagues.

Prime ministers are aware of the infamous reputed Mafia adage to 'keep your enemies close'. The times when prime ministers are often at greatest risk are when the obvious successor has left the cabinet and is free to campaign openly on the backbenches. Menzies might have followed that line in 1939, had Lyons not died a mere three weeks after his resignation. Fraser's resignation in 1971 led to Gorton's downfall. Peacock left the Liberal cabinet in 1981 and for 12 months collected the numbers until he failed in an attempt to dislodge Fraser. In those 12 months the prospect of a challenge hung over the government. Keating's sojourn on the backbenches was, everyone knew, only an interlude to a second challenge. He took the opportunity to challenge some of Hawke's cherished initiatives, particularly the attempt to restructure the way the Australian federal system works, which he declared to be counter to Labor tradition. He duly took Hawke on again and just succeeded. Being in cabinet stifles the oxygen of independent action.

Prime ministers can also use cabinet to integrate the factional differences that might exist in any initial stage. Even if the Liberals do not have formally recognised factions, there have at different times been identifiable groupings of common interest, sometimes based around states, sometimes personalities, sometimes policy directions. In cabinet these groupings may argue but will then follow the common line. Thus there can be little apparent difference between the wets and the dries when cabinet announces its policy.

Cabinet, too, is where the coalition is maintained. That has not always been easy. In 1939 there was a great rift between Menzies and the Country party over national insurance; in the end Lyons sided with Page and the Country party, leading to the resignation of Menzies. When Lyons died three weeks later and Menzies was elected leader of the UAP, Page refused to continue the coalition. Only a change of Country party leadership led to a resumption of good relations. In 1951 the Country party ministers in cabinet bitterly opposed any revaluation of the pound, arguing that 'they could not be in the cabinet and in the Country party' if cabinet accepted such a policy. Whether this was a serious threat or not, it worked. Even though cabinet debated the issue at length and once voted in favour (although some Liberals joined the Country party in opposition), Menzies was not prepared to push the issue in the face of such strident opposition. In 1968 McEwen announced that the Country party would not serve under McMahon. McMahon did not contest the leadership; in 1971 he checked that the embargo had been lifted before he stood against Gorton.

Being in the Country party has always given some degree of independence to its ministers. 'You can get away with a lot,' said one in the late 1970s, 'if you are senior enough ... and in the Country party'. McEwen was able to oppose the government line on revaluing the dollar. Anthony could threaten to leave the coalition in late 1971, again over revaluation, and win the day. But these events are remarkable for their rareness. The coalition has been stable since it returned to government in 1949 because Liberal prime ministers have been conscious of the need to manage the process and ensure that the junior party is never overwhelmed by sheer numbers. Even when Fraser had sufficient parliamentary support to form an exclusively Liberal government in 1975, he preferred to maintain a coalition. It has helped that, in McEwen, Anthony and Nixon, the Country party has had some of the smartest political operators in the cabinet and that prime ministers, as much from choice as necessity, have paid attention to their views and interests. Some observers note that it is hard to tell, in cabinet debates, which minister is from which coalition party.

In the Labor party the management of factions in cabinet may be harder, because the ministers are not entirely dependent on the prime minister for their presence there. But there are tactics available to bypass them or to coopt them. All Curtin's principal cabinet committees were chaired by ministers who were his supporters. In this way he could hold Ward at arm's length. Chifley could allocate portfolios to ministers that kept them away from the principal economic action. Hawke initially made Brian Howe minister for defence support (putting a leftwing pacifist in charge of defence procurement!). Later, seeing his talent, he brought him into the centre of government, not only giving him a senior portfolio, but including him on the ERC, so that the Left was committed to the tough decisions which that committee had to take.

The essence of political management for prime ministers is to maintain the continued unity and support of cabinet. They want it not only when ministers think they are right, for that type of support is easy to give. Prime ministers want it when ministers think they are wrong, but are prepared to trust the leader because of his record of being right most of the time. Every prime minister has a store of political capital, derived from a history of winning and from personal debts from those who have been promoted. If the prime minister chooses he can, in effect, say at times, 'this is what we are going to do'. Sometimes ministers want that decisiveness. On other occasions, however uneasy, ministers will agree. But a prime minister cannot use the tactic too often, particularly if those initiatives do not work. Eventually, too many failures exhaust the capital and he has to listen more, and attend to other views more. On the other hand, if he was right and the ministers were wrong, then his political capital and scope for independence is further enhanced. Everyone backs a winner who can get the government re-elected.

Prime ministers also use cabinet to manage issues, to ensure that the ministers are all 'on song'. Some of the discussion in cabinet may be to inform ministers and allow them to think aloud about the issues. The lengthy debates over foreign affairs in the early Menzies years were not intended, it seems, to lead to a policy decision, but rather to a sense of involvement and participation. Bruce was explicit that he let ministers, however uninformed, talk as a means of ensuring their support. Hawke and Keating allowed general debates without any prescribed topics. The idea was that a sense of priorities was allowed to emerge.

As prime ministers become more comfortable in office, more experienced and more confident, they may relax their detailed controls. But there is no certainty that length of service gives comfort. Political levers have to be used constantly, support garnered and duchessed, colleagues satisfied. Maintaining support is a constant challenge, a continuing and searching examination that most prime ministers eventually fail when they are forced from office rather than choosing the time of their own departure.

There is no one way to do the job. Prime ministers may be selected precisely because their skills and approach are different from the person they are replacing. Hughes and Bruce, Hawke and Keating were contrasts in style. Each successor brought unique skills to circumstances where their predecessor was out of favour. A senior prime ministerial adviser was struck by:

> ... how powerful they can be – a prime minister has more votes than his cabinet colleagues put together. I thought the process was a tad more democratic [than this] but even in a country like Australia, one man can wield a hell of a lot of authority. It's only when people lose confidence in the person making the decisions that that authority is dissipated.

The sting of course was in the last sentiment.

The purpose then is to balance the political and the administrative, the policy and the partisanship. Too much emphasis on either could be disastrous because it leads to a lack of perspective. It is worth recalling Howard's judgment of the Fraser cabinet:

> One of the tensions that I found as a senior minister in the Fraser government was the balance between the political role and the administrative role. The extent to which too frequent a number of cabinet meetings and too cumbersome an administrative procedure can paralyse one's political activity and one's political effectiveness is a real constraint.

So prime ministers seek to keep that balance, working through cabinet. The rhetoric will always be collective, even if some ministers are less persuaded of its reality. Prime ministers need the ministers to run the departments, to maintain a balance, to protect their portfolios. They need their continued political support. Using cabinet as a sounding board to gain their views, to provide a sense of involvement and to lock in ministers often strengthens their position. If ministers are part of the process most of the time, they will give prime ministers scope for independent action when they choose to use it. Cabinet activity is not a sign that prime ministers are weak, although at times floundering prime ministers may become bogged down in cabinet. Rather, it can be the process by which they retain the government's strength through collective action and commitment.

15 CORE EXECUTIVES: IS AUSTRALIAN CABINET DIFFERENT?

Peter Shergold, secretary of the PM&C, has commented that only in Australia have the traditions of cabinet government been maintained. That is an arresting proposition in that he is suggesting that in other Westminster governments such as Britain and Canada and elsewhere, the form of government that is recognisably cabinet government has been replaced by another phenomenon. Can such a proposition be sustained?

Cabinet is a familiar term in the lexicon of governments. It can be found in presidential systems, in the coalition governments of Europe and in the parliamentary Westminster systems of Canada and Britain. In each case cabinet means different things. In the United States, cabinet has status but no collective weight. In Europe, coalition governments are shaped by the demands of systems of proportional representation; the ensuing coalition agreement may limit the ability of the collective to overrule the individual minister. Neither of these models may tell us much about the characteristics of the Australian cabinet. The comparison works best with Westminster systems because the traditional conventions of Australia were derived, at one stage, from the British experience and ministers talk about Westminster systems as though they are from the same stock. Working from the Kipling principle of 'what can they know of England who only England know?' we can ask how the experience in Australia resembles the cabinet experiences in those countries and what those comparisons can tell us about the effectiveness of cabinet government in Australia?

Reading the recent literature it would seem that there is little to compare, despite the familiarity of the terminology. A common diagnosis of the state of government in Britain and Canada declares that cabinet government is dead. Prime ministers Jean Chrétien (1993–2004) and Tony Blair have dispensed with the support of cabinet and ruled with fewer constraints than their predecessors. Cabinet has become little more than a cipher, held briefly each week more for the purposes of show than as a decision-making forum. These two leaders are seen to be the epitome of prime ministerial power.

In 2001 Jeffrey Simpson argued in *The Friendly Dictatorship* that Chrétien was merely the last, and most obvious, manifestation of dominant prime ministers able to govern in Canada with few limitations on their ability to get their own way. Cabinet had become little more than a focus group in which some ideas might be considered, but it did not meet for long and was not a deliberative or decision-making institution. Cabinet committees could decide on new policies, but they were not funded at that time. Rather, they were put into a basket of new initiatives and the prime minister and the minister of finance would determine at budget time which policies would be taken up. Once ministers were asked to list their 'top ten' of the programs approved, but not funded in order to provide guidance to the prime minister and minister for finance, they were not told the outcome of this survey.

Within their portfolios ministers were left to their own devices, but wherever the prime minister wanted to become involved, he determined the direction and content of policy. Simpson argued that 'cabinet government presupposes collective decision-making and responsibility, a collection of equals, with some inevitably being more equal than others because of the importance of their portfolios'. But the prime minister has become far too powerful for such a description to be applicable now. Simpson's polemic builds on the work of Donald Savoie, whose magisterial work, *Governing from the Centre: The Concentration of Power in Canadian Politics*, provides a detailed account of the growth in the power of the central agencies in Canada, and the significance of the prime minister and his office. Cabinet has a series of set agenda items: discussion, presentations, nominations and then the endorsement of committee decisions (which are rarely disputed). But it does no more. Savoie builds a case that these changes mean the prime minister is '*Primus*: there is no longer any *Inter* or *Pares*'. These conclusions are based on the premise that cabinet should be the core decision-making forum. Others see it more as a representation of the federation and dealing with national, rather than operational, questions.

A similar debate can be found in Britain, where Blair's cabinet still meets weekly but for shorter periods and with a more limited agenda than in earlier regimes. There are a number of standing items for cabinet but few policy issues brought there for decision. Cabinet government, say the observers, has declined under Blair. The prime minister makes the crucial decisions; any belief in collective debate has gone. Blair's biographer John Rentoul comments:

> Blair's management style ushered in a new low in the history of cabinet government in Britain. That style was 'hub and spoke' rather than collegiate, reducing most meetings of cabinet to just forty minutes of approving decisions taken elsewhere, parish notices and short speeches either delivered by the Prime Minister or vetted by him in advance.

A Blair aide claimed:

> Cabinet died years ago. It hardly works anywhere else in the world. It is now a matter of strong leadership at the centre and creating structures and having people do it. I suppose we want to replace the Department barons with a Bonapartist system.

Similar comments were made about the imperial style of Mrs Thatcher who did not welcome debate, but wanted decisions. Peter Hennessy claimed that 'she has put Cabinet government temporarily on ice'.

But then there is the suggestion in many of these accounts that this state of affairs is an aberration. Hennessy goes on: 'the old model could be restored in the few minutes it takes for a new prime minister to travel from Buckingham Palace to Downing Street'. Rentoul also seems to believe that 'Cabinet government was not dead of course; it was only sleeping. It could clearly reassert itself if the prime minister's authority or popularity slipped, as it did over Thatcher.'

It was just, the arguments seems to run, that cabinet government did not operate under Thatcher and Blair, the two most dominant leaders their parties had seen in a century. On the other hand, it worked most obviously under Callaghan and Major, the two prime ministers in the weakest of positions with their cabinets in disarray, after the IMF crisis in 1976 and the currency crisis of 1992 respectively.

The traditional model of cabinet – perhaps best epitomised by Hennessy's old model of collective debate – provides a different picture from these current practices; it is sometimes presented as description, sometimes as normative prescription, of the way that government *should* work. George Jones, for instance, declares that British government is ministerial government. Formal authority is vested in ministers who therefore make the decisions on behalf of government. An implicit condition is that, as *ministers have the statutory responsibility* to make decisions, then it must in reality be theirs to make, not the prime minister's. This view argues that, in a proper system of cabinet government, prime ministers manage the cabinet process to ensure that the system works smoothly, not to direct policy. Thus Jones notes the prime minister's role 'is to help forge politically acceptable solutions and to relate policies together in an order of priorities by providing a coherent theme, tone or philosophy. His contribution is not to be a substitute for his ministers but a supplement ... A prime minister cannot help cabinet colleagues arrive at a unified decision if he is a protagonist of a particular line'.

So if prime ministers are driving the policy, perhaps with the ministers playing a secondary role, then cabinet government is in decline because prime ministers are taking over the proper ministerial responsibility. That is why Jones likes to talk of ministerial government. Unfortunately for such theories, no one told the prime ministers that they were not meant to direct the game when they were interested in doing so; both Thatcher and Blair have driven select areas of policy with a coterie of colleagues. Prime ministers go where they want; few will gainsay them.

If cabinet is no longer the source of authority in these accounts, is there an alternative explanation for the way that decisions are made? One explanation is through the consideration of government by core executive:

> The core executive approach ... defines the executive in functional terms. So, instead of asking which position is important, we can ask which functions define the innermost part or heart of government. For example, the core functions of the British executive are to pull together and integrate central government policies and to act as final arbiters of conflicts between different elements of the government machine. These functions can be carried out by institutions other than prime minister and cabinet; for example, the Treasury and the Cabinet Office. By defining the core executive in functional terms, the key question becomes, 'who does what?'.
>
> The term 'core executive' directs our attention, therefore, to two key questions: 'Who does what?' and 'Who has what resources?' If the answer for several policy areas and several conflicts is the prime minister coordinates policy, resolves conflicts and controls the main resources, we will indeed have prime ministerial government.

There is again a prior assumption: 'that the core functions of the British executive are to pull together and integrate central government policies and to act as final arbiters of conflicts between different elements of the government machine'. If that is accepted (and it should not be without dispute) then, as Rhodes explains, different networks may be responsible for decisions across areas. Some decisions may be made in the PMO, others in cabinet committees. In economic matters the prime minister and chancellor will determine strategy, advised by Treasury officials; in defence by chiefs of staff and intelligence supremos. Senior officials may be far more significant than junior ministers. There is no assumption that cabinet is the crucial forum; rather it is just one of several forums. The traditional model was decentralised, but still assumed (even required) the belief in political superiority. The core executive approach argues that others – officials, staff at No. 10, as well as ministers – may be crucial and that decisions may be effectively taken in a wide variety of networks.

This approach may have explanatory clout when practices in Britain and Canada are considered. Cabinet in Britain meets once a week, often for only one or two hours. Much of the meetings may be taken with the regular reports on foreign affairs and parliamentary business. Few decisions are taken. Effective decision-making is done in committee, with the ministerial chairs of cabinet committees liaising with the prime minister, hence the Bonapartist tag. This interpretation fits the Rhodes description of networks. Different groups of ministers and officials are involved in the development of economic policy or foreign affairs.

But we need to be aware of how far practices have really changed. The disaggregated British system may not be entirely new. Andeweg has argued that British government was already more segmented than other similar models. Further, cabinet government has never been a synonym for *primus inter pares*. Prime ministers have always been able to win; where they choose to exercise their authority depends on what they want. Savoie gave a concession in his analysis of Chrétien:

> To be sure prime ministers do not always bypass their cabinets or only consult them after the fact. They pick and choose issues they want to direct and, in some circumstances, may decide to let the Cabinet's collective decision-making run its course ... These are the issues on which a prime minister may hold no firm view, and decide that it is best to keep one's political capital in reserve for another day and another issue.

It was ever thus. Every prime minister in every country has chosen a number of subjects – war, security, nuclear policy, devaluations, budgets – which are discussed in a closed environment that will include crucial ministers and perhaps other advisers. None would regard such a tactic as a derogation of cabinet government. Cabinet was never intended to be democratic. As Graham White so colourfully has put it;

> At first blush the idea that Canadian cabinets should be in the least democratic is as improbable as the notion that after ministering to the downtrodden of Calcutta, Mother Teresa spent her leisure hours on a supercharged Harley-Davidson riding with the local Hell's Angels chapter for a little mayhem and debauchery.

Nor did the *Guide For Ministers and Secretaries of State*, released by Chrétien nominally as a rule book, leave any doubt about his perception of the powers and prerogatives of the prime minister. Prime ministers with great political standing and extensive interests (say, one that won three elections in a row (Chrétien) or three of the party's biggest ever electoral wins (Blair)) have a store of capital that is vast if they choose to use it. Yet they did not work alone; chancellors or finance ministers, always working with their prime ministers, not necessarily harmoniously, determined budgets; the level of cabinet participation has been limited at best. Foreign policy was always shared, with prime ministers being involved where they chose and representing their countries at conferences abroad. These debates reflect the obvious reality that the influence of prime ministers has varied over the decades. There have been powerful and weak, active and presiding, prime ministers.

What determines those tactical choices will, in part, be a matter of personality. The interests of prime ministers vary. Some care about a few things; others have broader agenda. Some concentrate on the big picture, the key initiatives and delegate the rest; others want to be constantly involved in detail. So will their approach to governing vary. It will also depend on the lessons, both positive and negative, that people have learnt from the past. Chrétien was an instinctive and pugnacious politician; he had vast experience; he was first sworn in as a minister on the same day as Trudeau and Turner, two of his predecessors, in 1967. But he was not comfortable having rambling policy discussions, reminiscent of a university seminar, which was the way Trudeau liked to run the cabinet. He preferred an efficient and speedy process and was less inclined to reflect on the processes, rather than the results.

Blair had never been in government, but he had immediate past models from which to select: the collegiate approach of two weak prime ministers in Callaghan and Major; or the directive lead given by Thatcher. Given those models, what leader would not look at the lessons and longevity of Thatcher and assume that here was a well-charted path to pursue?

The variations cannot be explained by constitutional theory. Certainly, observers make comments on what prime minister should do. 'The self-restraint of co-operative government ... is part of the job description'. Prime ministers should not pursue their own polices; their role is to hold the ring. These prescriptions may suit some ideal of a prime minister, or fit a model of practice for cabinet governments. But prime ministers do what they can, consistent with the ability to maintain collective support. In institutions that are constantly evolving it can only be expected. Noticeably, even in countries that have a constitution, cabinet may not be mentioned; it remains a conventional part of the political scenery.

Crucial factors are the national political traditions and the way they affect the position of the prime ministers. In Canada, cabinet has fulfilled a variety of functions; it has always been regarded as a representational body, with ministers to act as the voice for a number of provinces, languages and even sections of provinces. Because of this function, an inner cabinet was for long regarded as unacceptable because it suggested that some ministers, and therefore some regions, had greater input than others. With numbers rising to 40 at times, cabinet has never acted as a decision-making or even authoritative forum. Indeed, it is often not expected to be one. In the Privy Council Office (PCO) the culture requires that most issues be negotiated outside the cabinet room. Bitter argument between ministers in cabinet is a sign that the PCO has failed. Ministers are not used to being directed by cabinet within their own portfolios. In the program review exercise in 1995, ministers fought to protect their departments from cuts; Ralph Goodale, Minister for Agriculture, asked the program review committee: 'What gives you the right to act as judges on what generations of other people have created? From what divine right do you derive the power to decide that 50 of my scientists will be without work tomorrow?'

Ministers in Britain would not challenge the decision of a budget committee so passionately because their experience of a cost-cutting committee review is more regular; besides, the prime ministers give the committees that divine right (as Chrétien had done this time in Canada). So in that sense cabinet has never been the centre of decisions in Canada and the prime ministers have for decades, from Sir John A. Macdonald onwards, shown both a detailed interest in the decisions of ministers and arranged the processes of government around the cabinet system. Chrétien's comment: 'The prime minister is the prime minister and he has the cabinet to advise him. At the end of the day, it is the prime minister who says, "yes" or "no",' would not be acceptable in other systems, even if prime ministers would like to think it is true. They have used different vehicles for decision as the issue and circumstances required.

In both countries, officials see cabinet as a territory across which decisions are made, not a single forum. The two definitions of cabinet government, provided from interviews with officials in Canada and Britain, give an emphasis that takes into account these varieties. To reiterate, they argued:

- cabinet government is the arrangements the prime minister makes to ensure that decisions are made in the interests of the general, rather than the individual minister, with a view to presenting a unified program for legislation and supply (Canada)
- cabinet government is a shorthand term for the process by which government determines its policy and ensures the political will to implement it (Britain).

These definitions are process neutral. They accept the need for political support and for coherent policy, but appreciate the mix will change from time to time. How the prime ministers use cabinets to achieve these objectives will differ from person to person. Some take individual initiatives; others work through the cabinet. Some discuss in a meeting of ministers; others work in and around the cabinet itself. The location of decisions does not matter. The prime minister's offices, with increased capacity, may be as significant as any cabinet committee.

The essence of both definitions of cabinet is that prime ministers always need support and policy coherence and must work to achieve it. They need ministers to run departments day-to-day. That sharing of power is the core element of a cabinet system. But again there is no prescription for the way and extent to which power and decisions must be shared. For a long time Chrétien gave a degree of influence to the minister of finance, Paul Martin. Blair has given chancellor Gordon Brown extensive autonomy. The delegation may have been reluctant, but Martin and Brown were seen as successors to the incumbents and each had their own power base in the party. They held crucial economic portfolios that reflected their significance and had to be treated with care. Relations between the prime ministers and these colleagues are sometimes strained, but they can never be consistently ignored.

The extent to which power is shared with other ministers depends on the interests of the prime ministers and the quality and standing of those other key ministers. In most cases ministers are required to get on with the job for which they have statutory responsibility. Sometimes, far from complaining about excessive interference, ministers complain of the difficulty of attracting the prime minister's interest when they want to take an initiative. Some regard it as a sign of competence that they do not involve the prime minister in day-to-day business. But they know that where the prime minister shares an interest they will be required to work in cooperation with them and they usually relish the opportunity to do so. In each case the initiative will lie with the prime minister, not the minister.

Maintaining collective support is an end that can be achieved by a variety of means, of which debate and information exchange in cabinet has always been but one. Powerful leaders achieve it through their authority, of which there may be few public signs. There is too much activity for prime ministers to know all that is going on; they can take support for granted, for a time at least. But there is a need to avoid equating prime ministerial weakness with collective weight: often the times when collective government is reputedly at its strongest are when governments are in crisis and when prime ministers' political power is circumscribed because of internal or external constraints. The problem then is that no one exerts authority, not that it has leached from prime minister to cabinet. It does appear to be perverse to advocate normatively a form of collective decision-making that signifies a government under siege.

Cabinet remains a useful forum for maintaining that collective support; that still seems the most persuasive reason for regular meetings of cabinet, whether they are seen as a focus group or a political forum. These traditional political functions of cabinet – exchanging information, taking the political temperature, geeing up ministers, providing a sense of solidarity, setting the tone, emphasising the current issues and their resolution, ensuring they all sing from the same hymn sheet – can be undertaken almost independently of policy functions. Hence the fact that often when big issues come to cabinet, the intent is as much to solidify support as to determine any direction. Every government still uses cabinet for these political purposes and must do so as insurance and to lock in support.

The pressure and complexity of modern government mean that to some a weekly meeting of busy ministers no longer seems the best way to make timely and sophisticated policy. So prime ministers choose to work with the principal players in and around those regular meetings. Some take the budget out of the hands of cabinet and merely inform it of decisions. Policy areas are further segmented, with the prime ministers at the hub. The weaknesses of cabinet are, as Kavanagh and Seldon note, well established: too much information, too little time, too many busy people. Modern practices take this pressure into account by segmenting and organising the decision-making. The process may, *de facto*, now be closer to Dell's image of collective purpose, with crucial policy decisions made around, rather than in, the cabinet. Cabinet itself is used to forge unity and collective purpose, rather than decide on a course of action.

Canadian and British prime ministers have an additional asset; they are almost invulnerable from internal revolt. Canadian party leaders are elected by a party convention. MPs are a small minority among the delegates. The prime minister does not owe his position to the parliamentary caucus. Ministers may wonder who the successor might be, but they can do little to influence the timing of that vacancy, even if the prime minister is, according to the opinion polls, massively unpopular and leading the party to ruin. Trudeau, Mulroney and Chrétien decided when they would leave and, in effect, handed a poisoned chalice to their successors, none of whom was able to become established. If a prime minister is constantly successful, as Chrétien was, his position is much safer.

As both of the major British parties (Conservatives and Labour) move to leadership elections that are broader than just the parliamentary party, so they too will consolidate the position of the party leader. Those that do not elect can hardly remove. Even when it could, Thatcher's cabinet revolted only *after* the electoral college had required her to go to a second ballot. So prime ministers are becoming safer from internal revolt and their position is thus strengthened. Both Canadian and British prime ministers are far less vulnerable than their Australian counterparts.

Even without that change in the process of election the conventions and practice of cabinet have always been in the hands of the prime ministers who exercised the power in ways that they saw best for the future of their government and for their own position. All the evidence suggests that cabinet government is a malleable institution and has been for a long time; that is a major explanation for its survival.

Is cabinet government more sustainable in Australia?

So, to revert to Shergold's claim that cabinet government is alive and well only in Australia, how does its experience compare with those of its constitutional cousins? There is a need for some historical perspective. According to Andeweg, the British cabinet has always been more segmented than its counterparts in Canada or Australia, and the Australian cabinet has put a greater emphasis on collective government than either of the others. Therefore, if his diagnosis is correct, the concept of the core executive and networked government is more likely to be applicable and we should be looking for explanations about why Australia is more collective in its cabinet practices.

Cabinet appears on several criteria to be more vital in Australia. First, it meets regularly and for a period of some hours on vital issues. Submissions fulfil the requirement of informing ministers what is to be considered. There is greater involvement in budget considerations, even if the vital papers on the economy are circulated and collected at the same meeting to ensure secrecy and final decisions on spending may be made by the prime minister and treasurer.

Some committees, such as the ERC, may act as a gatekeeper to cabinet. Others, particularly those dealing with defence/intelligence/foreign affairs/security, may make final decisions. These cases provide some evidence of a segmented polity, but they are also not the norm. More often the recommendations of working parties or *ad hoc* committees go to cabinet for endorsement; approval there may be automatic, but it does provide an iota of cabinet involvement. There have been over the years many attempts to create effective committee systems; most have collapsed or fallen into disuse because of the desire to discuss controversial issues in full cabinet.

That intent does not mean that prime ministers do not manage the process. Bruce's discussions with ministers, Chifley's management of his ministers, Menzies' decisions to write the memo after debates on foreign affairs, ERC decisions finally settled in Keating's office: these are all examples of decision in the environs of cabinet, rather than in the cabinet room.

Others are involved as well. Senior officials from the Treasury, senior staff in the PMO, defence chiefs all have direct influence. Officials there have commented that they were initially surprised by the degree of influence that the prime minister could exert. It should not be surprising. Prime ministers may well be as powerful as their counterparts overseas. It is hard to find occasions when they have been clearly overruled by their cabinets. Chairing the cabinet, summarising the conclusions, and dictating the decisions gives Australian prime ministers authority. Like their counterparts they have a growing private office that controls many of the activities of government. Vital debates may take place within that private office or in bilateral discussions with senior colleagues and officials. But they are certainly publicly and rhetorically committed to the forum and processes of cabinet government.

That may be concluded from the absence of any debate about the viability of cabinet government in Australia, compared to the vigour of the arguments in Canada and Britain. Kelly argues that Howard's development of the prime minister's power is the end of a long process. It is indeed a process as long as the history of Australian government. Federal politics has certainly seen some dominant prime ministers: Deakin, Hughes, Menzies, Whitlam, Fraser and Hawke. But they still all chose, at least partly, to work through cabinet, to hold regular meetings, to listen to their colleagues. Apart from Hughes they did not make a habit of acting unilaterally, even if they could have (for a time anyway). Australian prime ministers work through and with their colleagues to a greater extent than their counterparts. That does not make them less powerful, they just exert their power through different channels.

In any case there are institutional limitations. Like the Canadian leader, Australian prime ministers must deal with state premiers with an independent power base and different interests. They may have to negotiate with a Senate that has equal powers to the House of Representatives if the government does not have a majority there.

But the reasons within cabinet go further. First, the culture is different. Cabinet is a forum where rugged debate is expected. In Canada, the PCO feels it has failed if there is a fight between ministers in cabinet. In Australia central agencies are required to isolate the hard issues that need a cabinet decision by determining the facts and letting cabinet decide on the direction. The hard arguments are then common in cabinet.

Second, cabinet serves a variety of representational functions. Senate and state inputs can be significant, particularly where the other side of the political divide holds power in the states or in the Senate. A variety of perspectives is useful.

Third, the party plays a more constant and participatory role. There is a *quid pro quo*. In exchange for participation in the party room and the ability to question ministers on a weekly basis there, party members sustain a level of party discipline in the public forum of parliament that is absolute. The very occasional vote against the party line is noted because it occurs so rarely. Prime ministers know that the party will vote solidly. That is one of their great strengths; there are few backbench revolts like those that occur in Britain.

Fourth, there are geographical considerations. When parliament moved to Canberra in 1927, most departments were still housed in Melbourne. The cabinet room was in the prime minister's suite in Parliament House. Ministers worked from their parliamentary offices. When a new Parliament House was opened in 1988, the ministers were all accommodated in the Executive Wing. The Press Gallery was in the building, too. Not only was it far easier to summon ministers to sudden cabinet meetings, but prime ministers needed to ensure they were clear about government decisions. Ministers could so easily meet journalists as soon as they left cabinet. Ministers never worked in their departments, even after they shifted to Canberra. The cabinet was thus geographically and politically concentrated, with the PMO in the middle.

But, most importantly, Australian prime ministers know that they depend for their futures on the support of the parliamentary party and can be removed by a vote at any time in the party room. As long as they win elections, or seem likely to win, they are secure. However, there is a record of successful and unsuccessful challenges, even to prime ministers like Hawke who had won three elections, more than any other Labor leader. Faced daily by those who elected them, prime ministers are conscious of the need to keep the minsters involved. Prime ministers must therefore be aware of the opinions and standing of their cabinet colleagues. The rules of engagement are thus different. The parliamentary party has, from 1901 and in both parties, been regarded as more involved in the process of governing and the approval of government polices and legislation. Australia created its own traditions and built on those foundations, while still remaining well within a Westminster format.

Institutional imperatives, based on political assumptions about the role of cabinet and the dependence of prime ministers on their colleagues, therefore lead to a different constellation of forces. The ends that prime ministers seek may be similar in Australia to Canada and Britain; the means they adopt are shaped by the national traditions. Consequently, the trajectory of cabinet government has, from the beginning, diverged from British and Canadian experience. There is much that remains common in language and style, but methods of collective commitment and discipline remain uniquely Australian.

16 CONCLUSION: TRENDS AND FUTURES FOR CABINET GOVERNMENT

Barton would be amazed by the layers of bureaucracy that surrounds cabinet and the complexity of the issues considered in 2006. It presents a very different picture from that cosy meeting of colleagues that established the federal government in 1901. It is tempting to suggest that the two cabinets are really separate and different bodies with little but history to connect them. They operate differently. That case can be made by identifying all the new things that cabinet has developed over the century, initiatives born of the belief that change was needed to ensure that cabinet can perform adequately.

An alternative view might look back with nostalgia to the way that cabinet once worked and to contrast that period (usually ill defined) with the inadequacies of the present. So Bunting, writing in the 1980s in defence of cabinet government of an earlier time, bemoaned the increasing cabinet control over the activities of once-powerful ministers. The history in this book suggests that by contrast minsters always were subordinate to cabinet and brought items there from the beginning to gain wide support and approval.

Both views are anyway too simple. Cabinet certainly has changed over the century as it faced demands of war, depression and globalisation, as it had to deal with modern communications and immediate scrutiny. At the same time the essential demands have remained almost the same, even if now achieved by different means. This conclusion therefore seeks to identify:

- the areas where there has been linear change
- the subjects that have been a source of continuous experimentation
- the activities that were essentially unchanged because they go to the core of what cabinet government is still seeking to achieve.

In that assessment it is important to retain a sense of history. Menzies once gave some fatherly advice to Bunting:

> Lad, the thing is, if you are taking over from someone, to assume that he knew what he was doing. You can disagree later if you want to and make a change, but if you are wise about it you will discover his reasons for his actions before you disagree. You may well find those reasons convincing. In any case, it is always a gross error to assume that your predecessor was a species of fool.

It is reasonable to assume that prime ministers and cabinet secretaries were each, according to their own lights and in the circumstances of the time, trying to govern or serve cabinet effectively. Changes were often needed when existing practices came under pressure; new governments provided the opportunity to fix what had been perceived to be wrong the last time the party was in power. That approach is likely to continue as prime ministers and cabinet secretaries change. Change is not necessarily always improvement.

First, then, the infrastructure and bureaucratic professionalism of cabinet procedures have been one-directional; that is, in essence, though not in detail, infrastructure and bureaucratic professionalism are likely to be sustained by any future government because they fill a need. Cabinet began with a prime ministerial notebook, developed a formal agenda and the circulation of papers in advance, created a secretariat, and then began to prescribe the form and content of submissions. The *Cabinet Handbook* began with a page of exhortations, became more detailed and then spun off additional rulebooks such as *A Guide on Key Elements of Ministerial Responsibility*. Decisions were recorded first by the prime minister, then by a ministerial secretary of cabinet, by a single official notetaker and now through the services of four officials in cabinet. The cabinet secretariat was initially responsible for the circulation of papers and explicitly had no policy role. Now it includes the cabinet implementation unit that reports on progress on cabinet decisions. CABNET, the computerised network for the negotiation and circulation of cabinet submission, is but the latest technical innovation to facilitate the processes of cabinet decision-making. The running of cabinet has become professional and routine. That has an impact on the way it works.

Also uni-directional is the trend associated with cabinet to provide policy advice for the prime ministers and the ministers. Ministers always relied on their departments, but advice at the centre was initially limited. From 1950 onwards that lacuna has been filled, first by the gradual development of a policy advising capacity in PM&C, as well as by the advent of ministerial staff. Prime ministers want people close to them who see the world through their eyes and others who are absolutely committed to the future of their government. The appointment of a political cabinet secretary to provide a political slant to the management of cabinet was an acknowledgment of the overlap of the procedural and the political. So staff and press secretaries provide support and spin, advisers can drive particular policies of interest to the prime minister and comment on other issues.

Each of these changes was a reaction to a sense of need, of a requirement for support in regular activities. Better records, wider advice, more careful consideration of decisions, more professional presentation of items for consideration: these are all worthy objectives. It seems unlikely that any of these trends will be reversed because the need they meet will continue to be present.

Second are those areas where there has been a constant push for better ways of managing pressures. Most contested are the schemes designed to develop strategic directions in cabinet. How to strike the right balance between the short and the long term, between the policy and the politics, is one of those wicked problems of government. Different strategies have been tried: day-long meetings dedicated to a single topic, discussions of priorities at meetings without other submissions and exploratory meetings of emerging issues. The forums can change too: from meetings of the full ministry, to a selection of senior ministers, to charter letters sent to ministers by the prime minister. The debates can be participatory or directive. Who is involved, where the debates take place, how effective they are will vary from government to government, and will depend heavily on the personality and style of the prime minister. It is a matter of labelling, rather than a crucial distinction about the existence of cabinet government. What is certain is that some of the initiatives introduced by Howard will, in time, be superseded by a new scheme, seen as more compatible to his successor. In part it will be introduced just because his successor is *not* Howard and wants to distinguish his regime, in part it will be because the new methods will be designed to avoid whatever flaws are seen in the current process. There is no one best way to establish priorities, to balance the short and the long term, to work through difficult and complex problems. Far from always being partisan, cabinets sometimes may just not know how to solve a problem; as Heclo noted sagely 'governments not only "power"; they also puzzle. Policymaking is a form of collective puzzlement on society's behalf'. Prime ministers and cabinets will continue to try, in their own way and with varying success, to meet the policy challenges, but no single process will suffice. Experimentation will continue.

So, too, will processes vary with the interpretation of the principles of collective and ministerial responsibility. We again need to avoid a nostalgia that posits better days or a more principled politics. A century of federal politics is bespattered with ministerial resignations, not one of which was caused by the administrative failings of officials. In the first 40 years some ministers fell out with their colleagues and chose to resign, starting with Kingston in 1903. Forrest wanted to pull Deakin out from reliance on Labor in 1907, Tudor objected to conscription and left two months before the split. But those types of resignation have almost entirely disappeared since 1950. Ministers hang in and accept the cabinet decision; only Ellicott in 1978 resigned when he opposed a cabinet decision, and he soon returned to the government. Interpretation of ministerial responsibility for departmental actions has been consistent: ministers may explain, they do not resign and never have. Officials may now be more explicitly blamed at times, but this is part of the greater scrutiny of government. Whether that makes government better or worse will be contested. It is hard to argue that an indication of responsible cabinets should be the number of ministers they lose through resignation. What matters is the degree by which a cabinet is held accountable, rather than any specific means for doing so. Interpretations will change with the rise and fall of Senate majorities, with the changes in the media and with changes in social attitudes.

Few of these changes in interpretation should be surprising. Cabinet is a working institution, not a frozen constitutional relic. It had to adapt to meet new challenges in its organisation, and the interpretations of conventions also were amended as new pressures emerged. Media demands may be as significant as any pressure that parliament can bring to bear on an incompetent minister. Interpretations of procedure, experimentation about process will all be designed to achieve the basic purposes of cabinet.

Third are those activities, the management of governing and the winning of elections, that have not changed, and are not likely to change. They are the core functions of cabinet government: the need for collective support and coherent policy. The question is how best to achieve it, not whether it is required. All the systems, procedures and interpretations of conventions are designed to that end. Prime ministers and ministers must work together; the leader needs loyal and effective lieutenants. Ministerial effectiveness can be interpreted in different ways: in their ability to represent states or interests, in their policy creativity or their brutality as political toughs. A cabinet needs all sorts for it to maintain discipline on the backbench and know how to select the right alternative. The drive for better procedures and support, the never-ending search for ways to resolve the core dilemmas faced by governments, are all part of this need to answer policy challenges and ensure re-election. They are not two different objectives, but part of the same calculus.

If, as asserted earlier, one of the key determinants of the Australian political reality is the election of party leaders, and hence prime ministers, by the parliamentary party, and if the practice remains that a contest can in effect be called on at any time, then the mutual dependence of prime ministers and their senior cabinet colleagues will ensure that the prime ministers need to maintain support all the time and must work at sustaining it. Yet cabinet is regarded as more than a means of bolstering party support; governing through cabinet is more than a rhetorical flourish. Prime ministers have all taken seriously the responsibility to make cabinet work and to allow ministerial participation. It is part of the political culture that, in their own way, they take seriously. It is difficult, in those conditions, to see the reduction of cabinet to a forum where only reports take place and where not even the appearance of decision-making occurs.

Prime ministers will continue to set the direction, control as many details as they choose, and sometimes pre-empt cabinet decisions. They will appear the dominant and decisive figure – that is what strong leadership requires and cabinets work best when led. Yet, with the exception of Hughes, the most effective prime ministers have still chosen to work through the cabinet because they know that it strengthens their hand and usually secures their position. Collective cabinet government will survive in Australia because it is underpinned by perceptions of good government and by self-interest.

APPENDIX 1

Cabinet and committees – frequency data

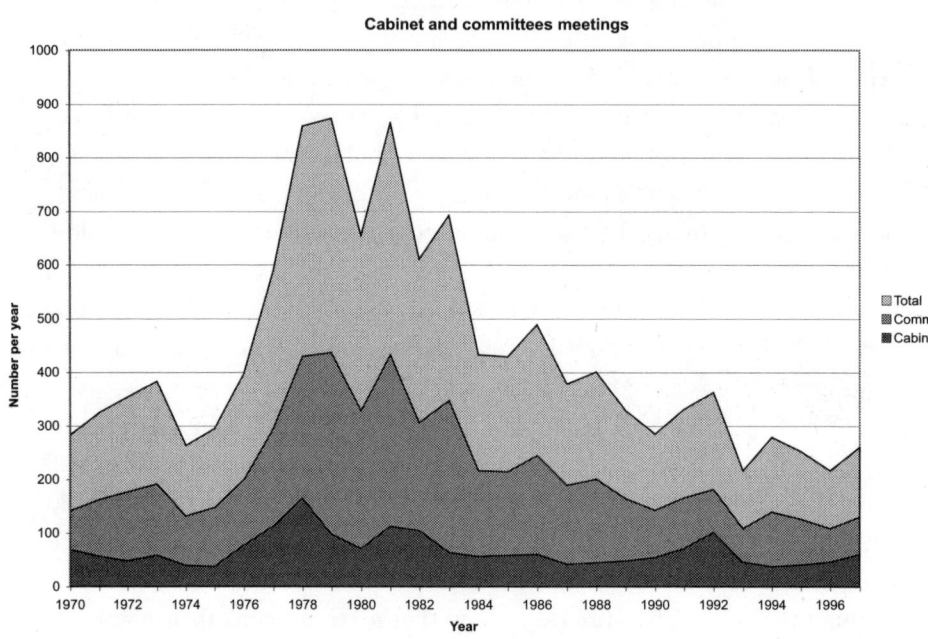

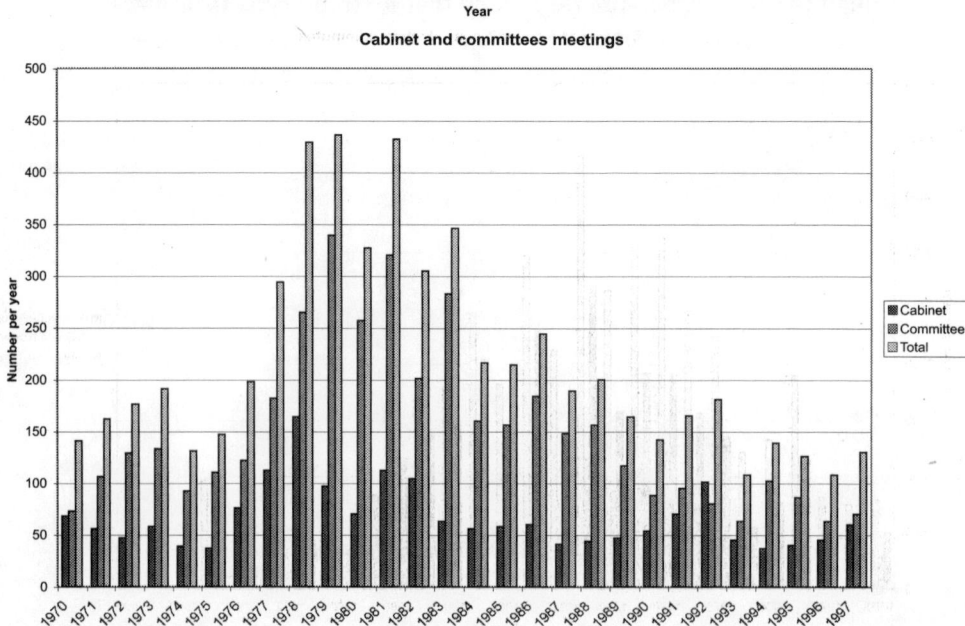

APPENDIX I 287

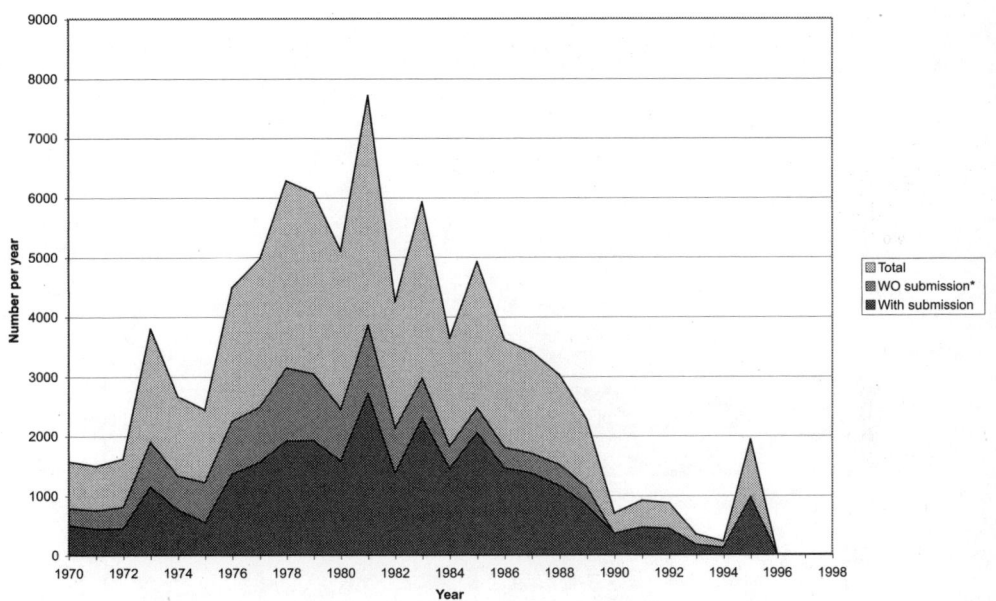

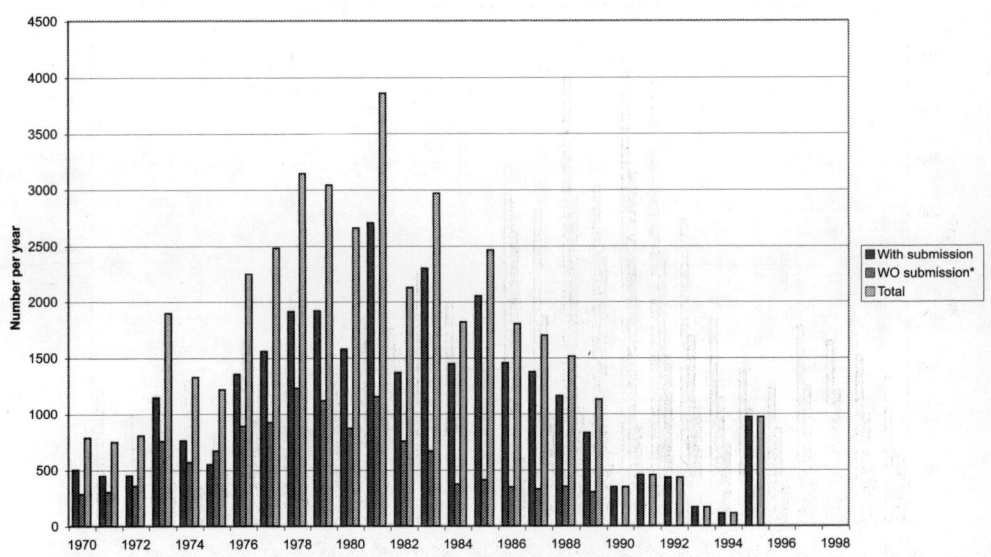

* Numbers of WO submission are not available after 1990

Cabinet and committees business

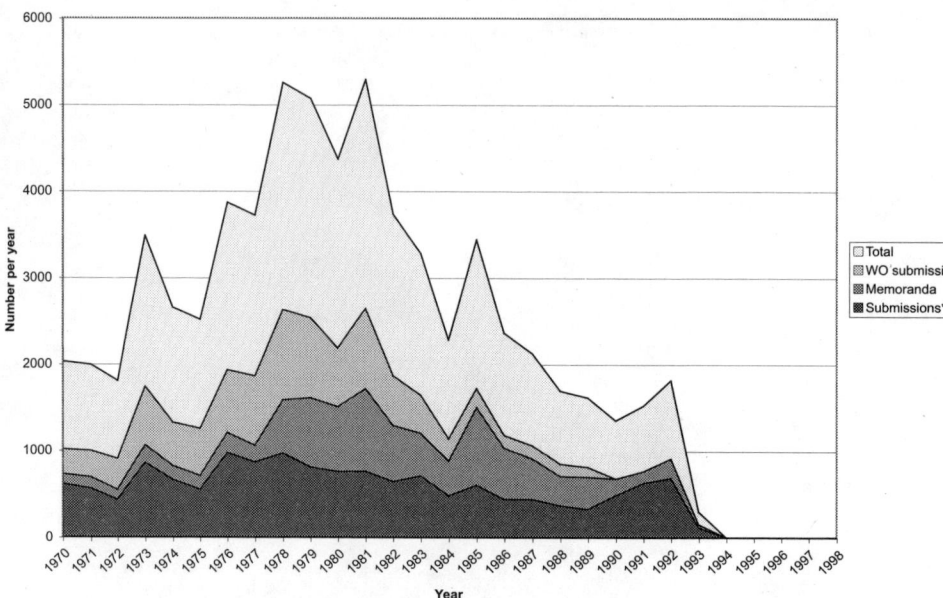

Cabinet and committees business

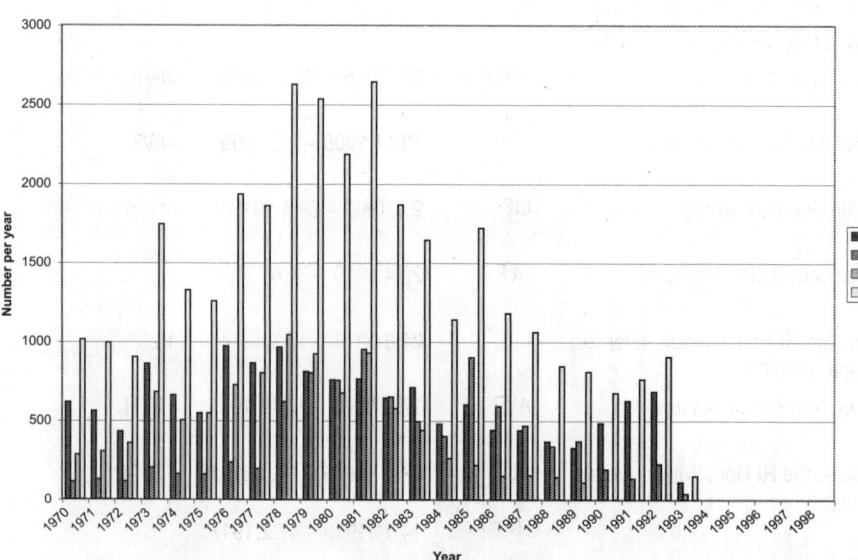

* Number of submissions includes legislative memorandums
+ WO submission numbers are not available after 1990

APPENDIX 2

Australian prime ministers

Name	Party	Period of service	Years/Months/Days
Barton, the Rt Hon. Sir Edmund, GCMG, KC	PROT	1.1.1901 – 24.9.1903	2/8/24
Deakin, the Hon. Alfred	PROT	24.9.1903 – 27.4.1904	–/7/4
Watson, the Hon. John Christian	ALP	27.4.1904 – 17.8.1904	–/3/21
Reid, the Rt Hon. George Houstoun, KC (later Sir George, GCB, GCMG)	FT*	18.8.1904 – 5.7.1905	–/10/18
Deakin, the Hon. Alfred	PROT*	5.7.1905 – 13.11.1908	3/4/9
Fisher, the Rt Hon. Andrew	ALP	13.11.1908 – 2.6.1909	–/6/21
Deakin, the Hon. Alfred	LIB	2.6.1909 – 29.4.1910	–/10/28
Fisher, the Rt Hon. Andrew	ALP	29.4.1910 – 24.6.1913	3/1/26
Cook, the Rt Hon. Joseph (later Sir Joseph, GCMG)	LIB	24.6.1913 – 17.9.1914	1/2/25
Fisher, the Rt Hon. Andrew	ALP	17.9.1914 – 27.10.1915	1/1/11
Hughes, the Rt Hon. William Morris, CH, KC	ALP	27.10.1915 – 14.11.1916	7/3/14
	NAT LAB	14.11.1916 – 17.2.1917	
	NAT	17.2.1917 – 9.2.1923	

Name	Party	Period of service	Years/Months/Days
Bruce, the Rt Hon. Stanley Melbourne, CH, MC (later 1st Viscount Bruce of Melbourne)	NAT*	9.2.1923 – 22.10.1929	6/8/14
Scullin, the Rt Hon. James Henry	ALP	22.10.1929 – 6.1.1932	2/2/16
Lyons, the Rt Hon. Joseph Aloysius, CH	UAP	6.1.1932 – 9.11.1934	
	UAP*	9.11.1934 – 7.4.1939	7/3/2
Page, the Rt Hon. Sir Earle Christmas Grafton, GCMG, CH	CP*	7.4.1939 – 26.4.1939	–/–/20
Menzies, the Rt Hon. Robert Gordon, KC	UAP	26.4.1939 – 14.3.1940	2/4/4
	UAP*	14.3.1940 – 29.8.1941	
Fadden, the Rt Hon. Arthur William (later Sir Arthur, GCMG)	CP*	29.8.1941 – 7.10.1941	–/1/9
Curtin, the Rt Hon. John Joseph Ambrose	ALP	7.10.1941 – 5.7.1945	3/8/29
Forde, the Rt Hon. Francis Michael	ALP	6.7.1945 – 13.7.1945	–/–/8
Chifley, the Rt Hon. Joseph Benedict	ALP	13.7.1945 – 19.12.1949	4/5/7
Menzies, the Rt Hon. Robert Gordon, KC (later Sir Robert, KT, CH, QC)	LIB*	19.12.1949 – 26.1.1966	16/1/8
Holt, the Rt Hon. Harold Edward, CH	LIB*	26.1.1966 – 19.12.1967	1/10/23
McEwen, the Rt Hon. John (later Sir John, GCMG, CH)	CP*	19.12.1967 – 10.1.1968	–/–/23
Gorton, the Rt Hon. John Grey, CH (later Sir John, GCMG, AC)	LIB*	10.1.1968 – 10.3.1971	3/2/–
McMahon, the Rt Hon. William, CH (later Sir William, GCMG)	LIB*	10.3.1971 – 5.12.1972	1/8/25
Whitlam, the Hon. Edward Gough, AC, QC	ALP	5.12.1972 – 11.11.1975	2/11/7
Fraser, the Rt Hon. John Malcolm, AC, CH	LIB*	11.11.1975 – 11.3.1983	7/4/–
Hawke, the Hon. Robert James Lee, AC	ALP	11.3.1983 – 20.12.1991	8/9/10
Keating, the Hon. Paul John	ALP	20.12.1991 – 11.3.1996	4/2/20
Howard, the Hon. John Winston	LIB*	11.3.1996 –	

* Coalition government.
Source: http://www.aph.gov.au/library/handbook/historical/prime_ministers.htm

Chronological listing of Australian ministries since 1901

Ministry	Period	Party
1. Barton	1.1.1901 – 24.9.1903	Protectionist
2. Deakin	24.9.1903 – 27.4.1904	Protectionist
3. Watson	27.4.1904 – 17.8.1904	Alp
4. Reid–McLean	18.8.1904 – 5.7.1905	Free trade–Protectionist
5. Deakin	5.7.1905 – 13.11.1908	Protectionist
6. Fisher	13.11.1908 – 2.6.1909	Alp
7. Deakin	2.6.1909 – 29.4.1910	Protectionist–Free Trade–Tariff reform
8. Fisher	29.4.1910 – 24.6.1913	ALP
9. Cook	24.6.1913 – 17.9.1914	Lib
10. Fisher	17.9.1914 – 27.10.1915	ALP
11. Hughes	27.10.1915 – 14.11.1916	ALP
12. Hughes	14.11.1916 – 17.2.1917	National Labour
13. Hughes	17.2.1917 – 8.1.1918	Nationalist
14. Hughes	10.1.1918 – 9.2.1923	Nationalist
15. Bruce–Page	9.2.1923 – 22.10.1929	Nationalist–CP
16. Scullin	22.10.1929 – 6.1.1932	ALP
17. Lyons	6.1.1932 – 9.11.1934	UAP
	9.11.1934 – 7.11.1938	UAP–CP
18. Lyons	7.11.1938 – 7.4.1939	UAP–CP
19. Page	7.4.1939 – 26.4.1939	CP–UAP
20. Menzies	26.4.1939 – 14.3.1940	UAP
21. Menzies	14.3.1940 – 28.10.1940	UAP–CP
22. Menzies	28.10.1940 – 29.8.1941	UAP–CP
23. Fadden	29.8.1941 – 7.10.1941	CP–UAP
24. Curtin	7.10.1941 – 21.9.1943	ALP
25. Curtin	21.9.1943 – 6.7.1945	ALP
26. Forde	6.7.1945 – 13.7.1945	ALP
27. Chifley	13.7.1945 – 1.11.1946	ALP
28. Chifley	1.11.1946 – 19.12.1949	ALP
29. Menzies	19.12.1949 – 11.5.1951	Lib–CP
30. Menzies	11.5.1951 – 11.1.1956	Lib–CP
31. Menzies	11.1.1956 – 10.12.1958	Lib–CP
32. Menzies	10.12.1958 – 18.12.1963	Lib–CP
33. Menzies	18.12.1963 – 26.1.1966	Lib–CP
34. Holt	26.1.1966 – 14.12.1966	Lib–CP
35. Holt	14.12.1966 – 19.12.1967	Lib–CP
36. McEwen	19.12.1967 – 10.1.1968	Lib–CP
37. Gorton	10.1.1968 – 28.2.1968	Lib–CP
38. Gorton	28.2.1968 – 12.11.1969	Lib–CP

Ministry	Period	Party
39. Gorton	12.11.1969 – 10.3.1971	Lib–CP
40. McMahon	10.3.1971 – 5.12.1972	Lib–CP
41. Whitlam	5.12.1972 – 19.12.1972	ALP
42. Whitlam	19.12.1972 – 12.6.1974	ALP
43. Whitlam	12.6.1974 – 11.11.1975	ALP
44. Fraser	11.11.1975 – 22.12.1975	Lib–NCP
45. Fraser	22.12.1975 – 20.12.1977	Lib–NCP
46. Fraser	20.12.1977 – 3.11.1980	Lib–NCP
47. Fraser	3.11.1980 – 7.5.1982	Lib–NCP
48. Fraser	7.5.1982 – 11.3.1983	Lib–NCP
49. Hawke	11.3.1983 – 13.12.1984	ALP
50. Hawke	13.12.1984 – 24.7.1987	ALP
51. Hawke	24.7.1987 – 4.4.1990	ALP
52. Hawke	4.4.1990 – 20.12.1991	ALP
53. Keating	20.12.1991 – 27.12.1991	ALP
54. Keating	27.12.1991 – 24.3.1993	ALP
55. Keating	24.3.1993 – 11.3.1996	ALP
56. Howard	11.3.1996 – 21.10.1998	Lib–NPA
57. Howard	21.10.1998 – 26.11.2001	LIB–NPA
58. Howard	26.11.2001 – 26.10.2004	LIB–NPA
59. Howard	26.10.2004 –	

SOURCE http://www.aph.gov.au/library/handbook/historical/ministries/index.htm

REFERENCES

Prologue – Cabinet in 1901 and 2006

p. 2   *Convention Debates*, 17 September 1897, p. 787.
p. 4   For Barton's claim of carrying the administration in his briefcase see Bolton, G. 2000, *Edmund Barton*, Sydney: Allen & Unwin, p. 229.

Chapter 1 – Understanding cabinet government

p. 7   Encel, S. 1962, *Cabinet Government in Australia* (1st edition), Melbourne: Melbourne University Press. *Ibid*, 1974 (2nd edition).

p. 9   Bagehot's description of cabinet as the hyphen and buckle from Bagehot, W. 1963, *The English Constitution*, London: Fontana and is also discussed in Macintosh, J.P. 1977, *The British Cabinet* (3rd edition), London: Stevens, p. 68. Discussion of the relationship between minister and parliament in Britain with its unwritten constitution can be found in Woodhouse, D. 1994, *Ministers and Parliament: Accountability in Theory and Practice*. Oxford: The Clarendon Press. The absence of reference to prime minister and cabinet in the Australian Constitution, as well as the derivation of ministerial power from section 64 of the Constitution is discussed in Forrest, J. and G.S. Reid 1989, *Australia's Commonwealth Parliament*, Melbourne: Melbourne University Press. For an argument on how to tighten the debate, see Weller, P. 1999, 'Disentangling Ministerial Responsibility', *Australian Journal of Public Administration*, 58, 1, pp. 62–4. Encel, S. 1974, *Cabinet Government in Australia* (2nd edition), Melbourne: Melbourne University Press. Mackintosh, J.P. 1977, *The British Cabinet* (3rd edition), London: Stevens.

p. 10   French, R. 1979, 'The Privy Council Office: Support for Cabinet Decision Making', in R. Schultz et al. (eds), *The Canadian Political Process* (3rd edition), Toronto: Holt and Rinehart. The formality of cabinet proceedings brought on by time pressures is addressed in Baker, A. 2000, *Prime Ministers and the Rule Book*, London: Politico's and also in Weller, P. 2001, 'Ministerial Codes, Cabinet Rules and the Power of Prime Ministers', in J. Fleming and I. Holland (eds), *Motivating Ministers to Morality*, Aldershot: Ashgate.

p. 11   The department versus office distinction relating to prime minister's supporting agencies is discussed in Weller, P. 1983, 'Do Prime Minister's Departments Really Create Problems?', *Public Administration*, 61, 1, pp. 59–78. For discussion of the presumption of strengthening of prime ministerial power brought on by institutional presence, see Savoie, D. 1999, *Governing from the Centre*. Toronto: University of Toronto Press and Holliday, I. 2000 'Is the British State Hollowing Out?', *The Political Quarterly*, 71, 2, pp. 167–76; the opposite view that there remains a hole in prime ministerial advice is provided in Kavanagh, D. and A. Seldon 1999, *The Powers Behind the Prime Minister: The Hidden Influence of Number Ten*, London: Harper Collins.

p. 12   Dell, E. 1980, 'Collective Responsibility: Fact, Fiction or Façade?', *Policy and Practice: The Experience of Government*, London: RIPA. Sir John Hunt's comments cited in Hennessy, P. 1995, *The Hidden Wiring*, London: Indigo. Assistance given by central agencies is discussed in Davis, G. 1995, *A Government of Routines*, Melbourne: Macmillan. Examples of reflections by former advisers and cabinet officials on how cabinet could work better are given in the following: Donoughue, B. 1987, *Prime Minister*, London: Jonathan Cape; Blackstone, T. and W. Plowden 1988, *Inside the Think Tank: Advising the Cabinet 1971–1983*, London: William Heinemann; Hogg, S. and J. Hill, 1995, *Too Close to Call: Power and Politics – John Major in No. 10*, London: Little Brown. Lindquist, E. and G. White 1997, 'Analysing Canadian Cabinets: Past, Present and Future', in *Agenda Formation* (W.H. Riker, ed.), Ann Arbor, MI: University of Michigan Press, p. 129. Australian studies of cabinet showing cabinet decisions and subsequent tensions include: Weller, P. 1989, *Malcolm Fraser Prime Minister*, Ringwood: Penguin; Mills, S. 1993, *The Hawke Years*, Ringwood: Viking; Edwards, J. 1996, *Keating: The Inside Story*, Ringwood: Viking; and Watson, D. 2002, *Recollections of a Bleeding Heart: A Portrait of Paul Keating PM*, Milsons Point NSW: Random House. Weller, P. 1985, *First Among Equals: Prime Ministers in Westminster Systems*, Sydney: Allen & Unwin.

p. 13   Arguments that power has shifted to the prime minister include: Crossman, R.H.S. 1963, 'Introduction' to W. Bagehot, *The English Constitution*, London: Fontana; Macintosh, J.P. 1977, *The British Cabinet* (3rd edition), London: Stevens; and for Australia, Kelly, P. 2005, *Re-thinking Australian Governance – The Howard Legacy*, Occasional Paper Series 4/2005, Canberra: Academy of the Social Sciences in Australia. Foley, M. 1993, *The Rise of the British Presidency*, Manchester: Manchester University Press, and Foley, M. 2000, *The British Presidency*, Manchester: Manchester University Press. The term 'ministerial government' is used in Jones, G. 1979, 'The Prime Minister's Aides', *Hull Papers in Politics*, 6, p. 1. The argument that cabinet can readily reassert itself after a dominant prime minister is given in Hennessy, P. 1986, *Cabinet*, London: Fontana. On ministerial power, see Bunting, J. 1988, *R.G. Menzies: A Portrait*, Sydney: Allen & Unwin. The levers of power analysis, especially on the use of cabinet committees, is given in Mackie, J. and Hogwood, B. (eds), 1985, *Unlocking the Cabinet*, London: Sage.

p. 14   Rhodes, R., 1995, 'From Prime Ministerial Power to Core Executive', in R. Rhodes and P. Dunleavy (eds), *Prime Minister, Cabinet and Core Executives*, London: Macmillan. The quote is from p. 12 but for the first exposition of the core executive see also Dunleavy, P. and R.A.W. Rhodes 1990, 'Core Executive Studies in Britain', *Public Administration*, 68, pp. 3–28. Burch, M. and I. Holliday 1996, *The British Cabinet System*, Hemel Hempstead: Prentice Hall. Andeweg, R. 1997, 'Collegiality and Collectivity: Cabinets, Cabinet Committees and Cabinet Ministers', in P. Weller et al. (eds), *The Hollow Crown*, Basingstoke: Macmillan.

p. 16 Definitions from officials are sourced from interviews conducted in 2001 with senior cabinet officials in both Canada and Britain. The Australian definition comes from Keating, M. and P. Weller 2000, 'Cabinet Government: an Institution Under Pressure' in M. Keating et al. (eds), *Institutions on the edge? Capacity for governance*, St Leonards NSW: Allen & Unwin, pp. 45–73. French, R. 1979, 'The Privy Council Office: Support for Cabinet Decision Making', in R. Schultz et al. (eds), *The Canadian Political Process* (3rd edition).

Chapter 2 – Setting the arrangements: 1901–14

p. 20 On the first executive council meeting, see Garran R.R. 1958, *Prosper the Commonwealth*, Sydney: Angus & Robertson, p. 143. Bolton G. 2000, *Edmund Barton*, Allen & Unwin, pp. 229–30. Barton cabinet records 1903 NLA MS51-2-951-S4. Deakin cabinet notebooks NLA MS51-2-951-S4.

p. 21 The issue of the Marquis of Tullibardine's horse is A6006, CRS A6 item 01/861. 'To cabinet' quote from A6006. Travelling expenses of ministers CRS A461 item 03/2/3. Travel allowance for parliamentarians' wives CRS A106 item G23/1525. Letter from American company CRS A8 item 01/311/[1].

p. 22 Cable to London in relation to Boer prisoners CRS A1 item 03/1833. Cabinet leak A34 NN. Discussion of estimates A34 NN. All of these are on NAA microfilm A6066 Roll 1. Barton Cabinet records NLA MS51-2-951-S4.

p. 23 Barton's memo to his secretary contained in NLA MS560. Barton's report on the 1902 Colonial Conference NAA A5954 item 431669. Election date, Deakin Cabinet notebooks NLA MS1540/15/2012. Cabinet memo relating to Defence Dept officer CRS A571 item 032866 contained in NAA microfilm A6006 Roll 1. Barton's Cabinet records NLA MS51-2-951-S4.

p. 25 ALP Caucus Minutes cited in Weller P. 1975, *Caucus Minutes 1901–1949. Volume 1 1901–1917*, Melbourne University Press pp. 125–38. Hughes' comments about first Labor cabinet meeting are cited in Hughes W.M. 1950, *Policies and Potentates*, Sydney: Angus & Robertson, pp. 141–2.

p. 26 Payment for Sunday work Minute CRS A571 item 15/11172. Dispute with Justices of High Court CRS A2863 item 1916/39. Both these items are on NAA microfilm A6006 Roll 1. Deakin cabinet notebooks July 1905 – June 1906 NLA MS 1540/15/2012, June 1906 – Nov 1908 NLA MS 1540/15/2013-2018.

p. 27 Deakin cabinet notebooks June 1909–1910 NLA MS 1540/15/2019-2021. Comments by Deakin's secretary are contained in Memoirs of M.L. Shepherd NAA Series A1632 item 1 Part 1.

p. 28 Relationship between caucus and cabinet cited in Weller P. 1975, *Caucus Minutes 1901–1949. Volume 1 1901–1917*, Melbourne University Press, p. 24. Childe V. 1964, *How Labour Governs: A Study of Workers' Representation in Australia* (2nd edition), Melbourne: Melbourne University Press, pp. 46–7.

pp. 29–30 Discussion on relationship between caucus and cabinet is cited in Weller P. 1975, *Caucus Minutes 1901–1949. Volume 1 1901–1917*, Melbourne University Press, pp. 115, 224, 252–318. Discussion relating to Prime Minister's Department and division of External Affairs Department in 1910-11 NAA A463 1957/1613 Part 1. Memoirs of M.L. Shepherd NAA Series A1632 item 1 Part 1.

pp. 31–32 Discussion in relation to World War 1 is included in NAA microfilm A6006 Roll 1. Note: There is no NAA Series number recorded; however, a handwritten note refers to Australian War Memorial 3 DRL 6673.

Chapter 3 – Stretching the limits: 1914–23

p. 33   Discussion on relationship between caucus and cabinet is cited in Weller P. 1975, *Caucus Minutes 1901–1949. Volume 1 1901–1917*, Melbourne University Press pp. 372–427.

p. 34   Fisher's resignation cited in Fitzhardinge L.F. 1979, *The Little Digger 1914–1952. A Political Biography William Morris Hughes Vol. II*, Sydney: Angus & Robertson, pp. 40–1. Naturalisation of enemy aliens over age 60 CRS A1 item 21/16414 (NAA microfilm A6006 Roll 1). Kitchener's troop request, no item number available (NAA microfilm A6006 Roll 1). Pearl luggers CRS A1 item 17/12225.

p. 35   Discussion on syphilis CRS A3 item 16/2836. Cablegrams re Deakin representation at Panama Exhibition CP 290/1 Bundle 1 item 2. All items on this page are on NAA microfilm A6006 Roll 1.

p. 36   Atlee Hunt's memorandum CRS A1 item 15/3264. Refugees from Syria CRS A2 item 1916/3742. Compensation for accidental death CRS A571 item 16/23116. British wives of Australian troops MP 367/1. Mahon and secretary's memoranda CRS A1 item 15/3101. Internment of enemy subjects MP 472/1. All these documents are on NAA microfilm A6006 Roll 1.

p. 37   Discussion on relationship between caucus and cabinet is cited in Weller P. 1975, *Caucus Minutes 1901–1949. Volume 1 1901–1917*, Melbourne University Press, pp. 428–47.

p. 38   Higgs' and Hughes' comments re conscription see Fitzhardinge L.F. 1979, *The Little Digger 1914–1952*, p. 179. Example of role of cabinet secretary see CRS A571 item 16/13572. Protection of 'Anzac' CRS 432 item 29/3484. For an example of annotation by Pearce see CRS A2 item 19/494 and MP367/1. National City Bank of New York CRS A571 item 17/13931. Disenfranchisement of persons of enemy birth CRS A456 item W9/5/58.

p. 39   War Profits Tax CRS A4719 Vol. 4. Hughes expected return A4719 Vol. 4. Desertion of Australian troops MP367/1. All these documents are on NAA microfilm A6066 Roll 2. Memoirs of M. L. Shepherd NAA CRS A1632 item 1 Part 2.

p. 40   Metropolitan race meetings no. NAA series number recorded – document found on NAA microfilm A6006 Roll 2. Pearce annotation 26 July 1918, CRS A2.

pp. 40–45 Telegrams between Hughes and Watt while Hughes was overseas NAA CRS CP360/8/1 and NAA CRS CP4/11 item 243053.

p. 46   Hungerford T., cited in Laurie V., 'Fighting Spirit' in *The Australian*, 23–24.4.2005, p. R9. Telegrams between Hughes and Watt while Watt was overseas NAA CRS CP4/11 item 243053.

p. 47   Composition of cabinet agendas NAA CRS A2717 Volume II. Cabinet decision in relation to rail passes NAA microfilm A6006 Roll 1.

pp. 47–48 Letter from Hughes to Bruce 27.10.21 NAA CRS A1492 item 202752 and CRS A1494 no item number.

p. 49   Bruce's account of cabinet meetings is set out in Edwards C. 1965, *Bruce of Melbourne. Man of Two Worlds*, London: Heinemann, pp. 63–4.

p. 50   1921 cabinet documents NAA CRS A2717 Volume III.

pp. 50–51 Bruce's account of cabinet meeting is cited in Edwards C. 1965, *Bruce of Melbourne. Man of Two Worlds*, London: Heinemann, pp. 64–5.

p. 51   Decision re Maltese immigrants CRS A2219 Volume 27 is contained in NAA microfilm A6006 Roll 4.

Chapter 4 – Consolidation, with hiccups: 1923–41

p. 52   Bruce–Page coalition history in Page, ECG, 2001, *Truant Surgeon: The*

Inside Story of Forty Years of Australian Political Life (new edition), Melbourne: Black Inc. p. 125.

p. 53 Bruce's comments on cabinet and details of cabinet processes see *Department of the Prime Minister and Cabinet Annual Report 1983–84*, pp. 52–3. 1925 cabinet practices NAA CRS A2718 Volume 1. Establishment of Cabinet Secretariat in 1927, see Department of the Prime Minister and Cabinet, *Annual Report 1983–84*, p. 53.

pp. 54–55 Draft document setting out establishment of Cabinet Secretariat NAA microfilm CRS A2718 Vol. 3 Roll 2.

p. 55 Cabinet processes NAA CRS A664 item 161425. Document setting out establishment of Cabinet Secretariat NAA microfilm CRS A2718 Vol. 3 Roll 2.

p. 56 Documents in relation to 1929 Premiers Conference CRS A461 item AF326/1/3 on NAA microfilm A6006 Roll 7. Cabinet document leaked to *Canberra Times* NAA CRS A432 item 214225. Cabinet discussion in relation to industrial powers NAA microfilm CRS A2718 Vol. VI, Roll 5.

p. 57 Caucus meetings Weller P. 1975, *Caucus Minutes 1901–1949. Volume 2 1917–1931*, Melbourne University Press, pp. 348–439. Scullin government's alternate cabinet arrangements, Department of the Prime Minister and Cabinet, *Annual Report 1983–84*, p. 54, and NAA CRA A3264. Note from Blakeley NAA CRA A3264. Note from Treasury CRS A461 item S344/1/4 NAA microfilm A6006 Roll 7.

p. 58 Decision re reading of Minutes of Cabinet NAA CRS A3264. Proposed changes to Cabinet Secretariat, 1930, *The Department of Prime Minister and Cabinet Annual Report 1978–79*, p. 36. Cabinet meetings January 1930 NAA CRS A3264.

p. 59 Cabinet meetings, February, March, 8 and 21 May 1930 NAA CRS A3264. Caucus meeting 8 and 21 May 1930 in Weller P. 1975, *Caucus Minutes 1901–1949. Volume 2 1917–1931*, Melbourne University Press, pp. 370–4. Cabinet meetings, including reappointment of Gibson and meeting held at Scullin's home 1930 NAA CRS A3264.

pp. 60–61 Caucus meetings in Weller P. 1975, *Caucus Minutes 1901–1949. Volume 2 1917–1931*, Melbourne University Press, pp. 356–410. Cabinet meetings 1930 NAA CRS A3264. Caucus meetings 1930, including issue of Gold Bonus and so on in Weller P. 1975, *Caucus Minutes 1901–1949. Volume 2 1917–1931*, Melbourne University Press, pp. 356–410.

pp. 60–63 Cabinet meetings 1931 NAA CRS A3264. Caucus meetings in Weller P. 1975, *Caucus Minutes 1901–1949. Volume 2 1917–1931*, Melbourne University Press, pp. 410–39. Denning W. 1982, *Caucus Crisis: The Rise and Fall of the Scullin Government*, Sydney: Hale & Iremonger.

p. 64 Re-establishment of Cabinet Secretariat by Lyons government NAA CRS A2694 Volume 1. Details of cabinet meetings, procedures 1932–1934 NAA CRS A2694. Discussion on operation of Lyons cabinet NAA CRS A2694 Volume 2. Types of cabinet memoranda see NAA microfilm A6006 Rolls 9 and 10.

p. 65 Memorandum re school milk CRS A192 item 15 in NAA microfilm A6006 Roll 10. Budget discussions are in NAA microfilm A6006 Roll 9. Sir Maurice Hankey's comments cited in Martin A.W. 1993, *Robert Menzies. A Life Vol. 1*, Melbourne: Melbourne University Press, pp. 127–8.

p. 66 Resignation of Fenton NAA microfilm A6006 Roll 8. Massy Greene's illness NAA CRS 2270 item 18. Lawson's appointment in NAA CRS M2270 item 15.

p. 68 Stanley Bruce's role as London minister NAA CRS M2270 item 8. Gullett's resignation NAA CRS 2270. Communication while the prime minister was overseas NAA CRS CP 290/5/1 item 7 and microfilm A6006 Roll 10.

p. 69 Relationship between Lyons and Latham cited in Martin A.W. 1993, *Robert*

Menzies. *A Life* Vol. 1, Melbourne: Melbourne University Press, pp. 127–8. Standing Committee for Defence CRA MP 1217 Box 991 in NAA microfilm A6006 Roll 11. Constitution of a war cabinet CRS MP 1217 in NAA microfilm A6006 Roll 11.

p. 70   Creation of cabinet committees NAA CRS A2694 XMI Vol. 19 Part 2. Lyon's invitation to Bruce cited in Martin A.W. 1993, *Robert Menzies. A Life* Vol. 1, Melbourne: Melbourne University Press, p. 256.

p. 71   National insurance problems for cabinet and the Menzies resignation cited in Martin A.W. 1993, *Robert Menzies. A Life* Vol. 1, Melbourne: Melbourne University Press, pp. 256–60.

pp. 71–72   Interactions between full cabinet and war cabinet NAA microfilm CRS A2697 Vols. 1. 2 and 3, Roll 1.

pp. 72–73   Cabinet practices 1940–1941 NAA microfilm CRS A2697 Vol. 5 and 6 Rolls 2 and 3.

pp. 73–74   Memorandum in relation to cabinet arrangements and letter from Menzies to Fadden in relation to cabinet arrangements NAA CRS A461 item A16/1/1.

p. 75   Cabinet meetings details NAA microfilm CRS A2697 Roll 4.

p. 76   Menzies' resignation cited in Martin A.W. 1993, *Robert Menzies. A Life* Vol. 1, Melbourne: Melbourne University Press, pp. 380–2.

Chapter 5 – Fighting war and managing mavericks: 1941–49

pp. 77–78   Cabinet discussions including Curtin's initial cabinet speech, budget and cabinet solidarity NAA A2703 item 227916. Scullin's caucus motion in Weller P. 1975, *Caucus Minutes 1901–1949. Minutes of the Meetings of the Federal Parliamentary Labor Party* Vol. 3 1932–1949, Melbourne University Press, p. 294.

p. 79   Details of caucus meetings and Labor National Conference in Weller P. 1975, *Caucus Minutes 1901–1949. Minutes of the Meetings of the Federal Parliamentary Labor Party* Vol. 3 1932–1949, Melbourne University Press, pp. 304–15.

p. 80   Discussion on Communist party NAA A2703 item 227917. Discussion on Commonwealth Bank NAA A2703 item 227919. Caucus discussion on Commonwealth Bank in Weller P. 1975, *Caucus Minutes 1901–1949. Minutes of the Meetings of the Federal Parliamentary Labor Party* Vol. 3 1932–1949, Melbourne University Press, pp. 349–52. Chair of caucus meetings in Weller P. 1975, *Caucus Minutes 1901–1949. Minutes of the Meetings of the Federal Parliamentary Labor Party* Vol. 3 1932–1949, Melbourne University Press, pp. 363–496.

pp. 80–82   Cabinet discussions on Bretton Woods agreement NAA CRS A2703 item 227919 and 227921/2. Dedman D. 1968, 'The Practical Application of Collective Responsibility', *Politics*, Vol. 1, No. 2, November, pp. 148–62. Caucus discussions in Weller P. 1975, *Caucus Minutes 1901–1949. Minutes of the Meetings of the Federal Parliamentary Labor Party* Vol. 3 1932–1949, Melbourne University Press, pp. 404–6.

p. 83   For number of war cabinet and advisory war cabinet meetings, minutes and agenda items see Horner D. 1996, *Inside the War Cabinet. Directing Australia's War Effort 1939–45*, Sydney: Allen & Unwin p. 197; for the Horner quote see p. 5.

p. 84   For Shedden quip by Menzies, see Horner D. 1996, *Inside the War Cabinet. Directing Australia's War Effort 1939–45*, Sydney: Allen & Unwin, p. 136. 1942 Production Executive Report NAA microfilm CRS A2700 Vol. 4 Roll 2.

p. 85   Horner D. 1996, *Inside the War Cabinet. Directing Australia's War Effort*

p. 86 *1939–45*, Sydney: Allen & Unwin, pp. 136–7. Interaction between full cabinet and war cabinet NAA CRS A2703 Vol. 1B.
Establishment of sub-committees NAA CRS A2703 item 227920. Cabinet procedures 1944 and 1945 NAA CRS A2703 items 227919 and 227920. Crisp L.F. 1960, *Ben Chifley. A Biography*, London: Longmans, pp. 258–9.
p. 87 Prime minister's statements to cabinet NAA CRS A2703 Vol. 1C.
p. 88 Ward's retort to Curtin on being told he had not voted for him is sourced from Horner D. 1996, *Inside the War Cabinet. Directing Australia's War Effort 1939–45*, Sydney: Allen & Unwin p. 94. For Ward's attack on Curtin re conscription see Day D. 1999, *John Curtin: A Life*, Pymble NSW: Harper Collins p. 491. Conflict between Curtain and Ward NAA CRS A2703 Vol. 1C.
p. 89 Banking Bills NAA microfilm CRS A2700. Post-war reconstruction NAA CRS A2700 Vol. 3 Roll 2.
p. 90 Appointments of Ross and Bruce NAA CRS A2703 item 50. Appointments of Beasley, Makin and Wilson NAA CRS A2703 Vol. 3A item 227920. Ward's complaint re appointment of Governor-General and powers of prime minister NAA CRS A2703 item 53.
p. 91 Discussions in relation to roles of prime minister and ministers – issues of 'Brisbane Line' and peace treaties NAA CRS A2703 Vol. 1D and CRS A2703 Vol. 113. Minutes of cabinet meeting 3 August 1942 NAA CRS A2703 Vol. 1C.
p. 92 Prime minister's statement on consumption of beer NAA CRS A2703 Vol. 1C.
p. 93 Crisp L. F. 1960, *Ben Chifley. A Biography*, London: Longmans, p. 239.
p. 94 Interview with John Dedman, 11 May 1973. Filed telegram, NAA CRS A2703.

Chapter 6 – An emperor and three pale shadows: 1949–72

p. 95 Restructure of Prime Minister's Department NAA CRS A447, A1946/2659.
pp. 96–97 Handbook of cabinet and cabinet committees NAA CRS A4917 item XMI.
p. 98 Menzies' appeal to ministers, cabinet notebook NAA A11099, 1/13. Formation of two committees in Department of Prime Minister and Cabinet, *Annual Report 1983–84*, p. 64.
pp. 98–99 Brown's quotes, as well as Lee's observation, are from Lee D. 1995, 'Cabinet', in *The Menzies Era: A Reappraisal of Government Politics and Policy*, in S. Prasser, J.R. Nethercote and J. Warhurst (eds), Sydney: Hale & Iremonger, p. 131–2.
p. 99 Menzies' comments on cabinet, cabinet notebook NAA A11099, 1/19. Separation of cabinet from ministry, Department of Prime Minister and Cabinet, *Annual Report 1983–84*, p. 69.
p. 100 Wilson's comments to cabinet in cabinet notebooks NAA A11099, 1/3, prime minister's question to Wilson A11099, 1/14; chiefs of staff attendance in cabinet in NAA A11099, 1/14, Mt Lyell mining representatives in cabinet NAA 11099, 1/30.
p. 101 Use of notebooks – Watt NAA A11099, 1/1, Brown's reminder memo NAA A11099, 1/9. Brown's briefings with prime minister in NAA microfilm CRS A4905, Vol. 1, Roll 1 and Vol. 7, Roll 3. Supporting officials on cabinet committees A11099, 1/6 and 1/28; Brown's briefing to Secretary of Air in NAA microfilm CRS A4905, Vol. 7, Roll 3. Brown's assessment of the Alcan deal is from memorandum from Brown to prime minister NAA microfilm CRS A4905 Vol. 7 Roll 3.

p. 102 Brown's proposed changes NAA CRS A6708/1 item 1. Comments by Chair of Public Service Board W.E. Dunk, *Notes re Prime Minister's Department – re-organisation* 20.9.50 CRS A447 item A1946/2659. Memorandum on Treasury advice and cabinet program NAA CRS A6708/1 item 1.

p. 103 Issues dominating cabinet in cabinet notebooks NAA A11099, 1/12 and NAA A11099, 1/13. Government's strategy re communism in cabinet notebooks NAA 11099 1/3 and A11099 1/5. Menzies' proposal re introduction of communism bill in cabinet notebooks NAA A11099, 1/3; McLeay's comments A11099, 1/5.

p. 104 Discussions re proposed double dissolution A11099, 1/12; further strategies re the double dissolution bill A11099, 1/12; communists and the public service A11099, 1/16; proposed introduction of television A11099, 1/16. Petrov affair cabinet notebook NAA A11099 1/18.

pp. 105–7 Discussions re the pound in cabinet notebooks NAA A11099, 1/3; continuation of discussions re the pound in cabinet notebooks on 12 September and 25 September 1950 A11099, 1/5.

p. 107 Economic debate 22 February 1951 A11099, 1/12; cabinet vote A11099, 1/12.

p. 108 Continuation of economic debate July 1951 A11099, 1/13; comments by McEwen and Fadden A11099, 1/13. Cabinet on foreign aid debate, cabinet notebooks NAA A11099, 1/19.

p. 109 Foreign policy discussion A11099, 1/1. Discussions in relation to Vietnam and Anzus in cabinet notebooks NAA A11099, 1/18.

pp. 110–11 Continuation of discussions in June 1954 A11099, 1/19. Spender's commitment of Australia to the Korean war in Spender, P. 1972, *Politics and a Man*, Sydney: Collins, pp. 282–4, and Martin A.W. 1993, *Robert Menzies. A Life Vol. 2*, Melbourne: Melbourne University Press, pp. 157–9.

p. 111 Crisis in Egypt, cabinet notebooks NAA A11099, 1/30; defence expenditure A11099, 1/5.

p. 112 Purchase of aircraft A11099, 1/8. Continuation of discussion on aircraft, cabinet notebooks NAA A11099 1/8; tension between economic and foreign policies A11099, 1/12; discussion re Egypt A11099. 1/27; discussions re Korea A11099, 1/27; defence discussions – Menzies A11099, 1/14.

p. 113 Defence discussions – McEwen A11099, 1/17. Menzies response to McEwen, cabinet notebooks NAA A11099, 1/17; meeting between Treasury officials and Defence Minister A11099, 1/30.

p. 114 Memorandum from prime minister regarding problem in gaining support over universities estimates, NAA CRS A4940 item C435. Budget papers NAA CRS A4940 item 706767. Holt comments on McMahon proposed condition for cabinet submission procedures NAA CRS A4940 item C4368.

p. 115 Issues presented at last moment, cabinet notebooks, NAA A11099 1/14; academics visiting China A11099 1/15, 1/16 and 1/17; 'north' Italian immigrants A11099, 1/9; further comments on immigrants A11099, A/13. Comments on Japanese wives, cabinet notebooks NAA A11099, 1/14.

p. 116 Federalism issues A11099 1/3; uniform tax A11099 1/15; UNESCO A11099 1/27; comment on cabinet decision-making while prime minister overseas A11099, 1/29; cabinet process A11099 1/30; creation of foreign affairs standing committee A11099, 1/27; Spooner's complaint about Treasury A11099, 1/14.

p. 117 Appointment of permanent head of external affairs cabinet notebooks NAA A11099, 1/17; prime minister's requests to cabinet A11099 1/5, direction of debate A11099 1/15, visitors to cabinet A11099 1/17, cabinet decisions A11099 1/13; Spicer's comment to Beale A11099 1/28.

p. 118 Holt and Menzies on Holt's leadership in Frame T. 2005, *The Life and Death of Harold Holt*, Crows Nest, NSW: Allen & Unwin, p. 143 and p. 224.

VIP planes affair in Hancock, I. 2004, *The V.I.P. Affair 1966–67: The Causes, Course and Consequences of a Ministerial and Public Service Cover-up*, Canberra: Australasian Study of Parliament Group.

p. 119   Election of Cabinets NAA CRS C4940 item C4473. Gorton's view on leadership in Hancock I. 2002, *John Gorton. He Did it His Way*, Sydney: Hodder, p. 154. Public explanation for splitting cabinet office and prime minister's department in Department of Prime Minister and Cabinet, *Annual Report 1983–84*, p. 72.

p. 120   McMahon's statement in *Hansard* (Representatives) 15.3.1971, p. 836. Gorton and McEwen fighting Treasury over industry development corporation in Hancock I. 2002, *John Gorton. He Did it His Way*, Sydney: Hodder, pp. 270–4. Comments by two ministers on Gorton's cabinet style in Hancock I. 2002, *John Gorton. He Did it His Way*, Sydney: Hodder, p. 402. Hasluck's assessment of McMahon is in Hasluck P. 1997, *The Chance of Politics*, Melbourne: Text Publishing, p. 188.

p. 121   McMahon's comments on function of prime minister on beginning his term, Department of Prime Minister and Cabinet, *Annual Report 1983–84*, p. 73. McMahon comments during 1972 campaign on what he had learnt as prime minister: Oakes L. and Solomon D. 1973, *The Making of an Australian Prime Minister*, Melbourne: Cheshire, p. 269.

Chapter 7 – Dashed hopes: 1972–75

p. 123   Contemporary comment on reasons that movements for a 'spill' were frustrated in 1975, see Kelly P. 'No Time for a Spill in the Cabinet', in *The Australian*, 30 May 1975, p. 9. Whitlam's comment on cabinet half the size and discussion of 1975 caucus committee recommendations on cabinet, see 'PM set for Major Shake-up', in *The Age*, 4 June 1975, p. 1.

p. 124   Caucus report on cabinet where Hayden supporting Whitlam's endorsement of reduced cabinet size, but other ministers opposed: 'Caucus Ducks Cabinet Issue', in *The Age*, 30 September 1975, p. 3.

p. 125   Wilenski's quotes on committee framework, as well as Whitlam's description of the proposed system, sourced from Solomon D. 'Aiming to Increase Ministerial Control' in *The Canberra Times*, 12 January 1973, p. 2.

p. 126   For an account of the inflation meeting held at the prime minister's house, see Haupt R., 'PM Wants Kitchen Cabinet', in *The Australian Financial Review*, 14 June 1974, p. 1.

p. 127   Estimates of possible submissions for general administrative committee are from Smith, R.F.I. 1977, 'Australian Cabinet Structure and Procedures: The Labor Government 1972–1975', *Politics*, Vol. 12, 1, pp. 23–7 with the quote on the modelling of the priorities and planning committee on Canadian federal cabinet located on p. 25. Wilenski's views on priorities and planning committee in Solomon D. 'Aiming to Increase Ministerial Control', in *The Canberra Times*, 12 January 1973.

p. 128   Attraction of Sydney meeting quote in Haupt R. 'PM Wants Kitchen Cabinet', in *The Australian Financial Review*, 14 June 1974, p. 1.

p. 129   Whitlam's outline of ERC committee functions in Prime Minister's Press Statement, no. 436, 28 January 1975.

p. 131   Submission circulation standard procedures and exceptions in Smith, R.F.I. 1976, *Australian Cabinet Structure and Procedures*, Royal Commission on Australian Government Administration, Appendix 4, pp. 207–11.

p. 132   For the case study of the 1974 budget discussed in relation to the eclipse of Crean's Treasury department see Hawker, G., Smith, R.F.I. and Weller, P. 1979, 'The Politics of Advice and the Making of the 1974 Budget', in *Politics and Policy in Australia*, St Lucia Queensland: University of Queensland Press.

Chapter 8 – Working all hours: 1976–83

p. 135   The material on Fraser draws generally on the following files: LC2 Cabinet Procedures; LC294 Planning and Co-ordination Committees; LC272 Economic Committee; LC2542 Co-ordination Committee; LC2198 Review of the Cabinet System. These files were all used in writing *Malcolm Fraser PM* and the material here was published therein.

pp. 136–7 Programs and arrangements drawn from LC222 Cabinet Program for week of 18 September 1978; LC2234, 25 September 1978; LC2239, 2 October 1978; LC2250, 9 October 1978; LC2252, 16 October 1978; LC2283, 6 November 1978; LC2545, 7 December 1981; LC3560, 13 December 1981; LC3565, 12 January 1982; LC3566, 19 January 1982; LC3630, 6 April 1982; LC3641, 13 April 1981; LC3653, 3 May 1982; LC3662, 10 May 1982; LC3663, 17 May 1982; LC3672, 31 May 1982.

p. 137   Anthony's special treatment found in LC3663.

p. 138   Fraser's letter to Yeend on submission length and timetable in M1255/12.

p. 139   Discussion of Lynch as agenda setter is part of the cabinet review by Yeend in LC2198.

p. 140   Fraser's comment on the inadequacy of the contingency planning submission in M1255/12. Details of ministry meetings and agenda are in LC2432 Ministry meetings: general discussions.

p. 141   Discussion of access of ministers to cabinet is found in LC2. Creation of ethnic television service is in LC2197 Establishment of an Ethnic TV Service.

p. 142   For details on number and hours of meetings see LC3641, LC1702 and LC3263.

p. 143   The table is sourced from Weller, P. 1989, *Malcolm Fraser PM: A Study in Prime Ministerial Power*, Ringwood Victoria: Penguin Books, p. 125, which extracted the material from LC3263 Peacock Resignation.

p. 145   Fraser's comments on the committee system from Fraser, J.M., 1978, 'Responsibility in Government', *Australian Journal of Public Administration*, Vol. 37, No, 1, pp. 1–11.

p. 146   For the agenda of the co-ordination committee see LC2542 while the details of its activities can be sourced from M1268/SV.

p. 148   Peacock's criticisms were made in parliament in *Commonwealth Parliamentary Debates*, 24 April 1981.

p. 149   The term 'partial cabinet' was coined by former British minister Patrick Gordon Walker in his 1972 book, *The Cabinet*, London: Fontana, pp. 87–101.

pp. 150–4 Weller, P. 1989, *Malcolm Fraser PM: A Study in Prime Ministerial Power*, Ringwood Victoria: Penguin, p. 138. The Nixon quote is from the same source. Ministerial perspectives on Fraser p. 142.

p. 154   'Decision by exhaustion' and Fraser on decision-making, Weller, P. 1989, *Malcolm Fraser PM: A Study in Prime Ministerial Power*, Ringwood Victoria: Penguin, p. 141. Yeend on seas and submerged lands is from Weller, P. 1989, *Malcolm Fraser PM*, p. 143.

p. 155   The request for cabinet decisions on the Seas and Submerged Lands issue is in M1268/24: Requests to Secretary PMC.

p. 156   The brief to Lynch is in the Lynch Papers: General briefing.

Chapter 9 – Contrasting styles: 1983–96

p. 159   The 1981 Labor Party taskforce report is discussed in Weller, P. 1983, 'Transition: Taking Over Power in 1983', *The Australian Journal of Public Administration*, Vol. 42, No. 3, pp. 303–19 and the reference is Australian

	Labor Party, 1982, *Report of the Taskforce in Government Administration*, Canberra, September.
p. 160	The quote from the report and the recommendation, see Australian Labor Party, 1982, *Report of the Taskforce in Government Administration*, Canberra, p. 3. Hawke's quality of government policy is based on Australian Labor Party 1983, *Labor and the Quality of Government*, policy presentation by Bob Hawke, 9 February.
p. 161	Solicitor-General advice in Weller, P. 1987, 'Assistant Ministers and Mega-departments', *Canberra Bulletin of Public Administration*, 52, pp. 18–23. More information on the restructure can be found in various articles in CBPA, 1987, *Canberra Bulletin of Public Administration*, 52, October.
p. 162	Table 3 Activity in Hawke Cabinet is sourced from Weller, P. 1990, 'The Cabinet', in C. Jennett and R.G. Stewart (eds), *Hawke and Australian Public Policy: Consensus and Restructuring*, South Melbourne: Macmillan, p. 19.
p. 163	The government's White Paper 1983, *Reforming the Australian Public Service: A Statement of the Government's Intentions, December 1983*, Canberra: Australian Government Publishing Service, p. 6.
p. 164	The quotes by Blewett from 23 June and 14 July are from Blewett, N. 1999, *A Cabinet Diary: A Personal Record of the First Keating Government*, Kent Town South Australia: Wakefield Press, pp. 154 and 175.
p. 167	Walsh's account of ERC processes outlined in Walsh, P. 1995, *Confessions of a Failed Finance Minister*, Milsons Point NSW: Random House, pp. 120 and 139. Blewett's views on the ERC are from Blewett, N. 1999, *A Cabinet Diary: A Personal Record of the First Keating Government*, Kent Town South Australia: Wakefield Press, p. 206.
p. 168	Quote on cabinet–caucus consultation is from Australian Labor Party 1982, *Report of the Taskforce in Government Administration*, Canberra.
p. 169	The rewritten definition of the principle of collective responsibility after the Stewart West affair is in Department of the Prime Minister and Cabinet 1983, *Cabinet Handbook*, Canberra: Australian Government Printing Service, p. 3. The extension of the relaxed definition of collective responsibility to non-cabinet assistant ministers who could debate in caucus in 'areas apart from their portfolio' is in the Cabinet Office 1988, *Cabinet Handbook* (revised edition), Canberra: Australian Government Printing Service, p. 4.
p. 170	Keating's plea for cabinet secrecy is from Blewett, N. 1999, *A Cabinet Diary: A Personal Record of the First Keating Government*, Kent Town South Australia: Wakefield Press, p. 32. Keating's comments against Simon Crean from Edwards, J. 1996, *Keating: The Inside Story*, Ringwood: Viking, p. 413. The Ray–Bilney exchange in Blewett, N. 1999, *A Cabinet Diary: A Personal Record of the First Keating Government*, Kent Town South Australia: Wakefield Press, p. 269–71.
p. 173	Keating's adviser's comments on the power of the treasurer is from Edwards, J. 1996, *Keating: The Inside Story*, Ringwood: Viking, p. 168. Keating's views on the roles of prime minister and cabinet chairman are from Kitney, G. 1993, 'Small Fuse, Big Row', *Sydney Morning Herald*, 4 June 1993, p. 17.
p. 174	John Edwards' descriptions of Keating's cabinet chair role are in Edwards, J. 1996, *Keating: The Inside Story*, Ringwood: Viking, pp. 466–7. Keating's domination of cabinet from *Sydney Morning Herald*, 29 April 1995. Keating on the republic, see Kitney, G. *Sydney Morning Herald*, 15 April. Keating on airports authority, see *Sydney Morning Herald*, 24 September 1994. Keating on tax increases and Commonwealth bank decision, see *The Age*, 28 April and 24 June 1995.
p. 175	Keating's disinterest in cabinet chair role is from Watson, D. 2002, *Recollections of a Bleeding Heart: A Portrait of Paul Keating PM*, Milsons Point NSW: Random House, p. 196. Hawke fitting the 'ideal' job description

of prime minister is discussed in Weller, P. 1985, 'Chapter 9 – is there a job description', in *First Among Equals: Prime Ministers in Westminster Systems*, Sydney: Allen & Unwin. Blewett's summation of Hawke's cabinet management style is quoted in Blewett, N. 2000, 'Robert James Lee Hawke', in M. Grattan (ed.), *Australian Prime Ministers*, Sydney: New Holland, pp. 391–2.

p. 176   Blewett's exchange with Gareth Evans is from Blewett, N. 1999, *A Cabinet Diary: A Personal Record of the First Keating Government*, Kent Town South Australia: Wakefield Press, pp. 183–4.

Chapter 10 – Discipline and control: 1996–2006

p. 179   Kelly's discussion of ministerial responsibility is from Kelly, P. 2005, *Re-thinking Australian Governance – The Howard Legacy*, Occasional Paper Series 4/2005, Canberra: Academy of the Social Sciences in Australia, p. 11.

p. 183   Howard's observations on the national security committee and details of its meetings during the East Timor peacekeeping operation are located in Kelly, P., 2005, *Re-thinking Australian Governance – The Howard Legacy*, Occasional Paper Series 4/2005, Canberra: Academy of the Social Sciences in Australia, pp. 14 and 15.

p. 184   The purpose of the annual strategy meeting of the Howard cabinet and Howard's allocation of time at the beginning of cabinet to consider strategic issues is discussed in Howard, J. 2002, 'Strategic Leadership for Australia: Policy Directions in a Complex World', Address to the Committee for the Economic Development of Australia, 20 November, p. 1.

p. 185   Kelly's description of how Howard runs cabinet is from Kelly, P. 2005, *Re-thinking Australian Governance – The Howard Legacy*, Occasional Paper Series 4/2005, Canberra: Academy of the Social Sciences in Australia, p. 4. Comments against the time allocated at the beginning of cabinet for strategic discussions are given in Wanna, J. and Hanson, S. 2006, 'Enabling the Australian Cabinet: Supporting Cabinet Capabilities, draft paper, p. 6.

p. 186   Where ministers obtain their advice is from Kelly, P. 2005, *Re-thinking Australian Governance – The Howard Legacy*, Occasional Paper Series 4/2005, Canberra: Academy of the Social Sciences in Australia, p. 8. The tasks of the CPU are outlined in Department of Prime Minister and Cabinet 2004, 'Cabinet Implementation Unit', 23 June, www.pmc.gov.au/docs/implementation.cfm

p. 187   The CPU head's observations on the purpose of the CPU are from McClintock, P. 2003, 'The Australian Approach to Policy-making', *Canberra Bulletin of Public Administration*, No. 108, June, p. 15. Table 4 is sourced from Department of Prime Minister and Cabinet.

p. 188   For Cabinet Implementation Unit see, Department of Prime Minister and Cabinet 2005, 'Cabinet Implementation Unit – special article', *Annual Report 2004/05*, pp. 107–12.

Chapter 11 – Cabinet, party and parliament: The threads of accountability

p. 192   Australia's description as a system of responsible party government is discussed in Parkin, A. 1980, 'Pluralism and Australian Political Science', *Politics*, XV (1), pp. 50–3.

p. 205   The Quick and Garran quote is cited in Codd, M. 1990, 'The Role of Secretaries in Departments in the APS', *PSC Occasional Papers No. 8*, Canberra, p. 2.

p. 206	The Bury statements and resignation vis-à-vis Menzies comments on collective responsibility are found in Encel, S. 1974, *Cabinet Government in Australia*, (2nd edition), Melbourne: Melbourne University Press, pp. 113–15.
pp. 207–8	The sections 2.1 and 2.3 are from the Cabinet Office 1988, *Cabinet Handbook* (revised edition) Canberra: Australian Government Printing Service, p. 4.
pp. 208–9	Section 2.8 and 2.9 of the *Cabinet Handbook* dealing with public statements by ministers is from The Department of the Prime Minister and Cabinet 2004, *Cabinet Handbook* (amended 5th edition), Canberra: Commonwealth of Australia, p. 5.
p. 209	The Lord Salisbury declaration is from Encel, S. 1974, *Cabinet Government in Australia* (2nd edition), Melbourne: Melbourne University Press, p. 107.
p. 210	Snedden's quote on ministerial responsibility is from Crisp, L.F. 1965, *Australian National Government*, Croydon, Victoria: Longmans, footnote 8, p. 321.
p. 211	Definition of ministerial responsibility is from Prime Minister 1998, *A Guide on Key Elements of Ministerial Responsibility*, Canberra: Department of the Prime Minister and Cabinet, p. 13.
p. 212	Thanks are due to Professor John Dewar for the information on the principle of constructive notice in equity law. On ministerial responsibility and admitting error, see also Garland, R.V. 1976, 'Relations between Ministers and Departments', ACT R.I.P.A. *Newsletter*, 3, 3, pp. 15–35.

Chapter 12 – The rules of cabinet

p. 216	The 'power and majesty of the cabinet minute' quote is from Hennessy, P. 1989, *Whitehall*, London: Secker and Warburg, p. 65.
p. 218	Department of Prime Minister and Cabinet 1999, *Legislation Handbook*, (incorporating No. 1 Update of May 2000), Canberra: Commonwealth of Australia; Department of Prime Minister and Cabinet - Federal Executive Council Secretariat 2005, *Federal Executive Council Handbook*, Canberra: Commonwealth of Australia; The Prime Minister 1998, *A Guide on Key Elements of Ministerial Responsibility*, Canberra: Department of the Prime Minister and Cabinet.
p. 219	Section 1.1 of the *Cabinet Handbook* is from The Department of the Prime Minister and Cabinet 2004, *Cabinet Handbook* (amended 5th edition), Canberra: Commonwealth of Australia, p. 1. Standards of ministerial conduct are sourced from The Prime Minister 1998, *A Guide on Key Elements of Ministerial Responsibility*, Canberra: Department of the Prime Minister and Cabinet, p. 10.
p. 223	The minister's observations on how cabinet worked under Menzies and Bunting is from Weller, P. and Grattan, M. 1981, *Can Ministers Cope? Australian Federal Ministers at Work*, Richmond Victoria: Hutchinson of Australia, p. 129.
p. 224	Bunting's description of cabinet is in Department of the Prime Minister and Cabinet, *Annual Report 1983–84*, p. 70.
p. 225	The acting cabinet secretary's explanation of the contents of cabinet handbooks to a court in 1993 can be found in *Commonwealth of Australia v Northern Land Council and Another*, 112 Australian Law Reports (ALR) 409, 21 April 1993.
p. 228	Yeend's comments from Yeend, G.J. 1979, 'The Department of the Prime Minister and Cabinet in Perspective', *Australian Journal of Public Administration*, Vol. 38, No. 2, pp. 142–3. The description of the PMC brief under the Fraser government is from Weller, P. 1989, *Malcolm Fraser PM:*

A *Study in Prime Ministerial Power*, Ringwood: Penguin Books, pp. 35–6.

p. 229 Bunting's description of the supremacy of ministers during the Menzies' period is from Bunting, J. 1988, *R.G. Menzies: A Portrait*, Sydney: Allen & Unwin, p. 84, while his recognition of the growing complexity of government is from p. 75.

p. 230 Holt's quote on reading the prime minister's department note as well as Bunting's conclusions about the preservation of ministerial versus cabinet government are from Bunting, J. 1988, *R.G. Menzies: A Portrait*, Sydney: Allen & Unwin, p. 83.

Chapter 13 – Making policy in cabinet

p. 234 Howard's assessment of the Fraser government's policy-political balance in Howard, J. 1990, 'Reflections on the Cabinet Process – I', in B. Galligan, J.R. Nethercote and C. Walsh (eds), *Decision Making in Australian Government: The Cabinet & Budget*, Canberra: Australian National University – Centre for Research on Federal Financial Relations.

p. 244 Tange's cabinet committee experience with Chifley on Bretton Woods is from Edwards, P. 2006, *Arthur Tange: Last of the Mandarins*, Sydney: Allen & Unwin, p. 37.

p. 245 Section 2.11 of the *Cabinet Handbook* on collective responsibility is from The Department of the Prime Minister and Cabinet 2004, *Cabinet Handbook* (amended 5th edition), Canberra: Commonwealth of Australia, p. 5. British cabinet secretary citation and discussion of Canadian cabinet experience is from d'Ombrain, N. 2004, 'Cabinet Secrecy (The Essence of the Cabinet Secrecy Convention)', *Canadian Public Administration*, 47, 3, pp. 332–60.

p. 246 Bagehot's claim that cabinet is an efficient part of the constitution is from Bagehot, W. 1963, *The English Constitution*, London: Fontana; consideration of access to cabinet notebooks is from *Commonwealth of Australia v Northern Land Council and Another*, 112 Australian Law Reports (ALR) 409, 21 April 1993. Leaking and Labor party crises is discussed in Encel, S. 1974, *Cabinet Government in Australia* (2nd edition), Melbourne: Melbourne University Press, pp. 124–33.

p. 247 Discussion of destruction of cabinet notebooks from Blewett, N. 1999, *A Cabinet Diary: A Personal Record of the First Keating Government*, Kent Town South Australia: Wakefield Press, p. 195. Section 2.12 of the *Cabinet Handbook* on ministerial memoirs is from The Department of the Prime Minister and Cabinet 2004, *Cabinet Handbook* (amended 5th edition), Canberra: Commonwealth of Australia, p. 5.

p. 248 Comment from senior Liberal in the 1980s on cabinet system and solidarity is from Weller, P. and Grattan, M. 1981, *Can Ministers Cope? Australian Federal Ministers at Work*, Richmond Victoria: Hutchinson of Australia, p. 136.

Chapter 14 – The power of prime ministers: Cabinet as contest

p. 250 Mackintosh's perspective on prime ministerial government is from Mackintosh, J.P. 1962, *The British Cabinet*, London: Stevens & Sons, pp. 451–2. Crossman's description of cabinet government as prime ministerial government is from Crossman, R.H.S. 1963, 'Introduction', in W. Bagehot, *The English Constitution*, p. 51.

REFERENCES TO PAGES 229–272 • 307

p. 254 Blewett's observation on the prime minister's political office is from Blewett, N. 1999, *A Cabinet Diary: A Personal Record of the First Keating Government*, Kent Town South Australia: Wakefield Press, p. 205.

p. 256 Fraser's novel cabinet approval process for establishing a high commission in Lusaka can be found in Weller, P. 1989, *Malcolm Fraser PM: A Study in Prime Ministerial Power*, Ringwood: Penguin Books, pp. 119–20.

p. 257 Howard's commitment to putting the tax question on the agenda is cited in Grattan, M. 2000, 'John Winston Howard', in M. Grattan (ed.), *Australian Prime Ministers*, Sydney: New Holland, p. 455.

p. 260 Bunting's analysis of decision-making based on weight of opinion and his tale of Chifley's 'government by exhaustion' are from Bunting, J. 1988, *R.G. Menzies: A Portrait*, Sydney: Allen & Unwin, pp. 93 and 94.

p. 261 Bunting's memo to the Secretary from NAA A4960 item 706767.

p. 262 Fraser's assessment of ministerial alignment with him and Anthony, in Weller, P. 1989, *Malcolm Fraser Prime Minister*, Ringwood: Penguin.

p. 265 Country party independence quote from Weller, P. and Grattan, M. 1981, *Can Ministers Cope? Australian Federal Ministers at Work*, Richmond Victoria: Hutchinson of Australia.

p. 266 Hasluck, P., 1997, *The Chance of Politics*, Melbourne: Text Publishing.
Power of prime minister quote from M. Grattan (ed.), *Australian Prime Ministers*, Sydney: New Holland, p. 16.

p. 267 Howard's judgment of the Fraser cabinet from Howard, J. 1990, 'Reflections on the Cabinet Process – I', in B. Galligan, J.R. Nethercote and C. Walsh (eds), *Decision Making in Australian Government: The Cabinet & Budget*, Canberra: Australian National University – Centre for Research on Federal Financial Relations, p. 27.

Chapter 15 – Core executives: Is Australian cabinet different?

p. 269 Simpson, J. 2001, *The Friendly Dictatorship*, Toronto: McClelland and Stewart, and for his quote on collective decision-making, see p. 62. Savoie, D. 1999, *Governing from the Centre*, Toronto: University of Toronto Press, and comment on cabinet agenda items see p. 647. Different conclusions regarding cabinet are from Hodgetts, J.E. 1973, *The Canadian Public Service: A Physiology of Government 1867–1970*, Toronto: University of Toronto Press.

p. 270 On Blair's management style, see Rentoul, J. 2001, *Tony Blair: Prime Minister*, London: Warner Books, p. 540; and for his comment on cabinet government see p. 640. The Blair aide comment on cabinet government is from Kavanagh, D. and Seldon, A. 2000, *The Powers behind the Prime Minister: The Hidden Influence of Number Ten*, London: HarperCollins, p. 291. For Hennessy's comments on cabinet government, see Hennessy, P. 1986, *Cabinet*, Oxford: Basil Blackwell. Hennessy's model of cabinet as collective debate is from Hennessy, P. 2000, *The Prime Minister: The Office and its Holders since 1945*, London: Penguin.

p. 271 The views of George Jones are from Jones, G. 1981, 'Review of Rose and Suleiman', in *Public Administration*, Vol. 57, 2, pp. 219–20. The quotes and discussion on the core executive are from Rhodes, R. 1995, 'From Prime Ministerial Power to Core Executive', in R. Rhodes and P. Dunleavy (eds), *Prime Minister, Cabinet and Core Executives*, London: Macmillan.

p. 272 Andeweg's assessment of cabinet in Andeweg, R. 1997, 'Collegiality and Collectivity: Cabinets, Cabinet Committees and Cabinet Ministers', in P. Weller et al. (eds), *The Hollow Crown*, Basingstoke: Macmillan. Savoie's

p. 273   concession in his analysis of Chrétien is from Savoie, D. 1999, *Governing from the Centre*, Toronto: University of Toronto Press, p. 650.

p. 273   The Graham White quote is from White, G. 2001, 'Mother Teresa's Biker Gang, or Cabinet Democracy in Canada', paper presented at the 'Canada Today: A Democratic Audit' conference, Ottowa, p. 1. Canada 2002, *A Guide for Ministers and Secretaries of State*, Ottawa: Privy Council Office. Chrétien as an 'instinctive and pugnacious politician' is from Martin, L. 1995, *Chrétien: The Will to Win*, Toronto: Lester Publishing.

p. 274   Self-restraint of cooperative government is from Rose, R. 1980, 'British Government: The Job at the Top', in R. Rose and E. Suleiman (eds), *Presidents and Prime Ministers*, Washington, DC: American Enterprise Institute, p. 340. Inner cabinet of Canada discussed in Bakvis, H. 2000, 'Prime Minister and Cabinet in Canada: An Autocracy in Need of Reform', *Journal of Canadian Studies*, Vol. 35, No. 4, pp. 60–79. Ralph Goodale quote in Savoie, D. 1999, *Governing from the Centre*, Toronto: University of Toronto Press, p. 180.

p. 275   Chrétien's quote is from Savoie, D. 1999, *Governing from the Centre*, Toronto: University of Toronto Press, p. 202.

p. 277   The weaknesses of cabinet are outlined in Kavanagh, D. and Seldon, A. 2000, *The Powers behind the Prime Minister: The Hidden Influence of Number Ten*, London: Harper Collins, p. 321; Dell, E. 1980, 'Collective Responsibility: Fact, Fiction or Façade?', *Policy and Practice: The Experience of Government*, London: RIPA.

p. 278   Andeweg's assessment of cabinet in Andeweg, R. 1997, 'Collegiality and Collectivity: Cabinets, Cabinet Committees and Cabinet Ministers', in P. Weller et al. (eds), *The Hollow Crown*, Basingstoke: Macmillan, p. 80.

p. 279   Australian prime ministers' reliance on the parliamentary party, see Weller, P. 1993, 'Party Rules and the Dismissal of Leaders', *Parliamentary Affairs*, Vol. 47, No. 1, pp. 133–43.

Chapter 16 – Conclusion: Trends and futures for cabinet government

p. 282   Menzies advice to Bunting is quoted in Bunting, J. 1988, *R.G. Menzies: A Portrait*, Sydney: Allen & Unwin, p. 4.

p. 283   The quote is from Heclo, H. 1974, *Modern Social Politics in Britain and Sweden: From Relief to Income Maintenance*, New Haven: Yale University Press, p. 305.

BIBLIOGRAPHY AND SOURCE NOTES

Official files

Commonwealth Cabinet records, including papers prepared for cabinet submission and those not formally presented as submissions but considered by cabinet nevertheless, records of cabinet meetings – Minutes and Agenda, records of the Department of Cabinet Office and the records of the Department of Prime Minister and Cabinet are all available in the National Archives of Australia. These were accessed through microfilm, digitisation and through personal searches at the National Archives in Canberra. Additional sources were in the National Library of Australia. Throughout the book, for sources from the National Archives of Australia series, numbers are cited and where available item numbers are added. For material sourced through the National Library of Australia the collection number is cited. Where applicable, for example the Hughes papers, a series number is cited, and when available, item numbers have also been included.

National Archives of Australia

Microfilm

There is no complete sequence of records prior to 1941; however, records to this point often contain informal documents and papers. As a more formalised system of record-keeping was introduced after 1941, records thereafter tend more to reflect the official processes and fewer informal documents are available. A considerable number of the cabinet documents for the period 1901–1956 are contained on microfilm. The main series is A6006 and it covers this entire period. Other files relating to each ministry up to 1956 also were accessed through microfilm. The principal series are:

A6006 – covers the period 1901–1918. This series contains cabinet papers, including submissions, decisions, agenda, minutes and peripheral papers for the prime ministerships of Barton, Deakin, Watson, Reid, Fisher, Cook and Hughes' first ministry.

A2712 and A3277 – covers the period 1918–1923. Included in these series are submissions, decisions, agenda, minutes a chronological list of cabinet meetings and supporting documentation relating to the second Hughes government.

A2718 – covers the Bruce–Page government between 1923 until 1929. Series A3264 follows and covers the Scullin Ministry from 1929 to 1932. This series primarily contains minutes and submissions.

A2697 contains the cabinet materials from the Menzies–Fadden ministry between 1939 and 1941. These series contain papers from the full cabinet, the economic cabinet and various sub-committees of cabinet.

The Curtin, Forde and Chifley ministries between 1941 and 1949 are considerably large and are disbursed over a number of series. These series are A2700. Contained in these series are records of cabinet sub-committees relative to trade and employment, Production Executive, Advisory War Council and the Ministry of Post-War and Reconstruction. These series also contain a number of index cards and agenda subject cards.

The final set of microfilm is related to the early Menzies era up to 1956. It contains records of the fourth Menzies ministry from 1949 to 1951, and part of the fifth Menzies ministry from 1951–1956. The series numbers are A4940.

Cabinet secretariat

Another extensive source of archival material was the Cabinet Secretariat files. Commonly known as 'pinks' these are the correspondence files of members of the Cabinet Secretariat, principally those of Sir John Bunting. The series number for these files is M319.

Cabinet notebooks

Prior to World War 2 only cabinet members attended cabinet meetings and a minister was appointed to take notes. However, during the war Frederick Strahan, the Secretary of the Department of the Prime Minister, was appointed to attend cabinet meetings and was responsible for taking notes of decisions. In 1950 prime minister Menzies approved new cabinet procedures that included regulation of submissions and other papers, arranging meetings and recording minutes. The secretary also takes notes of discussions, but only informally. Accordingly, cabinet notebook records are available from 1950.

The cabinet notebooks from 1950 to 1954 were accessed through the National Archives digitisation service and throughout the book are cited according to their series number. It is important to note that notebooks often extend over two years; for example, part of 1953 and part of 1954, as individual notetakers were used at different times. As well, different notetakers often recorded various aspects of the same meeting, and at other times two notetakers might record meetings simultaneously. Hence, there is often overlap in detail.

The series covering 1950 are A11099 1/1 to A11099 1/9. Those covering 1952 are A11099 1/10 to A11099 1/14 and A11099 1/27 – 1/28. The 1953 notebooks series numbers are A11099 1/14 to A11099 1/16 and A11099 1/27 to A11099 1/30. The 1953 records are series numbers A11099 A/16 to A11099 1/17 and A11099 1/30 and A11099 1/31. The 1954 notebooks are numbered A11099 1/17 to A1109 1/20.

National Library of Australia

Cabinet diaries and personal papers of prime ministers Edmund Barton, Alfred Deakin and William Hughes proved a useful source. They were accessed primarily through the Manuscripts Room at the National Library of Australia. Barton's diaries are referenced as MS 51. The papers of Alfred Deakin are primarily in collection MS 1540. This collection contains both general papers and Deakin's diaries throughout his time as prime minister. Hughes' papers are contained in MS 1538. Within this collection a number of series were used. Series 16 covers the period 1916–1922. Series 24 contains memoranda and reports presented to the war cabinet and series 4 contains Hughes personal diaries. There is also a second collection of Hughes papers MS 1538 that contained correspondence files and cabinet submissions, the latter are copies of those contained in microfilm A3227 and A2717 in the National Archives.

In addition to these a number of other sets of papers were examined. Atlee Hunt's papers are in collection MS 52. Robert Garran's papers were accessed through MS 2001, Patrick Glyn's papers through MS 4653. Earl Page's papers, including diaries, are in MS 1633. The papers of Thomas Bavin were accessed at MS 560. Joseph Cook's papers are in MS 2212. George Reid's papers were accessed at MS 7842 and Chris Watson's papers through MS 451. Scullin's papers through MS 5194.

For later years parts of the series of Robert Menzies were accessed through MS 4936, Joseph Lyons' papers through collection MS 4851 and John Gorton's papers through MS 7984.

Bibliography

Andeweg, R. 1997, 'Collegiality and Collectivity: Cabinets, Cabinet Committees and Cabinet Ministers', in P. Weller et al. (eds), *The Hollow Crown*, Basingstoke: Macmillan.
Australian Labor Party 1982, *Report of the Taskforce in Government Administration*, Canberra, September.
Australian Labor Party 1983, *Labor and the Quality of Government*, policy presentation by Bob Hawke, 9 February.
Bagehot, W. 1963, *The English Constitution*, London: Fontana.
Baker, A. 2000, *Prime Ministers and the Rule Book*, London: Politico's.
Bakvis, H. 2000, 'Prime Minister and Cabinet in Canada: An Autocracy in Need of Reform', *Journal of Canadian Studies*, Vol. 35, No. 4, pp. 60–79.
Bebbington G. 1989, *Pit Boy to Prime Minister. The Story of the Rt. Hon. Sir Joseph Cook P.C, G.C.M.G.*, University of Keele, Staffordshire: Centre of Local & Community History.
Blackstone, T. and W. Plowden 1988, *Inside the Think Tank: Advising the Cabinet 1971–1983*, London: William Heinemann.
Blewett, N. 1999, *A Cabinet Diary: A Personal Record of the First Keating Government*, Kent Town South Australia: Wakefield Press.
Blewett, N. 2000, 'Robert James Lee Hawke', in M. Grattan (ed.), *Australian Prime Ministers*, Sydney: New Holland.
Bolton, G. 2000, *Edmund Barton*, Sydney: Allen & Unwin.
Bunting, J. 1988, *R.G. Menzies: A Portrait*, Sydney: Allen & Unwin.
Burch, M. and I. Holliday, 1996, *The British Cabinet System*, Hemel Hempstead: Prentice Hall.
Cabinet Office 1988, *Cabinet Handbook* (revised edition), Canberra: Australian Government Printing Service.
Cabinet Secretariat 1980, *The Department of Prime Minister and Cabinet Annual Report 1978–79*, Canberra: Commonwealth of Australia.
Canada 2002, *A Guide for Ministers and Secretaries of State*, Ottawa: Privy Council Office.
CBPA 1987, *Canberra Bulletin of Public Administration*, 52, October.
Chester, A. 1943, *John Curtin*, Sydney: Angus & Robertson.
Childe, V. 1964, *How Labour Governs: A Study of Workers' Representation in Australia* (2nd edition), Melbourne: Melbourne University Press.
Codd, M. 1990, 'The Role of Secretaries in Departments in the APS', *PSC Occasional Papers No 8*, Canberra.
Commonwealth of Australia 1983, *Reforming the Australian Public Service: A Statement of the Government's Intentions, December 1983*, Canberra: Australian Government Publishing Service.
Crisp, L.F. 1960, *Ben Chifley. A Biography*, London: Longmans.
Crisp, L.F. 1965, *Australian National Government*, Croydon, Victoria: Longmans.
Crossman, R.H.S. 1963, 'Introduction' to W. Bagehot, *The English Constitution*, London: Fontana.
Davis, G. 1995, *A Government of Routines*, Melbourne: Macmillan.
Day, D. 1999, *John Curtin: A Life*, Pymble NSW: Harper Collins.
Dedman, D. 1968, 'The Practical Application of Collective Responsibility', *Politics*, Vol. III, No 2, November, pp. 148–62.
Dell, E. 1980, 'Collective Responsibility: Fact, Fiction or Façade?', *Policy and Practice: The Experience of Government*, London: RIPA.
Denning, W. 1982, *Caucus Crisis: The Rise and Fall of the Scullin Government*, Sydney: Hale & Iremonger.

Department of the Prime Minister and Cabinet 1983, *Cabinet Handbook*, Canberra: Australian Government Printing Service.
Department of Prime Minister and Cabinet 1984, *Annual Report 1983–84*, Canberra: Commonwealth of Australia.
Department of Prime Minister and Cabinet 1999, *Legislation Handbook* (incorporating No. 1 Update of May 2000), Canberra: Commonwealth of Australia.
Department of the Prime Minister and Cabinet 2004, *Cabinet Handbook* (amended 5th edition), Canberra: Commonwealth of Australia.
Department of Prime Minister and Cabinet – Federal Executive Council Secretariat 2005, *Federal Executive Council Handbook*, Canberra: Commonwealth of Australia.
Department of Prime Minister and Cabinet 2005, 'Cabinet Implementation Unit – Special Article', *Annual Report 2004/05*, Canberra: Commonwealth of Australia.
d'Ombrain, N. 2004, 'Cabinet Secrecy (The Essence of the Cabinet Secrecy Convention)', *Canadian Public Administration*, 47, 3, pp. 332–60.
Donoughue, B. 1987, *Prime Minister*, London: Jonathan Cape.
Dowsing, I. 1968, *Curtin of Australia*, Australia: Acacia Press Pty Ltd.
Dunleavy, P. and R.A.W. Rhodes 1990, 'Core Executive Studies in Britain', *Public Administration*, 68, pp. 3–28.
Edwards, C. 1965, *Bruce of Melbourne. Man of Two Worlds*, London: Heinemann.
Edwards, J. 1996, *Keating: The Inside Story*, Ringwood: Viking.
Edwards, P. 2006, *Arthur Tange: Last of the Mandarins*, Sydney: Allen & Unwin.
Encel, S. 1962, *Cabinet Government in Australia* (1st edition), Melbourne: Melbourne University Press.
Encel, S. 1974, *Cabinet Government in Australia* (2nd edition), Melbourne: Melbourne University Press.
Fadden, A. Sir. 1969, *They Called Me Artie. The Memoirs of Sir Arthur Fadden*, Australia: Jacaranda Press.
Fitzhardinge, L.F. 1964, *That Fiery Particle. A Political Biography William Morris Hughes 1862–1914 Vol. 1*, Australia: Angus & Robertson Publishers.
Fitzhardinge, L.F. 1979, *The Little Digger 1914–1952. A Political Biography William Morris Hughes Vol. II*, Sydney: Angus & Robertson.
Foley, M. 1993, *The Rise of the British Presidency*, Manchester: Manchester University Press.
Foley, M. 2000, *The British Presidency*, Manchester: Manchester University Press.
Forrest, M. and G. Reid 1989, *Australia's Commonwealth Parliament 1901–1988*, Melbourne: Melbourne University Press.
Frame, T. 2005, *The Life and Death of Harold Holt*, Crows Nest, NSW: Allen & Unwin.
Fraser, J.M. 1978, 'Responsibility in Government', *Australian Journal of Public Administration*, Vol. 37, No. 1, pp. 1–11.
French, R. 1979, 'The Privy Council Office: Support for Cabinet Decision Making', in R. Schultz et al. (eds), *The Canadian Political Process* (3rd edition), Toronto: Holt and Rinehart.
Garland, R.V. 1976, 'Relations between Ministers and Departments', *ACT R.I.P.A. Newsletter*, 3, 3, pp. 15–35.
Garran, R.R. 1958, *Prosper the Commonwealth*, Sydney: Angus & Robertson.
Glass, M. 1997, *Charles Cameron Kingston. Federation Father*, Victoria: Melbourne University Press.
Gordon Walker, P. 1972, *The Cabinet*, London: Fontana.
Grassby, A. and Ordonez, S. 1999, *The Man Time Forgot. The Life and Times of John Christian Watson, Australia's First Labor Prime Minister*, Australia: Pluto Press.
Grattan, M. 2000, 'John Winston Howard', in M. Grattan (ed.), *Australian Prime Ministers*, Sydney: New Holland.

Hancock, I. 2002, *John Gorton. He Did it His Way*, Sydney: Hodder.
Hancock, I. 2004, *The V.I.P. Affair 1966–67: The Causes, Course and Consequences of a Ministerial and Public Service Cover-up*, Canberra: Australasian Study of Parliament Group.
Hasluck, P. 1997, *The Chance of Politics*, Melbourne: Text Publishing.
Haupt, R. 1974, 'PM Wants Kitchen Cabinet', *The Australian Financial Review*, 14 June, p. 1.
Hawker, G. Smith, R.F.I. and Weller, P. 1979, *Politics and Policy in Australia*, St Lucia Queensland: University of Queensland Press.
Hazlehurst, C. 1979, *Menzies Observed*, Sydney: George Allen & Unwin.
Heclo, H. 1974, *Modern Social Politics in Britain and Sweden: From Relief to Income Maintenance*, New Haven: Yale University Press.
Hennessy, P. 1986, *Cabinet*, London: Fontana.
Hennessy, P. 1989, *Whitehall*, London: Secker.
Hennessy, P. 1995, *The Hidden Wiring*, London: Indigo.
Hennessy, P. 2000, *The Prime Minister: The Office and its Holders since 1945*, London: Penguin.
Hodgetts, J.E. 1973, *The Canadian Public Service: A Physiology of Government 1867–1970*, Toronto: University of Toronto Press.
Hogg, S. and J. Hill 1995, *Too Close to Call: Power and Politics – John Major in No. 10*, London: Little Brown.
Holliday, I. 2000 'Is the British State Hollowing out?', *The Political Quarterly*, 71, 2, pp. 167–76.
Horner, D. 1996, *Inside the War Cabinet. Directing Australia's War Effort 1939–45*, Sydney: Allen & Unwin.
Howard, J. 1990, 'Reflections on the Cabinet Process – I', in B. Galligan, J.R. Nethercote and C. Walsh (eds), *Decision Making in Australian Government: The Cabinet & Budget*, Canberra: Australian National University – Centre for Research on Federal Financial Relations, pp. 23–33.
Howard, J. 2002, *Strategic Leadership for Australia: Policy Directions in a Complex World*, Address to the Committee for the Economic Development of Australia, 20 November.
Hughes, W.M. 1950, *Policies and Potentates*, Sydney: Angus & Robertson.
Hungerford, T., cited in Laurie V., 'Fighting Spirit', in *The Australian*, 23–24 April, 2005, p. R9.
Jones, G. 1979, 'The Prime Minister's Aides', *Hull Papers in Politics*, 6.
Jones, G. 1981, 'Review of Rose and Suleiman', in *Public Administration*, Vol. 57, 2, pp. 219–20.
Kavanagh, D. and A. Seldon 2000, *The Powers behind the Prime Minister: The Hidden Influence of Number Ten*, London: Harper Collins.
Keating, M. and P. Weller 2000, 'Cabinet Government: An Institution Under Pressure', in M. Keating et al. (eds), *Institutions on the Edge? Capacity for Governance*, St Leonards NSW: Allen & Unwin, pp. 45–73.
Kelly, P. 'No Time for a Spill in the Cabinet', in *Australian*, 30 May 1975, p. 9.
Kelly, P. 2005, *Re-thinking Australian Governance – The Howard Legacy*, Occasional Paper Series 4/2005, Canberra: Academy of the Social Sciences in Australia.
La Nauze, J.A. 1965, *Alfred Deakin. A Biography*, Vols 1 & 2, Victoria: Melbourne University Press.
Lee, D. 1995, 'Cabinet', in *The Menzies Era: A Reappraisal of Government Politics and Policy*, in S. Prasser, J.R. Nethercote and J. Warhurst (eds), Sydney: Hale & Iremonger.
Lee, N. 1983, *John Curtin. Saviour of Australia*, Melbourne: Longman Cheshire.
Lindquist, E. and G. White 1997, 'Analysing Canadian Cabinets: Past, Present and Future', in W.H. Riker, (ed.) *Agenda Formation*, Ann Arbor, MI: University of Michigan Press.
Lyons, Dame E. 1965, *So We Take Comfort*, London: Heinemann.

Mackintosh, J.P. 1962, *The British Cabinet*, London: Stevens & Sons.
Mackintosh, J.P. 1977, *The British cabinet* (3rd edition), London: Stevens.
Mackie, J. and Hogwood, B. (eds), 1985, *Unlocking the Cabinet*, London: Sage.
Marr, D. and M. Wilkinson 2003, *Dark Victory*, Crows Nest NSW: Allen & Unwin.
Martin, A.W. 1993, *Robert Menzies. A Life, Vol. 1 and 2*, Melbourne: Melbourne University Press.
Martin, L. 1995, *Chrêtien: The Will to Win*, Toronto: Lester Publishing.
McClintock, P. 2003, 'The Australian Approach to Policy-making', *Canberra Bulletin of Public Administration*, No. 108, June, p. 15.
McMinn, W.G. 1989, *George Reid*, Melbourne: Melbourne University Press.
Menzies, Sir R.G. 1970, *The Measure of the Years*, London: Cassell.
Murdoch, J. 1998, *A Million to One Against. A Portrait of Andrew Fisher*, London: Minerva Press.
Mills, S. 1993, *The Hawke Years*, Ringwood: Viking.
Oakes, L. and Solomon, D. 1973, *The Making of an Australian Prime Minister*, Melbourne: Cheshire.
Page, E. 1963, *Earle Page*, Melbourne: Angus & Robertson.
Pearce, G.F. Sir 1951, *Carpenter to Cabinet, Thirty-Seven Years of Parliament*, Australia: Hutchinson & Co. Ltd.
Page, E.C.G. 2001, *Truant Surgeon: The Inside Story of Forty Years of Australian Political Life* (new edition), Melbourne: Black Inc.
Parkin, A. 1980, 'Pluralism and Australian Political Science', *Politics*, XV, (1), pp. 50–3.
Prime Minister 1998, *A Guide on Key Elements of Ministerial Responsibility*, Canberra: Department of the Prime Minister and Cabinet.
Reid, A. 1971, *The Gorton Experiment*, Sydney: Shakespeare Head Press.
Reid, G.H. 1917, *My Reminiscences*, London: Cassell & Company Ltd.
Rentoul, J. 2001, *Tony Blair: Prime Minister*, London: Warner Books.
Reynolds, J. 1948, *Edmund Barton*, Melbourne: Bookman Press.
Rhodes, R. 1995, 'From Prime Ministerial Power to Core Executive', in R. Rhodes and P. Dunleavy (eds), *Prime Minister, Cabinet and Core Executives*, London: Macmillan.
Robertson, J. 1974, *J.H. Scullin. A Political Biography*, Perth: University of Western Australia Press.
Rose, R. 1980, 'British Government: The Job at the Top', in R. Rose and E. Suleiman (eds), *Presidents and Prime Ministers*, Washington, DC: American Enterprise Institute.
Ross, L. 1977, *John Curtin. A Biography*, South Melbourne: Macmillan.
Rutledge, M. 1974, *Edmund Barton*, Melbourne: Oxford University Press.
Savoie, D. 1999, *Governing from the Centre*, Toronto: University of Toronto Press.
Simpson, J. 2001, *The Friendly Dictatorship*, Toronto: McClelland and Stewart.
Smith, R.F.I. 1976, *Australian Cabinet Structure and Procedures*, Royal Commission on Australian Government Administration.
Smith, R.F.I. 1977, 'Australian Cabinet Structure and Procedures: The Labor Government 1972–1975', *Politics*, Vol. 12, 1, pp. 23–7.
Solomon, D. 1973, 'Aiming to Increase Ministerial Control', *The Canberra Times*, 12 January, p. 2.
Spender, P. 1972, *Politics and a Man*, Sydney: Collins.
Walsh, P. 1995, *Confessions of a Failed Finance Minister*, Milsons Point NSW: Random House.
Wanna, J. and Hanson, S. 2006, 'Enabling the Australian Cabinet: Supporting Cabinet Capabilities, draft paper.
Watson, D. 2002, *Recollections of a Bleeding Heart: A Portrait of Paul Keating PM*, Milsons Point NSW: Random House.
Weller, P. 1975, *Caucus Minutes 1901–1949. Minutes of the Meetings of the Federal Parliamentary Labor Party, Volume 1 1901–1917, Volume 2 1917–1931, Vol. 3 1932–1949*, Melbourne: Melbourne University Press.

Weller, P. 1983, 'Do Prime Minister's Departments Really Create Problems?', *Public Administration*, 61, 1, pp. 59-78.
Weller, P. 1983, 'Transition: Taking Over Power in 1983', *The Australian Journal of Public Administration*, Vol. 42, No. 3, pp. 303–19.
Weller, P. 1985, *First Among Equals: Prime Ministers in Westminster Systems*, Sydney: Allen & Unwin.
Weller, P. 1987, 'Assistant Ministers and Mega-departments', *Canberra Bulletin of Public Administration*, 52, pp. 18–23.
Weller, P. 1989, *Malcolm Fraser PM: A Study in Prime Ministerial Power*, Ringwood: Penguin.
Weller, P. 1990, 'The Cabinet', in C. Jennett and R.G. Stewart (eds), *Hawke and Australian Public Policy: Consensus and Restructuring*, South Melbourne: MacMillan.
Weller, P. 1993, 'Party Rules and the Dismissal of Leaders', *Parliamentary Affairs*, Vol. 47, No. 1, pp. 133–43.
Weller, P. 1999, 'Disentangling Ministerial Responsibility', *Australian Journal of Public Administration*, 58, 1, pp. 62–4.
Weller, P. 2001, *Australia's Mandarins: The Frank and the Fearless?*, Crows Nest, NSW: Allen & Unwin.
Weller, P. 2001, 'Ministerial Codes, Cabinet Rules and the Power of Prime Ministers', in J. Fleming and I. Holland (eds), *Motivating Ministers to Morality*, Aldershot: Ashgate.
Weller, P., H. Bakvis, and R.A.W. Rhodes (eds) 1997, *The Hollow Crown: Countervailing Trends in Core Executives*, Basingstoke: Macmillan.
Weller, P. and Grattan, M. 1981, *Can Ministers Cope? Australian Federal Ministers at Work*, Richmond Victoria: Hutchinson of Australia.
White, G. 2001, 'Mother Teresa's Biker Gang, or Cabinet Democracy in Canada', paper presented at the 'Canada Today: A Democratic Audit' conference, Ottowa.
White, K. 1987, *Joseph Lyons*, Melbourne: Penguin.
Whyte, W.F. 1957, *William Morris Hughes. His Life and Times*, Sydney: Angus & Robertson.
Woodhouse, D. 1994, *Ministers and Parliament: Accountability in Theory and Practice*, Oxford: The Clarendon Press.
Yeend, G.J. 1979, 'The Department of the Prime Minister and Cabinet in Perspective', *Australian Journal of Public Administration*, Vol. 38, No. 2, pp. 142–3.

INDEX

Aboriginal land rights 174, 225, 246
abortion reform 257
ad hoc committees 97, 99, 128–30, 146, 238
Advisory War Council 84–85
alcohol 87, 92
ALP *see* Australian Labor Party (ALP)
Anthony, Doug 120, 137, 152, 156, 157
apartheid 239, 259
Atkinson, J. A. 53–54
AUSSAT 142, 145
Australian Capital Territory (ACT) 56
Australian Constitution, Section 64 9, 99–100, 161, 196–97, 209
Australian Council of Trade Unions (ACTU) 91
Australian Democrats 209
Australian Labor Party (ALP)
  ban on Communist Party 80
  caucus and national conference 200
  centenary of first party meeting 3
  chronological listing of ministries 291–92
  factional system 161, 198
  first Labor government 24
  lack of experience in government 122
  preparation for government 159
  relaxing of collective responsibility at national conferences 169
  second Labor government 24
  support for Deakin 24
  walkout by Billy Hughes and supporters 38, 39
  see also cabinet–caucus relationship
Australian State Regional Relations Committee (ASRRC) 128
Australian Wheat Board (AWB) 211
Australian Workers Union (AWU) 34, 91

Barton, Sir Edmund 1, 2, 4, 20–24, 193, 194, 289, 291
Batchelor, Egerton 24
Bavin, T. R. 29
Beasley, K. (Snr) 60, 62, 63, 77, 90
Bilney, Gordon 170
Blair, Tony 269–71
Blakeley, Arthur 57
Blewett, Neal 167–68, 247
Bolte, Henry 150
Bowen, Lionel 161
Bretton Woods Agreement 80–82, 201, 206, 237, 243
Brisbane Line controversy 76, 91, 198
Britain, cabinet government in 9, 11, 14, 16, 268–72, 274, 277, 280
British 'presidency' 13
Broome (WA) 34
Brown, Allen 86, 95, 98, 99, 101–103, 116, 223, 225
Brown, Gordon 275
Brown, John 212
Bruce, Stanley 47–56, 67–68, 72, 194, 217, 255, 290
Bruce–Page (Nationalist–CP) ministry 52–56, 59, 203, 291
Bunting, Sir John 119, 120, 223–24, 227, 229–30, 249, 260, 261, 281–82
bureaucratisation of cabinet 229–31
Bury, Les 206
Button, John 161, 170

cabinet committees
　attendance of supporting officials 101
　during Fraser government 239
　during Hawke government 164–68, 239
　during Howard government 182–84, 240
　during Lyons government 238
　during Menzies Lib–CP coalition government 98, 238
　during Whitlam government 238–39
　established on continuing basis 69
　frequency of meetings (1970–1996) 286
　ineffectiveness of 98
　number of decisions (1970–1996) 286
　role of 97, 238–40
　see also ad hoc committees; co-ordination committees; standing committees
cabinet decisions
　during early 1950s 117–18
　formal changes to structure of decision making in 1940 73–75
　implementation of 245
　rules for records and decisions 222–26
　statistics (1970–1996) 286
　vote counting 260
cabinet government
　acceptance for Commonwealth of Australia 2
　Australian system compared to Canada and Britain 278–80
　defined 6–7, 16
　development from ministerial government 229–30
　reliance on support of parliamentary party 192
　trends and futures 281–85
　in wartime *see* war cabinet
cabinet government, analysis and interpretations of
　combining various approaches 17–18
　constitutional theory or legal approach to 8–10, 15
　network approach 13–15
　political science approach 12–13
　public administration or positional approach 10–11, 15
　public policy approach 11–12, 15
Cabinet Government in Australia 7–8
Cabinet Handbook 165, 169, 208–209, 210–211, 218, 219, 245, 247, 282
cabinet implementation unit 188
'Cabinet of Kings' 1–2
cabinet leaks

　during Hawke government 165
　first inquiry into 22
　on governing arrangements for ACT 56
　regarding cabinet secretariat 70
　and cabinet secrecy 245–47
cabinet meetings
　attendance of officials during early 1950s 100–103
　during 1940 72
　during Bruce–Page ministry 54–55
　during first Lyons government 64
　during Fraser government 142–45
　during Hawke government 162
　during Hughes ministries 47
　during Scullin ministry 59
　first records 4, 20–21
　frequency and issues in early years 21–24
　frequency of meetings 1970–1996 286
　number of decisions 1970–1996 286
　regularity and frequency 235–37
　support of officials during early 1950s 100–103
cabinet membership
　and accommodation of state interests 199
　election and dismissal of ministers 196–200
　factional representation during Hawke-Keating government 161
　and process of cabinet-making 67, 118–19
　selection of cabinet in Howard government 178–80
cabinet notebooks 95–96, 102, 225–26, 246–47
cabinet operations, arrangements during World War II 73–75, 83–85
cabinet and parliament 202–204
cabinet policy unit (CPU) 186–87, 224
cabinet procedures
　in 1949 handbook 97
　abolition of cabinet secretariat by Scullin ministry 57–59, 217, 227
　adoption of more systematic processes during inter-war years 52, 53–56
　automation with development of CABNET 180, 181, 282
　commitment to process during Hawke government 165
　creation of cabinet secretariat and set of rules 54–6, 217
　during Curtin and Chifley governments 83–94, 218, 227
　during Fraser government 135–41

during Hawke government 162–63
during Howard government 180–82
during Hughes' ministries 39, 40, 48–51
establishment and consolidation of norms under Deakin 24–27
formal changes to structure of decision making in 1940 73–75
guidelines for 216–20
informality in the early years 22–23
management of 4–5
opinion of Sir Maurice Hankey 66–67
reestablishment of cabinet secretariat under Lyons government 64–65, 218, 227
rules of procedure 4–5
and cabinet secrecy 246
under acting prime minister Watt 39–40
see also Cabinet Handbook
cabinet records
deterioration in record keeping in 1940 73, 223
during Chifley government 87
during Curtin government 86
during Menzies Lib-CP ministries 95–96, 101–103
earliest documents 20–21
of first cabinet 20–21
incompleteness during Scullin ministry 57
lack for early ministries 25–26, 222
notebooks 95–96, 102, 225–26, 246–47
rules for records and decisions 222–26
cabinet rules
causes and consequences of bureaucratisation 229–31
challenges to ministers 215–16
guidelines for cabinet and ministers 216–20
of procedure 4–5
for records and decisions 222–26
role and function of 214
for submissions 220–22
see also Cabinet Handbook
cabinet secrecy 245–47
cabinet solidarity 78, 168, 207
cabinet structure
during Menzies Lib-CP ministries 96–100
during World War II 83
implications for prime ministers 195
cabinet submissions, rules for 220–22
cabinet support

advising cabinet as a whole 240–43
need for coherence and strategy 247–8
attendance support of officials at cabinet meetings 100–103
rules for support of cabinet process 226–29
support for prime minister and cabinet in Howard government 186–88
see also Department of External Affairs; Department of Prime Minister and Cabinet (PM&C)
cabinet–caucus relationship
during Chifley ministries 80–83
during Curtin ministries 80
during Hawke government 134, 161, 163, 168–69, 198, 201
during Scullin ministry 57–64
during second Fisher ministry 28–32
during third Fisher ministry 33–34
during Watson ministry 24–26, 28, 29
during Whitlam government 122–24, 134, 168, 201
early clashes 28
election of ministers to cabinet 29, 197
and Labor's theory of representation 200, 208
removal of ministers 198
split over conscription in 1916 37–38, 57
Cairns, Jim 123, 198
Calwell, Arthur 79, 80, 81, 83, 84, 90, 197
Cameron, Clyde 198–99
Canada
cabinet government 10, 11, 12, 14, 16, 127, 164, 245, 268–69, 272–75, 277, 279
federalism 125, 127
Casey, R.G. 66, 107, 111
caucus *see* cabinet–caucus relationship
charter letters 196, 218, 242
Chedden, Fred 73
Cherwell, Lord 117
Chifley (ALP) ministries, periods of 290, 291
Chifley, Joseph Benedict 80–82, 93–94, 131, 193, 198, 201, 206, 243, 248, 260
Chipp, Don 209
Chippindall, Giles 84
Chrétien, Jean 269, 272–73, 275
co-ordination committees 146–49, 164
coalition governments, problems for prime ministers 194–95
collective government 39, 40, 158, 249, 285

collective responsibility
   in cabinet 55, 68, 78, 168–70, 192, 201, 245
   defined by prime minister 47, 209
   distinction between cabinet and non-cabinet ministers 207–208
   explained 204–5
   and individual responsibility 249
   of ministers to parliament 9, 63
   opposition to 82, 206–207
Collins, T.J. 73
Colombo plan 108
colonial governments, and development of cabinet government 2
Combe–Ivanov inquiry 173
Commonwealth Bank 59–60, 80, 174
communism, in trade unions 103
Communist Party of Australia 80, 103–104, 115
Conciliation and Arbitration Bill 21, 25, 205–206
conscription 37–38, 79
constitutional conventions 2, 249
constitutional theorists, interpretation of workings cabinet 8–10, 15
constructive notice, principle of 212
Cook (Lib) ministry 30–32, 203, 291
Cook, Sir Joseph 39, 193, 195, 289
Coombs, Nugget 100
Copland, Prof. Douglas 74, 100
core executive, government by 271–72
Costello, Peter 179–80
Country Party (CP) 51, 71, 193, 255, 264–65
   see also CP–UAP coalition; Lib–CP coalition
CP see Country Party (CP)
CP–UAP coalition, ministries 291
Crawford Industry Report 145
Crean, Frank 132
Crean, Simon 170, 197
Culley, C. 62, 63, 206
currency appreciation 103, 105–108
Curtin (ALP) ministries, periods of 76, 198, 203, 291
Curtin, John Joseph 58, 79, 88, 193, 197, 201, 290

Dawson, Anderson 24, 25 (QLD)
Deakin, Alfred 1, 2, 4, 20–21, 24, 26–27, 35, 193, 194, 289
Deakin ministries 291
Dedman, John 82, 89, 89–90, 94
defence policy 109–113
Dell, Edmund 12, 248
Democratic Labor Party (DLP) 203

Denning, Warren 63
Department of Defence 111
Department of External Affairs, support for prime minister and cabinet 29–30
Department of Finance 183, 240
Department of Immigration 211
Department of Immigration and Ethnic Affairs 179
Department of Post-war Reconstruction 94, 227, 253
Department of Prime Minister and Cabinet (PM&C) 131, 132–33, 136–38, 149, 150, 181, 187–88, 218, 228, 253
Department of Treasury, relationship with cabinet 54–55, 57–58, 114, 116, 133–34, 146, 237, 240
Depression 57
Duffy, Sir Frank Gavin 61
Duke of Gloucester 90, 259

Earle, John 50
Economic and Industrial Committee of Cabinet 73–75
education, Williams report 145
Edwards, John 174
Ellicot, Bob 207
Encel, S. 7–8
Evans, Gareth 175
Evatt, Herbert Vere 61, 88, 90, 193, 243
executive council, first meeting 20
expenditure review committee (ERC) 128, 130, 164, 167–68, 182–83, 184, 239–40, 244

Fadden (CP–UAP) ministry 76, 203, 290, 291
Fadden, Sir Arthur 74–75, 106, 194, 207, 244, 290
Fahey, John 197
Federal Executive Council Handbook 220
federalism, and fiscal relations 115–16
Fenton, James 59, 60–61, 63, 67, 206, 255
Fisher (ALP) ministries 291
Fisher, Andrew 21, 24, 28–36, 51, 193, 198, 289, 291
Foley, Michael 13
Forde (ALP) ministry 291
Forde, Francis Michael 77, 80, 193, 290
foreign affairs and defence committee 146
foreign policy 103, 109–113, 259
Forrest, John 1, 4, 27, 32, 39, 193, 206

40-hour week 68
Fraser, John Malcolm 135, 194, 207, 259, 262, 290
Fraser ministries
  commitment to institution of cabinet 135
  the committee system 145–49
  management of cabinet 149–56, 256
  overview of cabinet 156–58
  periods of 292
  running of cabinet 142–45
  setting cabinet arrangements 135–41
Free Trade Party *see* Free Trade–Protectionist coalition
Free Trade–Protectionist coalition 291
Full Cabinet 73–76, 83–84, 85, 87–88
functional committees, during Hawke government 164

Gibson, Sir Robert 59, 60
Goodale, Ralph 274
goods and services tax (GST) 204, 237, 257
Gorton (Lib–CP) ministries 207, 291–92
Gorton, Sir John Grey 119–20, 135, 193, 194, 197, 200, 202, 290
Governing from the Centre: The Concentration of Power in Canadian Politics 269
Greene, Walter Massy 48, 67
Griffith, Sir Samuel 24
Grimes, Don 161
A Guide on Key Elements of Ministerial Responsibility 210, 218, 282
Guide for Ministers and Secretaries of State 273
Gullett, Sir Henry 68, 206
gun control 257

Hankey, Sir Maurice 66–67
Hanson, Pauline 180
Hasluck, Paul 118, 120–21, 193, 263
Hawke government
  collective responsibility and cabinet policy 168–70
  factional representation in cabinet 161
  meetings of full ministry 163–64
  overview of cabinet 175
  power to sack ministers 199
  restructuring of cabinet 161–2
  running of cabinet 159, 171–73
  size of cabinet 160
  use of strategic retreats 239–40
Hawke, Robert James Lee 173, 175, 193, 194, 237, 257, 290, 292

Hayden, Bill 124, 128–29, 164, 198
Hennessy, Paul 270
Hewitt, Lenox 119, 227
Higgs, William 38
High Court 24, 26, 61
HMAS Voyager, sinking 118
Holloway, E.J. 62–63, 206
Holt, Harold Edward 114, 115, 118, 193, 194, 207, 290
Holt (Lib–CP) ministries, periods of 291
Howard government
  cabinet meetings 185–86
  cabinet procedures 180–82
  guidelines for ministerial conduct 178–79
  leadership succession 179–80
  maintaining the coalition 180
  periods of 292
  politics and strategic planning 184–85
  selection of cabinet 178–80
  support for prime minister and cabinet 186–88
  use of cabinet committees 182–84
  use of strategic debates 42
Howard, John Winston 147, 156, 177, 189, 195, 256, 261, 290
Howse, Sir Neville 54
Howson, P. 200, 202
Hughes, William Morris
  actions in Bruce–Page government 56
  attendance at caucus meetings 25
  attitude towards collectivity 39
  and caucus split over conscription 37–38, 57, 195
  dominance over cabinet members and procedures 39, 40, 48–51, 197, 262
  as health minister in Lyons government 66
  independent action as PM 255
  as Labor prime minister 291
  lack of diplomacy 42–44
  leadership style 36–37, 45, 51
  loss of support of colleagues 51, 52
  as Nationalist prime minister 39–51, 291
  periods and duration of service as prime minister 194, 289
  relationship with Andrew Fisher 35–36
  relationship with Stanley Bruce 47–51
  relationship with W.A. Watt 39–47
Hungerwood, Tom 46
Hunt, Atlee 20, 29, 36
Hunt, Sir John 12

Immigration 114, 115
Immigration Restriction Bill 25
implementation of cabinet decisions 245
Implementation Unit 245
individual responsibility 249
industrial disputes 65
Industry Development Corporation 120
inflation 126
intelligence and security committee 146
International Monetary Fund (IMF) 80–81
International Trade Organisation 81
Iraq War 183, 187

Jensen, Jens 44
Jones, George 270–71

Keating (ALP) ministries, periods of 164, 169–70, 292
Keating, Paul John 159, 171, 172, 173–74, 193, 194, 199, 209, 257, 290
Kelly, Ros 212
Kerr, John 259
Killen, Jim 153
Kingston, Charles 1, 4, 21, 206, 236
Kirribilli House 163
Kirribilli rules 163
Kokoda track 79
Korean War 109, 243

Labor Party *see* Australian Labor Party (ALP)
Labor and the Quality of Government 160, 239
Land Rights Act 1976 225
Lang government (NSW) 62
Lang, Jack 62
Latham, John 68–69
Lawson, Sir Harry 67
Legislation Committee 145
Legislation Handbook 218
Lib–CP coalitions, chronological listing of ministries 291–92
Liberal Party of Australia (Lib) 195, 202
Lynch, Phillip 147, 150, 152, 156
Lyne, William 1, 2, 20, 22
Lyons, Joseph Aloysius 58, 59–61, 70, 71, 193, 197, 206, 255, 290
Lyons (UAP) ministry 63, 291
Lyons (UAP–CP) ministries 71, 291

McClelland, Jim 128–29
Macdonald, Sir John A. 275
McEwen (Lib–CP) ministry, period of 291

McEwen, Sir John 105–106, 108, 120, 206, 207, 290
McGregor, Gregor 25
McMahon (Lib–CP) ministries, period of 292
McMahon, Sir William 114, 115, 120–21, 193, 290
Major, John 270, 274
Marr, Major C.W.C. 54, 64, 65
Martin, Paul 275
media, attention on prime minister 254, 257–58
Melbourne Cup Day 23, 71
Melville, Prof. L.G. 80–81, 243
Members of Parliament (Staff) Act 224
memorandum for cabinet 64, 65
Menzies (Lib-CP) ministries 84–85, 99–100, 103, 105–108, 203, 290, 291
Menzies, Robert Gordon 69, 70, 108, 118, 193, 194, 195, 202, 206, 256, 290
Menzies (UAP-CP) ministry 73–76, 291
ministerial conduct, guidelines on 178–79
ministerial power, decline of 249
ministerial responsibility 9–10, 209–212, 284
ministerial staff, accountability of 211–12
ministries, chronological listing since 1901 291–92
monetary policy committee 146
Moore-Wilton, Max 181
Morshead report into defence organisation 100
Murdoch, Keith 38
MX missile commitment 173

National Archives, cabinet record 7
National Crimes Authority 164
national insurance scheme 71, 206, 237
National Labour Party 291
National Party of Australia (NPA) 180 *see also* Lib–NPA coalition
national security committee (NSC) 182, 183–84, 240, 244
national service 104
Nationalist Party 195, 291
Nationalist–CP coalition, Bruce–Page ministry 291
native title 204
Nauru 43–44
Nelson, Brendon 178
network analysts, interpretation of workings of cabinet 13–15
New Parliament House Committee 145
Niemeyer, Sir Otto 60

Nixon, Peter 147, 152
Nixon, Richard 117
Nock, H.K. 72
Northern Land Council 225, 246
NPA *see* National Party of Australia (NPA)

O'Connor, Richard 4, 24
officials in cabinet 243–44
O'Malley, King 37, 198
overseas ministers 67–68

Packer, Kerry 142
Page (CP–UAP) ministry, period of 291
Page, Sir Earle 51, 52, 71, 193, 194, 290
parliamentary business committee 182–83
parliamentary revolts 203
parliamentary tactics, in early cabinet 23
parties *see* political parties
Patterson, Kay 178
Peacock, Andrew 148–49, 194, 199, 207, 209
Pearce, George 34, 37, 38–39, 40, 41, 52, 255
pearling industry 34
pension levels 78
Petrov affair 104–105
policy development committees, during Hawke government 166
policy-making in cabinet 232–35
political parties
  cabinet accountability to party meetings 200–202
  creation of modern party system 24
  electing and dismissing leaders 193–95
  and interdependence of cabinet 3, 192
  party leadership challenges 193–95
  as source of cabinet legitimacy and centre of accountability 213
politics of cabinet
  management of 3, 91
  political tactics and manoeuvres in early years 23
post-war reconstruction 89–90
power
  cabinet as a source of 2–5
  within a political system 4
power realists, interpretation of workings of cabinet 12–13, 15
precedents, timing and conditions of cabinet meetings 4
Premiers' Plan 62–63
presidential government 6, 249
Prime Ministers of Australia
  election and dismissal of party leaders 193–95
  party and period and duration of service 289–90
  uncontested handovers 24
Prime Minister's Department 29–30, 95, 217, 227, 240, 253
Prime Minister's Office (PMO) 186, 188, 229
prime minister's power
  cabinet and political support 263–67
  as focus of media 254, 257–58
  over timing and conditions of cabinet meetings 4, 55
  patronage 252, 254
  as *primus inter pares* 6, 249
  resources to bolster 253–54
  scope for independent action 254–58
  to appoint and dismiss department heads 253
  to control cabinet 251, 258–63
  to define collective responsibility 47, 209
  to remove ministers 76, 123, 198
  to veto initiatives of ministerial colleagues 257
Prince of Wales, sinking of 85
Priorities Review Staff 241
Privy Council Office (PCO) (Canada) 274
Production Executive (of cabinet) 83, 84, 89–90, 92, 236
proportional representation, introduction in the Senate 3–4
Protectionist Party
  periods and duration of ministries 291
  see also Free Trade–Protectionist coalition; Protectionist–Free Trade–Tariff Reform coalition
Protectionist–Free Trade–Tariff Reform coalition 291
public administration school, interpretation of workings of cabinet 10–11, 15
public policy advocates, interpretation of workings of cabinet 11–12, 15
public servants, and ministerial responsibility 211
Public Service Act 1999 210, 253
public service appointments 117, 139

Qantas, privatisation of 201

Ray, Robert 170
Reagan, Ronald 256
Reforming the Australian Public Service 163

refugees 68, 257–58
Reid, Sir George Houstoun 27, 28, 289
Reid-McLean (Free Trade–Protectionist) ministry, period of 21, 24, 26, 291
Rentoul, John 270
the republic 174, 257
Repulse, sinking of 85
Reserve Bank 146
Resources Committee 128, 130
responsible cabinet government, acceptance of principle 2
responsible government 192
responsible party government 192
Review of Commonwealth Functions Committee (Razor Gang) 145, 155
Robb, Andrew 178
roles and functions of cabinet
  in 1949 handbook 96–97
  as an arbiter and patchwork of influence 13–15
  as a constitutional actor 8–10
  as a formal administrative institution 10–11
  as a forum for policy decisions 11–12
  as a political battleground 12–13
Ross, Lloyd 90
Ryan, Susan 161

Sandys, Duncan 117
Savoie, David 269
Scullin (ALP) ministry 52, 203, 291
Scullin, James Henry 77, 197, 198, 255–56, 290
security 240
  see also national security council (NSC)
Senate
  and control by cabinet 3–4
  introduction of proportional representation 3–4
  opposition to cabinet 203–204
Shakespeare, A.T. 56
Sharp, John 212
Shedden, Fred 73, 84, 87, 89
Shepherd, Malcolm 29, 39
Shergold, Peter 268
Simpson, Jeffrey 269
Sinclair, Ian 147
Sinodonis, Arthur 188
Social Welfare Committee 145
Spender, Percy 107, 108, 110–11
standing committees
  during Hawke government 166
  during Whitlam government 124–28
  establishment of Economic and Industrial Committee 73–75

establishment of standing committee for defence 69, 71
establishment of standing committee for finance 71
role of 97
under Fraser government 145, 146–49
State premiers, power of 2
Stevenson, J.D. 65
Strahan, Frank 68, 72–73, 74, 86, 227
strategic retreats 241–42
sugar tariffs 33
syphilis 35

Tange, Arthur 80, 117, 243–44
taxation
  goods and services tax (GST) 204, 237, 257
  tax summit 173, 237, 257
  uniform tax system 115–16
Thatcher, Margaret 270, 271, 274
The Friendly Dictatorship 269
Theodore, Ted 58, 59, 60, 61, 62, 63, 200
trade unions, and communism 103
Treasury *see* Department of Treasury
Trudeau, Pierre 125
Tudor, Frank 38
Turnbull, Malcolm 178
Turner, George 1

UAP–CP Coalition, ministries 291
under-the-line items 162–63, 182
UNESCO 116
uniform tax system 115–16
United Australia Party (UAP) 67, 193, 291
Uranium Committee 145
uranium policy 145, 201, 207, 237
US missile testing 256

Vanstone, Amanda 178
Vietnam, foreign policy on 109

wages committee 146
War Cabinet 69–70, 72, 73–75, 236, 243
War Precautions Act 200
Ward, Eddie 62, 77, 79–84, 88–91, 198, 206
Watson (ALP) ministry 21, 24–26, 197, 291
Watson, John Christian 26, 193, 289
Watt, W.A. 39–47, 220, 255
Webster, William 37
West, Stewart 207–208
Westminster systems of government 268

Wheeler, Fred 80–81, 243
White Australia policy 90, 118
White, T.W. 70
Whitlam (ALP) ministries
   ad hoc committees 128–30
   advice for cabinet 241
   election of undivided cabinet 123–24
   and opposition in the Senate 203
   overview of cabinet 133–34, 159
   periods of 122–34, 292
   standing committees 124–28
Whitlam, Edward Gough 130–33, 197–98, 198–99, 203, 259, 260, 290
Wilenski, Peter 125–26, 127–28, 238
Wilson, Roland 89, 90, 100, 113, 244
Withers, R. 212
women
   going without stockings at work 87
   removal of marriage bar for female public servants 118
World Bank 80–82

World War I
   caucus split over conscription 37
   commitment of Australian contingent by cabinet 31–32
   disenfranchisement of persons of enemy birth 38
   landing of AIF in Egypt 34
   Peace Plan 42
   pearl industry 34
   use of *ad hoc* committees 238
World War II
   Advisory War Council 84–85
   components of cabinet system 83
   defence force readiness 71–72
   establishment and operations of war cabinet 69–70, 72, 73–75, 83–85
   impact on format and running of cabinet 69

Yeend, Sir Geoffrey 137, 138, 139, 227, 228